DEFENDING A
KING
~ HIS LIFE & LEGACY

DR. KAREN MORIARTY

outskirtspress
DENVER, COLORADO

Dedication

To Robert,
my in-house inspiration,

&

To Michael Jackson,
who changed my life.

*David Nordahl graciously and generously approved the reproduction
of his original life-sized drawing of Michael Jackson for this book ~
in Michael's memory.*

ACKNOWLEDGEMENTS

My primary goal in writing *Defending A King ~ His Life & Legacy* has been to create a worthy tribute to the incomparable Michael Jackson. To play a small part in celebrating his life and fashioning his legacy is one of the greatest honors of my professional career. This book is a work born of gratitude.

My husband Robert had more faith in me than I had in myself when I began this adventure toward successful completion of a unique and caring book about Michael Jackson. Robert has unconditionally supported every major activity that I have undertaken; I'm grateful beyond expression.

Other primary supporters have been Irene McDonald (Florida), Luke Russell (Tennessee), Guadalupe McDougald (Illinois), and Therese Ryde (Sweden), who have steadfastly provided me with both emotional and substantive help. Bill Harte, my Chicago attorney, has been a special asset to this project and to me; for many years he has been extraordinarily helpful and supportive. I feel special, heartfelt gratitude toward Thomas Mesereau, whose integrity, intelligence, humanity, and compassion are an inspiration to me; he provided me with encouragement and invaluable input at a critical juncture in the progress of this book and then all along the way.

I would like to thank Michele Taylor, Elizabeth Michelle Billeaudeaux, David Nordahl, Larry Nimmer, Roberta Hennessy, Gerald and Mary Anne Moriarty, John and Drina Gruber, Susan Yu, Eric Otero, and especially Norma Rumberger for their unique contributions to my journey. For moral support and friendship, thanks to Kelley Bost and her daughters Jennifer and Julie, Maureen Cummings, Judge James Heiple, Lonnie Johnson, Valerie Benton, Carol and Russ Walker, Ed and Terry Wodecki, Jack and Lorraine Beagley, Shirley and Fred Beck, Bernadette and Lorelle Hadaway, Ellen Mertens, Wanda Polatty and Charles Radloff, Judy and John Rowan, Eileen Dyson, Susan Campbell, and Helene Douglas. For their being special, thanks to Samantha Moriarty; Bridget, Kelly,

Katie, and Jack McNamara; Brittany and Brooke Jamrozik; and Peyton, Lexi, and Kendall Moriarty. For their strong support of this book, I am grateful to Debbie Kunesh, Sherilynn Black, Rev. Barbara Kaufmann, Rev. Dr. Catherine Gross, Lauren Trainor, Brenda Jenkyns, Mary Singer, Debolina Raja Gupta (India), Jacqueline Minarick, Akiko Shimada (Japan), and Qian Zhang.

To the relatively few media people who, in spite of earning lesser notice and monetary rewards than those of your colleagues, were objective, ethical, and fair-minded toward Michael Jackson—such as Charles Thomson and Linda Deutsch—I laud and thank you for your efforts. You were traveling the "high road" and that is probably your true reward.

I would like to acknowledge Michael Jackson's fans everywhere. In my experience, you are the most open-minded and open-hearted people I've known. It has been a joy for me to join the fold, knowing that it is truly worldwide in scope and pervasive in its sense of kinship and purpose.

Michael Jackson longed to bring unity, peace, harmony, and love to this planet, to countries of all shapes and sizes, to people of all shades of color, belief systems, and ways of life. The Michael Jackson community—strengthened by his passion and example, by his tragic passing—is working to continue his vision.

He deserved better and more than he got from this world that he worked so diligently to improve and heal. In a kinder, gentler time, Michael Jackson will be more appreciated. With the dust settled on the travesties surrounding the Conrad Murray trial, Michael Jackson will be remembered for the exceptional human being and extraordinary entertainer that he dedicated himself to becoming.

Perhaps his music tells his story best of all. We're listening, Michael.

**The least I can do is to speak out
for those who cannot speak for themselves.**

— Jane Goodall

**This book is humbly offered
as one gem, among many,
for the crown of a man
who deserves to be a king
in his enduring legacy.**

— Dr. Karen Moriarty

**Show me a hero
and I'll write you a tragedy.**
— F. Scott Fitzgerald

CONTENTS

CONTENTS

Introduction

A king under siege—by those near and far who wanted a piece of his kingdom for themselves—was a humble, soft-spoken, and vulnerable man. His closest subjects shielded him from anyone who might challenge their coveted control of him or prevent their self-seeking agendas from unfolding. A greater, expanded empire was in sight for the king ... and for themselves. Victory and glorious, unparalleled acquisition were on the horizon.

The kindhearted, gentle king—who was no stranger to betrayals from every quarter—chose to cling to love and good works. Lesser men would have become embittered, but not he. Children, the poor, the suffering, and the downtrodden were his true mission. He wanted to heal them and the world. Lofty goals—but the fire for accomplishing these beautiful visions burned within him.

Night after night, he could not sleep, this monarch of melody, music, and dance. The king's burly bodyguard brought to him a doctor, from another realm. This doctor was commissioned by the king's advisers to keep him in sync with their campaign to conquer the world, to reap untold benefits, and to line their pockets. The doctor lusted after riches, prestige, and exclusive control of the beloved king.

Administered a powerful poison by the imported doctor, the king finally fell asleep. He did not awaken. And millions of people, inside his kingdom and without, mourned and grieved.

How could this happen to a king?

Michael Jackson was gone from this earthly realm. People from around the globe were halted in their tracks. They were shocked, stunned, and confused. They tried to understand this man who became a King. He was adored and attacked; admired and vilified; regal and human.

Michael Jackson is like a modern-day Rorschach Inkblot Test. Just as individuals see vastly different things in the mysterious shapes of these inkblots, used in personality assessments by professional psychologists, individuals perceive Michael Jackson in wildly varying ways. "Angel" or "devil," or some of both—Michael Jackson is a complexity of visual and auditory talents, searing memories, and unforgettable images, both in his professional works and in his very private personal life.

Tell me what you think and feel about Michael Jackson, what you see in him, and I can tell you much about yourself. How open is your heart, how wide is your perspective, how perceptive is your mind, how tolerant are your attitudes.

As a psychologist and therapist for many years, I have been told that I am an "easy grader" of people. When you hear the deepest secrets, greatest fears, desperate goals, and private failures from people who open their lives to you in therapy sessions, you come to view the human condition in a fuller, much less judgmental way. To be helpful to people, you must. It might be said that you develop rose-colored glasses onto the world of humankind.

Nothing about Michael Jackson's lifestyle is weirder than what I have heard in routine therapy sessions from people considered normal and average; some are pillars of their community. I can couple that statement with the truthful assertion that *I have never met a person who was more persecuted than Michael Jackson.*

He gave "controversial" new meaning. Michael Jackson did everything big; he could not even think small. He lived and performed with audacity and boldness. Unfortunately, these characteristics translated to his reputation and image in distorted ways. A whirlwind of Michael Jackson controversy blew through the years, especially in his home country, both during his life and after his death.

$$* \quad * \quad * \quad * \quad * \quad * \quad * \quad * \quad *$$

Michael Jackson wore his heart on his sleeve. He was a complex individual living a pinnacle and precarious life. He coped in ways unavailable to everyday people; he chose to be a man with a childlike heart. Like all of us, he did what he had to do to survive in *his* world, and his world was *unlike any other*.

Unlike us, Michael Jackson was a "king of prey." The predators who surrounded him were like hyenas. In Africa, the hyena is the arch-enemy of the lion—king of jungle and savannah—and is hated by native people for good cause. The hyena is the only wild animal that will start to devour you before you're dead. Cagy, hyenas stalk their kill; they pounce and start consuming the arm or leg of their live prey; they bite off a chunk of their vulnerable victim before the other hyenas can grab theirs. They also kill their own when it suits their purpose.

Michael lived in a unique jungle. He was the quarry of the grasping, the conniving, the ill-intentioned and unscrupulous. Opportunists and sycophants surrounded him, manipulated him, and grabbed their piece of him when they could. Media hyenas stalked him incessantly; they tried to get their chunk of Michael Jackson before the others of their kind.

At the Conrad Murray manslaughter trial in late 2011, Michael Jackson's heretofore private life was blown open, and he was turned into a victim to his own death! Although ruled a homicide, Michael's death was blamed on him by many in the media and in court by defense attorneys who tried unsuccessfully to save their client Conrad Murray from prison. Blaming Michael seemed cosmically unjust and sickened millions of people. He had already paid the price of misplaced trust *with his life*. How could people of integrity, with any sense of humanity, now demand that Michael Jackson pay another price *with his death?*

"There's no revenge so complete as forgiveness," a sage once wrote. Michael Jackson sought no revenge against anyone; he always took the high road. He issued no public statements against any of the people who chose to become his enemies or who tried to ravage him, even though he could have commanded a public platform and free publicity in an instant if he had chosen to do so.

As a society, we are iconoclasts who love to destroy our heroes. We enjoy it even more when they destroy themselves. The political arena and the entertainment industry are replete with individuals who have obliged our generalized lust for the downfall and disintegration of those who have been catapulted to a pedestal of admiration and devotion. Tiger Woods, Lindsay Lohan, former Senator John Edwards, and Arnold Schwarzenegger are only a few recent examples of fallen idols who captured front pages of media for months, but they are too numerous to list here, and it would serve no purpose to attempt a more complete line-up.

Michael Jackson was at the top of this list. An innocent victim of rapacious individuals in authority positions and media jobs, Michael was savaged for fun and profit. His predators ensured that his perceived idiosyncrasies eclipsed his amazing talent, stratospheric musical accomplishments, and global humanitarianism. This was— and is—a travesty and a tragedy.

The real man, however, had to deal with not only that dreadful, painful reality of his existence but with other onslaughts and ordeals that were hidden from public view. *Defending A King ~ His Life & Legacy* presents the torturous life of Michael Jackson with an emphasis on his *triumphs* over the unique adversities and challenges that came with his double-edged fame ... and his fate.

Through the good, the bad, and the ugly of his life, Michael Jackson maintained a nobility of spirit and a dignity of the soul that are amazing victories in his life-long fight for normalcy and a slice of happiness. He continued to choose love and forgiveness when most people would succumb to hatred and bitterness. The child in Michael Jackson, the part of himself that he cherished, saw the good, the possible, the divine on this earth. He decided to become a part—even a prophet and messenger—of that beauty, of harmony and peace, of unity and love.

"I used to walk around holding baby dolls," Michael Jackson once confessed to an interviewer, "I wanted children so badly; I was holding them." He added that he was "not territorial" because he loved not only his own, but all children. He wanted to be the voice of the voiceless and to use his music as a force for healing. His ubiquitous armband was the symbol that he used to remind people of the plight of children and of our responsibility to help them.

Admittedly, it sounds corny to say that Michael Jackson was the king of love, the champion of children everywhere, with deep passion and missionary zeal. The unsettling response to hearing or reading this assessment that we feel is more a reflection of our jaded society than anything else. It's just not okay to attribute an all-encompassing love for children to a man in this culture; it seems suspicious or even dirty. If and when we suspend this learned, quick and harsh judgment, however, we can begin to understand the real man who was Michael Jackson.

Defending A King ~ His Life & Legacy represents an attempt to place a pebble, perhaps a boulder, on the end of the playing field that has been so tilted against Michael Jackson for so many years by jaundiced, self-serving, greedy media. Supported and assisted by many people who really knew Michael the real person, this author ardently hopes that this book will cause a major tilt in the right direction. Michael Jackson deserves no less.

Today, in spite of volumes of printed material, toxic airwaves, and a world of cyberspace about Michael Jackson, there is little published information available about the real, flesh-and-blood man from first-hand witnesses. This is a man who deserves to have his praises sung; to have revealed his genuine love for the planet and

all of its children, men and women; to have his humanity rightfully
bestowed and restored as a glorious, enduring memory.

Imagine what Michael Jackson experienced during his remarkable
life, one that was literally unlike any other. He saw the richest of the
rich, the poorest of the poor, the sickest of the sick, the highest of the
high, and the lowliest of the low. He interacted with royalty, heads
of state, celebrities at the top of stardom, the rich and famous. He
made it his business to interact with the suffering, the orphaned, and
the dying on every continent, praying with them, giving them his
money and his love, and offering them hope. He traversed countries
of every size and shape. He left his lasting impact upon people from
every walk of life, of every religion and shade of color. He reached
out to everyone, and he did it quietly, passionately, and reverently.

Along the way, a few fortunate individuals were able to
accompany Michael during part of his journey, in ways through
which they glimpsed the heart and soul of this brilliant, enigmatic,
talented, loving, and pervasively misunderstood man. They came
to view Michael Jackson's "eccentricity" as the man's survival
techniques and his pinnacle-level fame as dehumanizing and even
toxic. They discovered that what some called his "paranoia" was
the reasonable reaction to continuous, insidious assaults from
various quarters—frivolous lawsuits by the gross, avaricious sharks
in suits, vulturous media, and crazies too numerous to describe.
They marveled at the mismanagement of his affairs by others, the
questionable financial practices by those who supposedly had his
best interests at heart, and the dangerous, who gained his trust and
did him in.

Michael Jackson felt the same feelings as any human being. He
experienced the gamut of joy and suffering, gain and loss, achievement
and failure, marriage and children, love and betrayal. The difference
is in the sheer *scope, scale, and magnitude* of everything related to
Michael Jackson and experienced by him. He made it to the *Guinness
World Records* twenty-three times; he should be in *Ripley's Believe
It or Not!* for the incredible richness, complexity, and absurdities in

his life. It could be argued that, in his fifty years, Michael Jackson experienced the equivalent of many lifetimes.

Although these judgments may appear to be hyperbolic, this book will demonstrate that they are not. *Defending A King ~ His Life & Legacy* allows a peek into the Michael Jackson world from his perspective, his unique personal journey, and his deep humanity.

It is time for a paradigm shift. The reader of this book should be prepared for it. Neither a "tell-all" book nor sensationalistic, *Defending A King ~ His Life & Legacy* focuses on the normalcy in a man who was turned into a caricature, on the creative genius that permeated every aspect of his life, and on the extraordinary coping mechanisms that he was compelled to adopt in his unique struggle to survive. Michael Jackson wanted what most people want—a chance at happiness, the opportunity to raise his kids and watch them grow into adulthood, to be loved, and to make a difference in this world.

Bizarre circumstances demand bizarre behavior. Michael Jackson lived in the most bizarre of circumstances ... like no one else on earth.

Defending A King ~ His Life & Legacy emphasizes the *goodness* of this man ... in addition to his generally acknowledged *greatness*.

Imagine what he could have left to us if he had lived. He was planning and working toward a glorious return to performing, to producing new music and films, and to advancing other works for the betterment of this planet.

This book is a sympathetic, empathic, and hopefully insightful look at Michael Jackson, who was both more and less than his public image. It is designed to celebrate his life and to perpetuate his legacy as the *transcendent* man that he was and is.

His fans, whom he so genuinely and deeply appreciated, deserve to know him better. The fans were the one true, lasting love affair of his life ... and beyond.

This book was put together by people who love him. If you say those words after reading *Defending A King ~ His Life & Legacy*, we will have done our job.

*   *   *   *   *   *   *   *   *

What you will discover and learn from *Defending A King ~ His Life & Legacy*....

"The Back Door" presents the circuitous route taken by this author in assuming the task of producing this book. It is the story of a serendipitous entry into the daunting project of writing about Michael Jackson. The major contributors to this book, people who knew Michael intimately, are introduced.

"Protecting Mr. Jackson" describes the surprising, unique, and extreme measures that were required to protect Michael Jackson and his children in their everyday lives. Tragically, Michael was the ideal target for some demented individual or group that would seek more than their "fifteen minutes of fame."

"Michael Jackson the Man" delves into the real person behind the celebrity. Little-known facts about Michael are presented in addition to a recap of major aspects of his personal history and life. There is very little coverage of his medical condition(s), out of respect for the man and his posthumous privacy. There are ample resources available to the reader about this topic, some of them fabrications and some valid.

"Daddy" discloses how Michael Jackson fathered his children, who were the most important aspect of his life. Everyone who contributed information and insights to this book describe Michael as his best self with his children.

"Michael Jackson & His Family" presents a view of Michael's relationships with his nuclear family, the Jacksons, particularly during his last years of life. Michael is revealed as a sometimes reluctant member of a large, confusing entertainment family with special pulls and tugs and conflicts.

"Michael Jackson's TSUNAMI: The Trial" covers the media-saturated 2005 criminal trial, in which Michael was wrongly accused of fourteen counts of misdemeanors and felonies, including child molestation. He was found *not guilty* of all charges. This chapter reveals the reasons for his acquittal and the incredible toll that the process took on him; he never fully recovered. "Don't rehash the trash" was the underlying principle of this chapter, and no attempt was made to describe details of the lurid and salacious allegations against Michael. To do so would serve no good purpose.

"The Back Story: Surprises" gives the reader a rare inside look into the true human stories and dynamics behind the scenes of the 2005 trial. Some never-before disclosed information is presented, and the reader will emerge with a wholly new perspective on the trial and what really went on.

"The Morass of Michael Jackson's Finances" explains the many moving parts of Michael Jackson's finances—his assets, debts, liabilities, and turbulent financial life. Surprises include the "king's ransom" that he kept within arm's reach and why he felt he needed it. The bottom-line realities are presented in order to separate *fact* from *fiction*.

"Flypaper: *Sticky Lawsuits* & Such" may shock the reader in terms of their number and scope. This chapter gives a good idea of what Michael Jackson had to contend with on a daily basis, of the precariousness of his financial position, and of the inescapable frustration and pain he had to endure from legal affronts of all kinds, many of these from former employees and "friends."

"Nothing But the Facts ..." outlines the chronology of Michael's last four years—arguably the most mysterious of his life—including where he and his children went, what he did, and how he spent his time. Although sometimes an isolate, Michael was *not a recluse,* and this chapter sets out to prove that assertion, in contradiction to media myth. Michael's path toward a triumphal return to the stage and to public life is revealed.

"Healer & Humanitarian" spells out the incredible level and scope of Michael Jackson's charitable acts, financial contributions, and philanthropic activities during his adult years. Some of the individuals whom Michael helped include children whose lives he saved and others to whom he personally gave the precious gift of hope.

"Artist & Entertainer" focuses on the genius of Michael Jackson in many areas of accomplishment and on his major artistic achievements. Even those well versed in Michael Jackson musical history are apt to be surprised by some of the inclusions in this chapter.

"Bizarre Behavior" is normal in bizarre circumstances. As a major theme of this book, this concept is explored in depth as it relates to Michael Jackson. The author humbly and respectfully offers psychological analysis of some of Michael's primary personality characteristics and behavioral patterns. It is written in layman's terms to the extent possible to make the various points in the discussion.

"The Paragon of Paradox" is an original, in-depth portrayal by the author of the unique paradoxical aspects of Michael Jackson, his career, and his life. This chapter is more "heady" than the others; readers who enjoy analytical approaches and more abstract concepts may especially appreciate this unique characterization of the complex and fascinating man who was both the dazzling, electrifying King of Pop and the humble genius-boy from Gary, Indiana.

"Michael Jackson & His Fans" celebrates Michael from all angles, in relationship with his fans, who range from music colleagues and other celebrities to paparazzi to people from every corner of the world. His fans were the only continuous love affair of Michael's life.

"The Unwanted Chapter" is the most difficult portion of this book for the author. As the title implies, it represents a painful reality—Michael Jackson died too early, at too young an age, and at the hands of a man he trusted. A summary of the Conrad Murray Trial for manslaughter is presented. Vindication for Michael Jackson has finally arrived....

"The Legacy of Michael Jackson" describes the enduring, evolving, and expanding legacy of the mega-star. What the future holds for Michael's image and for his admirers is predicted and explained.

"Ruminations" are the author's concluding thoughts and feelings about Michael Jackson the man.

Obviously absent is the chapter about Michael Jackson and His Friends. If there were such a chapter, it would be entitled "'You Are Not Alone' But Michael Jackson Was." After June 25, 2009, a horde of celebrities scampered and scurried to spotlights and microphones to proclaim and reclaim their friendship with the legendary King of Pop. During his post-trial years, Michael Jackson stood abandoned and ignored by many of those people, and others, whom he considered friends. The irony, of course, is that Michael Jackson was a best friend to the world; he will be remembered and honored for his unbridled love and unending loyalty. He never faltered on that path....

When the reader considers that Michael Jackson experienced so many of the events and hassles covered in these discreet chapters—organized by theme—*at the same time*, it becomes apparent that he led the most amazingly, almost unfathomably, challenging life possible. *He never lived a day free from crisis.*

*   *   *   *   *   *   *   *   *

When the dust finally settles from all of the ugliness of the Conrad Murray Trial, we will hopefully realize that Michael Jackson was a genuine victim who was forced to pay a huge price *for his death*. He not only lost his life but he was put on trial in a court of law for that very tragedy! The consummate irony and injustice of those realities were not lost on his family and his fans and admirers.

The painful mourning continues for this beautiful human being to whom much of the public never gave a break. We can now begin to celebrate him with renewed awe and greater understanding.

**We can hope to weave the colorful threads
and torn pieces of his life
into a rich fabric
that can deservedly be admired.**

"THE BACK DOOR"

**I was a seedling [of a fan] before;
now I'm an oak tree
with growing roots and branches.**

"Was Michael Jackson happy?"

I traveled 2,240 miles from Ponte Vedra Beach, Florida, to the desert of Las Vegas to hear the answer. When I met with Boyd Williams and Baron James for the first time, on Valentine's Day of 2011, I had my first question about Michael Jackson ready for them. I so hoped that these two men would assure me that Michael had overcome the trauma of his 2005 trial to the point of achieving some level of content.

In truth, I made this journey not only to seek a truthful, valid answer to this query. I went to interview with the security men who had protected Michael Jackson and his young family during the critical months before his tragic decision to move to Los Angeles to begin preparations for his "come-back" concerts in London. To most of Michael's fans, he had never really been gone, but the prospect of his renewed performing career excited and, yes, *thrilled* people everywhere.

In March 2009, an exuberant Michael Jackson held a press conference, standing-room-only, in London to announce his planned series of concerts, to begin in July. Because I was confined to bed and sofa by my physician, with my right leg in a cast and elevated above the level of my head for twenty-three hours per day, I watched television for hours and hoped that my ankle, broken in six places, would soon heal. Michael's high-spirited announcement was played over and over again throughout the day on various news programs. Each time I felt joy for him. *Way to go, Michael!* I thought, delighted that he had seemingly overcome his great adversities post-trial to the point of a glorious return to the stage.

Little did I know at the time about the specifics of those adversities. I would soon learn from a variety of sources that Michael Jackson dealt with more challenges, pain, and assaults against him than most people can even imagine, much less endure themselves....

Although I admired Michael Jackson and enjoyed his music for decades, I didn't yet refer to myself as *a fan*; I considered the term demeaning; and it smacked of teenage years. During the five-month circus of his trial in 2005, however, I found that I could not watch any televised coverage of it. I had to leave the room or change the channel immediately when there was reportage because the suffering on Michael's face was so apparent. *If anyone appeared to need painkillers, it was Michael Jackson.*

He was surrounded by security guards as every day he walked stonily to and from the packed courtroom through the hordes of people outside. The sight reminded me of a fettered lion cub, robbed of his dignity, being led by his keepers to a performing arena for the amusement of blood-thirsty spectators. I felt the same reaction to defendant Michael Jackson that I experience when a tortured animal is shown on a commercial or *Animal Planet* program. I felt as if someone was squeezing my heart, and I fled.

After Michael Jackson's death in June 2009, I found myself mourning from a depth I had not yet explored, from a place within that I had not yet discovered. I began reading and researching about the man; listening to his music; and buying his short films. I studied him with the same level of thoroughness that I had brought to the variety of subjects in graduate school, when I worked toward and completed a doctoral degree which qualified me to become a psychologist. When I learned about Michael's philanthropy and humanitarian works, his genuinely loving heart, and his immeasurable, ubiquitous impact on the world, I became ... *a fan.*

While watching his concert *Live in Bucharest* especially, I marveled as Michael Jackson sang "Heal the World," surrounded by orphan children. The audience—men and women of all ages and races—wept. Then he performed "Man in the Mirror," and the security attendants could not keep up with the fainting and overcome individuals; they were carried out to unseen medical tents for treatment, 3,500 of them! *More casualties here,* I reflected, *than in most natural disasters, such as hurricanes and earthquakes.* These were willing casualties, however, with no permanent injuries, thankfully. *They had seen Michael Jackson perform live.*

At his emotion-wracked Memorial service on July 7, 2009, I was amazed and deeply touched by the genuine outpouring of love for this man from all who knew and admired him. It was an epic event. His children emerged that day like beautiful butterflies from a cocoon for the world to see for the first time, as a newly-public family. People marveled at their dignity and grace. Michael Jackson had done right by these children; they were living testament to his dedication and abilities as a father.

He became a real human being to me that day, no longer just the King of Pop on a light-drenched stage but a true giver of love, an inspiration, a role model.

Time passed, and in mid-September of that year I almost lost my husband also. Robert suffered at least one heart attack—perhaps several during weeks of bouts of severe chest pain—which resulted in his need for quadruple by-pass surgery to save his life. *It was a scary time.* Robert was my confidante, lover, cheerleader, caregiver, and listening ear for more than three decades. While he was in the hospital for one week and then recovering at home, in rehab activity for many weeks afterwards, I set aside two hours every night—actually, early morning from 2:00 to 4:00 A.M.—for a break. During that allocated time I watched concerts from the Michael Jackson *Ultimate Collection*—32 DVD's and a CD of 97 songs—which Robert had given me for my birthday two weeks before his surgery.

During those two hours, when Michael Jackson sang, danced, and gave his all, I found that I could not worry or feel bad … about anything. It was a precious respite; it provided much-needed "head-vacuuming"; I became addicted. And, then I felt overcome by gratitude. *Michael Jackson as therapy!*

While, thankfully, my husband fully recovered, I did not! With my college roommate Lupe McDougald, dear friend Irene McDonald and her daughter Lori, I made the pilgrimage to Los Angeles on June 25, 2010. There we joined the Michael Jackson Tribute Tour and visited his Encino family compound (Hayvenhurst), the Holmby Hills home where he died, Neverland, the Staples Center, and Forest Lawn Cemetery. We left sunflowers at every site, where throngs of people were gathered, many of them bringing flowers, teddy bears, and other meaningful offerings.

Back home, with friends, I visited the Jacksonville Zoo for a behind-the-scenes tour. There I sought out Ali, the huge Indian elephant who had been transported here from Neverland Ranch after its closing. For many years, Ali had roamed freely with his companions Baba and Gypsy—the latter elephant a surprise gift to Michael Jackson from Elizabeth Taylor—on vast, hilly, verdant landscapes, along with tigers, lions, orangutans, giraffe, llamas, and numerous other species.

I watched Ali, now confined to a few sparsely-treed acres where he can only retrace his own steps in an endless manner, his large ears constantly, gently flapping. I wondered if Ali remembers the kind hand of Michael feeding him leafy branches and green bananas from days long ago. Like Ali, Michael was garrisoned in close quarters, at least as compared to his Neverland kingdom, during his nomadic post-acquittal years.

Earlier, in March 2010, I watched security guards Boyd Williams, Baron James, and Michael Garcia on two back-to-back *Good Morning America* programs. [The real names of Boyd Williams and Baron James have not been disclosed in this book.] They talked about their days with "Mr. Jackson" and "his little ones"—a span of many months during which they shared in Michael Jackson's life to the surprisingly significant extent that their boss allowed. The three men spoke about how they immutably bonded with him and his three children in a profound way that they had never known before. I wept.

Some months passed; I looked unsuccessfully for the book that they were writing about their experiences and interactions with Michael Jackson, "the real man"; and I decided to take action. I sent them a proposal, thanking them for their intentions and efforts on behalf of Michael Jackson and offering my help. They wanted to present the human Michael to the world, the good man whom they had come to know, and I hoped to assist them.

To my delight, Boyd Williams telephoned me on a sunny Sunday in early 2011. He told me, "We know more about Michael Jackson than his family, not bad things about him, but just things that no one else knows.

"We are doing this book because it is the last thing that we can do for Michael Jackson. We're doing it for him ... and for his fans. They deserve it."

"*I'm on a plane!*" a voice said in my head. I wanted to meet with these men to discuss my becoming their ghost writer—on a *pro bono* basis. Boyd explained that they had gotten thousands of hits to their website after their *GMA* program airing as well as overtures by would-be publishers for their proposed book. There was a catch, however, for the publishers; they wanted a scandal. *Here we go again....* The media world, at least the segment that is willing to put out money, wants Michael Jackson as a villain or at least a miscreant or weird creature.

"Michael Jackson was amazingly normal," Boyd told me during our introductory phone conversation. After he further elaborated on the themes of their book, I happily responded, "It sounds like you will be continuing the love affair between Michael and his fans."

On the night of our first meeting in Vegas, Boyd and Baron came to the Excalibur Hotel, where I was staying. Michael Garcia, the third member of the security team and the driver of Michael Jackson's weapons-filled back-up vehicle, left the project during that week. I did not have the opportunity to meet up with Mr. Garcia until the summer of 2011. Boyd, Baron, and I met for four hours, until 1:00 A.M. the next day; we talked about "the boss" and their memories of specific times and experiences with him.

They both look like security guards, I thought immediately upon our first handshakes. Both were noticeably scanning the casino environment, frequently looking right and left—an occupational hazard, a learned behavior that cannot be turned off like a faucet. Boyd directed the hostess to seat us in a reserved area of the restaurant so that we could have dinner and talk without any chance of being overheard. They whispered stories about Michael Jackson's financial affairs, lawsuits, exploitative managers, and the extreme measures that were necessary to protect him. They seemed relieved to be able to share with me these various matters and "inside stories."

Boyd struck me as a rare combination of "Don't mess with me" and "I could become your friend." He was guarded—pun intended—and had a penetrating gaze, but he also occasionally spoke with warmth that was comforting. Boyd, forty-seven years old, is a big, burly man with a barrel chest and arms the size of palm tree trunks. The sign posted next to the front door of his home, he explained, is strangely appropriate; it displays the unfriendly end of a gun with the warning "Never Mind the Dog—Beware of Owner!"

Baron looked like a professional actor of hero parts. At 6'4", 235 pounds, the thirty-four-year-old has the stature and bearing of a formidable, confident man. He smiles readily and comfortably in spite of the professional requirement for him to appear forbidding at certain times while guarding a client. Boyd described Baron as "the quiet storm," explaining that his friend is to be feared when he is confronted or angry.

Baron wore a knit cap that hugged his head and seemed strange in light of the warm weather. His arms were covered with tattoos, elaborate and highly detailed figures from shoulder to wrist. Near his shoulder resided an image of his mother, about five inches long, and he was quick to point her out to me. "This is my mother," Baron said proudly. "We are very close. Even when my mother is wrong about something, she is not wrong *to me*."

When Baron began his service with Michael Jackson, he was the father of a newborn daughter, only one month old. He has two other children, a teenaged daughter and a young son. As a single father, he shares in the care of his children with their mothers.

During our lively, intense conversation about Michael Jackson and their prospective book, I felt excited, energized, and hopeful. We smiled; laughed a bit; and at one point cried together. Baron provided the Kleenex, while Boyd, a bit embarrassed, shook his head from side to side and muttered, "Grown men shouldn't cry." As they were leaving we hugged.

The two men are African-American single fathers; they could easily identify with Michael Jackson. They empathized with his joys, worries, and challenges as a single parent.

On February 16, 2011, two days after our meeting, Boyd took me to see Michael Jackson's "primary house" during his months of service; it was located in Summerlin. I walked the streets that flanked the property and took photos. Boyd pointed out all of the various rooms in the house and elaborated on the security measures and personnel used in protecting Mr. Jackson and his children. He talked about the signal that Mr. Jackson used to communicate that he was retiring for the night. Boyd described the night that he met Michael Jackson and explained how "the boss" had tested his loyalty. During the car ride, he regaled me with stories that were interesting and poignant, including Mr. Jackson's secret trips to the Strip just to watch the everyday people and his ritual in reading his fan mail.

When Boyd returned me to my hotel, he informed me that he and Baron wanted me to work on their project. What an incredible opportunity for me to do something for Michael Jackson and for his fans, I thought with pride and eager anticipation.

When I had left my home days earlier, I perceived Michael Jackson as a human Bambi—fragile, vulnerable, deserted, in need of protection, alone—in a perilous environment. By the time I returned, I perceived Michael as Bambi's little brother.

Williams and James had devoted themselves to the safety and welfare of Michael Jackson across the span of time that they shared with him. Both appeared to be haunted by the question, *If June 25, 2009 had been on our watch, would Michael Jackson still be alive?* They will never know....

Boyd, Baron, and I worked together intensively on the book via emails. During the weeks of full-time writing, I felt angry, confused, and agitated, and I sometimes cried. I was stunned by what Michael Jackson had to endure in his complicated, tumultuous life.

In mid-April 2011, I returned to Las Vegas to work with Boyd and Baron on more material for their book. The two men, Boyd's assistant Angela, and I met at the Rio Hotel for dinner. Unfortunately, we never got around to the work that was the articulated goal and plan....

As before, Boyd instructed the restaurant hostess to seat our group in an unoccupied area. In the vast restaurant, the four of us sat at a table against the far wall. Baron ordered a bowl of boiling water, which the waiter promptly served us. To my amazement, without a word spoken, he collected all of our silverware and immersed it in the steaming water. Minutes later, explaining that he always engages in this precautionary ritual, he returned our silverware. *What kind of experiences*, I wondered, *has caused this unusual pattern of behavior?*

On the following night, the four of us met in the condo where I was staying. Baron had offered to bring the refreshments for our group.

"I'd like coke—nothing else," I told him. Both he and Boyd burst into broad smiles, blurting simultaneously, "You want *coke?*"

"No, no," I hastily replied; "I want *Coca Cola.*" Their smiles faded and I realized that we live in different worlds.

"I love her passion," Baron exclaimed several times to the others during our meeting. In spite of those welcome and complimentary words, it became apparent to me that they were not sufficient to bridge our divergent visions for a book.

Our four-hour meeting together included colorful, "salty" language and it turned emotional for everyone. The men pepper their conversation frequently with interesting expressions, such as "yo," "hey," "dude," and "bro." At one point, Baron suddenly left the room and the condo, after exclaiming, "I have anger issues!" He returned—after ten tense minutes for the remaining three of us— and we resumed our debate. We had *opposite* opinions regarding Conrad Murray, and I struggled with my strong, immutable feelings of anger over Murray's role in Michael Jackson's death.

Finally, exhausted and talked-out, we reached the conclusion that we were "not on the same page" regarding the content of their proposed book. I could neither embrace some of the directions that they wanted to take nor the limitations of scope and perspective. The draft that I presented them served as the focal point around which our differences were clarified. We parted, with hugs, at 1:30 A.M.

My impression was that they were still suffering from strong feelings that included anger—not generally directed at Michael Jackson but at his "people"—particularly over their allegedly not having been paid in a timely manner.

In the wake of our disagreements, my profound desire to present Michael Jackson in a very different and comprehensive manner to his fans and non-fans alike was intensified. I felt inspired to return to the drawing board, to start all over again, and to create my own book about Michael Jackson. I wanted to focus on a celebration of the man, focusing upon his last years and the complexities and herculean challenges with which he struggled. I hoped to propose probable explanations for his decisions and behavior and to shed light upon those characteristics of the man that reveal both his humanity and nobility of spirit.

Sitting at my kitchen table the week of my return from Vegas, I felt myself flooding with memories. *Flashback* to 1995, when I jumped into the controversial media-driven Baby Richard case in Chicago, Illinois. On a *pro bono* basis, I had become the psychologist-therapist for the four-year-old child and his biological parents,

Otakar and Daniela Kirchner, Czech immigrants. The state's highest court ruled the adoption of Baby Richard, when he was a newborn, by a "WASP" couple who called themselves Mr. and Mrs. John Doe in court documents, as "failed" and "fraudulent." Accordingly, the little boy, at the age of four, was suddenly transferred to his father Otakar and mother Daniela, who had married each other during the drawn-out custody battle. My job was to help the child and his birth parents become a family.

The media, however, had decided to champion the adoptive parents and to excoriate Otakar and Daniela Kirchner. Friendless, they became an underground family, dealing with death threats, hate mail, and rejecting potential employers. The paradigm was set: Baby Richard, whose real name was Danny, was described as a boy who would "never be normal," who was "doomed to a life of mental illness" due to his traumatic hand-over to "unsavory" people, away from "loving suburban parents." I realized, across many months, that these people didn't have a chance. They had been vindicated and supported by the Illinois Supreme Court, but they were harshly judged and condemned roundly in the media.

The truth was that Danny, from his first days in his biological parents' home, rapidly gained weight, got on with the life of a four-year-old, and thrived. His parents dearly loved him; worked hard and devotedly; avoided the media and the public; and managed to eke out a decent, respectable life. In my opinion, however, they did not recover from the grossly sullied images of them—including the innocent child Danny—that were manufactured in the media. It was heartbreaking to witness ... across years. The media won; these struggling good people lost.

From this deeply disillusioning experience, I viewed the phenomenon of Michael Jackson as Defendant during his 2005 trial. I knew that he didn't have a chance either to ever recover from the media-set perception of him as suspicious at best and criminal at worst. I ached for this man whom I didn't know, but with whom I felt deep empathy. It seemed cosmically unjust. I was convinced that he was an innocent with a kind heart, gentle spirit, and an incredibly, uniquely vulnerable life situation....

Michael Jackson has been the indisputable underdog in the media, who love it that way. Their ratings, sales, and profits have been astronomical ... at Michael's expense. As the life-long champion and rescuer of stray cats, I identified with the media-created plight of this man who was deservedly at the top of the world in his field but undeservedly an outcast in the court of public opinion.

After the 2011 court proceedings that addressed the senseless death of Michael Jackson, who was a victim *once again*—a victim to the doctor who killed him and a victim to media that exceeded all bounds of decency and respect in their coverage of Michael during the manslaughter trial of Conrad Murray—I felt heartbroken again....

Michael Jackson's influence on me was profound, I realized with a mixture of surprise and gratitude. Because of his example, I was inspired to volunteer every week at my local humane society, working to help potential adopters of the homeless cats and kittens. I also began feeding, on a daily basis, a colony of feral cats who live in a vacant field near my home. Now attending a Buddhist center to learn meditation, I have made new, close friends, individuals who value their spirituality and bring to the experience an open, probing mind. I go out of my way to give money to every homeless person whom I see; I remember that, from the time he was a teenager, Michael Jackson sought out homeless people to give them food or money. I've increased my donations to charities and try to do random acts of kindness. And, I've formed new, engrossing friendships with fans of Michael Jackson from Sweden, Russia, Germany, Australia, Tennessee, Louisiana, Nevada, Illinois, New York, California, and Florida. I try new things and attempt to "think outside the box" when making decisions in my everyday life and in considering my future.
Thank you, Michael.

*   *   *   *   *   *   *   *   *

In May 2011, I had launched a campaign to speak to people who really knew Michael Jackson intimately and to renew my reading and researching, at the same level of dedication and work from my years in college and graduate school.

Thomas Mesereau, the attorney who directed Michael's defense team at his criminal trial in 2005, telephoned me—in response to a letter I had sent him—from his Los Angeles office on a Sunday afternoon. He asked me pointed questions about my intended book, the resources that would be utilized, and the people who would be interviewed. Satisfied with my answers, Mr. Mesereau consented to meet with me to share information, insights, and behind-the-scenes material with me for this book. With genuine and deep affection for his client, he believes strongly that Michael Jackson deserves a legacy of well-earned respect, admiration, and love.

Calling the trial "a disgrace," Thomas Mesereau anguished over the horrendous mistreatment of his famous client by the authorities who dogged him, the media that tried to destroy him for their own gain, and his pathetic and perjured accusers. Mr. Mesereau felt powerless to control these factions, but he committed himself completely and tirelessly to defend the very life of Michael Jackson. He and his brilliant law partner, Susan Yu, led a team of attorneys, private investigators, researchers, and assistants in their quest to bring about justice for Michael Jackson—a full acquittal.

Mesereau and Yu succeeded. They set aside their egos; avoided the media; took control of the defense preparations, replacing those who were less skilled and less selfless vis-a-vis Michael Jackson; and avoided the circus-like machinations that are typical of high-profile celebrity cases. They ignored the inner circle of Michael Jackson.

Michael put his faith in them, and they did not let him down. They worked with uncompromising zeal and a special level of wisdom, instinct, and skill on Michael's behalf.

Thomas Mesereau spent many hours of his time with me in person, on the telephone, and in email communications in his unselfish commitment to contribute to this book "defending" Michael Jackson. Mr. Mesereau knew Michael Jackson in a way unlike anyone else. He understood Michael's feelings, core values, and belief system; he discovered nearly everything about his client's personal life. Thomas Mesereau's input has been invaluable to me.

While in Los Angeles, I had the great pleasure of meeting Susan Yu also, in the offices that she shares with her law partner Thomas Mesereau. We spoke and hugged, and I felt a special bond with this woman who was the behind-the-scenes heroine during Michael Jackson's trial.

Larry Nimmer, a professional filmmaker who was commissioned by Mesereau and Yu to videotape Neverland for the jury in Michael Jackson's trial, also gave unsparingly of his time toward this book. We met in person in Los Angeles and then continued to correspond across subsequent months.

Describing himself as "indifferent to Michael Jackson" at the time of his accepting the assignment to capture Neverland on film in a full, complete manner, Larry met Michael, "got a feeling of him as a man," and soon became a disciple of Michael Jackson. Larry has posted 43 videos of Michael Jackson on his Facebook site, and he has started a "Mike Like" organization of people who perform acts of kindness and charity in Michael's honor.

Larry remembers Michael Jackson as slim and graceful, "looking like a Boy Scout in the hallway of the courthouse," and as "kind, humble, gentle, and thoughtful." He was genuinely impressed with Michael as a human being. According to Larry, Michael Jackson had an inner strength that he came to admire. Michael would give an Eastern bow to Larry, one of his typical gestures that communicated deference and respect for other people—something Larry never expected from a mega-star.

His videotape of Michael's Neverland Ranch and home was critically important to the trial. The judge had refused Mesereau's request for the jurors to visit the Ranch; instead, he ruled that a visual representation could be presented in court. Larry took his job very seriously. He testified for two days on the witness stand, interpreting the footage, explaining the beauty and innocence of the place.

Most of the employees at the Ranch were Mexican Americans, and many were long-time staff members. "They were all nice, down-to-earth people, and they expressed warm feelings toward 'Mr. Jackson.'"

Larry would hear Michael's children laughing and giggling in their bedrooms, which were off-limits to the filming for the sake of the young ones' privacy.

"The smile on his face was so sincere when he was with kids," Larry says. "He was a spectacular person in so many areas—as a humanitarian, talent-wise, as champion of the disadvantaged and the sick, as advocate for the environment."

Larry Nimmer felt sorry for Michael because of what he had to endure throughout the trial months. Today, he has dedicated himself to advancing the legacy of Michael Jackson.

David Nordahl, an artist from Santa Fe, New Mexico, evolved into Michael Jackson's full-time personal artist. The relationship spanned two decades, during which David moved into Neverland for weeks at a time and sometimes traveled with Michael. He became a father figure to Michael. The men shared a gentleness of spirit and felt a strong mutual bond that was based upon creativity and a love of beauty. The two men would have long talks together, often throughout the night and early morning hours, when Michael could not sleep. Today, David will do anything that he can toward the goal of advancing Michael Jackson's legacy. He has been supportive and helpful to me beyond description. David told lovely stories about Michael that I had never heard or read before. The artist not only had special experiences with his younger friend, but he gained unique insight into Michael's heart and soul. "I always learned something new from him," he marvels.

Reverent June Juliet Gatlin, based in Los Angeles, became Michael Jackson's spiritual adviser during a span of many months before his death. As a healer and seer, she became a confidante to Michael. Reverent Gatlin spoke openly to me and shared her feelings and insights about Michael; she obviously felt fiercely protective of him. This interview and other information from Gatlin provided a wealth and depth of information for this book.

Each of the contributors to this book occupied a special niche in Michael Jackson's life.

In addition to the major contributors, I have interviewed seemingly countless other people, ranging from a driver of his vehicle to a man who was his friend as a child to fans from all over the world, whose lives were changed by Michael Jackson. I am grateful to everyone for their unique additions to *Defending A King ~ His Life & Legacy.*

We are never so defenseless against suffering as when we love.
— Sigmund Freud

Don't compromise yourself.
You are all you've got.
— Janis Joplin

PROTECTING MR. JACKSON

> **No one knew more about security than Michael Jackson.**
>
> — Boyd Williams

> **They're so quick to call you strange and weird, but it's almost as if you're forced to be different—because it's not normal life.**
>
> — Michael Jackson

To keep him safe. To keep him private. These were the marching orders for Boyd Williams, Baron James, and Michael Garcia during the last year-and-a-half of Michael Jackson's incredible life—while Las Vegas served as his geographical base. It was the most mysterious of times....

When he left Vegas for Los Angeles and the preparations for his comeback concerts, Michael Jackson became more visible to the public, if only by degrees. Up to that point, however, he chose to keep a low profile, and it was the job of his security guards to ensure that their boss's agenda would be fulfilled.

If their mission was to keep him *private*, why have Williams, James, and Garcia gone public via television interviews and Internet interactions that disclose both their glimpses and full-participation involvements in Michael Jackson's personal life? They offer the explanation that "someone needs to come forward" to present a view of their boss that is authentic and positive, revealing the good man and father that they observed and came to know intimately. When they began their public disclosures in early 2010, they were arguably among the relatively few people who were in fact speaking up for Michael Jackson, saying that he was a wonderful man. Now, however, since the Conrad Murray trial began roaring across global airwaves, telecasts, and cyberspace, a good number of Michael Jackson's friends and acquaintances *have* come forward. On a vast array of programs, they have revealed their "special" relationships with the King of Pop, nearly all of them paying tribute to his core goodness as a man and his effectiveness as a father.

During their watch, Williams, James, and Garcia successfully kept Michael Jackson and his children safe at all times. They devotedly contributed on a daily basis to the well-being and comfort level of Mr. Jackson and his three little ones. Now, they say that the reason for keeping Michael Jackson private has evaporated. Because, tragically, he is no longer with us, he does not require privacy any longer. Then, he was attempting to live in a way that was as close to normal life as possible, within the constraints of his unique burdens; precious days of anonymity were required for him to have even a small chance to achieve his goal for "ordinary life." His myriad security guards across decades tirelessly worked toward their boss's quest for privacy.

Boyd and Baron, calling themselves "two ordinary men pulled into an extraordinary life," feel that they are uniquely qualified to bring to light an important, factual segment of the historical legacy of Michael Jackson the man, father, and friend. During the span of their service, they claim, they saw more of Mr. Jackson and his children than almost anyone else; they knew him in a special, authentic way; and for those realities, they consider themselves "blessed."

More recent descriptions of Michael Jackson's life have been heard from his various employees from the witness stand at the Murray trial. Michael Amir Williams (Michael's personal assistant for two years), Alberto Alvarez (director of logistics/security guard for six months), and Faheem Muhammed (head of security for ten months) testified about Mr. Jackson's pattern of behavior and activity during his last six to eight months of life. They described his elaborate security structure during his residence in Los Angeles and his rented Holmby Hills home (at 100 North Carolwood).

The security precautions needed to protect the most famous man on the planet serve as evidence of the truly unique burdens of his personal life. Many years earlier, Michael affirmed, "I have ... had to live my whole life in a fishbowl." He had intrusive, prying people—paparazzi, would-be hangers-on, and fans—following him around, stalking him, and staking out his residences on a daily basis.

Protecting Mr. Jackson At Home

On December 23, 2006, unanticipated and unannounced, Michael Jackson quietly moved to Summerlin, an upscale Las Vegas community, with his beloved young children, Prince, Paris, and Blanket. After having stayed in dozens of places in a variety of countries, he came back to the U.S. as a changed man from the settled-in homebody he had been when he left the country many months before.

From the time of Michael Jackson's arrival in the United States after his self-imposed exile abroad, Boyd Williams, an eighteen-year veteran in the security business, became his "jack-of-all-trades protector" and the daily gatekeeper between Mr. Jackson and his new environment. Baron James and Michael Garcia, also experienced security men, joined up with Williams to form Michael Jackson's core Las Vegas security team.

Baron became Mr. Jackson's driver and his second go-to man. Michael ("Mike") served as the driver of the back-up vehicle that routinely followed the boss's vehicle and carried "enough weapons and surveillance equipment to wage a small war." The weapons vehicle transported firearms, sub-machine guns, thousands of rounds of ammunition, tasers, counter-surveillance devices, and body armor for the guards.

A job that usually demands little intimate contact with the client, one that is generally "devoid of emotional attachment," strangely blossomed into a "surreal," all-consuming life of dedication for the men. Loyalty, respect, admiration, affection, empathy, and sympathy—Williams, James, and Garcia found themselves transformed by a surprising amalgam of all of these powerful feelings while they were working to ensure the safety and privacy of the Michael Jackson family. They spoke about their having developed a commitment that transcended the assignment. They talked about their dedication with great pride on national television in 2010, as they recounted stories of Michael Jackson's private life and revealed their personal feelings.

From the beginning of their service—they explained—the three men jumped onto the roller coaster of their mega-famous, world renowned, charismatic boss's life, becoming his eyes and ears, daily helpers, trusted allies, confidantes, and then "friends." They dutifully and faithfully served as the buffer between Michael Jackson and the outside harsh and perilous world. Often they protected him from a scary segment of the public and from determined, manic paparazzi, and surprisingly sometimes from members of his own family.

Amazingly, in Las Vegas there was no entourage surrounding the most successful entertainer in the world. The three security guards became Michael Jackson's full-service attendants. Not only protecting him from physical harm in myriad ways, they also ran errands, assisted him with his email communications, and ushered financial and business records to and from a horde of Mr. Jackson's "people."

It became for these men an unforgettable journey with a brilliant, complex, talented, loving, and pervasively misinterpreted man. The security guards marveled at the mismanagement of his affairs by others off-site and at questionable financial practices by those who supposedly had Mr. Jackson's best interests at heart.

"Where is everybody?" Michael Garcia says that he and his colleagues would often ask each other. Williams, James, and Garcia would talk among themselves; they were supremely puzzled over the lack of any visible assistants in their boss's immediate environment.

Ironically—as they reported on national television—the three men went unpaid for weeks that turned into four months while they worked for Michael Jackson. They never blamed him, they explained, because they came to know the complications of his financial empire; his absentee kingdom was in jeopardy; and he suffered from the ambiguity more than they. Because they bonded with the man and his little ones, they could not walk away. The stark reality, they believed, was that shockingly Michael Jackson had no one else to lean on, no one else to be there for him.

Bodyguards are prepared to "take a bullet" for their boss, if necessary. That's part of the unwritten job description for personal security guards. The unparalleled level of Michael Jackson's international fame, the extraordinary degree of controversy that surrounded him, and his ubiquitous fans and followers made their jobs more difficult, challenging, and worrisome than would be the case for any other client.

Early on, Williams, James, and Garcia realized the uniqueness of their jobs protecting the most famous entertainer of their lifetimes.

The protocol for personal security of a top-level client calls for reporting to a designated place at a designated time without having foreknowledge of the identity of that client. Once the security detail begins, the use of personal cell phones and computers is discontinued entirely. Total focus must be on the safety, security, and comfort-level of the client. While they are on duty, all electronic communications by security personnel should be limited to those exclusively for use on behalf of the client.

Often, the assignment of a bodyguard to a well-known celebrity, athlete, or politician comes by telephone and from a blocked number. Not even the origin of the phone call is revealed. A personal assistant, manager, or secretary of the client places the call to an individual whom he or she has vetted and approved as competent and trustworthy of the job.

If a high-profile, recognizable client arrives by plane, the lead security man arranges for secure, discreet transportation by the necessary vehicles. He is provided the number and name of the incoming airplane, the destination address, and the name of the auto service company that has been assigned to pick up and transport the client. The auto service is not made aware of the identity of the client or, often, even of the destination. It is the lead security man who is responsible for ensuring that the vehicles are in place on time at the airport and also for determining the most secure route to the client's destination.

Boyd Williams had decided on the best route from the airport to what would become the new home of his unknown client on a still and starry night in early winter of 2006. With a professional colleague, he determined the number and locations of traffic lights, stop signs, and road closers all along the proposed route—essential considerations for this detail. The men carefully drove the route together, alert to every stop, turn, congested area, and potential impediment along the way.

Private vehicles, armed security men, tarmac access, and complete secrecy were all part of the process that evening. Curious anticipation— *Who is this client?*—is typical for security personnel, and it grows through the hours of systematic preparations for his or her arrival.

It was Saturday, December 23, 2006. It was cold at 10:30 P.M., at the private executive terminal of McCarran International Airport. A small jet plane broke the silence and landed on the air strip, arriving after its long flight from Dublin, Ireland.

The door of the plane opened. Out came the client, a man, accompanied by three children, and a woman who was probably the nanny. The man was dressed in black from head to toe; his face was covered by a black scarf. *Could this be Michael Jackson? No....*

There had been no news of Michael Jackson's return from Europe. He had been in Bahrain, Japan, Ireland, and other faraway places in the eighteen months since his lengthy trial and acquittal. *Where are the paparazzi that always precede and then follow Michael Jackson everywhere? Where are the fans who always seem to know about the King of Pop's arrivals? Where is the entourage?*

The mysterious man seemed to flow effortlessly into the vehicle. The motorcade of shiny, black security vehicles exited the airport, covert and quiet, and headed west toward Summerlin in the outskirts of Las Vegas.

Summerlin would appear to offer an ideal setting for a family man and his little children. As a master-planned community of fewer than 100,000 residents, it is one of the best-selling communities in the country. Named for Howard Hughes's grandmother, Jean Amelia Summerlin, it is surrounded by mountain peaks and distinguished by 150 neighborhood and village parks. With tree-lined streets and distinct villages, Summerlin is a quiet, safe, suburban-type community that appeals to families with children.

After twenty minutes of leisurely progress in the dark of night, the vehicles pulled up to a large, lavish home, its many palm trees decorated in holiday lights. (Well-known Vegas "deal-maker" Jack Wishna and his wife Donna had made arrangements for the Christmas decorations, including a big tree in the living room with wrapped presents underneath for the newly-arriving residents.)

The impressive house was surrounded by an eight-foot concrete wall with a twelve-foot wrought-iron entrance gate. As the front gate opened, the lead car pulled in and around the paved, circular driveway; the other vehicles followed in tow. It was after the five passengers had entered the house and all of their luggage had been carried inside that Williams realized that his client has been *Michael Jackson*! But where are the assistants, managers, groundskeepers, security guards, cooks, chefs, butlers, maids, drivers—all of the expected human accompaniments of tremendous wealth and fame?

Still in a state of disbelief, Boyd felt a dramatically heightened awareness of security needs, as anyone would in this situation.

Soon Williams found himself invited inside by his client's assistant, and then he was shaking hands with Michael Jackson. He felt star-struck, a new feeling for him. Boyd confesses, "The hair on the back of my neck stood at attention."

The two men enjoyed a brief, pleasant, and amazingly relaxed conversation. The result was that this slender, elegant man with the soft voice became his boss!

Boyd was alone, the only security scheduled to stay that first night. He was shocked to discover that the house had neither a functional alarm system nor an electronic surveillance system. The neighboring houses were located less than thirty feet away from the perimeter walls around this home.

It was obvious that security was not a priority in the vetting of this residence for Michael Jackson and his family. *Something was very wrong here.* Mr. Jackson's security men would later discover that this manifestation of mismanagement was—as the Alaskans are prone to say—"just the tip of the iceberg."

Before too long, however, additional security guards were hired and on site at the Michael Jackson home. Baron James began his employment on Mr. Jackson's security team only days after Boyd Williams. At the house, when Baron met Michael Jackson, a mask covered his face! He related this story, with a broad smile, during a television interview. With a mixture of surprise at the casual appearance of his new masked boss and deeply-felt awe, Baron gladly agreed to stay on. Michael Garcia happily became the third member of the core team that was responsible for protecting Michael Jackson and his family of three little children.

The security men immediately familiarized themselves with the layout of the house, every exterior corner and planting, and with the surrounding neighborhood. Astoundingly, during the first weeks, there were no visitors, no fans, no paparazzi lined up at the gate, as one would expect.

Their first priority was to establish a comprehensive and systematic plan to ensure the safety and well-being of Mr. Jackson and his three little ones. They installed state-of-the-art electronic equipment of various kinds and in various locations. They formulated behavioral rules that would direct all security personnel in their responsibilities. The men reviewed every aspect of the house exterior and grounds, of the house interior, and of the immediate locale and neighboring homes. They checked out all vehicle routes for ingress and egress.

They were alarmed by the full visibility of the glass-paned, quadruple-door front entrance of the Summerlin home from the street. They considered the portal from every angle. The front wrought-iron gate near the street curb consisted of bars through which an ill-intentioned person might hurl an object or, even worse, shoot a firearm. The men decided with conviction that Michael Jackson must be prohibited from using his own front door for his own protection and safety.

Thus began Mr. Jackson's consistent routine of using only the back door to the pool area or the door to the attached four-car garage, and only after the surrounding outside areas had been thoroughly checked by his security team.

Michael Jackson could not enter or exit his own front door.

Not ever.

*   *   *   *   *   *   *   *   *

They called him "Mr. Jackson." Williams, James, and Garcia decided that while others would refer to Michael Jackson as "Michael," "Mike," or "MJ," they would bestow upon him the respect he deserved, not just because of his superiority of position but because of their deeply felt regard and admiration for the person they knew. Even with each other, they remained consistent when they spoke about him by name. They did also call him, with real affection, "the boss." This did not seem deferential to the men; it was the reality that they worked for him, of course, but "the boss" also meant to them that they would gladly do his bidding and devotedly take care of him … and his children. And, of course, they routinely responded to their boss with the respectful term "sir."

Once the word got out that Michael Jackson was living in Las Vegas, daily life, as his security team knew it, changed dramatically. Paparazzi were climbing the trees that encircled the Jackson rented mansion, just as they were known to do everywhere they encountered his presence. They tried to take photographs of anything they could inside the perimeter walls that surrounded the property. Many of them attempted to scale the high wall.

Fans camped outside of the front gate and also across the street on the pebble-stoned easement with its few tall trees spaced evenly apart. They came and set up chairs; they ate their meals and stared at the wrought-iron, barred gate, through which the house's front doors were partially visible. Some of them wept; some paced; and some even passed out. It could get as hot as 120 degrees in the sun. Some fans fainted from heat exhaustion, others from intense emotions, and many from a combination of the two.

Sometimes an individual or two would approach one of the security men to cajole him to allow them to meet Michael Jackson. Every once in awhile, a fan would saunter up to the big front gate and casually ask to see Michael Jackson or even assert that he was expected by the superstar.

Williams, James, and Garcia knew that Mr. Jackson was not fond of his new Las Vegas home. He could never feel totally secure because of its corner location and close proximity to the two intersecting streets and to its immediate-neighbor houses. He hated the necessary prohibition on his use of the front door, but he dutifully utilized only the side door into the garage for the sake of his own safety. It would take only one deranged or publicity-seeking individual, some punk determined to make a place for himself in history books, to kill Michael Jackson or to maim him.

Mr. Jackson knew all of the details pertaining to the 1980 assassination of John Lennon, whom he admired as a gifted musician and messenger of peace. Michael had befriended young Sean Lennon after the tragic death of his father. Yoko Ono took her son to visit Michael at his Neverland Ranch, where he and Sean spent quality time together. Michael Jackson hoped to help fill the void in Sean's life that was left by his father's untimely passing. John Lennon, at the age of forty, had been gunned down in front of his own residence in New York City.

There were days when Michael Jackson never left his house, but his hard-core fans remained in their chosen places nearby, from early to late hours ..., waiting. Nothing would deter Mr. Jackson's fans from their encampment outside of his house.

The neighbors, unhappy with the continuous presence of strangers who settled in on the areas near their homes, called the police on many occasions. Although the authorities responded to these calls, of course, the fans, who were generally well-behaved, either stayed if they were on public property, or left and returned only minutes later.

Sometimes when he could see the police interacting with his fans from his window, Mr. Jackson watched the dynamics with obvious concern. Several times he directed one of the security team to approach the scene to ensure that the fans were all right. Michael Jackson had always demonstrated a paternal and protective attitude toward his fans throughout the years. His security teams carried out his directives to stay alert to any problems of potential danger to his admirers and followers.

When the security team took Mr. Jackson out for a ride, the fans would rush the vehicle, sometimes risking injury to themselves, in their efforts just to get a close-up view of the King of Pop. It was always tense inside his SUV at these times, especially when the little ones were in the vehicle. Although the majority of the fans were respectful and exercised restraint, some others became aggressive and rude, causing the security guards to become more assertive and forceful.

"Be nice to my fans," Michael Jackson would continually remind his security guards across the years, wherever he went. He remained adamant in his insistence that they "always be good to the fans," but doing so was not always the correct method to his security personnel. They realistically feared that, left unchecked or uncorrected, some of the fans would get carried away with their excitement to the point of becoming dangerous.

Mr. Jackson was known for insisting on stopping the vehicle nearly every time that his fans approached, even if it was just to say "hello" to them through his car window. He often received gifts from them. The women especially would give him teddy bears, balloons, flowers, original artwork, cards with special messages written to him, and other sentimental items to express their admiration and love.

During their first days on the job, as their greatest priority, his security guards made elaborate arrangements for a full-scale electronic surveillance system. They installed video cameras onto the exterior of the mansion so that every square foot surrounding the exterior was monitored. Twelve screen monitors displayed the area on a 24/7 basis; they took turns watching the monitors around the clock. The grounds were secured by an infrared laser detection system that was so sensitive that if so much as an empty pop bottle was tossed over the perimeter wall, they could detect its presence and location immediately.

Panic buttons were installed within the house in various locations, including every bedroom. In the event of an emergency, such as an intruder or fire, it would be a simple task for Mr. Jackson or one of his children to bring the security guards running to the scene. In fact, on several occasions one of the kids pushed the button, either by mistake or to test the guards' mettle, and the worried men appeared in seconds with their guns drawn.

The house rules for the security guards included that they were to enter the home only upon invitation or for a special reason, such as making a delivery or escorting a pre-approved visitor. The family members' bedrooms were like their sanctuaries, and they were never entered by security personnel except for an extraordinary reason. This way the Michael Jackson family could enjoy some privacy even with a number of men always on the premises. The guards used the large deluxe security trailer, parked near the garage, as their base of operations. It was well equipped with amenities that included kitchen facilities, a bathroom with shower, and sleeping quarters.

"We respected Mr. Jackson's privacy," Mike Garcia explains. "The bedrooms were off limits to us, ... and we didn't get too involved in family business."

Boyd Williams, Baron James, and Mike Garcia ran trial drills, simulating the evacuation of Mr. Jackson and his children from the house through its back and side doors. They also tested the use of the door that was located in the solid, concrete perimeter wall surrounding the house. It was always kept locked from the inside, of course, but when needed, it could open to the side street. This door was close to the pool and backyard area. It would be utilized if and when the Michael Jackson family needed to leave the mansion fast and the front door and garage exits were blocked by some unfortunate circumstance or menacing people.

The battery of Michael Jackson's employed security men ensured that guards were always on duty and available, on a 24/7 basis. Often staying at the house for twenty-four consecutive hours, they rotated brief sleep times; while one slept in the trailer, the others were on active duty. Williams and James, as members of the core security team, were always "on call," even when they left the premises of Mr. Jackson's home to return to their own residences and families.

Williams and James rotated nighttime shifts with the perimeter security team—two designated men who watched the house at all times. These positions were staffed by the same, well-vetted individuals. They were not permitted to interact with Mr. Jackson or the children except in an emergency or when directly addressed by a member of the family. Although all four Jacksons knew who they were, of course, there was very little interaction between the perimeter guards and the family.

Mike Garcia worked full-time as both a bodyguard and as the driver of the back-up vehicle that followed Mr. Jackson on every outing. Only after many weeks of service by Garcia would Mr. Jackson entrust "Mike" to accompany his children on outings without their father. Garcia explains that he was required to maintain frequent telephone contact with his boss, however, to ensure him that the little ones were okay.

Needless to say, the core security team spent the vast majority of their time on duty; they went home only for short periods of time; and, unfortunately, they sometimes missed out on seeing special milestones in the lives of their children. This was the job....

It took some time for Mr. Jackson to open up to his new security team in his new Vegas residence. During the honeymoon period with new security guards, Michael Jackson spoke only briefly and his words were short and simple.

As a single father with three young children, Mr. Jackson's only physical connection to the world at large was dependent on the attentiveness and conduct of his security team. They understood the importance of their role in his life.

Michael Jackson had security teams since he was a young boy. In fact, from the time he was only ten or eleven, he could not go anywhere without them. His incredible level of celebrity as the lead member of The Jackson 5 created special security challenges everywhere. For his own safety, he was never left alone; even then the fans were relentless in their efforts to get close to their idol; and their frenzy often got so out of hand that it became downright scary. Michael Jackson required medical treatment for injuries caused by his overly zealous fans on a number of occasions.

At the 2,700-acre Neverland Ranch, there was an army of security guards and also hundreds of security cameras throughout the grounds. The hidden cameras were necessary because of the many visitors to Neverland when Michael Jackson was in residence and also when he was away. Many incidents had occurred across the years wherein people tried to gain access to private areas at the ranch and then hide out there. There were both stalkers and intruders onto the property.

In Las Vegas, Mr. Jackson required his bodyguards to bring back from their regularly-scheduled shooting-range practices the big targets to demonstrate to him their level of skill and progress. This behavior by their boss was reminiscent of his having drilled his dancers, one at a time, during preparations for his tour concerts. Michael Jackson would tactfully critique each dancer toward the goal of improvement and perfection. His security guards would present to their boss their respective targets for his inspection; it was, to them, a little like showing "dad" their report cards. Mr. Jackson wanted to feel safe, for himself and his young children, in their hands. When they'd had a good day and done well, they were very proud. The boss would praise them enthusiastically.

Michael Jackson had gotten to the point that bodyguards were like the furniture, always there and available for his use when needed. He learned to ignore their presence for his own peace of mind and freedom of movement, even if that movement was confined to a small place, such as a hotel room. His frequent lack of interaction with them was just adaptive behavior rather than a social snub or message of disdain.

Within a couple of months, the men report, Mr. Jackson grew sufficiently comfortable with Boyd, Baron, and Mike and trusting of them to the point of discussing everyday matters, sharing some laughs with them, and even shedding a few tears in their presence.

The men found themselves becoming a formidable buffer for him, between Michael Jackson and members of the outside world. From fleeing the seemingly ever-present paparazzi to maneuvering around frenzied fans, to sometimes avoiding his own extended family, Mr. Jackson relied on the three security guards to carry out his wishes and protect him in myriad ways.

During their watch, there were no on-site assistants or household domestic staff to help with various necessary tasks. When Michael Jackson and his little ones lived at Neverland, there were dozens upon dozens of employees to provide the complex array of services required by a large home, vast grounds, elaborate recreational facilities, and frequent hordes of guests.

It was obvious to the men that the boss needed them for a wide range of duties that exceeded the expected, typical security detail. They helped him with his personal and business correspondence, emails, grocery shopping and packaged-meals acquisition, and errands of all kinds. Their services ranged from helping with the care of the family pets to reconfiguring the rooms of the house for special uses, such as creating a classroom for the children and music and dance studios for Mr. Jackson.

The security team washed and polished the SUV's daily so that they always looked clean and shiny. The men wore ironed shirts and dress pants, and, when taking Mr. Jackson out in public, they wore suit coats even when the Las Vegas temperatures soared into the one-hundred range.

Boyd was occasionally commissioned to buy clothes for Mr. Jackson's little ones. The boss would provide him with articles of clothing that fit each of the children, and, armed with those items, Boyd shopped for stylish clothing of the same size. In the stores, he would hold up a dress or pants or shirt, guess the size, and then try to match it to similar items from the racks of clothes.

Williams and James constructed Mr. Jackson's dance studio in the large room located on the other side of the garage wall. All of his security men were fans of Michael Jackson music, but to hear him dancing and singing—through the wall—was "a blessing and an honor."

The men never got used to the surreal experience even though Mr. Jackson would practice almost every night. As soon as the bodyguards heard the music start up, they knew it would be followed by the sounds of his dance steps. They often looked at each other with that knowing smile that meant "That's our boss, the King of Pop!"

*   *   *   *   *   *   *   *   *

Mr. Jackson was noticeably concerned—and worried—about security, often surprising the men with his personal involvement. They would detect him walking throughout the large house between 3:00 and 4:00 A.M. Mr. Jackson would be checking to ensure that the doors were locked, even though he knew that armed security guards were monitoring and patrolling his property at all hours. Outside in the dark, the bodyguards would be standing together near the side door, and they would startle when the door knob jiggled.

"That's the boss," one would say to the other. Then they would smile as if the door checker were a lovable frightened child.

Williams, James, and Garcia discovered early on that their boss suffered from chronic insomnia. From the time of his earliest fame, when he was not much more than twenty, Michael Jackson would engage in various activities throughout the very early morning hours, such as writing music or making phone calls, because he was unable to sleep.

His head of security arranged for a simple signal to be used for the guards to know when Mr. Jackson would be going to bed for the night. Whether he was able to sleep or not, when he wanted them to know that he had turned in for the night, Mr. Jackson would turn off a certain lamp in his bedroom. The men knew that they would not likely be needed by their boss any more that day, and they would continue to monitor and patrol the grounds in the routine manner.

Not that anything was really considered "routine" by his security team. The men remained ever-vigilant to every sound and car headlight during their assigned shifts. They knew that at any time, in spite of the elaborate electronic surveillance equipment, a determined, skilled individual could successfully climb over the eight-foot perimeter wall and forcibly gain entrance to the house, especially if undetected for a span of minutes. Years before, a crazed fan had somehow gotten into Michael Jackson's Neverland home, hiding out in a closet for four days, coming out only at night to use a restroom and raid the refrigerator. She was caught and removed, of course, but her successful home invasion served as a message that the best security program can be breached.

Boyd Williams, Baron James, and Mike Garcia were abundantly aware of the far international reach of Michael Jackson's fame and of his incredible, unprecedented inspirational and commercial value to the entire world. Above all, however, they understood how much their loving father meant to Prince, Paris, and Blanket. As single fathers themselves, Boyd and Baron intuited Mr. Jackson's all-consuming devotion to his children; he showed his love every day.

One afternoon as they were driving on the highway, Mr. Jackson directed James to pull the SUV to the curb. Dutifully, the driver obliged and brought the vehicle to a stop. Mr. Jackson explained to his security guards how much his children meant to him. He extracted promises from them to protect his children at any cost.

His bodyguards knew well that, although their boss was loved and even revered by millions, there were those among the public who loathed him. He was perceived as very different; he elicited a level of excitement like no one else; and some people despised him for his unusual *persona* and undeniable charisma. Nothing brings out the crazies more than celebrity, and some people want to destroy what they don't understand. Some men likely hated him because of the stirrings he may have aroused that surprised and dismayed them.

Then there were those people who believed the media bias against him and the ugly reports and accusations. Although he was acquitted of all charges by a jury at his 2005 trial, many thought he was guilty, at least of *something*—a *where there is smoke, there is fire* kind of reasoning. Some believed he was guilty of serious misconduct. Boyd, Baron, and Mike knew their boss was a kind and gentle man with an always-open heart for children and people in general, even in spite of the raw deal that he had gotten during those terrible recent years. But the general public could never observe what they did on an everyday basis, and many people would just go on hating. There is always some percentage of those people who can turn to violence to act out their own rage....

Mike Garcia has been especially vocal in expressing his perceptions of his former boss as loving, caring, and gentle; he has referred to him as "an innocent." Often surprised at Mr. Jackson's obvious shyness, Mike witnessed the immediate metamorphosis of his boss to "confident and exuberant" as soon as he would begin to perform a song.

Securing Mr. Jackson's safety became "more than a job" to his guards. It was a personal responsibility that came with an inestimable price if they would fail. Besides, they not only *were* protective of him as their job, they *felt* protective of him.

His security team especially appreciated the thoughtfulness of their boss. Because Mr. Jackson realized that the men worked long hours for him every day, he often personally brought out plates of food and bottles of water to them. The guards realized that this behavior was unusual for a client, and they felt real affection for this gentle and considerate man who was their boss.

Mr. Jackson often asked Williams, James, and Garcia about their families, and he listened to their responses with genuine interest. He then wished them all well by saying something kind and sending along his warm wishes. "God bless you," he often told them.

Mr. Jackson even bought for the teenaged daughter of his head of security her first cell phone, an unforgettable gift for the grateful girl.

After the first weeks of their employment with Michael Jackson, there were mostly times when Mr. Jackson would interact with Williams, James, and Garcia in a comfortable, friendly manner, as if they were all buddies exchanging stories and jokes, but at other times he was quiet and detached. At first, the security guards assumed that these periods of aloofness were the arrogance of stardom, but they came to understand that Mr. Jackson struggled with anxiety, loneliness, and a host of problems related to his worrisome financial status and sullied image. He would periodically confine himself to his room for days at a time. He may well have interacted with his children at those times, because the security men had witnessed his consistency in being accessible and loving to them, but he remained secluded from all others.

When rare visitors came to the Las Vegas house, the head of security was always notified beforehand. The security guards would watch for the guests and then inspect them and their vehicles when they arrived. No one was getting into that house that was not expected and examined.

When repair persons, installers, and other service people were needed at the house, Williams would make the necessary arrangements. Everyone was required to sign what might be called an *industrial-strength confidentiality agreement* before gaining access to the Michael Jackson home. The agreement, which carried the power and enforceability of a contract, was intended to guarantee that service providers would not divulge the location of Michael Jackson's residence or specifics about his house. Even more important, these individuals were prohibited from revealing any information they might obtain regarding Mr. Jackson or his family while they were on duty at his home. Breach of the agreement would result in a king's ransom in financial penalties.

In addition to the verbal and written precautions taken by his security team when service providers came to Michael Jackson's house, at least one of the bodyguards would accompany the worker at all times. Even when the individual needed to use a washroom while at the home, a security guard would accompany him and, while averting his eyes, stand at the worker's elbow until the personal mission was accomplished!

Mr. Jackson and his children often enjoyed going out onto the roof of the Summerlin house, because there they could breathe the fresh air and see across the entire expanse of land that included a patch of Vegas desert in front of the concrete-and-lights downtown area. There was an ample deck fashioned into the house's sloping rooftop that accommodated sitting and lounging there.

It was even more fun for the children because they had to use a secret door in their father's bedroom to access the special spot. The kids and their daddy would sometimes eat candy bars and drink soda pop while they shared the joy of togetherness, watching the entire landscape before them. When Paris and her father enjoyed "alone time" together on the roof, it was a special, unforgettable treat for her; she would later refer to it as one of her best memories.

His security guards worked hard to prevent problems for their boss, and sometimes they kept information from him that would be troubling. This kind of manipulative behavior was common for those surrounding Michael Jackson.

After a particularly upsetting telephone conversation, Mr. Jackson threw the phone across the room. Boyd, who stood nearby, was startled by this atypical outburst; he just watched, feeling helpless. Mr. Jackson sometimes showed his frustration and anger in the privacy of his home.

"Why won't they just leave me alone?" he would say. Of course, there was no good answer … except that he was *Michael Jackson*.

Everyone seemed to want a piece of him for so many reasons, financial and emotional.

It was well known that Michael Jackson hated conflict and avoided it at almost any cost. His security guards also realized, however, that the boss knew how to fire people, although he never did the deed himself. One of his managers or attorneys would deliver the bad news to an employee who was to be terminated, either by phone call or written communication. By design, Mr. Jackson would not be around at the time; he was too sensitive and caring to become involved in the traumatic event; and he had people on his payroll who were readily available to carry out his wishes. The Las Vegas security team witnessed the comings and goings of a number of Michael Jackson's assistants and managers.

In fact, Mr. Jackson had become accustomed to expressing his desires to one of his "people," who would immediately and invisibly arrange for their fulfillment. A plane would be arranged for his travel; a new vehicle would arrive with all paperwork having been completed by someone else; and deliveries of furniture, accessories, and clothing would just happen. Most of the time there was no signature needed and no receipt provided. It happened like magic.

His security guards realized that their boss had lived this way for his entire life. Through no fault of his own, he had never learned to arrange for "things" by himself. He did not need to complete forms or fill out applications. One of his security men made arrangements for Mr. Jackson to obtain his first personal credit card during the period of time that he resided in Las Vegas. He had apparently lived for nearly fifty years without a personal credit card.

Occasionally Mr. Jackson would borrow a cell phone from one of his security guards for his own use or for one of the children. Later he might sheepishly apologize and inform the guard that the phone was "lost somewhere in the house" and that the man would need to order a new one.

Every day classical music played throughout the house; Mr. Jackson found it soothing and inspirational. At Neverland, Mr.

Jackson's favorite classical music was always played, not only in his home but through one hundred speakers hidden in rocks around the grounds. Who would have thought that the King of Pop listened to classical music all of the time?

As a self-proclaimed lover of books and knowledge, Mr. Jackson read at every opportunity. His security team observed the boss reading from the *Holy Bible* nearly every day; he also seemed especially to enjoy history, art, science fiction, and biographies.

"We learned something new from him every day," explains Boyd, the admiration for his boss apparent in his voice.

Protecting Mr. Jackson Out & About

"Guarding Michael Jackson in public in real life," explains Boyd Williams, "was *nothing* like you see on TV. The onrush of fans trying to see and touch him, the fainting women, and the stampeding people coming from all sides were all very scary." All of Michael Jackson's security teams encountered mass hysteria, from time to time, during their service to the King of Pop. A real-life mob scene is impossible to predict or to control once it gains momentum. Security personnel feel powerless in the face of it, and their only rational response is "to run, to get him out of there as fast as possible."

His security guards were always ready to move fast; they previewed every potential exit from every building into which they took their boss; and, on numerous occasions, they all wound up running. Even when Michael Jackson was wearing a disguise in the hopes of remaining undetected, someone would always recognize him. He had "a distinctive swagger" and the fans recognized it. At those times, the swagger would turn into a full run until he got away from the electrified, frenzied fans. Typically, his final escape was achieved when he would seemingly flow gracefully into the waiting vehicle, which then sped away.

Michael Jackson loved live entertainment of all kinds. "That's why I love Las Vegas," he explained to an interviewer; "it has such great shows."

At another time, he was asked, "What are you doing in Vegas?"

"Working my way through all of the magic shows," he answered, not as facetiously as it may sound.

Michael especially enjoyed watching David Copperfield; he had known and admired the world-class magician for many years. Copperfield worked as an illusionist and consultant for Michael Jackson on several of his projects, including the *Liberian Girl* short film and the *Dangerous* concerts. Michael Jackson had always loved magic; he was fascinated by it; and he especially savored the idea of transmutation. Michael specialized in transforming himself; he continually and dramatically changed his own physical appearance, attire, dance moves, and songs. He wanted to push the envelope with everything he did. Magic opened up new possibilities for him and unleashed his creativity.

He loved live concerts and the theater. Celine Dion was surprised one night when, from the stage, she saw Michael and his security team walk down the center aisle and take reserved seats. Knowing that he cherished his anonymity, she struggled with the decision of whether to announce his presence. Ms. Dion did acknowledge him: "Ladies and gentleman, we are honored to have Michael Jackson here with us tonight."

The audience went wild with excitement. "I was afraid that people would actually jump down from the balcony to see him," she explained. Michael was very gracious and shook the hands of many people on the aisle.

After her performance, Michael visited with Ms. Dion in her dressing room, where he asked her questions about the advantages and disadvantages of sustaining a long-run series of concerts in Las Vegas. He listened intently because he was considering such an opportunity for himself.

That night—as always when Michael Jackson chose to attend a performance without a disguise—it proved to be a nerve-wracking experience for his security team. Whether he was accompanied by three guards or more than six, the security detail required complete focus and elaborate anticipation for anything that might go wrong.

His security team would collectively breathe a sigh of relief when Mr. Jackson was returned safely to his home after an outing to enjoy professional entertainment. The idea of his going to a restaurant after the event was out of the question. His presence would undoubtedly draw a crowd or mob, seeking photos, autographs, and physical contact.

"Anyone who has entered the realm of being a professional security person can only dream, but never really imagine, protecting the King of Pop," his head of security revealed. In the videos of Michael Jackson's concerts, it is apparent that there are legions of police, military, and security guards that were required. Literally thousands—reportedly 20,000!—individuals were assigned to his ironically-named *Dangerous* concert in Bucharest, Romania, to provide the necessary security for 70,000 attendees and, of course, for Michael Jackson and his touring company. (This concert was broadcast to millions in dozens of countries.)

Because of the level of security measures necessary for the protection of Michael Jackson, there is no training program available that can adequately prepare an individual for a position on one of his security details. On-the-job learning was more important for his security men than their formal training because protecting the King of Pop was in a league of its own. Street savvy had an important role, as did specific input from Mr. Jackson himself; the boss had become exceptionally knowledgeable about all aspects of security work.

Before Mr. Jackson would travel from his house to any designated destination, his security team would perform a dry run of the trip. They would drive the entire route, taking note of every traffic light, stop sign, crossroad, congested area, shrouded curbside, and building along the way. They would plot alternate routes in the event that detours became necessary. They familiarized themselves with the nearest hospitals, police stations, and ambulance services as standard precautionary activity; they had the telephone numbers to these facilities at the ready. The security men communicated with each other through earphones and two-way radios; they were in constant contact with each other whenever they were driving the SUV's and/or taking Mr. Jackson anywhere.

After he moved to the Los Angeles area, Michael Jackson's security guards would ensure his safety and convenience through an "advance team." One of his vehicles, typically occupied by two bodyguards, would drive his anticipated route while communicating the condition of the roads and the best exits from the expressway to the security men who were driving the mother vehicle that carried Mr. Jackson.

In Las Vegas, Williams, James, and Garcia executed all of their preparations with extreme precision, priding themselves on their thoroughness. They were determined to be primed for any eventuality. If you plan for the worst, they believed, you will get the best outcome. No day was routine, and no detail was considered insignificant.

"Mr. Jackson paid great attention to detail," Mike Garcia recalls. This focus by their boss was mirrored by his security team members, who wanted to measure up to his standards and to ensure his safety at all times.

Whether they were driving across town to a movie theater or a bookstore or taking the little ones to Chuck-E-Cheese, the team adopted the mindset that any given day could bring a breach in security or an attempt to harm Michael Jackson and his family. "Not on our watch," they promised themselves.

The protocol for the transportation of Mr. Jackson was established in clear, emphatic terms. Mr. Jackson always sat behind the security man who was seated in the front passenger seat; this arrangement is the standard for executive protection. His head of security was the vigilant front-seat passenger, "riding shotgun." He understood that his position in the vehicle was intended as a shield for his client.

Baron James served as the driver of Mr. Jackson's vehicle, the mother car. When the children accompanied their father or rode in the vehicle with only the security men, they sat, with their seat belts tightly secured, in the back seat. Following the mother car was the back-up vehicle with surveillance and counter-surveillance equipment, weapons, and ammunition, driven by Mike Garcia or another regular on Michael Jackson's security personnel roster.

Each of Mr. Jackson's bodyguards carried a pistol under his shirt or suit coat. The men also carried tasers that could take down a big man.

In the event of any attempt to physically harm or to kidnap Mr. Jackson or his little ones, deadly force would have been employed by his security team as necessary.

Mike Garcia recounts that he realized that he had earned the trust of his boss when Mr. Jackson finally allowed him to take his children on local excursions without him. Many weeks passed before Michael Jackson permitted his children to leave with his security guards while he stayed at home.

When the security men took the children for an outing, they would try to be as inconspicuous as possible so that the kids could function in a normal way. The challenge was to remain close enough to them to afford ample protection but far enough that the children were not shadowed.

Although the boss's children could enter public buildings through the front door when they were accompanied by their nanny and/or the security guards, the team did not allow their father this freedom. It was too dangerous, they decided, for him to become the likely target for trampling fans, especially in light of their responsibility to jump in between as a buffer, when necessary. The guards, armed and wearing headphones for communication with each other, would escort Mr. Jackson through back entrances and hallways, always walking briskly.

They regularly had to endure the smell of kitchen waste and garbage; walk on filthy, greasy floors; and use service elevators that creaked and groaned. Michael Jackson was consigned to back doors, dimly-lit secondary hallways, and alleys.

Their boss couldn't enjoy the creative decorating or the comfortable furniture of fancy and elegant hotel lobbies. He rarely experienced them, and when he did, he was whisked through them by his bodyguards. Mr. Jackson would have enjoyed the architectural beauty of the buildings' interior spaces and their elaborate furnishings, they knew, but his safety was the priority—not his enjoyment—during these times of exposure in public places. The boss was always on a short tether.

"I can't remember the last time I entered a hotel or restaurant through the front door," Mr. Jackson would lament. Going to a park with his children or riding public transportation, such as a train or bus, was out of the question entirely. Michael Jackson wanted to ride a subway, but that was impossible. When Mr. Jackson would occasionally say something like he would someday just saunter into a bar and order a drink, the men would just look at each other, silently, as if their boss were a kid who was saying that he would someday become an astronaut and go to the moon.

Elaborate measures for his safety and security were necessary at all times. Michael Jackson had suffered injuries from his fans too many times in the past, sometimes requiring medical treatment, his security teams knew. In Germany, for example, when he made an aborted attempt to eat in a restaurant, he sustained an injury from rampaging fans that required him to use a wheelchair for days after the unfortunate failed experiment.

Before they escorted Mr. Jackson into any building, his security teams would always thoroughly check out his destination rooms, whether a hotel suite, meeting room, or private residence. They used counter-surveillance "bug" detectors to scan everything—walls, furniture, closets, draperies, mirrors, paintings, lamps, and bathroom fixtures. They carefully and systematically ran the scanners across the fronts, backs, and sides of every piece of furniture and under every table top.

When Mr. Jackson stayed at a hotel, he was typically registered in an assumed name. Sometimes one of his security men used his own name and credit card in the hope that the boss could remain anonymous during his stay.

His security guards installed tiny cameras across from Mr. Jackson's hotel suite door so that they could detect all comings and goings. From their own hotel rooms, they watched the camera monitors throughout the night. That way they avoided the necessity of being positioned there, as in the movies, which usually portray mammoth-sized, frowning men with folded arms, their backs straight and rigid against their boss's door.

When Mr. Jackson checked out of his rooms, his security team reviewed the entire area, again checking for hidden cameras or microphones. They removed any personal items left behind and uncovered the mirrors; the boss regularly blocked the hotel mirrors with a bed sheet. His head of security marveled over this unusual practice but he did not ask questions; it was not his place. *It's very curious and even paradoxical that the Man in the Mirror doesn't allow himself to see his own mirrored reflection.* He didn't know whether Mr. Jackson intended the mirror-veiling as a special precaution against hidden cameras or whether he didn't like to see his own image. As a teenager, Michael Jackson had avoided mirrors because of his self-consciousness and embarrassment over the acne condition that plagued him until post-puberty. He revealed this idiosyncrasy in his interview with Oprah Winfrey in 1993.

The "cloak and dagger" routines, as some critics called them, were in fact necessary for those protecting Michael Jackson. In September 2005, two air service men were indicted for recording conversations between Michael and his then-attorney Mark Geragos during their trip, via private jet, from Las Vegas to California in November 2003. These men, who confessed their guilt, were sentenced in 2006, the first to eight months in federal prison followed by six months in a halfway house and the second to six months of home detention. The presiding judge, A. Howard Matz, stressed the seriousness of the crime in his sentencing order.

Later, in March 2008, one of these defendants—the owner of Extrajet, the air charter company that had transported Michael and Mr. Geragos during the time of Michael's criminal trial preparations—was ordered in civil court to pay the sum of more than $12 million in damages. He had pled guilty to planting a device on the plane in order to tape Michael Jackson and his legal representative. The crime was discovered when Fox TV was offered the tape for an undisclosed amount of money.

The lesson learned from this unsettling event was that it is easy for ill-intentioned individuals to record private conversations if they are determined and greedy. The *Michael Jackson factor* was at play, of course, because a secret recording of the ubiquitously front-page star could command six figures from a media outlet or tabloid.

The tabloids prominently featured photos of Michael Jackson wearing disguises in public; the paparazzi loved capturing these images. Mr. Jackson used a variety of disguises to increase his comfort level in venturing into public places, such as bookstores or live shows. He was trying to enjoy an experience like a "normal" person, a non-celebrity. When he appeared in disguise, Boyd, Baron, and Mike did not ask their boss why he wore bandages, a mask, or a veil to cover his face. They knew that Michael Jackson loved the idea of transformation and he had a flare for whimsy. When he would come down the staircase wearing some costume, the men simply smiled and accompanied him to the waiting vehicle. Then off they would go to the planned destination for the day.

Mr. Jackson also occasionally used a wheelchair, which created media speculation about the state of his health. On one such occasion, he accompanied his children to a bookstore during regular hours. He probably believed that he would be less likely to be confronted by fans or anyone else if he was confined to a wheelchair. His security men pushed the chair and surrounded him on his way to and from the store, and they remained nearby as Michael and his children happily sampled the books.

Their boss bought so many books—many thousands of dollars' worth—that the men had to return with a trailer to transport them to his house or hotel suite. When they asked Mr. Jackson where he intended to store them, particularly when he was staying in a hotel, he just relied upon them to "make it work."

The ubiquitous umbrella, always very large and held over Michael Jackson's head by one of his security team, became a kind of trademark. For years people had wondered about it, and many reporters considered it an affectation or a narcissistic symbol of his self-importance. Royalty in many countries for centuries used servants to shield them from the sun with umbrellas and portable canopies. The truth is that Michael Jackson was hypersensitive to the sun, to the point of allergic reaction, and the umbrella was used for compelling medical reasons.

Not only was Michael Jackson a prisoner of his fame—unable to use his own front door; to leave his home for spontaneous excursions; or to enjoy a park, department store, or restaurant—he was also severely limited by his need to avoid direct sunlight. It was as if he had been cursed, this man who so loved nature, swimming, and amusement parks. He was limited in so many ways, his security guards knew, and it was their job to maintain those limits for his general welfare.

Once in awhile, however, Mr. Jackson wanted to see a movie in a theater like ordinary people. When he did, his security team underwent preparations that were anything but simple. In addition to the usual dry run with the vehicle along the proposed route to the theater, his security team contacted the manager and theater security; together they scrutinized the prospective seating arrangements, doors and aisles. Sometimes Mr. Jackson wanted to enjoy a big-screen movie as part of the audience, to feel the excitement and reactions of people in a full theater. Other times he wanted to enjoy a movie with only his three little ones. Either way, sneaking them into a movie theater always required detailed planning in order to avoid the otherwise inevitable fanfare and paparazzi. At times the family and their guards would purposely enter the theater a few minutes after the movie started in an attempt to avoid notice.

Las Vegas is well known for offering a wide range of opportunities, something for everyone. "What happens in Vegas stays in Vegas" has become the city slogan for visitors. One night,

Mr. Jackson spotted a young woman standing on a street corner as his security team drove him toward home. They were passing through a particularly nasty Vegas neighborhood as their most direct route back to Summerlin.

"I wonder if she is all right," Mr. Jackson called from the back seat to his bodyguards, who occupied their usual positions as front-seat passenger and driver respectively. "Why would she be out alone here so late at night?" he queried.

"She's a prostitute, sir," explained Williams over his shoulder.

Mr. Jackson seemed to be shocked at first; then he replied with surprise registered in his voice that she looked good enough to be taken home. His guards felt certain that their boss "knew what a prostitute was, but in Vegas they don't look like prostitutes." Mr. Jackson's first thought and concern had been for the woman's safety; his motivation was for rescue rather than predation.

Their boss continually surprised his security guards in one way or another. Early on, they learned about Mr. Jackson's consuming passion for classical music. It was one thing that it played continuously throughout his home, but he directed his security guards to play it for him in his vehicle all of the time. The men tolerated it, but they would have preferred to hear something more like Michael Jackson music! He was the boss, however, so they had to cope with classical music.

While Michael Jackson was the undisputed King of Pop as his global *persona*, his private self was secretly immersed in classical music! This seemed like the guy who paints houses during the week to earn a living, while he spends his off-time as a talented artist of beautiful pastel landscapes for his own pleasure. The analogy breaks down, of course, because Michael Jackson's unique brand of pop music incorporated lovely melodies and imaginative, evocative lyrics—nothing like the tedium of house painting.

It was both the King of Pop and Michael Jackson who required the constant dedication and preparedness of his security men. This often became apparent when his security team accompanied Mr. Jackson to a shopping center or mall. Within minutes after his entrance into the area, Mr. Jackson would typically be recognized by a fan. Shouts of "Michael Jackson!" would ring out. Then a mob would form and his bodyguards would need to jump into action; sometimes his head of security made an urgent call for the assistance of local security personnel and city police officers. Even bodyguards who had regularly provided security for other high-profile celebrities and athletes said that they had never seen the reaction of ardent Michael Jackson fans. It was an unparalleled event.

After Michael Jackson had left the country in 2005 and was not expected to return, the adulation and longing of his fans only increased exponentially. His unexpected presence in Las Vegas was heralded as a precious gift to the fans, who yearned to get even a glimpse of him.

When he was spotted in public, many people would cry, scream, and faint to the floor, their faces distorted by genuine passion. Although the scene would sometimes become uncontrollable because of the sheer number of people and their emotional abandon, it was obvious to his security guards that the fans wanted only to show him their love, support, admiration, and appreciation.

Mr. Jackson was well known for responding to his fans' adoration in his "trademark" warm and caring way. He would wave, give the sign of peace, and repeat: "I love you more; God bless you all."

When his excursion into the public realm turned into a mob scene, Mr. Jackson would leave the area immediately, having to abandon his plans in order to avoid the distinct possibility of someone getting hurt in the melee. He would run fast to the waiting SUV—his bodyguards both preceding and following him—and swiftly enter it as the first-arriving guard would open the door for him and then quickly shut it behind him. Then he would be returned to his home by the most direct route.

There were a lot of abbreviated nights for the King of Pop and his guards....

Even when he received his Star on the Hollywood Walk of Fame in 1984, his appearance there needed to be cut short. Thousands of fans, who had come from all over, started pushing and shoving to get a peek of their hero. For their safety, Michael Jackson decided to exit the scene rather than to give the acceptance speech that he had prepared.

Sometimes arrangements were made for Mr. Jackson alone to return to a shopping mall or particular store, after closing, to do some shopping. Of course, "alone" meant that he was accompanied by two or three security guards, but he otherwise had the stores to himself, with only gawking, excited managers and clerks available to him as the sole customer.

As a gentle man who rarely lost control, Michael Jackson did not yell or raise his voice to his employees. When he was upset, however, his long-time security men could feel the tension; they became very "tuned in" to his feelings. During jaunts when Williams, James, and Mr. Jackson were stuck in traffic together, sometimes for hours, there was time for them to speak on a "man-to-man" basis. They would talk about a variety of things. His bodyguards knew that Michael Jackson had spent most of his life "in a bubble," surrounded by people who catered to him or took advantage of him, or did both. He had said, with sadness, that people were "not really *themselves*" with him. At these times, however, while stalled in traffic, the trio spoke freely and naturally, and Mr. Jackson could enjoy some genuine interactions with "real" people.

Sometimes things got really ugly when Michael Jackson ventured into public places. On one such occasion, as Mr. Jackson and his children left a performance by the back door, a paparazzo was waiting. He snapped some photos in quick succession. Mr. Jackson was understandably upset. The man turned and ran away at full speed. Mr. Jackson's bodyguard chased him for quite some time before he caught up with the man and grabbed his camera.

Mr. Jackson seemed relieved, but the adventure had only begun for his security guard. Soon after that incident, five police officers appeared at the guard's front door. They informed him that the paparazzo was filing charges and claiming an injury from the scuffle.

Realizing that he would need to report this matter to Mr. Jackson now that the authorities were involved, the bodyguard timidly related the current status of affairs to his boss. The police had threatened to get a search warrant for Michael Jackson's home. Just the "button" that was sure to panic Mr. Jackson! The boss had been subjected in the past to horrific police invasions of his home, which included a humiliating "strip search" at Neverland that required Michael Jackson to stand completely naked and be thoroughly scrutinized and photographed from all angles. Michael Jackson had unsurprisingly called it "the worst experience of my life."

"What does he want? What does he want?" Mr. Jackson implored his security man, with panic in his voice. "Find out what he wants, please. What will it take for this to go away?"

The bodyguard discovered that the paparazzo had retained an attorney, who was then contacted. His demand was for $50,000 for his client to settle the matter.

Feeling that this demand was ridiculous to the extreme, the bodyguard, angry but dutiful, discussed with Mr. Jackson the "bottom line" of the paparazzo's attorney.

"Okay, settle it!" was the boss's response.

Thus the matter was brought to a conclusion ... to his security guard's chagrin but to the relief of his beleaguered employer.

Another incident that prompted aggressive initiative by Boyd Williams occurred when Mr. Jackson and his children arrived by plane when his own security vehicles were not available. Williams made arrangements for a local company to dispatch an appropriate vehicle and driver to transport his boss and little ones to their residence.

"May I borrow your cell phone?" Williams asked the driver when he appeared for duty. The man readily complied by handing over his phone.

"You'll get this back after you've completed this detail," Williams told him. He had confiscated the phone in order to avoid any potential notice of Michael Jackson's whereabouts to media or anyone else. It didn't take long for Mr. Jackson's security people to realize that nearly everyone wanted to make known that they had interacted with *Michael Jackson*!

Boyd immediately noticed that small cameras were mounted on the rear-view mirrors of the security vehicle; these were poised to capture video footage of the passengers. He insisted to the driver that he either disconnect them or turn them off immediately.

When the man informed Williams that he could not comply, the security guard phoned the manager of the company, who confirmed that the drivers were neither allowed nor able to dismantle the security cameras.

To avoid delaying Mr. Jackson and his children, Williams directed the driver to fulfill his assignment, and the group proceeded toward the boss's home. However, upon their arrival, Boyd took charge of the situation by announcing that the leased vehicle would be released after the camera footage of his client was turned over to him. Only the company's manager had a key to the box in the trunk of the vehicle that housed the camera equipment, and therefore only he or his designee could access the footage.

The security team kept the leased vehicle safely parked in Mr. Jackson's garage until the required key showed up and the video film was given to Williams and destroyed. The guard knew that this film could command six figures on the tabloid market, and that might cost Boyd his job for having allowed it to happen. It took a week for a man with the key to appear at the house. No doubt, for that entire time the leasing company charged Michael Jackson's account.

It was another example of the *Michael Jackson factor*. People who provided goods or services for him could over-serve and overcharge readily and easily. Mr. Jackson was unaware of these things, and those around him did not want to bother, worry, or upset him with the frequently irksome details related to his everyday life.

Michael Leary, a transportation specialist in Las Vegas, met with the author of this book in August 2011. He worked for Michael Jackson as a limousine driver long enough to get a surprising first-hand look at what for Leary were uncommon protocols but were commonplace for the King of Pop.

"One day I got a call for a job, driving the clients from Vegas to Los Angeles," explains Leary. "I was told to report to a Starbucks at a specific address. When I got there, I was greeted by a bodyguard, who put a written confidentiality agreement in front of me to sign." Leary felt confused, then worried about the document that he was to sign, and yet he wanted this job.

After signing the off-putting agreement, which guaranteed that he would not disclose the whereabouts of his imminent client, among other assurances, Michael Leary followed the bodyguard. Their two vehicles soon came to a gate, which opened for them, and they entered the area until they arrived in front of an impressive mansion. Leary wondered, *Who will be coming out of that building; who needs a confidentiality agreement for a limo ride?*

He barely finished his thought when Michael Jackson emerged from the front door, followed by his three children. The limo door was opened for them by a burly bodyguard, and all four got into his back seats, joined by the guard. *Wow!* thought Leary, who sat up straighter and gripped the steering wheel more tightly.

Then Leary's limousine, carrying the King of Pop and his kids, blended in with a motorcade of five other shiny vehicles, his taking the position of third in line. The other vehicles, he discovered, were carrying the Michael Jackson family's suitcases and a number of his "people." They crossed the desert, under a blazing sun, for three-plus hours until they reached the Beverly Wilshire Hotel.

"Michael Jackson was talking to his bodyguard along the way," Leary recalls, "but when we arrived, he made a special point to personally say 'thank you' to me for driving him." Leary felt honored, and he came away with a proud story to tell about the King of Pop.

Leary learned later that Michael Jackson regularly and personally expressed his thanks to those who provided any service to him or his children.

That was the first and last time that the transportation specialist signed a confidentiality agreement for a passenger or that his vehicle became the most important part of a king's caravan and entourage.

> **... Just leave me alone....**
> **Just stop doggin' me around.**
> — "Leave Me Alone,"
> Michael Jackson

When you're amazingly rich and famous,
you're amazingly vulnerable.
— Thomas Mesereau

MICHAEL JACKSON
THE MAN

**People think they know me,
but they don't.
I am one of the loneliest people
on this earth.**
— Michael Jackson

**I'm just like anyone.
I cut and I bleed.
And I embarrass easily.**
— Michael Jackson

After he tucked his children into bed at night, secure in the knowledge they were safe with bodyguards and often their nanny nearby, Michael Jackson would frequently ride in his SUV down the famed Las Vegas Strip. His security guards enjoyed these details because they knew their boss was fighting "cabin fever" and getting precious glimpses into a world so different from his own....

A virtual sea of lights shone over the buildings at all hours of the night. World-class casinos and hotels lined the Strip. Limousines, taxis, and all makes and models of automobiles filled the street, hustle and bustle all around. Gambling, shows, restaurants, and shops galore, glitz and bits of glamor everywhere.

Two black SUV's, Mr. Jackson's vehicles of choice for these excursions, would cruise slowly so that he could look out of the heavily-tinted windows onto the activity outside. No one could see inside these vehicles; from the outside, the windows reflected the viewer's own image, like a mirror; but Mr. Jackson could see everything. The back-up vehicle, ever present, followed along with its armed driver and the weaponry needed in case of a dangerous incident.

Some men and women, holding hands, walked lazily; some briskly. There was the occasional newly-wed couple, the bride attired in head-to-toe traditional white and the groom in black formal attire. There were teenagers in jeans; middle-aged people in brightly-colored outfits; and senior citizens in their city clothes. Couples of various kinds, sizes, and genders filled the walkways, coming and going. Sometimes a couple with a child in tow would be seen, past the little one's bedtime, heading for their hotel room. There were lots of people from all walks of life, able to meander wherever they liked, unhampered and unmolested.

Sometimes Mr. Jackson would lower his window just enough to see better and still not be seen. All around his vehicle, of course, were tourists, either on foot or in their own cars and taxis, all of them oblivious to the reality that Michael Jackson was so close by. He savored his anonymity at these times, but he was ultimately alone ... except for his protectors.

His security men knew that Mr. Jackson, night after night, would watch the lives of normal, everyday people playing out in front of him. Through his darkened window, he could regularly see the smiles and laughter of togetherness and of personal freedom. While Michael Jackson was observing real, unfettered lives only from behind this protective glass, millions of people, cozily at home, were watching television programs of fiction and fantasy, because they already enjoyed a "normal life" of easy comings and goings, which they largely took for granted.

Michael Jackson would never be among these carefree people that he observed, not without a mask or disguise, never as himself. The security men always felt a twinge of sadness from this awareness. *The boss was a helpless captive of his fame, a prisoner of his celebrity.* No one understood this better than his guards.

The Michael Jackson who returned from abroad at the end of 2006 was a different man from the Michael Jackson who had departed the United States in 2005 after his acquittal. Mr. Jackson had undergone the most painful experience of his life, fighting for his freedom, career, reputation, and children, for twenty months; during the last five of those months he suffered through a degrading and frightening trial. Every day, at the courthouse, he would have to walk in full view of the many hundreds of spectators—journalists, reporters, paparazzi, fans, and gawkers—and of the millions who watched the daily telecast reports. As a man who clung to his privacy so zealously, his obligatory daily attendance as a spectacle, in court, was a cruel punishment. The humiliation, fear, and trauma of the trial left him a shattered man ... in spite of having been fully acquitted of all charges against him. Michael experienced overwhelming feelings of total helplessness for the first time in his life.

The media coverage before, during, and after Michael Jackson's 2005 trial was devastating for him, both image-wise and emotionally. Sound bites of accusations, innuendo, and lurid speculation filled the airwaves in the skewed reportage of the proceedings. When the salacious accusations were discredited later, by testimony or court exhibits, the media failed to report the refutations. Always lingering, therefore, were the mud, the stain, and the appearance of guilt—all created by ruthless, self-serving media.

When it was finally over, some of Michael Jackson's people planned a dignified celebration for him at Neverland in honor of his acquittal and vindication. The guest list was comprised of approximately 300 invitees; many thousands of dollars were spent on preparations for the special, celebratory event; but only a few dozen individuals attended. Although many of Michael Jackson's friends and business associates supported him during the trial, many others did not. Perhaps from confusion, perhaps from the toxic environment that the media had created, many individuals chose to exclude themselves from his party and from his life. The public perception was that Michael Jackson was guilty of *something*, although few people, it seemed, could even articulate any of the specific charges of which he was ultimately found *not guilty*.

The widespread media reports were that "Hollywood turned its back on Michael Jackson." In reality, he *was* abandoned by people whom he considered friends and by business associates, professional colleagues, and some members of his extended family.

It's no wonder that he fled from all of this heartbreak, his security guards thought, as they assisted in their boss's re-entry to a painful world they could only partially understand. Michael Jackson's reluctant return from abroad was due to the upcoming 25th anniversary of *Thriller*, the world's top-selling album. Mr. Jackson was scheduled to remake the new release with some remixes that would include various contemporary artists by special invitation.

A soul-weary but determined Michael Jackson completed and released the *Thriller* anniversary album and tried to settle into a renewed life in Las Vegas. Boyd Williams, Baron James, and Mike Garcia, as the core of his security team, soon discovered that their boss was far from the strange, "wacko" individual depicted in the tabloids. Mr. Jackson despised the nickname "Wacko Jacko" that segments of the media fell in love with using when referring to him. He admitted, during a rare interview, that it not only hurt him deeply, but he wanted to protect his children from seeing such disrespectful, dismissive coverage of their father.

Michael Jackson avoided the tabloids to the extent that he would not even walk by the racks of these "rags" in a store, particularly when accompanied by his children. He asked the public not to buy them because they perpetrated untruths, distortions, and lies.

One day in particular, Boyd remembers receiving a faxed article from Mr. Jackson's assistant Raymone, who requested that he give it to his boss to read. As he held out the document for Mr. Jackson and told him that it was a recently-published article about him, the boss recoiled from it "like it was a poisonous snake." He pulled back his hand and looked into Boyd's eyes.

"Is it okay for me to read, Boyd?" he asked, seeking reassurance.

"Yes, sir," the guard responded. "Your manager says that it is very favorable about you." It was only then that Mr. Jackson would accept the paper to read it.

Mr. Jackson employed self-protective techniques of all kinds, and his "people," realizing that reality, worked to help him. They shielded him from certain people and things, and that required foresight, finesse, and also manipulation. His security people were an active part of that web.

Michael Jackson was understandably accustomed to the unique private life he had always known—constricted, highly structured, and protected. In some ways, of course, he was like everyone else; in others, however, Michael was truly unique, like no one else on the planet. *It's lonely at the top* is the apt expression for Michael Jackson's existence.

He really wanted nothing more than to be treated like the *human being* that he was—like the man he aspired to be—not the celebrity. He wanted to go out and about, to shop, browse the malls, and attend live entertainment, like Broadway and Vegas shows, with freedom. He longed to enjoy public attractions with his little ones without being stalked, chased, mobbed, or harassed by the curious and the fans.

"One of my dreams was to go ... shopping ... at a grocery store," Michael disclosed in his "Private Home Movies." "I want to see the real world and what it's like."

"Knowledge" was Michael's response when asked about his greatest goal in life. From the time of his early childhood, he was like a sponge, trying to absorb everything around him. He watched and listened; he asked many questions. He wanted to learn all that he could from experts and "knowers." Interestingly, his zealous pursuit of knowledge extended beyond the various areas of his craft as an entertainer. He longed to know "what made people tick," what motivated them; he wanted to hear about their childhood experiences. Most of his closest friends shared a bond with him related to a "lost" childhood and strong feelings of alienation.

Although he was often described as "reclusive," Michael Jackson made it his business to know what was happening in the world and in show business. He was an avid reader, determined to learn everything he could about the subjects of his greatest interest. He was also committed to instilling in his children a love of knowledge and reading.

Michael Jackson was a high school graduate, who did not attend college because of his soaring, all-consuming career. He was a self-educated man who not only read everything he could but passionately researched areas of his greatest interests.

His security team transported hundreds of books from stores; this activity became a regular part of their duties, of their unwritten job description. Mr. Jackson read the classics and books about human anatomy, financial wealth, history, science fiction, and art. He also read biographies to learn from the people whom he most admired. Michelangelo, Leonardo da Vinci, Mozart, John F. Kennedy, Martin Luther King, Thomas Edison, Albert Einstein, and Abraham Lincoln were among his favorites. When Neverland was raided by dozens of sheriffs in 2003, they found on his night table a book about Pope John Paul II. Mr. Jackson's Vegas security men often observed him reading the *Holy Bible*; it was the boss's frequent companion; and he would sometimes quote a favorite passage to them.

During the years at Neverland and subsequently, the Michael Jackson family did not watch much television. Listening to classical music and reading were the preferred modes of enjoyment. The computer was not often used, and Internet use for the children was strictly supervised by their father, nanny, or teacher. Mr. Jackson feared that his kids would be exposed to information about him—an infinite amount of it accessible—that would cause them anxiety, or worse. When he wanted information from the computer, their boss would usually ask one of his security people to retrieve it for him.

Christmas celebrations were intimate, with only Mr. Jackson, his three little ones, and sometimes employees in attendance, such as the children's nanny and/or security guards. The men felt heavyhearted when they saw only their boss, Prince, Paris, and Blanket—no other children, family, or friends—at the festive dining room table. Later, there would be gift-giving; the kids would open brightly wrapped items of all shapes and sizes; all four Jacksons would be giggling and laughing together.

Only yards away from the tight-knit family was the Gift Room, designated and used only for storing the hundreds of cards, letters, flowers, and presents of various kinds and sizes that were delivered in profusion to Michael Jackson the King of Pop. Ironically, Michael Jackson the father was alone with his little ones. Presents and other loving sentiments from all around the world waited in that special room for him; they were stacked up on the floor and on tables. While millions who had never met him loved him, not one of them would be a part of his holiday events, of course, nor would anyone else who had been or were currently in his life … except his kids.

Those who interacted with Michael Jackson in a variety of settings knew that he had two voices. Most of the time he spoke in a soft, almost whispery voice. He was humble, gentle, and polite. Nearly everyone who has been interviewed regarding their relationship with him has used these words to describe him. He used his second voice, of lower pitch and higher volume, with attorneys and business people. Either way, people always listened intently when *Michael Jackson* spoke.

Mr. Jackson did not use a tone of authority—not even with his employees—nor was he directly confrontational. On occasion, however, he did choose to disclose his most vexing feelings to his security guards in the privacy of his vehicle or home. He would call his head of security, sometimes in the middle of the night because of his chronic insomnia, to vent his feelings.

"Everybody's wanting a piece of Michael Jackson" are words from his song "Breaking News." In truth, he often lamented the reality of these words. "Why won't they leave me alone?" was his common theme.

When the boss occasionally chose to elaborate on his frustrations to his security men, they typically felt helpless and just listened to him. At least they could do this much for Mr. Jackson, just being there and lending a sympathetic ear.

Predictably, Michael Jackson the King of Pop regularly received invitations to attend celebrity-filled events. However, he was neither enthused about attending nor comfortable when he did accept and make a rare appearance. Being around Mr. Jackson every day led to his security guards' intuitive understanding of the man, his facial expressions, tone of voice, and body language. The men sensed his reasons for declining the vast majority of these invitations.

Many of the same people who wanted him to show up for a gala event as Michael Jackson the King of Pop would otherwise not accept his personal phone calls to them, nor would they return his calls. His security men struggled with their own feelings of disappointment and anger when they observed this paradoxical phenomenon regarding their boss. Mr. Jackson was undoubtedly hurt by the many people he considered friends who would neither reach out to him nor reach back in the aftermath of his horrendous trial.

In contrast, Nelson Mandela, retired president of South Africa, would call Mr. Jackson. His head of security was always impressed when he answered the phone and the greatly-respected and admired statesman was on the other end. Mr. Mandela's long-time friend Michael had performed several fund-raising concerts abroad, at the president's request, specifically for designated South African charities. Michael Jackson had stayed in Nelson Mandela's home when he was on tour in that country, and they got to know each other as men, apart from their public roles.

Miko Brando, son of Marlon, remained a friend of Michael. He had worked for Michael Jackson for many years, and he, along with several other bodyguards, put out the fire on top of Mr. Jackson's head at the ill-fated Pepsi commercial filming. Ever since that time, there was a special bond between the two men, and Mr. Jackson evidenced a special level of trust with his former protector. Miko Brando and his family had been regular visitors at Neverland, and

Miko continued his regular contacts with Michael during his last years.

Michael Jackson had generously offered Neverland Ranch as the site for Miko's wedding, with the condition that he could be his friend's best man. Miko gratefully accepted, and the gala special occasion remained as one of Brando's fondest memories of his friend with "such a big heart."

Religion & Spirituality

Michael Jackson was a practicing Jehovah's Witness from his earliest years until 1987, when at the age of twenty-eight, he felt he had to choose between his art and his religion. As a child, Michael regularly attended the Kingdom Hall for services with his mother, a devout Witness. In fact, the elderly Katherine Jackson was actively "in service" on the morning of Michael's death.

Even at the height of his success with *Thriller,* Michael went door-to-door proselytizing, in accordance with the expectations of his religion. Often he went in disguise in an attempt to reach people on a human level rather than as a celebrity.

The elders from his church were disapproving of Michael's film *Thriller* because of its supernatural theme. They interpreted as "demonic" the ghouls and ghosts rising from their graves and doing mischief. Out of fear of ex-communication, Michael attempted to stop the release of *Thriller,* but his attorney cleverly resolved the conflict by suggesting the addition of a disclaimer at the beginning of the short film: "Due to my strong personal convictions, I wish to stress that this film in no way endorses a belief in the occult."

Ironically, the short film of the best-selling album in world history was nearly sabotaged and killed before its release because of Michael's religious affiliation. He agonized and wept over this dilemma until his lawyer, John Branca, effected the ultimate creative solution, the upfront acknowledgment that the church elders' position against the occult was shared by Michael Jackson.

Later, when Michael worked on *Smooth Criminal,* the elders disapproved of several elements, including his use of a machine gun. It was at this time that Michael reached the painful realization that he could not continue as a Jehovah's Witness and pursue his artistic vision; the two were inevitably destined to conflict and limit his creativity. He left the fold of the Witnesses.

Until he was thirty-five, Michael never celebrated birthdays or holidays such as Christmas, in accordance with the proscriptions of the Jehovah's Witnesses. Every day was like every other day for Michael Jackson, including secular holidays celebrated by the general population. Therefore, when he spoke about his "lost" childhood, Michael was referring not only to the requirement that he work in the entertainment business on a full-time basis rather than play, have friends, or attend a regular school like most other children; he also meant that his childhood and early adulthood were devoid of celebratory events and rituals that were enjoyed and taken for granted by other people.

Throughout his life, Michael remained deeply spiritual, interested in religions, and desirous of learning from the holy books. He read the Christian Bible and sought messages for his own life from its pages.

Often when he received awards, he thanked God in his acceptance speeches. Immediately after his 2005 trial, his official statement referred first and foremost to the deity: "Without God, my children, my family, and ... my fans, I could not have made it through...."

During his interview with Oprah in 1993, she asked if he believed "in a higher power." Michael answered, "Absolutely; I believe in God, very much."

Michael Jackson studied religions, especially after his painful decision to leave the Jehovah's Witnesses. He had a deep, abiding respect for all religions, as he did for all races and ethnicities.

His first wife, Lisa Marie Presley, was a practicing Scientologist when she married Michael. She had turned to religion to help her through a tumultuous time in her life, including drug rehabilitation and "purification," when she was only eighteen. Lisa Marie attributed to Scientology her resolve and strength to "keep clean" afterward.

His second wife, Debbie Rowe, was a convert to Judaism long before she married Michael Jackson. His much older best friend, Elizabeth Taylor, was also Jewish, having converted from the Christian Science religion when she was twenty-seven.

Michael studied Judaism during the years when Rabbi Shmuley Boteach served as his spiritual adviser and became a friend. Michael had very young children at the time. He often attended services at the Rabbi's synagogue, and he was always warmly welcomed by the congregation.

He also studied Islam, at the urging of his brother Jermaine, who was a convert. Contrary to some erroneous reports in 2007, however, Michael did *not* become a Muslim. He took from the teachings of Islam the kinds of lessons and inspiration that he derived from all other religions that he investigated throughout his life. He believed that he could learn from all great teachers and all of the major world religions.

Michael Jackson saw the presence and influence of God everywhere. He expressed these beliefs in his beautiful, succinct essay on "God" in *Dancing the Dream*:

It's strange that God doesn't mind expressing Himself/ Herself in all the religions of the world, while people still cling to the notion that their way is the only right way....
For me the form God takes is not the most important thing. What's most important is the essence. My songs and dances are outlines for Him to come in and fill. I hold out the form. She puts in the sweetness.
... In that moment [of seeing the night sky and stars] I saw God in His creation. I could as easily have seen Her in the beauty of a rainbow, the grace of a deer ..., the truth of a father's kiss. But for me the sweetest contact with God has no form. I close my eyes, look within, and enter a deep soft silence. The infinity of God's creation embraces me. We are one.

To say that Michael Jackson was open-minded does not even come close to the reality of the depth and breadth of his spiritual consciousness. Seeing the divine in everything around him, he saw himself as "an instrument of nature."

Michael felt a natural affinity toward others who perceive the divine as everywhere, as embodied in all living beings. He often interacted with Buddhists and Hindus, especially in countries that he visited and where he toured, such as Japan and India; he went to many temples and shrines during those times. He especially admired and connected with the core values of these Eastern religions, which promote the cherishing of all forms of life. Michael's deep, enduring love of all species of animals seemed reflected in the beliefs of his Buddhist and Hindu "brothers" and "sisters," who consider some animals as genuinely sacred.

Known for saying "God bless you" to everyone, Michael also took on the habit of folding his hands together, as if in prayer, and gently bowing to people. This behavior was very endearing to those around him.

Deepak Chopra—a medical doctor and author of several best-selling books on spirituality—became a friend and spiritual adviser to Michael Jackson around 1990. He went to Neverland to teach Michael meditation. He was surprised to discover that Michael Jackson was very shy and introverted, but also very curious about consciousness and spirituality.

"We would talk about starving children in Mumbai, and he would start to cry," Dr. Chopra remembers; "or we'd … talk about the trophy-hunting of the grizzly bear, and he would start to cry." He would ask why people go to war, why there was genocide in the world, why there was racism and bigotry, and why we were killing the environment. Dr. Chopra stated that Michael Jackson was probably the most spiritual man he had ever met.

According to Chopra, he spoke to Michael during his last month of life, by telephone. Michael was reading the poems of Rabindranath Tagore, a Bengali who began writing as a young child. He was the first non-European Nobel laureate; he produced not only poems but paintings, hundreds of texts, and two thousand songs; Tagore died in 1941. His poetry is considered both spiritual and mercurial, lending him a prophet-like aura. Not many Westerners are familiar with Rabindranath Tagore, but Michael Jackson was reading his works.

Dr. Wayne Dyer—a teacher, author, and lecturer—got to know Michael well. He took all eight of his children and his wife to spend five days at Neverland in the early nineties. Dr. Dyer said of Michael:

> He was as kind and decent and spiritual a human being as I ever had the pleasure of spending any time with.... When you look at ... the commitment that he had to ending the world['s] hunger, for example, he personally was responsible for cutting the number of people starving to death on this planet IN HALF back in the 1980's and the 1990's with "We are the World"....
> This was a beautiful, beautiful human being.

During the last months of his life, Michael regularly consulted with Reverent June Juliet Gatlin, a Los Angeles "seer" and "healer" who takes on private clients and speaks to groups. She describes herself as a paranormal who has received special powers from both sides of her parentage. At the age of three, in her birthplace of Akron, Ohio, she was proclaimed to be a child of prophecy by officials of her church.

Today, Reverent Gatlin is considered a controversial figure with a unique, fiery, outspoken, and confrontational style. She prides herself on "bringing people's innermost feelings to verbal expression" and on "offering messages of hope, faith, enlightenment, and personal responsibility."

Reverent Gatlin came forward in 2010, on a nationwide television program, to reveal that she was Michael Jackson's spiritual adviser. She met him for the first time and did a reading for him in May 2008. She spoke about Michael's deep spiritual commitment to unity, love, respect, and peace. Reverent Gatlin described Michael's love for his three children as all-consuming and his first priority in life. She related that he expressed his desire to her that, if something happened to him, his mother or sister Janet should raise his beloved children.

In an exclusive telephone interview with this author in August 2011, Reverent Gatlin spoke about the journal that she keeps and in which Michael wrote her a grateful message. She cherishes that journal and is quick to remind, "It is *my* property, to keep in Michael's memory.

"Michael still lives inside of his mother," she says with great vigor, as if she is delivering a sermon. "She birthed him, bibbed him, raised him, gave him life." Reverent Gatlin knows Katherine Jackson and sees her "from time to time." She did not disclose the nature of their relationship but only the existence of it. "He trusted his *mother*," she assured her listener, while confirming that he could not really trust anyone else.

Michael shared with her his feelings of disappointment and anger over the shabby treatment he was receiving from those around him. That included deals made by his advisers that were not in his best interest and, in fact, in several cases were detrimental to him and even scary. He named names and got specific with her. Michael seemed to need someone to whom to vent, someone safe. He even allegedly used the "h" word with her ["hate"], a behavior for Michael that was totally out of character. Matters for him at the time must have been extreme and painful.

"We breathed the same air!" Reverent Gatlin exclaims when speaking about herself and Michael Jackson. This description is filled with great meaning for her, including the intimacy that it suggests, the empathy between them, and the fact that Michael was actually present with her, in the same room. "Fans and other people who didn't deserve to touch the hem of his garment are talking and writing about Michael Jackson," she declares in a venomous tone; "they didn't know him but they are presenting themselves as if they did.

"I give strength, I reach to the inner core of people, I touch the very cells of their being," she continues, as she relates what kind of interactions she had with Michael. She strove to impart to him not only spiritual strength but inspiration and encouragement. Michael had the loftiest goals for himself, Reverent Gatlin explains. They were not so much from ego as from his desire to be the best person he could be.

Drawing from her own background of childhood experiences and African-American family traditions, Reverent Gatlin became the strong, feisty, and formidable woman that she is today. She joined the short list of women to whom Michael seemed to feel close and connected—his mother, Diana Ross, Lisa Marie Presley, Debbie Rowe, Elizabeth Taylor—all of them strong, tested people who could hold their own with Michael Jackson and love him for himself.

Priding herself on having "absorbed" strength and wisdom from her upbringing, she works to foster and grow those qualities in her spiritual advisees. Reverent Gatlin explains that she felt an especially deep spiritual connection with Michael. She now feels the weight of a great loss.

"There will never ever be another Michael Jackson," Reverent Gatlin affirms. "He was so special and unique. I would tell him that...."

Michael strongly believed in the power of love and prayer. He believed that a combination of the two could bring about healing in people. He rejoiced when children with "incurable diseases" got better after they visited Neverland. There were verified stories of cures that were not otherwise explicable except for a "miraculous" recovery by children who learned to hope from Michael Jackson.

Michael and his own children prayed together before meals. He continued this practice—learned under the Jehovah's Witnesses' influence when he was a young boy—with his own family on a daily basis. Michael and his touring team of singers, dancers, and stage crew always joined hands and prayed together before each concert.

It was a cherished tradition for all of them, and it bonded them on a level that transcended the performances.

"I'm trying to imitate Jesus," Michael disclosed to Oprah Winfrey. He was quick to add, "I'm not saying I *am* Jesus but that I want to be *like* him." With this clarification, he was no doubt anticipating the predictable media twist on his words that was likely to follow.

The point, however, is that Michael Jackson always strove to be a good Christian man, to remain faithful to his core values, and to make a difference on this Earth.

Reverence

Michael Jackson admired many individuals to the point of deep feelings of reverence. He was old-fashioned in his ability and propensity to idolize people of talent and passion. He felt a childlike sense of awe when he thought about them; he held them on a pedestal in his mind and his heart.

Michael Jackson's heroes, mentors, and idols included Fred Astaire, Gene Kelly, Bette Davis, Gregory Peck, Charlie Chaplin, Jackie Wilson, James Brown, Sammy Davis, Jr., Henry Fonda, Little Richard, Chuck Berry, Otis Redding, John Lennon, Elvis Presley, Judy Garland, Katherine Hepburn, Frank Sinatra, Marlon Brando, Stevie Wonder, Clark Gable, Shirley Temple, Elizabeth Taylor, and Diana Ross. "The greatest education in the world," Michael asserted, "is watching the masters at work."

Because he was Michael Jackson, many of these individuals initiated contact with him to get to know the super-talented, shy man whose career reached the stratosphere. Michael overcame his timidity to meet and befriend many of his idols.

He met Fred Astaire immediately after the "Motown 25" telecast that catapulted Michael to international recognition for his "Billie Jean" performance, in which he immortalized his iconic dance steps, his "moonwalk." Astaire gave his highest praises to Michael, who then reportedly showed "the master dancer" how to do the moonwalk.

Five years later, Michael dedicated his 1988 autobiography *Moonwalk* to Fred Astaire.

Gregory Peck and his wife Veronique became regular visitors to Neverland. Michael referred to Gregory Peck as "a dear friend." While on tour in Europe, Michael visited with Charlie Chaplin's widow; he was delighted to take the opportunity to tell her how much he admired her late husband. Michael delivered a moving eulogy at the funeral of his greatly-admired friend and mentor James Brown. "I idolized him," Michael related when he spoke about watching James Brown, in complete awe of his talent, on his small family television set when he was a young child.

Michael Jackson held vigil with Henry Fonda's immediate family, including his famous daughter Jane—who had befriended Michael—on the day that the veteran actor passed away. He met Yoko Ono and Sean Lennon after the assassination of John Lennon, and, as a father figure, he spent time with Sean at Neverland.

Of course, Michael married Elvis Presley's only daughter—only child—Lisa Marie Presley more than two decades after their first introduction. He had first met Lisa Marie when her famous father took her backstage to meet Michael after one of The Jackson 5 concerts. Michael remembered her well:

We first met when she was seven … and I was 17… in Las Vegas…. The Jackson 5 was the only family show on the Strip, and she used to come … and sit right up front. She came quite often, and then she'd come backstage and talk. I thought she was sweet.

Katherine Hepburn gave Michael Jackson motherly advice when he got to know her, including how to handle his fame. She specifically recommended that he remove his sunglasses when on stage so that his fans could see his eyes.

Michael often invited Marlon Brando to stay at Neverland, and the actor accepted, sometimes staying for weeks. When he became aware that Marlon was worried about his finances, reportedly "down to his last $600,000," Michael asked his overweight and struggling friend to address the audience at his *Thirtieth Anniversary Concert* at Madison Square Garden. Brando also made a cameo appearance in Michael's *You Rock My World* short film, for which he was paid one million dollars. Michael found a way to give his friend this money without compromising his sense of dignity.

Stevie Wonder and Michael, both Motown prodigies, became friends; they recorded together and talked often about their shared love, music. Months after Michael's passing, when Stevie was performing "The Way You Make Me Feel," the always-professional singer broke down and could not finish the song. Seeming to understand Stevie's overwhelming grief over the loss of the man who had always been so kind to him, the audience gave him a standing ovation.

Shirley Temple, a famous, precocious child star like Michael, was a special favorite of his. He had his staff place posters of her in his dressing room when he was on tour. After years of staring at those posters, Michael sought out Shirley Temple Black, still a public figure and also a successful politician, to thank her for having been an inspiration to him for so long.

Boxer Muhammad Ali was quoted in a Norwegian newspaper in 2005 as a great admirer of Michael Jackson. "When people ask me where I get my strength from, I tell them that I look at the man Michael Jackson looks at when he looks at the man in the mirror," Ali revealed to the interviewer.

Michael Jackson was godfather to Nicole Richie, daughter of Lionel Richie, and to the son of Barry Gibb of the Bee Gees. He was a best man at the wedding of Liza Minnelli to her fourth husband, David Gest. Michael paid for and hosted a beautiful and extravagant wedding of 160 attendees on his Neverland property for his dear friend Elizabeth Taylor when she married her seventh husband, Larry Fortensky.

His Aura

"The energy in the room changed when Michael Jackson entered," many individuals have said about him at various times. It was palpable for most people ... and unforgettable.

"That aura was real," affirms musical director Michael Bearden; "the air would change...."

Remarkably, he was always unassuming and soft-spoken. It was his *presence* rather than his speech or behaviors that most impressed people.

Michael Jackson was unquestionably charismatic. There was an ethereal quality about him. So many people who really knew Michael described him as "seeming to be other-worldly."

On the negative side of that reality, Michael lamented that people were "not themselves" with him. This awareness contributed to his loneliness and general sense of isolation. Children, however, were natural, relaxed, and typically unimpressed by his celebrity. Michael loved that. Interactions with children gave him a break from his *persona* as the King of Pop; he could be the little boy from Gary, Indiana that he was in his heart. He could be *himself*.

Michael Jackson always wore perfume; he preferred scents for women. For years he had his own perfumes custom-made. He smelled good, and that was an important part of his image. Everything was thoughtfully and carefully executed by Michael. He was anything but casual about the way he presented himself to the world.

His Sexuality

Michael Jackson was a heterosexual man. He proclaimed his sexual preference on a number of occasions, from the time when he was in his mid-twenties.

Lisa Marie Presley confirmed that she and Michael enjoyed a normal sexual relationship during their marriage. In an interview with Diane Sawyer, conducted the year after their wedding, Lisa Marie said, "Do we have sex? Yes! Yes! *Yes!*" It was only after his death, however, that Lisa Marie also admitted that she had left her first husband, Danny Keough, for Michael. They married twenty days after her divorce was finalized, when she was twenty-six and Michael was thirty-five.

Michael developed what he called "a serious crush" on Diana Ross when he was eleven, and it lasted through his years as a teenager and well into his adulthood. He lived with Ms. Ross in California before his mother and younger siblings left Indiana to join the rest of the Jackson family when The Jackson 5 group was breaking into big-time stardom. Ms. Ross was maternal with Michael, spending time with him and encouraging him. She often took young Michael to art museums, where his life-long love and study of art were born and nurtured.

He thought that Ms. Ross was beautiful, elegant, and wonderful. She was a top-level celebrity as well, the most successful African-American recording artist at the time. Ms. Ross was a dedicated, hard-working, determined, strong, and assertive woman; she became a role model for Michael Jackson's work ethic. She assured her young charge that someday he would become a "great, great star." Michael worshiped her. To the surprise of many, Michael stipulated in his 2002 Last Will & Testament that Diana Ross should become the guardian of his three children if his mother Katherine would be unable to care for them.

Ms. Ross elicited Michael's first sexual feelings for a woman, although theirs was a platonic, mother-son kind of relationship.

Contrary to rumors and speculation fueled by tabloid media, therefore, Michael Jackson was not gay. Many persons who knew Michael well, including his parents, a number of his siblings, friends, and professional colleagues have affirmed that Michael was heterosexual. His Las Vegas security guards—Williams, James, and Garcia—and Thomas Mesereau, all of whom knew Michael well, have confirmed that he was not homosexual.

"Being a twenty-six-year-old virgin teen idol devoted to a sexually repressive religion is not easy, especially when show business dictates that a male celebrity be 'romantically involved' … with a woman," wrote his biographer J. Randy Taraborrelli.

Michael was often seen at celebrity events with the beautiful model and actress Brooke Shields, but theirs was a platonic relationship. He confessed to Oprah in 1993, however, that he had been in love with two women, and one of them was Brooke Shields.

The pressure was on Michael Jackson to declare himself when his solo career was making him a global celebrity and rumors were rampant....

In 1984, Frank Dileo held a press conference on behalf of Michael Jackson to "once and for all set the record straight [pun intended?]." His prepared statement was intended to address the widespread, unfounded rumors that Michael was gay. Calling the reports of Michael Jackson's alleged homosexuality "ridiculous," Dileo read his client's statement: "I plan to get married and have a family. Any statements to the contrary are simply untrue."

Five years earlier, Michael confronted a reporter himself, saying that he was not homosexual: "I'm sure I must have fans who are gay, and I don't mind that. That's their life and this is mine. You can print that."

Michael believed that his soft voice may have given rise to the rumors. He was accused in tabloids of taking female hormones to keep his voice high-pitched. Seth Riggs, Michael's voice coach, revealed that his speaking voice was "natural, male, husky." Riggs said, "We're all fed up with the lies and nonsense about this boy we love so much. Michael is different.... He's not of this world." He explained that Michael didn't like what he called his "frog" voice and, for personal reasons, he stuck with the higher voice that, while working with Riggs, he learned to reach and maintain.

Michael Jackson was allegedly a virgin until he was in his thirties. He was not only admittedly timid regarding sexual behaviors, but he internalized the teachings of the Jehovah's Witnesses, which prohibit premarital sexual relations. Michael quoted the Bible to reference his belief in abstinence from sexual intercourse until marriage.

He was conscientious, controlled, and perhaps even repressed when it came to sexual expression. Until 1993, when he was falsely accused of child molestation, Michael had a "squeaky clean" reputation. In that same year, he told Oprah Winfrey—in a telecast viewed around the world—that he had girlfriends but rarely went out in public with them; they visited in each other's homes.

"Are you a virgin?" Oprah directed the audacious question in a tactless, direct manner to the startled thirty-four-year-old man, who had never discussed such private matters in a public forum and certainly not on international television.

"I'm embarrassed," Michael responded in an honest and guileless manner. "I'm a gentleman," he continued; "call me old-fashioned but that is what I believe."

To that response, Oprah said that she interpreted his answer as his desire to keep such matters private, out of respect for the women.

Attorney Thomas Mesereau became intimately aware of Michael Jackson's sexual proclivities during the months of the 2005 trial that delved into every aspect of the superstar's private life. There was a massive and thorough intrusion into every event and piece of evidence that might reveal Michael's sexual preference and behaviors. All of the items at his Neverland home—books, magazines, videos, articles of clothing, laundry hamper, papers, safes, and personal effects—were searched, confiscated, studied, and/or filmed. Only some "girlie" magazines were found; nothing related to homosexual or child pornography was found—nothing. It is interesting to note that a photo of Marilyn Monroe was displayed on Michael's bedside table.

Thomas Mesereau affirms that "Michael Jackson was a 'red-blooded male heterosexual'; he was *not* a pedophile—nothing could be further from the truth."

Michael Jackson's Las Vegas security team also adamantly denounces any and all allegations that his love for children was anything but a sincere, innocent part of Mr. Jackson's pervasively-caring personality. He was thrilled by animals of all species, manifestations of nature, and children of all ages and races—all of which he perceived as wondrous. *Period.*

A legion of other people who came to know Michael Jackson's gentle, loving nature have testified to his innocence. He was kindhearted, generous of spirit and behavior, and caring at an amazingly deep level. He "saw the face of God" in every child.

In another culture and/or at another time, this special level of generalized love would be readily accepted at face value. "Not so much" in America, a country in which its citizens are quick to judge unusual behaviors as deviant or criminal. In fact, if Michael Jackson had been a *woman* who did the very same things he did with and for children, that person would likely be perceived and heralded as a Mother Teresa. A man does not enjoy the luxury of full expression of love and concern in this culture as does a woman.

In many other places—especially Third World countries where entire families share the same tiny quarters and bed—Michael Jackson would not be perceived as deviant or weird. He would be admired. We have become so jaded in our media-saturated culture that we believe the worst because we have been exposed, on a daily basis, to so many aberrations and violations of acceptable behavior. We look at events with a colored lens, a jaundiced eye, fashioned by our societal learnings.

His Las Vegas security team of three men has affirmed that "Michael Jackson was not gay."

"Men know men," they explained in a kind of shorthand to communicate that they got to know their boss intimately, and he obviously liked women. He would watch them from his vehicle, like any heterosexual man would do, and occasionally he would comment to his protectors on the attractiveness of various women.

Mr. Jackson maintained a relationship with each of two women during the many months of guard service by Boyd Williams, Baron James, and Michael Garcia. On national television in 2010, the three security guards openly spoke about the women who visited him regularly, sometimes engaging in what seemed to them as teen-like behavior in the back seat of the vehicle. Mr. Jackson and his female companion would be hidden from view by a curtain but audible to the front-seat guards. The men would occasionally hear sounds like giggling and kissing.

Known to his security team as "Flower" and "Friend," each would occasionally come to visit their boss. Mike Garcia speaks about driving them to meet up with Mr. Jackson when one of the women came to Las Vegas to spend private time with him. The three men believed that Mr. Jackson used nicknames for the women in order to protect their identities.

Michael Jackson did not typically entertain either of his female friends in the presence of his children nor did they come to his house. Nothing was more important to Mr. Jackson than the well-being of his family, and he did not want to impose a single/unmarried female guest—as his "date"—upon his young, impressionable children. This behavior was in keeping with his self-professed description as "old-fashioned" and "a gentleman."

It is fair to say that Michael Jackson was at the point in his life that he would not allow himself to open up thoroughly to any woman or to allow himself to fall in love. Doing so would bring a world of attention to his women friends, and the media would be relentless— *like a dog with a bone*—in chasing and hounding these women.

Ironically, it seems that the only ones—outside of his security team—who ever saw Michael Jackson and one of his female companions together did not recognize him. Thankfully, no photos were ever taken. This situation is a tribute to his security men, who worked so diligently and intelligently that Mr. Jackson and his special "friends" were not detected or revealed to the public.

When Mr. Jackson was visited by one of the women, the security team covertly made all of his requested arrangements. The guards escorted Mr. Jackson into the reserved hotel suite without the knowledge or cooperation of hotel management. It would be too risky to notify hotel personnel about the boss's identity; his rendezvous with his lady could be easily and quickly ruined by the onslaught of paparazzi. *"Michael Jackson with Mystery Woman!"*

For the guards, it was great to know they could provide Mr. Jackson with temporary peace of mind, which he so longed for and deserved. He could have someone he truly liked and she could reciprocate his feelings. They "acted like high school sweethearts," laughing, giggling, and joking around. They spoke on the telephone often, so much that Mr. Jackson accumulated huge monthly long-distance phone bills.

The revelation of Michael Jackson and women friends comes as no shock to most of the residents of Los Olivos, the closest town to Neverland, at a distance of five miles. There, among the townspeople, it was commonly known that their neighbor superstar was dating women. Michael and his female friends typically avoided public places, as was his *modus operandi* in general, but sometimes he was spotted with a woman companion, who was obviously a "date," and the Michael Jackson sighting would be passed by word-of-mouth. Soon everyone would hear about it in this peaceful, scenic town in "wine country" with only 1,100 residents. It is also interesting to note that, according to a recent U.S. Census Bureau report, the racial makeup of Los Olivos was 92.7% white, only one African American (.1%), and the remaining 7.2 % of individuals were of other races. Michael Jackson was unique within his local community in so many ways—the biggest celebrity, the wealthiest resident, and an anomaly as an African-American man.

When Michael Jackson was seen in the Los Olivos area, especially with a woman friend, it was always notable.

Women in His Life

To his great credit, Michael Jackson was capable of maintaining with women long-term, intimate relationships which were platonic, comfortable, and very special.

For many years, during the early stage of his solo career, he dated Brooke Shields. She jokingly reminded Michael that she started in the business even before he did, when she was just a baby. Ms. Shields accompanied him to a series of special events, including awards ceremonies. She kept in regular touch with him even when they were far apart for weeks at a time. Ms. Shields earned her permanent place in music history in 1984 by having been Michael's date at the Grammy Awards when he won a record-breaking eight Grammys. "This is the *Michael Jackson Show*!" quipped a comedian who was a presenter at the ceremony that night.

At his Memorial, Ms. Shields spoke, with breaking voice and deep affection, about her special relationship with Michael and the childlike fun they had together. Michael Jackson greatly enjoyed pranks, and he loved Brooke as his co-conspirator in the little dramas that they would create together, like sneaking a peek at Elizabeth Taylor's wedding dress while she was sleeping.

Jane Fonda became a friend of Michael, and she took him to visit the site of the movie that she was doing with her father, *On Golden Pond*. There she introduced the men to each other. Ms. Fonda and Michael discussed personal matters; he confided to her concerns he had about some of his family members that he had kept to himself. She remembers Michael as sensitive and fragile, very caring, and easily moved to tears when describing things that affected him deeply.

Diana Ross took Michael Jackson "under her wing" when his father and brothers moved to Los Angeles to produce records for Motown, Ms. Ross's label. Young Michael, a preteen, lived in Ms. Ross's home; spent quality time with her; and studied her movements and manners. He was star-struck, impressionable, and prone to hero worship. In that emotional soil, their relationship took root, and for the rest of his life—although he had little contact with her during his last decade—he admired her and considered her a great entertainer and mother figure. It was Diana Ross's prediction that he would be an unparalleled star that impressed Michael about his own abilities and the brightness of his future.

And then there was Elizabeth Taylor. A true and loyal friend to Michael Jackson in good times and bad, Elizabeth Taylor bonded with him in an extraordinary way.

Because he admired her from afar, Michael Jackson—in the early eighties—sent to Ms. Taylor complimentary tickets to one of his concerts. Unfortunately, because her seat turned out to be far from the stage, Ms. Taylor left his concert early. Disappointed, Michael telephoned her the next day; he apologized when she explained the problem; and that incident began their life-long, close relationship of genuine communications and candor.

Elizabeth Taylor accompanied Michael Jackson to many gala events and awards ceremonies. They were photographed together on red carpets, at restaurant tables, and sitting side-by-side in the front-row audience at various performances. She was someone whom he trusted, admired, and loved; he was always comfortable in her presence. Arm in arm or holding hands, the two mega-celebrities supported each other in front of the ever-present, eager cameras. Michael was shy; Elizabeth was tough and self-confident.

Calling Michael "the least strange man I know," during an interview with Oprah Winfrey, Ms. Taylor trumpeted to the listening world that her friend was "a good man," unchanged by his peak-level fame.

Elizabeth Taylor had happily served as the presenter of significant awards to her dear friend Michael, including the Soul Train Heritage Award with which she immortalized him. From the podium, Elizabeth Taylor coined the name "King of Pop" as the unforgettable honorific term that would carry Michael Jackson through his stratospheric career into infinity:

> ... [A]ll of his accomplishments, his rewards, have not altered his sensitivity and concern for the welfare of others, or his intense caring and love for his family and friends, and especially all the children the world over....
> He is always trying to learn. He is so intelligent that he is alarmingly bright....
> He's not really of this planet....
> He is filled with deep emotions that create an unearthly, special, innocent, child-like, wise man....
> ... [H]e is one of the least devious people I have ever met in my life—he is ... painfully honest—and vulnerable to the point of pain.... He is so giving of himself that, at times, he leaves very little to protect the beautiful inner core that is the essence of him. That is the thing that I love so much about him and that makes the world identify with him in the way it does....

[He is] an incredible force of incredible energy....
And just when you think you know him, he gives you more....
I think he is one of the finest people on this planet, and ...
he's the true King of Pop, Rock and Soul.

In 2009, Elizabeth Taylor—who had seven husbands and many other lovers—described her profound feelings for Michael: "I don't think anyone knew how much we loved each other. The purest, most giving love I've ever known."

It was Elizabeth Taylor who arranged for Michael Jackson, the former Jehovah's Witness, his first-ever celebration of Christmas when he was thirty-five. Ms. Taylor introduced Michael to a decorated Christmas tree and holiday gift-exchange. She festooned the rooms of Neverland with brightly twinkling lights, and she stacked colorfully wrapped presents under the tall evergreen tree that she had brought with her. Ms. Taylor gave Michael the newest water pistols on the market, super-soakers, the ideal gifts for her have-everything friend. After their shared fun and laughter, Michael excused himself and went to cry in the bathroom from his overwhelming ambivalence and feelings of guilt. He later revealed this self-disclosing story in his "Private Home Movies."

In 1993, Elizabeth Taylor flew to Mexico City, where Michael Jackson was scheduled to give a concert, when she realized that her friend was in trouble. Although he had always hated drugs, Michael issued a public statement in which he admitted that he had become addicted to painkillers. Ms. Taylor proudly announced to the media that she loved Michael "like a son" and that she personally had arranged for him to enter a rehabilitation program in an undisclosed facility. She and her husband Larry Fortensky accompanied the ailing Michael Jackson to a well-respected rehab center in London, where he checked in and began the prescribed program.

Theirs was an exceptional rapport and understanding of each other. Both had been child stars, who had to give up their childhood in exchange for hard work and fame; both had felt great loneliness; and both dealt with the ever-present restrictions of pinnacle-level celebrity. They each broke records for the volume of media saturation and sensationalized coverage of them. Elizabeth Taylor made international headlines when she allegedly broke up the marriage of Debbie Reynolds and Eddie Fisher, who left his popular wife Debbie for the voluptuous, violet-eyed beauty Elizabeth.

With Michael, Elizabeth was maternal, straightforward, take-charge, nurturing, and sometimes confronting. He yielded to her strong personality and felt warmed by her affection and caring. Even when they did not see each other in person, they spoke often by telephone.

Michael Jackson performed his original song, "Elizabeth I Love You," on stage at her lavish birthday party on February 27, 1997. He sang his lovely, intimate ballad only once because it was a unique, heartfelt musical expression for his one-of-a-kind relationship. Michael referred to his beloved Dame Elizabeth as "a combination of Mother Teresa, Princess Diana, the Queen of England, and Wendy [from Peter Pan]."

When Michael died in 2009, his seriously-ill friend Elizabeth was completely devastated. She was already packing her luggage to fly to London for his first O2 Arena "comeback" concert. Her security personnel heard her continuous shrieks coming through the bedroom door.

Ms. Taylor issued the following heart-wrenching testimonial:

My heart ... my mind ... are broken. I loved Michael with all my soul and I can't imagine life without him. We had so much in common and we had such loving fun together.... He will live in my heart forever but it's not enough. My life feels so empty.... Oh God! I'm going to miss him.... I keep looking at the photo he gave me of himself, which says, "To my true love Elizabeth, I love you forever." And I will love *him* forever.

Many people who knew Elizabeth Taylor believe that her death, twenty-one months after her much-younger best friend's untimely passing, was hastened by her enduring, debilitating grief.

Love of Children

It is well known that Michael Jackson loved children. He did indeed, and in a wholesome, deeply caring way. As verified by many people who knew him, Michael could not view television newscasts, primarily because it hurt him too much to see the pain and suffering of others. He especially could not bear to see a child suffering. Michael told his corrupt interviewer in "Living with Michael Jackson"—in outtake footage—that he avoided newscasts in order to protect himself from seeing the pain experienced by children everywhere in the world.

Michael explained that, in his family, when a baby was brought into the household for a visit, everyone would fight to hold that baby. His mother and father loved children; they had ten of their own, one of whom died only hours after birth, Marlon's twin brother Brandon.

In every city where he held a concert, Michael Jackson visited a hospital or orphanage. He personally passed out toys to the children; he gave out photos of himself and signed autographs. He would inquire as to the unmet needs of the facility, and then he would direct one of his security team to "take care of it." Michael Jackson provided expensive equipment, playground facilities, and other items that assisted in the medical treatment of the children. He also paid for surgeries, often anonymously, for children whose parents could not afford them.

"Michael would stay up all night long," explained Seth Riggs, "putting batteries into toys, making certain each one worked so that he could have them ready to give to kids backstage the next day. As if he didn't have enough to worry about." Michael always allowed handicapped children to be brought to see him before or after a concert performance; some were in wheelchairs, some on stretchers, and some were terminally ill.

What most people do not know, including many of Michael's fans, is that he would give his phone number to dying children so that they would have something to live for. Even if they lived an additional day or two, it was worth it to Michael to spend some of his time in telephone conversations, encouraging these children and telling them that he would see them again when he came back to their town.

"He's the most natural, loving person I've ever known, a very good person, as corny as that sounds," continued Riggs, who accompanied Michael Jackson on tour for many years.

His manager Frank Dileo told many heartbreaking stories of Michael's influence on sick and dying children. Dileo said that it was as though an unexplainable part within Michael was able to reach these kids, to make them smile, to cause them to forget their maladies, and to find hope.

David Nordahl and Michael would talk for "long hours together," across two decades of their close relationship. "Michael spoke about the many children in the world who were discarded, abandoned, and unloved," Nordahl remembers. "He would discuss with me what he was planning to help children in need, to improve their lives, to bring healing. This was the core of his very being. He was the most amazing person I've ever known."

In stark contrast to the adults in his life—family members, friends, acquaintances, professional colleagues, and business associates—children did not "have their hands out," seeking money or special favors from Michael. They did not try to manipulate him or to ingratiate themselves in devious, creative ways as so many adults in his life did as a matter of routine.

It was not so much that Michael Jackson did not "grow up"; it was that he did not *want* to grow up. "I *am* Peter Pan," he insisted more than once, to make his point. When he named his Santa Ynez Valley home "Neverland," Michael instituted himself as its Peter Pan resident.

Elizabeth Taylor succinctly analyzed her dear friend's personality with an insightful summary: "I think Michael appeals to the child in all of us, and I think he has the quality of innocence that we would all like to obtain or to have kept."

Love of Animals & Nature

From his earliest childhood years, Michael Jackson loved animals of all kinds and species. To Oprah, Michael elaborated that he loved the "purity and honesty" of animals—comparing these wonderful traits to those of children. "They don't want anything from you; it's sweet," he told her.

His first # 1 solo hit "Ben" was about a beloved pet rat, the theme of the movie with the same name. Michael Jackson—as the youngest artist ever to sing a nominated song at the Academy Awards—wowed the audience with his flawless performance of "Ben" in 1973. Not only was "Ben" nominated in the Best Original Song category for an Oscar, but it won the Golden Globe award for Best Song. It was eerily appropriate for the fourteen-year-old to sing about his love for his "best friend" rat. At the time, in reality, Michael's bedroom was filled with his own beloved pet rats, much to the chagrin of his mother and sisters who were living at home.

Michael also had a big snake, named Muscles, who roamed not only his room but the rest of the Hayvenhurst house. He often took Muscles with him to the recording studio, where the snake would coil himself around the equipment while Michael experimented with new sounds and tweaked his musical arrangements.

Then there was Bubbles, the baby chimpanzee whom Michael saved by adopting him from a cancer research center in Texas. Michael grew so fond of Bubbles that he regularly traveled with him, dressed him in designer clothes, and set up a crib in his bedroom, where the animal slept. Bubbles ate his meals at the Jackson family table, helped himself to food from the refrigerator, and occasionally swung from the chandelier.

The chimp watched Michael's rehearsals, including those for the *Bad* short film, which included wild dancing across the floors and stairs of the New York subway. Bubbles was reportedly well-behaved and genuinely interested in being a spectator. In addition, however, Michael taught his pet to do "the moonwalk," which Bubbles performed on a Dick Clark program. In Japan, when Michael was invited to a press conference with dozens of media personnel and the city mayor, he chose to take the chimp as his guest. The two "friends" sipped tea together at a huge table while the cameras snapped photo after photo of the mega-famous star and his unexpected companion. Bubbles had his own following of fans, including 300 people who greeted him at an airport in Japan when he arrived there in a separate plane from Michael's.

Michael Jackson brought in an impressive group of animals that included swans, giraffe, and lions to his Hayvenhurst home, which had five acres of land and sufficient personnel to accommodate them. Later, at Neverland, Michael had a private zoo with ample veterinarians and care-takers for a wide range of species of animals that included elephants, giraffe, lions, tigers, alpacas, llamas, sheep, alligators, a pot-bellied pig, colorful exotic birds, horses, a 34-inch-tall stallion, and a twelve-foot albino python. All of the animals had names that were chosen by Michael.

David Nordahl fondly remembers Jabbar, a giraffe whom Michael raised from a baby. Michael mourned his long-legged friend when the animal passed away—as he did all of his animals who died. "Michael fell asleep once with the head of a baby giraffe cradled on his lap," David recalls with tenderness in his voice.

Michael Jackson spoke about how he enjoyed watching the animals, observing their species-based behaviors. They brought him great joy. He so loved walking among his animals and watching children smile and squeal with delight at the sight of them.

"I respect the secrets and magic of nature," he often said. Unabashedly, Michael Jackson talked about the beauty of trees, the changing of leaves by season, and the reasonableness of people talking to their plants, as other living beings.

"Plants and grass and trees respond to music," he asserted in outtake footage of "Living with Michael Jackson." "They have emotion; they feel.... When they hear music, they grow more beautiful. The butterflies come around. The birds come around."

Perfectionism

"Top it!" "Make it better!" These are words that Michael Jackson's colleagues and collaborators heard from him all of the time. From his costumers to his back-up dancers, from the lighting specialists to the stage designers, from the recording engineers to the musicians, everyone was encouraged to exceed themselves.

"You had to be at your best at all times with Michael Jackson, or you would not be there," boasted the people who were talented, devoted, and lucky enough to be chosen to work with him.

Michael Jackson raised the bar for everyone. He would rehearse over and over again the same song and dance steps. The musicians on his recordings and on the live stage with him went over the songs hundreds of times, to the point that their performances were flawless. Michael would perform with his dancers and then just watch them and critique every gesture and movement. "Your arm should be stretched out more during the crescendo." "You should lean more to the right at the beginning of the bridge." It was hard work and long hours for everyone, but his dancers and musicians internalized the pride of being the best, like Michael Jackson.

"Good job!" he would tell them when they performed to his standard. Michael was known for complimenting his people, for recognizing their efforts.

Michael Jackson demanded of himself the same level of effort and perfection that he sought from them. He worked to the point of exhaustion. In fact, during his twenties, he would fast on Sundays and dance in his private studio at the Hayvenhurst home for hours at a stretch, until he dropped to the floor. These hours of rehearsal, he reasoned, would not only help him perfect his execution but increase his stamina for the all-out, nearly superhuman energy that was always a hallmark of his live concert shows.

"I'm a perfectionist," Michael admitted; "I'm never satisfied with anything."

Referring to Michael Jackson as "an amazing human being," Greg Gorman, a professional photographer for four decades, said, "Michael was a perfectionist beyond your wildest imagination.

Every time we would shoot, he would call me and we'd have a two-hour conversation to discuss what it was we were going to do and how we were going to go about it." Not only was he obsessive about the details, explained Gorman, but "he was very genuine" as a human being.

Adrian Grant, who many years ago began the Michael Jackson Fan Club in the United Kingdom [which led to his creation of the production *Thriller Live*], came to know his idol very well. "He … taught me to really reach for the stars, follow your dreams and be the best you can."

"He was a perfectionist," echoes Cris Judd, a choreographer, dancer, and producer who worked with Michael on his *Dangerous* and *HIStory* world tours. "... In rehearsal he would make each of us perform the entire two-hour-plus show, one at a time, in front of him.... And then he would give you some very precise correction. Like exactly where your thumb and middle finger should be on your hat!"

Michael's music engineers and producers were always impressed by his intense, full-out rehearsals. He performed with the same verve and energy as he did in front of an audience of one hundred thousand people. Also, according to Quincy Jones, Michael danced in the studio booth while he recorded a song; he couldn't help himself. Most singers would be too winded to perform at peak level while they were dancing, but not Michael Jackson; he belted out the song while dancing his heart out.

"Michael Jackson knew every element—instruments, notes and chords—in his music," explained Michael Bearden, who won the coveted job as musical director of *This Is It*. "He was extremely professional and detail-oriented." Yet, in spite of the complexity of the preparations, Michael used to say to Bearden, "When you're coming up with new arrangements for the songs, make sure they're simple. They gotta be able to hum it...." Michael Jackson wanted his music to be sung by eight to eighty-year-olds…, and he succeeded!

"MJ was brilliant in that he always wanted to grow and push boundaries," Bearden summarized. "He would always tell me to push him so that's what I did.... It was all done in love."

Today, the largest mirror in Michael Jackson's bedroom at his Holmby Hills home still bears the message, written on it by him: "TRAIN, *perfection*, March, April FULL OUT May." He often wrote or posted reminders and inspirational messages on his mirrors and walls in order always to keep focused on his goals toward being "the best."

Perfectionism blended with genius and unfailing intuition in Michael Jackson to result in his gifts to the world of unique creative expression.

Self-discipline & Determination

No one had a stronger work ethic or clearer vision of what he wanted from his career than Michael Jackson. He was intensely determined to achieve the heights in his profession; he was driven to deliver the best music and performances that would become his lasting legacy in this world. He was also committed to having his own family, to fathering children.

Michael worked around his genuine humility and gentleness of spirit to get what he wanted. Anyone who knew him well understood that he made things happen for himself.

He made telephone calls, hired the best people, got creative, and persisted. He preferred the phone—no eye contact, few physical distractions, and limited constraints on time spent in conversations at all hours of the day or night. No one was ever too busy to speak with *Michael Jackson.*

Lisa Marie Presley described Michael, posthumously:
He was an incredibly dynamic force and power that was not to be underestimated.... Mediocrity was not a concept that would even for a second enter Michael Jackson's being or actions.

He worked harder than anyone else to be the best and to give the most. From his first producer as a solo artist, Quincy Jones, to his last director and collaborator, Kenny Ortega, all of his colleagues spoke of Michael Jackson's consuming passion for his work, complete professionalism, total focus, and inexhaustible efforts.

Combining his self-discipline with high intelligence and amazing creativity, Michael Jackson soared into the stratosphere of recognition and fame. However, as he himself explained, he paid a huge price for his unequaled success. "It came with a lot of pain," he said; "a lot of pain."

The Greatest Show on Earth

Michael read *The Greatest Show on Earth* during the earliest stage of his solo career. He was so impressed by it that he told his attorney/manager John Branca that he wanted to become just that— "the greatest show on earth"—and that John's duty was to help get him there.

"All of the world is a stage," William Shakespeare wrote centuries ago. These words of the bard were adopted by Michael Jackson as his mission statement.

Every time he appeared in public, which occasions became more and more rare across the years of his life, Michael Jackson perceived himself as being on the world stage. He always knew that if any camera at all was in his general vicinity, photos would be captured of him. For the photographer, they would command the highest price on the open market for celebrity photos.

His appearance was always designed to make an impression. Whether he was wearing a disguise, a mask that covered the lower half of his face, or reflective sunglasses, Michael Jackson often hid behind something that would keep him semi-private in a public setting. Not only was he genuinely shy and adamantly averse to public speaking, but he savored the idea of keeping people guessing, of being inscrutable. His image was very important to Michael. Yet he did not want to disclose too much of himself—either with his physical appearance or from his personal life.

Michael was fascinated by the mysteriousness of the reclusive and germ-phobic Howard Hughes. He loved the genius and skills of

Charlie Chaplin, who evoked so much pathos with so little effort. "I *am* Charlie Chaplin," Michael said once, when overcome by his feelings of admiration for the talented English comic actor from the silent film era.

For many years, Michael was fearful of overexposure to the public. He labored over decisions related to public appearances; he was committed to keeping his availability very limited. In keeping with that decision, Michael Jackson turned down a lucrative offer by Pepsi-Cola to perform in commercials for their product. It was only after intense cajoling by his family members, led by his determined father, that Michael finally agreed. It was a time when celebrities typically did not sponsor products; Michael was arguably the first *major* entertainer to accept such an offer. His compensation was a staggering, unprecedented $700,000.

The filming of the first commercial—which featured Michael Jackson in concert, singing and descending from stairs with pyrotechnics overhead and behind him—went very wrong. Michael's hair caught on fire because of a technician's premature release of the pyrotechnics, and he was rushed to the hospital with second and third degree burns on his scalp. Pepsi promptly settled the matter with $1.5 million, all of which Michael donated to charity.

The commercial was ultimately completed and released, to great fanfare, but Michael had insisted that his face be shown for no more than four seconds. Although the Pepsi commercial was televised countless times, Michael kept his exposure to the public—at least his face, that is—limited to a flash of time. He turned his participation in the ad into a cameo appearance! People would have to view the commercial *fifteen times* to see Michael Jackson's face for a total of *one minute!*

Another interesting tidbit about his unprecedented success in the advertising arena is that the Michael Jackson Pepsi-Cola commercial was the first non-Russian advertisement to air in the former Soviet Union. In 1988, Michael Jackson became a symbol of American culture in that country.

In spite of his extensive efforts to limit his exposure in the media, Michael Jackson became the most recognized individual on the planet. Everything about him went big. The front pages of newspapers on six continents featured stories about him, many of them absurd, such as the hyperbaric chamber myth.

A photograph of Michael Jackson lying on his back in a special kind of oxygen chamber, one which is used to treat burn victims, was released by the Associated Press and the United Press International. The story was covered extensively on television and radio. The reportage explained that the singer regularly slept in this casket-sized, glass-covered box in an attempt to prolong his life to the age of 150. The truth behind the photo, however, was that Michael Jackson had donated this important life-saving equipment to a hospital burn unit, and when he later visited there, he tried out the unit to get a feel of what real burn victims experience. Thus, Michael's reputation as "weird" and "bizarre" blossomed and, thereafter, just continued to grow in that direction.

He was always a show-stopper, both on stage and in real life. By 1993, when Michael Jackson gave his first national interview in fourteen years—to Oprah Winfrey at his Neverland Ranch—he had turned himself into the most fascinating and mysterious celebrity anywhere. Viewed by more than ninety million people, the ratings-winning international broadcast remains today among the most-watched in U.S. television history.

When asked why it had taken him so long to consent to an interview, Michael humbly responded, "I felt that there wasn't anything really important for me to say." He may not have realized that people would tune in to a show to hear him talk about his favorite colors or his cereal preferences! Of course, Michael Jackson let his *songs* do his talking....

Michael's primary goal was to become the greatest entertainer the world has ever seen. He worked tirelessly to accomplish it. His genius, commitment, and work ethic were purposefully directed, from his early childhood, toward this consummate achievement. He had the "fire in his belly" to be the best.

From early on, Michael was concerned about his legacy. He did not want to be forgotten. Michael passionately wanted to leave something special for the world after he would leave this mortal realm.

The greatest entertainer made himself into the greatest show on earth. Sometimes, however, both achievements caused him great suffering and anguish. At what horrendous price does an individual reach these pinnacles?

The real, behind-the-scenes "greatest show" that was Michael Jackson was his humanitarian endeavors, his myriad philanthropic activities, and his private acts of charity, for which he sought neither publicity nor public acclaim.

At the Top

Royalty, heads of state, prime ministers, and other dignitaries sought out Michael Jackson both in the United States and abroad. During his visits to other countries, he graciously met with top-level officials whenever he was able to do so.

As early as 1972, Michael Jackson, then a young teenager, met the Queen of England when The Jacksons did a special performance for her. Michael called the event a great honor and one of the best experiences of his life.

President Ronald Reagan wrote a fan letter to Michael Jackson in February 1984, when he was recovering from the Pepsi-ad burn: "I was pleased to learn that you were not seriously hurt.... I know from experience that these things can happen on the set—no matter how much caution is exercised...." Among the thousands of phone calls, letters, and cards that Michael received, this one was the most noteworthy for him. The hospital where he was first treated reportedly was forced to add six volunteers to answer the volume of telephone calls from his fans and well-wishers.

Three months later, President Reagan and First Lady Nancy honored Michael Jackson at the White House by presenting him with an award for his accomplishments and humanitarianism. Michael gifted the president and Transportation Secretary Elizabeth Dole with the royalty-free use of his chart-topping song "Beat It" in their national D.A.R.E. drug/alcohol prevention initiative. In his personal journal, published many years later, the late president wrote that he was "most surprised at how shy" Michael Jackson was.

Jacqueline Kennedy was a woman whom Michael idolized from the time when he was a child. President John F. Kennedy, who was assassinated when Michael was only five years old, was one of his heroes. Michael always wanted to meet the iconic, elegant, and courageous woman, and finally fate provided him with an opportunity. When, as Jacqueline Kennedy Onassis, the famous former First Lady, visited Michael Jackson in 1983 at his Hayvenhurst home, it was for the purpose of asking him to write his autobiography. Ms. Onassis was an editor for Doubleday Publishing Company, and she was determined to capture Michael as an author. Katherine and Michael hosted her with great enthusiasm and respect, and the reluctant twenty-five-year-old, already a recognized global celebrity, consented. Michael had dated her daughter Caroline Kennedy once, probably in an attempt to meet her mother, and he could not say "no" to the woman who beseeched him in his own living room to publish the details of his personal life.

Michael Jackson and President Jimmy Carter served as co-chairmen of the "Heal Our Children" charity during the early 1990's. Michael appeared with former President Carter and his wife Rosalynn to meet a group of children in May 1993, in Atlanta, Georgia. He joined the Carters for the Atlanta Project's "Kid's Celebration," a concert that promoted vaccinations for low-income urban youth. Many thousands of these children living in poverty failed to be immunized against serious diseases. Michael never forgot that his beloved mother had polio as a child and, although she progressed well across the years, she continued to walk with a limp throughout her adulthood.

President George H. W. Bush honored Michael Jackson by presenting him with the Entertainer of the Decade Award in the summer of 1990 at the Museum of Children. In 1992, at the White House, President Bush presented Michael with the Point of Light Award for his unparalleled charitable involvements.

Michael Jackson accepted President Bill Clinton's invitation to perform at two of his inaugural events in 1993. He and the president shared the stage together, and Michael sang and danced—to the delight of the celebrants—at these festive historical events.

In 2000, at the Angel Ball in New York, Michael Jackson and President Clinton were honored together—with several others—for their work to fight cancer. The star-studded, black-tie dinner with 1,800 attendees was held with the expressed goal to raise four million dollars for a cancer foundation toward finding a cure for the dreaded disease. From the podium, Michael gave the president a warm tribute: "I'm honored, Mr. President, to receive this award in your presence.... You have been an incredible president and I love you."

For years, Michael Jackson maintained a private relationship with Princess Diana, sometimes speaking with her by telephone in the middle of the night for him (U.S. time). They commiserated on the savagery of the paparazzi and tabloids. They shared a common bond in that both were primary targets, in their respective countries, of judgmental, harassing media on a continuous basis. Michael encouraged her to "be strong" in the face of such onslaughts. He greatly admired Diana for her genuineness and love of children, her charity work, and her unique, trail-blazing approach to her role as a prominent member of British royalty.

Princess Diana and Prince Charles attended a sold-out *Bad* concert in London, after which Michael Jackson presented the princess with a check in the amount of £100,000 for her favorite charities. Before his performance, Diana had asked him if he was going to perform "Dirty Diana" that evening. He replied, "No, out of respect for you." The princess then expressed her regret because, as she explained, "I really like that song!"

In February 1998, Michael Jackson attended the investiture ceremony of then South Korean President Kim Dae-jung, one of the century's astute fighters for democracy and, later, the 2000 recipient of the Nobel Peace Prize. Michael explained that he was there because of Dae-jung's commitment to children. The former president praised and honored Michael Jackson on the day after Michael's death: "The world has lost a hero … and Korea also lost a beloved friend, who showed continued interest and supported unification of [the] Korean peninsula. Korean people are sad."

Michael was a "close friend" of Prince Albert of Monaco, and he knew several royal family members in the Middle East, including the King of Bahrain. Sheikh Abdullah bin Hamad Al Khalifa, son of the King, befriended Michael and hosted him and his children at his exquisite palace in Bahrain in 2005, after the family left their Neverland home. Princess Stephanie of Monaco sang the female part in the duet with Michael Jackson in his song "In the Closet."

A reciprocal admiration between Nelson Mandela and Michael Jackson came to light in 2005, when the former South African president spoke to a Danish magazine and disclosed the profound impact of his celebrity friend upon him:

When you are behind bars with no hope of release, you need to find strength wherever you can.... I found strength in Michael Jackson. Even to this day Michael Jackson is a constant source of inspiration.

In the early nineties, the two men became friends, while Mandela was president of his country. At the request of the consummate statesman, Michael Jackson performed concerts in Seoul and Germany for South African charities. These performances broke the record for the most-watched live Internet concerts in history.

Although Michael Jackson did not perform in person at the inauguration events for President Barack Obama in 2009, Michael's "Wanna Be Startin' Something" was played, like a celebratory anthem, at the Mid-Atlantic Ball to honor the president on the eve of his taking the oath of office. Later in 2009, Mr. Obama addressed Michael Jackson's passing by saying: "I'm glad to see that he is being remembered primarily for the great joy that he brought to a lot of people through his extraordinary gifts.... I still have all his stuff on my iPod. I think that Michael Jackson will go down in history as one of our greatest entertainers...."

"The High Road"

No matter what might be said about Michael Jackson by his detractors, it must be admitted that Michael always took "the high road" with his consistent forbearance and sterling example for others. Michael never uttered a harsh, reciprocal statement about the individuals from the media who so excoriated and criticized him, who so cruelly accused him of acts that ranged from silliness to criminal behavior. Michael never lashed out at his two ex-wives or at any member of his family. He never succumbed to the ever-present human temptation to "fight fire with fire," to counterattack his critics with retorts directed at their faults or foibles, or to rail publicly against the injustices he suffered.

Michael didn't name names when, on a very few occasions, he tried to defend himself from media lies and viciousness. He was a lamb; he was a sweetheart. Michael did in fact "turn the other cheek," in accordance with his religious upbringing and beliefs.

In his rare public statements, he addressed the facts and not the persons who were flinging mud at him. He spoke of his ex-wives hardly at all, and when he did, it was with restraint and respect, even during trying times.

Who else has so continuously restrained himself or herself from verbal retribution directed at attackers and maligners ... and for a span of *four decades*? Who among us would always resist the temptation to lash out against those who have so cruelly or manipulatively maligned us?

Factor in the reality that Michael Jackson, if he had chosen to retaliate, would have received priceless publicity for himself and his commercial products. The economic benefits to him of a battle of words in the media are inestimable. Every time he chose to utter some public words, they fled onto the pages of newspapers and tabloids and onto television screens. Within this context especially, his forbearance and manifest sense of dignity are truly astounding!

Michael Jackson reached a pinnacle in the world, in terms of his success and celebrity. *He also took the high road in getting there.*

Sense of Humor

The people who really knew Michael Jackson describe him as "funny," "fun-loving," and "a prankster." His mother remembers especially the times when young Michael played tricks on his siblings. One of his favorites was hiding his pet snake or a spider in a place where one of his sisters would surely find it and scream in horror.

As an adult, Michael enjoyed childlike fun, particularly when that included physical activity like running around outside or racing in go-karts. In his "Private Home Movies," which he released to the public in an attempt to counteract the devastating effects of the distorted image of him from "Living with Michael Jackson," Michael described his "favorite activity of all" as water balloon fights. At Neverland, he explained, nearly every visitor was required to get wet from falling into the pool or lake, getting squirted by a "super soaker," or preferably being drenched in a water balloon fight. Tongue in cheek, Michael prided himself on always winning these harmless contests and "never getting wet."

When working on his music with others, he would break the tension by telling a joke or teasing one of his colleagues. It would never be hurtful, however, as he always tried to avoid making anyone feel bad.

He loved to laugh and giggle, especially during the years preceding 2005. Michael's high-pitched, joyful laughter was readily recognizable and unforgettable to everyone he befriended. He enjoyed watching not only all kinds of cartoons but the *Three Stooges* from his expansive video collection of "the oldies." As a little boy, Prince had special fun with his dad, watching the antics of the three buffoons and laughing with abandon. In fact, according to his older brother Jermaine, Michael watched a *Three Stooges* movie immediately after his acquittal, just so that he could laugh once again. His sister Janet said that what she would miss most about her brother Michael was his laughter.

One day while he was riding along in his vehicle in Las Vegas, his security men turned on the radio. The broadcast was interrupted for an announcement that "Michael Jackson has died." The newscaster continued, "Let's have a moment of silence...."

"What's that?" the boss asked from the back seat, leaning forward.

"You died, sir," his bodyguard, from the front passenger seat, replied.

The boss just laughed out loud. "This kind of thing always happens to me," he said. Mr. Jackson didn't take himself too seriously, even when an outrageously inaccurate report was issued about him.

Creature Comforts

It is fair to say that, in general, Michael Jackson sublimated his sexuality through his art. He devoted himself with a rare level of drive and passion to his music—composing, arranging, producing, singing, and dancing.

He always occupied lavish quarters and surrounded himself with enviable accoutrements. Except for this one variable, however, Michael Jackson's creature comforts were quite limited.

It has been said that a person either "lives to eat" or "eats to live." Michael would be categorized in the latter description. "I don't eat much," he confessed to many individuals, and sometimes he failed to eat meals entirely when he was engrossed in his work.

Michael was a vegetarian for many years when he was a young man. By the time that his children were eating meals with him, he enjoyed a wider selection of foods. He tried always to make time for sit-down lunches and dinners with his children. Michael often personally made breakfast for them. He believed strongly that parents should eat with their children, that this shared focus and activity were important bonding times.

Kai Chase, Michael Jackson's chef during his last three months, at the Holmby Hills home, described his eating pattern. Michael drank specially-mixed, natural fruit and vegetable juices for breakfast; had lunch—which usually consisted of an elaborate salad—with his three children at 12:30 P.M.; and ate dinner with his family at the dining room table whenever he was able to do so within his busy rehearsal schedule. On Sundays the family would enjoy "comfort food," such as gumbo.

Kenny Ortega, his friend and the director of *This Is It,* would often personally ensure that Michael, who became totally immersed in his rehearsals and concert planning to the exclusion of everything else, would eat his meals on the set.

Michael's limited food preferences, during the early 2000's, are revealed in his standing order for the flight attendants on the private plane that he commissioned for his frequent use. The "passenger profile" indicated Kentucky Fried Chicken for every meal—breakfast, lunch, and dinner—specifically the "original chicken breasts," along with mashed potatoes, corn, and biscuits with strawberry jelly and spray butter. He would eat fruit, especially oranges, grapes, apples, and bananas, but rarely any other desserts. He also liked gum and mints instead of typical desserts.

His preferred beverages were 7-Up, Orange Crush, and fruit punch, and also white wine, always served in Diet Coke cans.

Michael did not want his children to see him drink an alcoholic beverage. If he drank wine—or the occasional tequila, gin, or Crown Royal—he consumed it discreetly, in "disguised" cans.

He would never eat chocolate, peanut butter, broccoli, or strong-scented foods.

Neither a gourmand nor a connoisseur, Michael Jackson liked a few "tried and true" foods and stuck to them, eating in great moderation.

With regard to his sleeping habits, he was cursed with profound insomnia from a young age. At times he could not sleep at all for days in a row. From the time of his early twenties, Michael was known to be active during the wee hours of the morning, such as 3:00 and 4:00 A.M. He would wander his house, venture outside in the darkness for short walks, work on his current projects, and make telephone calls to those who were receptive to middle-of-the-night conversations. Often Michael felt truly desperate for a good night's sleep; he could not turn off his racing mind; and he continued to hear the beat of the music that was forever playing in his head.

"You can't sleep after the show," Michael explained in "Private Home Movies." "The adrenaline is up there; I go through hell touring." With the continuous long-distance travel and different time zones, he had great difficulty adjusting to the physical demands. Unfortunately, this meant chronic sleeplessness, which continued when he returned home after months on a tour.

Michael avoided the sun and the beach—except for brief exposure and always with an umbrella over his head. Although he loved the out-of-doors and nature, he was doomed to limit himself to the shade or the indoors. His skin condition, vitiligo, and super-sensitivity to the pernicious effects of sun affected him greatly. He was not only uncomfortably self-conscious about it but he had to severely restrict his daily activities. David Nordahl and Thomas Mesereau, at different times, each saw Michael's back when he lifted his shirt to show his trusted friends the visible results of his disease, the brown and white splotches.

"He always wore long sleeves and cover-ups and used an umbrella," recalls Nordahl, "because the sun was not supposed to touch his skin at all. I was worried about him because I knew that he had what can be a deadly disease." [Michael also suffered from lupus erythematosus, which was likely the primary cause of the toxic effects of the sun upon him.]

Whereas many celebrities choose sybaritic, hedonistic lifestyles, Michael Jackson chose a quiet, as-private-as-possible life as the father of three young children. Except for his place of residence itself, the daily routines of his life were quite simple. Eating was almost incidental; sleeping often impossible; sexual expression sublimated through his work and music; and recreating seriously inhibited by his skin condition ... and his fame.

With his great wealth and incredible resources, Michael Jackson could have chosen to live in a profligate manner, filling his time with consorts, parties, nightclubs, casinos, resorts, and jet-setting to far-flung places for serial romantic liaisons and exotic vacations. Instead, he spent all of his available time interacting with his three children, immersing himself in his work, and attending to his charitable activities.

That was the real Michael Jackson.

An Isolate

Called "a recluse" throughout his adulthood, Michael Jackson did choose to keep his personal life as private as possible. In general, he avoided interviews; he restricted the capture of photos or footage of him through the skillful machinations of his security personnel, wearing masks and disguises, and declining most invitations to appear in public.

Michael Jackson's security guards were directed to keep him safe and to keep him private, except for the rare, explicit times that he wanted to be seen. They knew that he planned to be seen on a given day when his hairstylist would be invited to the house to assist him in his preparations.

During the last four years of his life, Michael Jackson was surprisingly active and interactive. He worked on his music—composing, arranging, dancing, and collaborating with other artists and musicians. He entertained a host of proposals that were submitted for his potential involvement, ranging from the creation of amusement parks to assuming a residence-based series of concerts in big cities that included Las Vegas and London. Michael traveled across the United States and in other countries, always taking his three children with him.

He worked in numerous recording studios with state-of-the-art equipment in his own homes, his friends' homes, hotels, and free-standing facilities in various cities. He attended musicals, magic shows, and concerts; he visited art exhibits, museums, historical sites, and scientific displays. He shopped frequently in bookstores and occasionally in antique and clothing shops. With his children, he visited amusement parks and enjoyed the rides, from the roller coasters to the bumper cars.

Michael watched movies at public theaters—as well as in the privacy of his home—and voraciously read books and some favorite magazines. He cared deeply about the problems of the world; he worried about the environment and the future of this planet. His poignant poem "Planet Earth" conveys his heartfelt concerns for the survival of beauty and Nature. He continued his philanthropic activities both on a private level by giving to certain individuals in need and on a larger scale by donating to organizations with a mission of helping and healing.

Michael Jackson rarely entertained people in his own homes during those last four years—in stark contrast with his all-out entertaining during seventeen years at Neverland. However, he maintained a relationship with each of two girlfriends, with whom he spent time in places away from the residences he shared with his children, such as hotels. He also visited other people from time to time. He and his children stayed for a span of many weeks with his long-time friends, the Dominic Cascio family, in New Jersey.

Wait for it now.... *Michael Jackson was not a recluse!* Just because we hardly ever saw him on television, the Internet, or media paper products, that does not mean that he was not out and about. A review of his activities in the chapter "Nothing But the Facts ..." will reveal his frequent geographical changes and many of the major involvements of the private King of Pop.

200 Years?

Michael circled the globe many times, visiting dozens of countries on six continents. He met people from the top echelon of society, and he made it his business to meet with the disadvantaged, the seriously ill, and the orphaned. He saw it all and, within the limitations of his existence as the most-watched celebrity on the planet, experienced it all. He gave of himself and his wealth everywhere he went. He left an unforgettable part of himself everywhere. Anyone who has met or seen Michael Jackson remembers him with clarity.

The highs and lows of human existence, joys and sufferings, the unimaginably wealthy and the unfathomably poor were not strangers to Michael Jackson. He thought seriously and felt deeply about all that he experienced. And it all confirmed his self-perception as an ambassador of love, a messenger of peace, and a harbinger of world unity. Michael Jackson believed in the power of his being on this planet; he knew that he would make a difference; and he tirelessly engaged in quiet, private acts of charity and caring.

In his personal life, too, he had incredible experiences within his large family; with his wives and children; and with his hundreds of "friends," most of whom were acquaintances in reality. In his "Private Home Movies," Michael said that he could count his real friends on one hand.

It was a badge of honor to know Michael Jackson throughout most of his life, and many people flaunted their familiarity with him … and exaggerated it. Yet, he did know myriad celebrities and other public figures around the world.

The fabric of Michael Jackson's life was like a tapestry of all colors and symbols, textures and shapes. *It was uniquely rich.*

At the age of fifty, Michael was taken from our planet way too early and so tragically. Michael Jackson experienced the equivalent of perhaps two hundred years of a more "average" person in terms of the richness, breadth, and depth of his life.

I was tough on him....
I wanted him to know that the world
was not a nice place....
He was so damn sensitive, ...
I was worried about him....
I would do it differently today....
— Joseph Jackson,
as quoted in *Michael Jackson—*
The Magic, The Madness, The Whole Story

"Daddy"

**Love is the answer
to all that I am.**
"You Are My Life,"
Michael Jackson

**Michael Jackson was not only
"the King of Pop"—he was
the King of "Pops."**

"Daddy" is what his children called him, always. Michael Jackson decided before he had his first child that his kids would call him "daddy." His own father had insisted that Michael and his eight siblings call him "Joseph"—never "father" or "dad" or "daddy." The young Michael felt that this requirement and the emotional distance it fostered were continually an impediment to his relationship with his father. He vowed that his own children would use a name for him that conveyed affection and affirmed him as a loving, approachable father.

Anyone who observed Michael Jackson as a father realized early on that he was very devoted, affectionate, and protective of Prince, Paris, and Blanket. He played with the children on their level, often sitting on the floor with them. He believed in the importance of eye contact with children, at their same level; it fostered bonding between father and child.

He read bedtime stories to his children and watched DVD's with them; they all shared a love of movies, ranging from Disney cartoons to Hollywood classics, especially those that featured children. He taught them to ride bicycles. Michael Jackson took great pride in his commitment to give them as normal a life as possible and to be the best father he could be.

When he had to leave his children in order to attend a business meeting or to work in a recording studio off-site, every time the little ones would see him off with "I love you, daddy."

"I love you more," he always responded, holding their faces in his hands and looking into the eyes of each one. There were hugs all around. When he would return, even if absent for only several hours, they would run to him as if they had just been rescued from a well.

"Daddy! Daddy!" the little ones would sing in chorus. It was heartwarming to observe their special bond playing out....

Michael Jackson's family members, David Nordahl, Thomas Mesereau, his Las Vegas security team, and many others have spoken with great admiration about Michael's special relationship with each of his children.

Michael was the one who buttoned up the kids' sweaters when the temperature fell. He always made certain that his kids wore scarves, gloves, and hats during the winter months. He brushed their hair. Kathy Hilton, mother of Paris Hilton, observed Michael in action as a father, and she described him as "so warm and wonderful," when she was interviewed in June 2011. Kathy visited Michael and his children often when they were living at the Bel Air Hotel, where she was also staying in late 2008.

"He did not have any nanny at all," she explains, during the weeks of their Bel Air residence. "And he was so fabulous at the hotel, up early every morning, playing with the kids," she continued. "There was not a kinder, more generous, loving, sweet, smart ... [person], the most wonderful father."

Ms. Hilton fondly remembers Michael in earlier times, when the two of them "were little kids," who made prank phone calls together and "got silly." They first met when she was thirteen and he was a year older. "We ... developed a friendship and a bond throughout the years. And we always kept in touch.

"He was a father who was so *with* his children."

The singer Akon also spent time with Michael, during his last years, working on new material for an album. He recalls:

> We recorded at his home studio, and his kids were always there. He was always monitoring them—making sure they were doing their homework, eating right. He would personally cook for them, always healthy stuff.... We could be in the middle of recording, and he'd drop everything to make sure they were good.

*   *   *   *   *   *   *   *   *

Although he loved all animals, including snakes, rats, chimps, and gorillas, Michael Jackson continued to be wary and nervous around dogs from the time of his childhood, when he was once bitten. However, he would gladly overcome his own reluctance to adopt a dog for the sake of his young children.

A chocolate Labrador puppy arrived at their Summerlin home shortly after the family's arrival to their new residence in 2006. He was a gift to Prince from his father. The little boy loved his new pet with gratitude, passion, and affection. He named the puppy "Kenya." How fitting a name it was! The East African country of Kenya is considered by evolutionists to have been the cradle of mankind, the birthplace of the human species. To Americans, it is the prime location for the photo safari, where the big wild animals roam free—lions, cheetahs, leopards, giraffe, herds of elephants, and forty species of antelope.

With Neverland's sprawling, exotic zoo only a fond memory to the Michael Jackson family, Kenya the pup represented their only link to the animal world, which they all deeply loved and keenly missed. Quite a responsibility for one little brown puppy!

Kenya, like all healthy pups, was full of seemingly boundless energy. When he got loose from time to time and ran off the property, the security guards would chase Kenya down the street and through the neighbors' yards. Regardless of the circumstances, they knew that they could not return without Kenya. Prince would have been devastated.

Once Prince had his own puppy, Paris wanted her own pet. If anyone could convince their dad to get them anything, the precocious Paris was the front runner. She held a special place in her dad's heart. Paris's presence brought a smile to everyone who encountered her. She was polite, kind, thoughtful, and enthusiastic. Her lake-blue eyes seemed to sparkle when she spoke. Everyone loved her.

Specifically, Paris wanted a kitten. Because there was no one else around to do it, the security guards were given the mission of obtaining a kitten for Paris.

The little girl named her new cat baby "Katie." Michael's mother, Paris's loving grandmother, was nicknamed "Kate" and sometimes also called "Katie." Paris shared her father's focus on the importance of names and of giving honor to special people.

A couple of weeks after the little family's enthusiastic welcome of Katie into her new home, Paris left a note for Boyd Williams, written in red crayon: "Boyd, I would very much like it if you could get more canned tuna for Katie because I only have #1 can left. Thank you so much [sic.] I appreciate it very much. From Paris." Williams kept that note and cherishes it to this day. He carried it with him to his *Good Morning America* interview to show his admiration for the little girl's warmth, politeness, and appreciation of kindnesses extended to her.

"This is why we stayed on the job," Boyd explained. "Though our pay was slow in coming, the reward of seeing an innocent child ask for so little and express such sincere appreciation was enough." His Las Vegas security team greatly valued and embraced their commitment to Mr. Jackson and his little ones.

Kenya made his television debut on the *Oprah Winfrey Show*—along with Joseph, Katherine, and Michael's three children—on November 10, 2010. Prince and Paris talked about their fondest memories of their father, while Blanket said little. The two older children affirmed that they "were okay" with wearing masks in public when they were younger; they understood their father's reasons.

This international exposure of his young children to the general public caused some fans, who had espoused the "death-hoax conspiracy" belief, to say, "Now we have *proof* that Michael Jackson is dead—his children were on *Oprah*!"

* * * * * * * * *

Michael Jackson had always kept his children's faces covered when they were in public or likely to be photographed. From the time of their infancy, he took elaborate measures to ensure that they wore veils. He suffered harsh criticism in tabloids and ridicule and cruel jocularity by comedians for this decision, but he held fast to it.

It was reported by at least one source that Debbie Rowe, the mother of the two older children, had initiated the idea and insisted on this veiling practice. The more prevalent opinion was that Michael Jackson made the decision, which is most credible because he greatly feared that they would be kidnapped, a potentially tragic event made more likely if they were readily recognizable.

Many commentators pointed out that the veils brought even more attention to the children than would their exposed faces. Some speculated that Michael Jackson's veiling practices were spawned by his desire to appear eccentric or to garner widespread publicity for himself.

Few, if any, among the public seemed to understand Michael's real motivation for concealing his children's identities from public awareness. If no one knew what his children looked like, they could occasionally go to various public places with security personnel, their nanny or teacher, and thereby have normal experiences. When they were not with their famous father, who was always recognized in public, they could be everyday kids doing everyday things. Michael Jackson so much wanted that normalcy for his children!

Michael Jackson was determined that his children would not be exploited in the same way that paparazzi harassed and used him from the time of his own youth. He had paid a huge price for his international celebrity, for his astounding artistic and commercial success. When he started breaking all records for accomplishments in the entertainment industry, the vicious portrayals, name-calling, belittling, and accusations began, and they continued non-stop across years. As a deeply sensitive man, he suffered both mentally and emotionally; it saddened and troubled him to have been turned into a late-night talk-show joke. He wanted to shield his children from all of the stress, pain, and humiliation that he endured.

The tabloids would no doubt have paid a king's ransom for an exclusive photograph of Michael Jackson's children. Consider the $14 million that *People* magazine paid to Brad Pitt and Angelina Jolie for the debut photo of their newborn twins in August 2008; the couple chose to donate this extraordinary windfall to charity. Jennifer Lopez was reportedly paid $6 million by *People* for an exclusive photograph of her infant twins earlier that year, in February 2008. *How much bounty would a picture of Michael Jackson's three little ones fetch on the open tabloid market? No doubt a fortune.*

Once such a photo would be published, most likely on the front cover of some unscrupulous tabloid, Michael Jackson's children would forever be denied the precious anonymity that he created and sustained for them by their consistent veiling.

His security personnel fully understood the real, beneficial effects of Michael Jackson's controversial decision. They could take the children to a movie, arcades, amusement parks, or on a field trip, and, with some extra precautions to camouflage their own identities as bodyguards, the kids could have fun, interact with other children, and act like regular non-celebrities.

Sadly, Mr. Jackson could not accompany his children on sojourns to everyday places like parks and restaurants. He sorely missed these opportunities for sharing in their fun and recreation. His security men would remind their boss that they could not protect him, or ultimately the children either, if he accompanied them to an open, unsecured public place.

Not that he needed reminding about security and his kids. Mr. Jackson was always fearful about the possibility of their getting hurt or carried away; he fretted. His security guards never asked why he was so frightened about something dreadful happening to the children. He did not explain; it was as if he was afraid that his mere utterance might trigger a horrible incident.

Michael Garcia describes a time when he took Prince, Paris, and Blanket to Circus Circus to enjoy the kid-friendly rides and attractions there. Their father stayed at home, eager for his children to enjoy themselves, unrecognized and uninterrupted. "Mr. Jackson would call again and again," recalls Garcia. "What are they doing now? Are they having fun?" their solicitous father would ask the bodyguard, anxious to hear from him specific reports about their smiles and laughter.

In all of the piles of mail that poured into his home, it was likely that there were "hate letters" and malicious threats made to the King of Pop and the children he loved.

Michael Jackson would ask his security guards to promise that they would always protect his children, no matter what. His Vegas team would promise to care for them like their own children.

* * * * * * * * *

Michael Jackson was superlatively creative. He always thought "outside the box" in his art, music and dance, songwriting, concert productions, and even in fatherhood. He put together a family for himself in an unconventional way.

Michael had longed to be a father, wanting his own children more than anything else in life. He overcame the obstacles to his becoming a dad in a unique, planned, and constructive manner....

Michael Jackson married Lisa Marie Presley, daughter of Elvis and Priscilla Presley, in May 1994, in a secret ceremony in the Dominican Republic. Their courtship was conducted across months, largely by telephone while Michael was touring and traveling extensively. Many people close to the couple confirmed that they genuinely loved each other. Early in the marriage, Michael publicly professed his love for Lisa Marie and she reciprocated. For various reasons, however, the couple officially separated in

December 1995; Lisa Marie filed for divorce in January 1996; and their divorce became final in August of that year.

Before their wedding, Lisa Marie, then twenty-six years old, had promised Michael—thirty-five and anxious to start a family—to bear his children. Soon after the nuptials, however, she recanted. Lisa Marie already had two young children from her first marriage, a one-year-old son and a five-year-old daughter. When he suggested repeatedly that they could adopt a child or employ the services of a surrogate mother, Lisa Marie firmly demurred. Michael's disappointment was profound.

In response to this unhappy development, Debbie Rowe offered to bear a child for Michael. Debbie had known Michael Jackson for many years. She was the nurse who assisted in his dermatological treatment for vitiligo, the non-contagious disorder that caused his skin to lose pigmentation, resulting in patchy white blotches over his body and face.

Through her professional contacts with him, which progressed to frequent personal telephone conversations and intimate discussions, Debbie's feelings for Michael grew into love. She filled her small apartment with posters and pictures of Michael Jackson, King of Pop. She considered him a dear friend and vehemently believed that he deserved to be a father.

Although at first reluctant, Michael accepted her unconventional offer to give birth to a child for him to raise. Debbie became pregnant but miscarried in early 1996. Within weeks, she conceived again, and—in accordance with their agreement—they kept her pregnancy a secret. However, Debbie made the mistake of confiding in one friend that she was carrying Michael Jackson's baby. Within hours the "friend" betrayed her trust by revealing the stunning news to a tabloid. Predictably, media around the world picked up the story for front pages of newspapers and lead stories on broadcasts.

Debbie Rowe, a stranger to public life and to the world of media frenzy, was devastated. She most feared the loss of her friendship with Michael for what she had done, albeit innocently.

Michael Jackson was on tour in Australia when the news broke. When she spoke with him on the phone, Debbie apologized profusely for her naivety and poor judgment in making her bombshell disclosure to the disloyal friend. To Debbie's amazement and delight, Michael not only forgave her immediately but reassured her that her only concern should be for her own welfare and the well-being of their unborn child. *How she loved this man!*

Katherine Jackson, having seen the media coverage, telephoned Debbie, although the two women had neither met nor spoken with each other. Michael's mother explained that, as a Jehovah's Witness, she believed in the sanctity of marriage; for the sake of the baby, she asked Debbie to marry her son. The conversation went well; the women liked each other; and Debbie understood and respected Katherine's point of view.

Soon after this conversation, Debbie flew to Australia to visit Michael. When she arrived, he asked her to marry him and she said "yes." They married hours later in his hotel suite, which he had filled with flowers, and he had ready a beautiful wedding ring. It was November 1996. Debbie returned to her California home after a few days of staying, apart from Michael, in her own hotel suite. He continued, as scheduled, to perform for sold-out concerts across Australia. Michael made certain that he would be present at the birth of his first child in California.

As soon as their son, Michael Joseph Jackson, Jr. ("Prince"), was born on February 13, 1997, Michael carried him home to Neverland. The baby was only a few hours old, but his mother and the hospital staff gave their approval. Michael had nurses and nannies already in place; they worked on a rotational schedule that he arranged and oversaw. Michael also fed his baby and changed diapers, sang to him, and rocked him to sleep.

Debbie Rowe was "not interested in being a mother"; she had this child for Michael. She moved, alone, into a $1.3 million house that Michael bought for her in Franklin Canyon, an enclave of Beverly Hills.

On April 3, 1998, Debbie gave birth to Michael's daughter, Paris Michael Katherine Jackson. As agreed between them and with the permission of hospital authorities, Michael cut the umbilical cord, and with the placenta still in place, within minutes of her birth, he took his baby girl home to Neverland. Michael personally washed the infant when they arrived there, and the nurses and nannies were on site to ensure the best care possible for her and her fourteen-month-old brother.

Debbie Rowe continued to live by herself; by design, she seldom visited her children at Neverland; and she accepted substantial monetary support from Michael. She was informed by her doctor that, for medical reasons, she could not have more children, after which upsetting news she and Michael obtained an amicable divorce in October 1999. Debbie Rowe received an estimated $10 million from Michael Jackson in the divorce settlement, and, in accordance with their original plan, he kept their children.

On February 21, 2002, Prince Michael Jackson II was born to an unidentified surrogate mother with whom Michael had entered into an agreement. Michael nicknamed his third baby "Blanket." The dark-haired, brown-eyed infant joined his two fair, then-blonde older siblings and proud father to become a family at Neverland Ranch. Michael Jackson fervently embraced his fatherhood and devoted himself with his heart and soul to his three children.

Even Michael Jackson's naming of his children caused widespread controversy. He was accused of grandiosity in choosing "Prince," an obvious term of royalty, for both of his sons, and "Paris," considered the most glamorous city in the world, for his daughter. It was not Michael Jackson's style to select common names like "Tom," "John," or "Emily" for his children. Though the naming is representative of his creative personality, there are also other compelling, meaningful reasons for his decisions. Prince is the name of both Michael's grandfather and great-grandfather, and Paris is the city that Michael and Debbie Rowe reportedly visited when their daughter was conceived. As for his youngest child, Michael nicknamed him "Blanket" not only to avoid confusion with two children named Prince in the household, but because Michael would often use the word in a precise, affectionate manner with his family, friends, and employees. "We will blanket them with love," he was known to say often when directing his staff members to take care of his visitors to Neverland. To his doting father, Blanket represented comfort, solace, warmth, and hope.

Lurid speculation about the biological paternity of the three children has run rampant through media, across continents. This issue, many believe, should never have made it to print and into newscasts at all. *Michael Joseph Jackson is the father of Prince, Paris, and Blanket; he has been and always will be their father.* Michael Jackson was legally, morally, behaviorally, and emotionally the father of each of these children. He loved them "more than life itself."

Questions about the biological parents of the children raged through the media after Michael Jackson's death in 2009. When Paris Jackson visits a beauty salon for a hair cut or style, her security guards sweep the floor, ensuring that every hair has been retrieved. This security routine prevents DNA testing of the child's hair by someone who would love to sell the results to a tabloid editor, hungry for the information and willing to pay six figures for an exclusive story. The sad reality is that this young girl and her brothers are encumbered by the daily precautions of their guardians and security to prevent massive intrusions into their privacy.

Ever struggling for normalcy, Michael Jackson planned and fought for a good life for his three little ones. At Neverland he had created a setting of privacy and seemingly unlimited space. After 2005, Michael's quest for a normal family life was hampered by a series of transitory residences, special security challenges, and his general sense of rootlessness.

Their father desperately wanted them to have the childhood he never had. He wanted them to have fun, but he also provided them with structure, routine, and discipline, administered with paternal understanding and consistency of values. Paris describes her father as "strict," but with obvious affection and appreciation in her voice.

Michael Jackson pervasively demonstrated his love and gentleness with his three children. His parenting reflected his commitments on a daily basis. Years ago, in a rare interview, Debbie Rowe revealed that, in her opinion, no one had read more about parenting than Michael Jackson, that he was a great father, and that she gladly birthed his two older children "just for him."

He not only believed in the importance of saying "I love you" to each child every day, he added that "it doesn't count" unless you look into your child's eyes when you say it. When the children said, "I love you, daddy," he always replied, "I love you more."

As his Las Vegas security team witnessed Michael Jackson's parenting on a regular basis, they delighted in how he would often be childlike with his little ones, playing, teasing, hugging, and laughing.

It was like watching four children at play. Michael Jackson knew how to play with his kids with joy and abandon. When riding in the back seat of the SUV together, they would seem like four puppies in a basket.

Michael was well known for his playful antics, practical jokes, and giggling by his mother, other family members, and professionals in the entertainment industry with whom he worked across decades. At the end of a shoot for his short films, for example, there would be water fights, pie-throwing, or other acting out. After Michael and his sister Janet completed the filming of *Scream,* they covered each other in whipped cream from head to toe.

After his trial in 2005, however, he changed; he confessed to his mother that he now trusted no one but her. Michael Jackson had an open and vulnerable heart, but he had been savaged in a public forum for many months. As the result, he was more subdued and guarded; he laughed less frequently; he seemed more pensive.

Paradoxically, only with his children could he be like the *old* Michael, when he was *young* and sometimes carefree. He would play hide-and-seek, tag, and similar active games with his kids.

Michael hated it when his children were "cooped up" in the house or a hotel suite. He wanted them to get out and be kids.

Although when accompanied by security, his little ones, unveiled, could go to a park or indoor adventure center in a generally casual way without their crowd-drawing father, Michael sometimes could not resist sharing the fun with them in spite of the elaborate safety precautions that were required.

Taking Mr. Jackson and his children to a public place during normal business hours could be a real error in judgment; it could become a security nightmare. For years, Michael's various security teams had made it a practice to work with the managers to close down public facilities for their boss's exclusive use for himself and/ or his kids. In fact, the managers often perceived this practice as a *win-win* because they realized that Michael Jackson's fans might inadvertently damage their facilities in the frenzy to get to him. One antique store owner *insisted* on closing his doors to the general public when Michael visited; he feared that his priceless antiquities would be broken. Michael had the entire store to himself, while fans pressed their noses against the large glass windows and took photos with their cell phones.

To minimize the risks, his security teams would sometimes make arrangements to take the boss and kids to an amusement park after it closed for the day and all regular customers were gone. Both in the U.S. and abroad, Michael Jackson visited amusement parks only after special security measures were arranged and in place.

The manager of a park usually agreed to keep it open and operational after its evening closing for two or three hours in return for a negotiated fee that Michael Jackson readily approved. The boss and his kids were always excited when they were told by his head of security about the "all-clear" decision. Often Mr. Jackson was the most excited of the four!

To his Vegas security team, seeing the boss in this state of exuberance was priceless. They knew about the daily burdens of his business dealings and the constant pressure on him of various competing interests. Nothing brought a smile from him like any opportunity to spend family time in public places with his kids, like a "normal" dad.

After the security guards' advance run, ensuring that the travel route looked safe, they would return to transport Mr. Jackson and his little ones to the amusement park. While the park was closed to the public, the security team monitored the front and rear entrances and continued to check all around for any lingering patrons. At least one bodyguard would follow Mr. Jackson and kids as they ran together to each ride. It was eerie to be present in an empty park that is usually filled with hundreds of families and children. It felt like an episode of *The Twilight Zone* to his security men.

Michael Jackson had always loved activities like riding down a 50-foot slide on burlap potato bags or racing his friends in go-karts. He visited Disneyland in California and Disney World in Florida many times across the years; these were his "favorite places." He called Disney World "the ultimate vacation" in the world—a surprising assessment from a man who had circled the globe again and again, visiting exotic, far-flung places. He felt that the Disney parks were the best places for sheer fun. Of course, he and his kids didn't have to stand in lines to enjoy the attractions.

Mr. Jackson was always grateful to his security team for making possible a safe, fun outing. He thanked them from his heart. When his children were sleepy and mellow, tired out from a good time and riding home in the SUV, as a family, their dad was content. These experiences were no doubt positively colored by their fond memories of Neverland and of their carefree shared moments there.

*   *   *   *   *   *   *   *   *

Especially after his children became old enough to join him, Michael Jackson enjoyed indulging in fast food. In their quest for normalcy, Mr. Jackson and children would be driven to a Kentucky

Fried Chicken, McDonald's, or Dunkin' Donuts. When the vehicle pulled up to the drive-thru speaker box, all four would compete for the privilege of placing the order.

"You ordered last time," one would say to the other in all earnestness. "It's my turn." They would then argue as to who ordered last time. Mr. Jackson enjoyed this kind of interaction with his children, teasing and bantering in real, or feigned, seriousness.

This would be the closest they would get to "normal" everyday fun together, the security guards knew, and their hearts lifted—and then ached—for their boss and his little ones.

Once in awhile, Michael Jackson's impulse to share in a good time with his kids would backfire. On one such occasion, Prince, Paris, and Blanket were enjoying themselves, with other kids, in a Chuck-E-Cheese Restaurant. After their father waited patiently for them in his vehicle for some time, he announced that he wanted to watch them having fun.

Accompanied by security guards, who watched from a small distance in an attempt to be inconspicuous, Mr. Jackson stood in a corner, his face covered, to observe his children playing with the others.

When Paris acknowledged her father's presence with a few words, one of the group of children cried out, "Is that *Michael Jackson*? Is he your father?"

"No, I *wish...*," Paris promptly replied. She had been taught to deflect this type of query from people in public places. This time, however, to no avail....

"It's Michael Jackson!" someone shouted. A stampede of people headed toward the mysterious figure, who had to flee out the door, followed by security. "Get him out of here!" one guard shouted to the other.

With a mob of people in pursuit, Michael Jackson ran across the parking lot to his waiting, parked SUV. After trying to open the vehicle door and discovering that it had been locked by his bodyguards, he ran across the street and into a retail store. His security team intervened by speeding to the front door of the store in the vehicle; the boss jumped into it; and they all drove away together, father and kids safe once again.

*   *   *   *   *   *   *   *   *

The pursuit of good times and fun for his children was accompanied by Michael Jackson's absolute commitment to their formal education and other learning activities. He personally supervised their home-schooling by working closely with their teacher to ensure that she was providing them with a comprehensive educational program.

Every weekday the children attended school in their home classroom. The teacher would arrive at the same time every day, in the early morning, and work with them until mid-afternoon. Prince, Paris, and Blanket had afternoon recess and homework assignments, and they were assigned to write book reports.

And they wore uniforms! Raymone Bain fondly remembers how proud the children were of their tidy, attractive uniforms—like the kids wore in the big schools. Their father believed in the importance and symbols of structure and discipline. He instructed their teacher to treat them like any other children, not to indulge them or excuse them from hard work.

During their years at Neverland and later in Nevada and California, their home schooling was conducted according to the State Board of Education requirements, which included the taking and passing of examinations that made them eligible to move on to the next grade. The only privilege they enjoyed was the one-on-one instruction, which, of course, greatly enhanced their learning. The kids were very smart—"like twenty-year-olds," according to Michael Garcia—and their father was adamant about their succeeding in their education.

Michael Jackson always believed that parents and teachers should be "tough but fair" with children. At Neverland, he was known by household staff to require his children to clean up a mess after themselves even when they were very young but able to do it. When he visited other people's homes with his children for overnights—for example, the Al Malnik family in Florida—he insisted that his kids make their own beds and straighten up their rooms even if maids were available for the job.

Early on, his security guards had assisted in the creation of a classroom on the second floor of the sprawling Summerlin home by converting a large bedroom into a colorful learning center with books, computer equipment, and other resources. Michael Jackson always wanted his children to have the setting, standards, and accoutrements of a typical classroom. His goal was for everything to be as much as possible like the education they would receive if they were enrolled in a public or private school. Even while the family was traveling and staying in hotels, a separate room was reserved and used specifically as a classroom for the three children.

For physical education, their teacher supervised the children in running laps around the huge backyard swimming pool. The security men also took them, accompanied by their teacher, on field trips to local museums, art exhibits, and historical sites. Paris especially enjoyed all displays of works of art; she shared with her father an appreciation of art; it was a special bond between them.

It would not be feasible for the children to attend a school away from home because of the security risks involved. If a skilled professional miscreant set about to kidnap or harm one or more of the Jackson children, there would be no realistic way to guarantee the prevention of such a disaster inside a public building or on an open playground. As long as these children were at risk with an emotionally and financially vulnerable mega-star as their father, a man who would pay any price to ransom his children, they should be schooled at home, where their safety and comfort could be virtually ensured.

Mr. Jackson worried, however, when the children exercised in the backyard for their physical education lessons because the two-story neighboring homes afforded a view of them from their large windows. When they swam in the pool, they would also be visible from some vantage points above the perimeter wall of the property.

The armed security guards, who were always present, would probably be sufficiently menacing to forestall an individual with violence as a motive; the likelihood of a serious problem was thereby minimized.

The three children understandably missed Neverland, which was such an ideal place for kids. There they had enjoyed such freedom of movement and variety of stimulation. The attractions ranged from exotic animals roaming the acreage to constant music playing throughout; from a private, old-fashioned steam-engine train to a fully-stocked candy store; from a Ferris wheel and other major-league rides to colorful go-karts; from a fresh-water lake to an immense in-ground pool. They even had their own private playground area with a tree house, miniature fort, swings and slides. On the fort was posted a sign that said "Daddy loves you." *What not to miss?*

With his heartfelt utterance to attorney Thomas Mesereau, "That place [Neverland] has been contaminated by evil," Michael Jackson closed the door, in 2005, to his fantasy-world estate for himself and his family. Both his tone and words communicated his deeply-felt pain from the distressing memories it evoked.

Michael Jackson could never return to his private kingdom even though it had been both haven and sanctuary for him for nearly seventeen years. Neverland became to him the symbol of betrayal, despair, and resultant rage, caused by his heartless, perjured accusers and the herd of law enforcement officers that callously raided and ransacked his beloved home.

In spite of this emotional shell-shock and heartache, Michael Jackson would continue to draw his artistic inspiration from his children. He had been creatively stimulated and emotionally moved by nature at Neverland Ranch. There he would regularly climb a special sprawling oak, "The Giving Tree," and compose songs, while straddling one of its thick, long branches, his legs dangling and his face toward the sky. With that gone, he would seek inspiration elsewhere, but it would not come from the Las Vegas house on a postage-stamp-sized lot in comparison to Neverland's 2,700 hilly acres.

Michael Jackson's profound love for his children found expression, though, no matter where he and they were living or staying. Always the most important consideration for him was that they were together. He was abundantly aware that he had almost lost them, after his criminal trial, to their biological mother, a child protection services agency, or a bureaucratically-determined placement in a foster home. *Very scary.*

Michael's transforming and transcendent love for all of his children is reflected in the heartwarming triumph of a song that he dedicated to his firstborn son Prince, when the boy was an infant. The lyrics of "You Are My Life" describe the profound and life-changing effects upon Michael of having a child. They include the self-awareness that "You help me understand that love is the answer to all that I am."

*   *   *   *   *   *   *   *   *

In contrast to the exaggerated tabloid reports of Michael Jackson's indulgence of his children and alleged over-the-top splurging, he tried to avoid spoiling his children. At Neverland they were allowed to go on the rides only for special occasions, as determined by their father. Yes, he loved to buy them things, to surprise them from time to time with unexpected treats or gifts. Mostly, though, he rewarded them for specific points of progress in their academic studies and for personal behavior that he valued, such as politeness and kindness. On an everyday basis, the three children *earned* most of their respective largesse from their father.

David Nordahl cherishes memories of his visit at Neverland for the celebration of Prince's seventh birthday in 2004. The little boy got presents from his father, Nordahl explains, but they were mostly things worth a couple of dollars, like play dough—things that would be considered stocking stuffers. The children would earn points for their schoolwork in order to play a video game or watch television. Prince would take three books at a time to bed with him; that routine was a big treat for him. "Michael wanted their lives to be as much like normal kids' as possible," Nordahl confirms.

From the mound of presents from his fans that would be delivered for his children on their birthdays or at holiday time, Michael Jackson would typically allow each child to choose and keep a favorite one. The other gifts would be sent to orphaned children or hospitals for less fortunate youngsters.

Birthdays were considered special by Michael Jackson, perhaps because he never celebrated them until he was thirty-five. His various security guards across the years would often arrange for the closing of a toy store so that the birthday child could shop undisturbed and select a memorable gift, or they would negotiate terms with a movie theater manager to provide a private showing of a newly-released film so that the family could enjoy it together by themselves.

Mr. Jackson usually prepared an extra treat or surprise for each of his children on their eagerly anticipated birthday. At the celebration there would be a dinner of the birthday child's favorite foods, with cake and ice cream. There would also be balloons and decorations, popcorn and cotton candy, and often a clown or a magician. Sadly, only the three children, Mr. Jackson, and his employees—such as the nanny, teacher, and several of the Vegas security guards—were participants. There were no other children in attendance; no neighbors, cousins, or friends. The children's grandmother, Katherine Jackson, came to visit every so often but not Mr. Jackson's brothers or sisters.

The paparazzi always knew when it was birthday time. Low-flying helicopters would hover over the house, the paparazzi leaning against the glass windows with their cameras poised in the hopes of a photo and big money for it. When the little ones were outside in the backyard, the bodyguards would rush them into the house until the helicopter and its predatory passengers flew away.

Mr. Jackson's security would joke that the helicopter paparazzi could probably qualify for frequent-flyer mileage rewards!

According to security personnel and others who knew them, Michael's three children were well-behaved and well-mannered in addition to being extremely bright for their ages. Prince and

Paris sought their father's approval for their good behavior and achievements. Blanket sometimes showed an "attitude," probably to compete with his older siblings for his dad's attention. Surprisingly, the children reportedly never asked for much; when they did, they were genuinely grateful for anything they were given. They always said "please" and "thank you" with a smile; they learned these behaviors from their father, who modeled them.

Echoing these laudatory assessments, Mike La Perruque, who was Michael Jackson's security chief from 2000 through 2004, spoke on national television in August 2011, disclosing that "being a dad was *the* role for Michael Jackson." La Perruque said that his boss went to great extents to make his kids feel normal and that they were great kids. Prince was "the adult looking out for the other two," Paris was "very mature," and Blanket was "quiet."

"He raised those children *all by himself*," Mike Garcia says, with great admiration for his boss's effectiveness as a loving father.

Without a telephone land line in the house, the children—and their father—used cell phones. Often they would borrow the phone of one of the bodyguards. Sometimes that phone would get lost in the big house somewhere. "Sorry, but you'll need to get a new phone," Mr. Jackson would sheepishly inform his security man. "Kids will be kids...."

Because the security team was the conduit for nearly all items that came into the Michael Jackson household, the children would sometimes cajole one of the men for special favors. "Daddy says"— they would invoke what they believed to be the magic phrase to get what they were seeking—"that you should get us some Oreo cookies," or "that you should get a new toy [or treats] for Kenya." The bodyguards would smile, and often they would submit to the request even though they knew that the boss was really "outside of the loop" in his little ones' harmless schemes. They realized that the children could never leave on their own to go in search of their desired treat.

Michael Garcia tells the story about his "mission" to buy an iPhone for his boss. "I waited in line for three hours," he says, just to get that phone. Excited about the new gadget, Michael Jackson sent Garcia to obtain one so that he could take photos of his kids to send to his mother. "He was a child himself," Garcia relates, with obvious affection; "he was a great father … and he had a heart of gold."

"I'm not territorial," Michael told his interviewer in the outtake portions of "Living with Michael Jackson." When asked what children mean to him, Michael answered, "The stars, the moon, the universe, but all children do, not just mine."

Michael Jackson wanted his own children to learn empathy for other people and to internalize sensitivity to the plight of the needy and suffering. He sometimes took Prince, Paris, and Blanket to hospitals, where they would interact with sick and dying children of all ages. His kids came face to face with human suffering and experienced the rewards of selfless giving with their father.

     *   *   *   *   *   *   *   *   *

On a regular basis, Michael Jackson bestowed upon his little ones the benefits of his own cooking. In Las Vegas, without a staff of employees, the family lived on a combination of packaged meals, delivered by security guards or restaurant vendors; take-out and drive-thru meals; the occasional services of a cook who came to the house; and the boss's own cooking. The children especially enjoyed the breakfasts that their dad made for them, according to Paris, who thought he made "the best French toast anywhere."

Even years before he had his own children, Michael Jackson recognized the importance of food to both parent and child as symbolic of love. He wrote the introduction to a cookbook, *Nourish This Child*, in which he emphasized the significance of nurturance for children:

To a child, food is something special.... Food is love and caring, security and hope.... Food is something we all need physically, but so is love, the deeper nourishment, that turns into who we are.... The food's proteins and minerals will turn into bones and muscles, but your feeling as you cook will turn directly into a soul. It makes me happy to think that the needs of children's spirits are at last becoming important in this world.... All they [children] can do is be themselves, to shine with gratitude and joy when love is turned their way.... You may think that your apple pie has only sugar and spice in it. A child is wiser—with the first bite, he knows that this special dish is the essence of your love. (*Pigtails & Frog Legs: A Family Cookbook from Neiman Marcus*, 1993)

*   *   *   *   *   *   *   *   *

While on vacation, the small entourage—Michael Jackson, three children, nanny, and security team—was riding in their vehicle in a rural area. To their collective dismay, they suddenly realized that they had gotten lost in the backwoods of Virginia. As they moved along, slowly winding their way, they spotted a group of rugged and seedy-looking men, four of them, who stood on the side of the road, scowling at the lone vehicle.

One of the children, frightened at the unusual, menacing situation, said, "Maybe they will try to hurt us."

"I hope they do," Mr. Jackson announced in a brave tone of voice. "I'll take care of *them!*"

His security men smiled but said nothing. They realized that this strong assertion by their father to his kids was his way of saying that he would keep them from harm. He was seeking their approval as father and capable protector. Everyone knew, of course, that his security guards would be the ones to do the job of protecting the group if it should come to that.

The children knew that their dad could perform karate moves, however, from having studied and practiced the martial arts as a young man. He not only liked karate but he believed that it enhanced his agility, balance, and dancing skill.

After some uncomfortable laughter among all of the passengers, their vehicle proceeded without further incident toward their destination, delayed but otherwise unhampered.

As a special treat, Mr. Jackson took his children on a hot-air balloon ride across the Virginia countryside. His security guards followed on the ground, their SUV serving as the chaser vehicle. The men could see that their boss and his kids were enjoying themselves, as they caught glimpses of the smiling family leaning over the edge of the gondola and looking down.

When they landed, the boss whispered to his head of security that he feared that the pilot of the air balloon had taken photos of him and the kids. When the bodyguard immediately turned to take care of the matter, Mr. Jackson stopped him by saying, "Wait until we are not around."

The boss always avoided direct confrontations, and he did not want his children to witness any unpleasantness. The bodyguard, obeying his boss's direction, waited until the family was out of sight and then dealt with the breach of security.

No photos were ever released of Michael Jackson and his three children on their hot-air balloon ride.

Michael Jackson's devoted, systematic protectiveness of his children is understandable from the life path he had taken. *He learned that the bigger the celebrity, the bigger the struggle; the more the success, the more the risk; and the greater the fame, the greater the danger....*

At Neverland, the large "army" of security guards patrolled the grounds systematically, but Mr. Jackson's rule there was "no firearms" because of his strong concern for safety. In Nevada and California, however, his security guards were usually armed, but the rule was that his children would not see their weapons unless it became necessary. Typically, the men wore holsters that held their guns inside their jackets, not readily visible.

*   *   *   *   *   *   *   *   *

Prince, Paris, and Blanket cherish fond memories of their dad. Paris's bedroom walls are covered with posters of her father. Prince remembers, with a deep sense of loss, the long walks on the beach in

Bahrain that he and his father enjoyed together every morning during the weeks they lived in that exotic country. Blanket says little, but can anyone doubt the hole in his heart from the sudden loss of so loving a father, one who was really both mom and dad to his kids?

Like his own mother had done, Michael worked to make each of his children feel special. He fostered Paris's love of art in a variety of ways that included their studying together and visiting art museums and shops. He commissioned a university professor to teach Prince and himself about movie directing, which was his son's hoped-for career direction. He often danced with Blanket, teaching the little boy his iconic steps and moves, including the moonwalk. Michael's youngest child seems not only interested in dancing but also talented, according to friends of the Jackson family.

Michael Jackson hoped that Prince, Paris, and Blanket would take a different path for themselves than show business, but he said that he would support them in any direction they might choose. In June 2009, Prince and Paris spent time working on music in a recording studio in Los Angeles, as arranged by their accommodating father. Like most parents, Michael devoutly wanted his children to be happy.

His children have been described by scores of people as bright, confident, affectionate, and considerate. They are also thoughtful, polite, and funny. Their father is reflected in all of these traits; he would undoubtedly continue to be proud of all three of them.

Prince, Paris, and Blanket were the lowest common denominator in Michael Jackson's life. Everything was ultimately about them and for them. They were his anchor; his daily encounter with genuine, reciprocated love; his family in every respect. In a way, Michael Jackson was growing up with his children, living his lost childhood by accompanying them on a loving journey—as their guide and companion—through theirs.

How many of us have had a father who refashioned and/or postponed his career in order to be with us all of the time? ... Who told us every day that he loved us? ... Who showed it in so many ways?

Those who have been blessed with such a father are the fortunate, taking from that special relationship the emotional foundation that gives us permission to love and be loved throughout our entire lives. Prince, Paris, and Blanket Jackson—although theirs is a loss that is consummately tragic and incomprehensible —can still be counted among the fortunate. Theirs was not a "concierge father," as might be expected from a superstar. Theirs was a real "Daddy."

What I think life is really all about:
I love and adore my children.
They mean everything to me....
I'm proud to be their dad.
— Michael Jackson,
"Private Home Movies"

One joy dispels a hundred cares.
— Confucius

MICHAEL JACKSON & HIS FAMILY

Family is often a blessing,
sometimes a curse,
and occasionally both at the same time.

— Anonymous

I realized I have family
all over the world—
the fans.

— Michael Jackson

"**P**erfection" is the word that Michael Jackson used to describe his mother Katherine. During his first telecast interview in fourteen years, Michael hosted Oprah Winfrey at his Neverland kingdom in 1993, and he graciously answered her pointed and prying questions about his private self. A record-breaking audience of more than ninety million people viewed the program in dozens of countries, not only because Michael Jackson was the biggest mega-star on the planet, but because he had kept his behind-the-music life so secret and provocatively mysterious.

Michael also said that his mother made every one of her nine children feel like an only child. Katherine somehow made time for each of her three daughters and six sons. She made a point of providing them, as much as she could financially afford, with things of their respective special interest, such as art books for Michael.

Having inherited his mother's heightened sensitivity for other people, Michael had deep feelings—even during his early childhood—about the plight of the poor, sick, dying, and underprivileged throughout the world. While watching a graphic televised program about the suffering multitudes in Africa, young

Michael turned to his tearful mother and assured her, "Mother, someday I'm going to do something about this."

In *Dancing the Dream*, Michael wrote the lovely poem "Mother," in which he dedicates his love to her:

And now that I have come so far
Met with every king and czar
Encountered every color and creed
Of every passion, every greed
I go back to that starry night
With not a fear for muscle or might
You taught me how to stand and fight
For every single wrong and right....
No matter where I go from here
You're in my heart, my mother dear.

Michael's father Joseph was cut from different cloth than Katherine. He ruled the family with an iron hand and used a strap to whip his children into line, especially his sons while they rehearsed for their performances as The Jackson 5. Joseph taught his sons skillfully to use a microphone, to work the audience, and to show appreciation for their fans. He also drilled them relentlessly to perfect their dance steps, singing, and harmonizing. He lectured them on the importance of being polite and adaptable.

The *end* seemed to justify the *means*, to the harsh father. He often resorted to physical coercion with his boys. In 2003, Michael confessed in "Living with Michael Jackson" that his father often hit him and his brothers.

In 1993, during his interview with Oprah Winfrey, Michael had first disclosed the physical punishments that he regularly endured at the hands of his father. He said that he had suffered so many physical affronts by his father that he became so afraid of the man that he sometimes would regurgitate upon seeing him.

"Forgive me, Joseph," he then said, looking straight into the camera. "I'm sorry," he added; "please don't be mad at me."

Michael felt ambivalent about this public disclosure of the abuse he had suffered from his father. "But I do love him and I am forgiving; I do forgive," he clarified. "I didn't know him," Michael explained further. "I *don't* know him.... I wish I understood him better."

In spite of everything, Michael forgave his father, as he forgave everyone in his family....

Michael Jackson's relationships with his siblings and parents were more complex and complicated than one might think from the picture that was projected to the outside world by the show-business family. When they went to work for Michael Jackson, his Vegas-based security team—like millions of others—believed that the Jacksons were the model of a close-knit African-American family who had made it to the big time despite great obstacles. They had been black, poor, unknown, and disconnected to anyone of prestige, wealth, or influence in the gritty, industrial city of Gary, Indiana, where Joe Jackson labored as an hourly worker in the steel mills. Katherine was a stay-at-home mom with nine children, all residing in the family house on Jackson Street—an interesting coincidence because the naming of the street had nothing to do with the Joseph Jackson family.

When international success came for The Jackson 5—Michael and his four brothers, Jermaine, Tito, Jackie, and Marlon—so suddenly, it seemed literally like an overnight phenomenon to Suzanne de Passe. She had been assigned to manage the boys for Motown Records; oversee their education, attire, and music; teach them manners; and coach them on interview techniques, on behalf of the record label. On one day, the musical group of kids was unnoticed as they went about their business; the next day, they could go nowhere without being mobbed by teenagers, to the point of real threat to their safety. From then on, they could go no place and stay nowhere without their security teams.

Michael Jackson continued, non-stop across the years, the challenging and restricted life that he had led from boyhood. His family was perceived to have become rich, not only in monetary terms but in culture, pride, fame, love, and success. On the surface, the Jacksons seemed to be exempt from struggles with the issues that plague the average American family, but in reality they were not so lucky.

Their family history is laced with in-fighting, family politics, hurt, anger, betrayal, disappointment, and self-seeking manipulation of each other. Yet, when push comes to shove, they stick together. They are a family first and foremost. Both parents inculcated this core value in their children, and they modeled their commitment to it by remaining married through good times and bad.

During their many months of service, Boyd Williams, Baron James, and Michael Garcia witnessed very few interactions between their boss and members of his family. It was not so much that the security guards were excluded from observing Mr. Jackson with his siblings or parents; rather, it was that the boss saw them so infrequently. Perhaps he felt emotionally close to them, or perhaps not, but their in-person interactions with each other were rare. Of course, Michael Jackson's relationship with *each* member of his family was a unique one, with its own complexity of interpersonal history and ever-changing feelings, as is always the case for human beings. From his public statements about his mother, however, it was absolutely clear that his relationship with her was continuously sincere, warm, loving, and strong. His relationships with the rest of his family members appeared anemic at best during his last few years.

Thomas Mesereau confirms that Michael loved his mother deeply and trusted her above everyone else. "She was his spiritual cheerleader," the attorney explains; "his moral support." During Michael's 2005 trial, his mother attended court every day across five months. Katherine never missed a day, rain or shine. She sat in the front row of the assemblage, listening to the torturous testimony and redeeming cross-examinations, always determined and stoical. She and Michael made meaningful eye contact early in the day in the packed courtroom, and they left together in the afternoon.

"God is on your side; the truth will come out," Katherine would assure her worried son during breaks from the testimony.

They would huddle together in the special private room set aside for the defendant and his family. They would talk and hug. "His mother was his rock," Mesereau reveals, in admiration of the then-septuagenarian woman who limped into and out of the courthouse daily to support "her boy."

During the trial, Michael's entire family "circled their wagons" and supported their beleaguered son and brother. They were there for him.

Michael's father and siblings attended days of the trial on a more sporadic basis than did their mother, but they appeared regularly, especially on important days of the proceedings. They presented a united front, and they communicated their absolute faith in Michael and in his total innocence.

A few weeks after Michael Jackson relocated to Las Vegas, his security detail noticed a vehicle passing slowly by the Summerlin mansion. The traffic on the intersecting roads in front of the walled property was sparse at all times. With no stores or commercial buildings of any kind in the vicinity of the Michael Jackson home, few cars drove by it during either daytime or overnight hours.

The mysterious vehicle returned and pulled right up to the wrought-iron gate that shielded the property from vehicle ingress. A male figure was observed getting out of the vehicle. The head security man, on duty as always, walked down to inquire about the unknown man's identity and purpose.

It was Joe Jackson, the boss's father, looking angry and determined. He insisted to the guard that he be permitted to see his son "immediately."

As directed by protocol, Michael Jackson was informed that his father was outside the gate. "Does he have an appointment?" Mr. Jackson asked in a flat voice.

"No, I don't believe so, sir," the guard replied.

"Tell him that he needs an appointment," the boss said. Mr. Jackson was not interested in drop-in visits by members of his family.

"Yes, sir," the security guard answered dutifully. The elder Jackson left, but not before he said some stinging words into the air.

In 2007, at his Las Vegas home, some of Michael Jackson's brothers and sisters attempted to stage an intervention with him. They showed up at the house, and Michael did meet with them. For the press, the Jackson family members denied the intervention at the time, but later they admitted to it, as circumstances would change in later years.

Although they did not know what was going on with the Jackson family or why Mr. Jackson appeared distant from them, his Vegas security team knew without a doubt that their responsibility remained always to ensure Mr. Jackson's safety, privacy, and comfort level. However, dealing with his family had to be done very diplomatically ... unless one or more of them would pose a physical threat. *That could happen*, the trained, experienced security personnel always knew....

On one occasion, the boss's brother Randy surprised and worried the security guards with his sudden appearance at the Summerlin estate. Before they realized what was happening, Boyd and Baron watched a large vehicle crash through the front gate and drive around the circular driveway. It came to an abrupt stop near them.

Boyd drew his weapon and prepared to open fire when he noticed that the invading vehicle's occupants were Randy Jackson, who was the driver, and a female companion in the passenger seat.

From the open window of his car Randy yelled out, insisting on seeing his brother Michael. He shouted something about Michael owing him a lot of money. Reputable media were reporting that Michael Jackson's baby brother had fallen on hard times. During Michael's trial, Randy had worked as a manager for his famous older brother. Later, however, he reportedly turned to doing a variety of odd jobs to earn his living.

Randy was quoted by media as saying that his brother owed him for loans that he had obtained from friends to help with Michael's exorbitant trial expenses. Randy was still living in the Hayvenhurst compound where he, Janet, and Michael had grown up together as the youngest Jackson children. Katherine and a variety of extended-family members were in residence there also.

Boyd, doing his job, confronted Randy politely but firmly. Randy responded by threatening to call the media … on his own brother.

Randy did not get out of his vehicle. The security guards were bristling with anger and anxiety; they were feeling the rush of adrenaline. Randy had breached security, the worst possible event for men whose job it was to protect and defend their client and his homestead. Emotions were so elevated that there was a good chance that, depending upon his behavior, Randy could have gotten thrown over the perimeter wall, or worse.

He must have realized that the security men, in accordance with required protocol, would have him arrested for trespassing. Randy obviously sensed the harsh reality of the situation that he had created, and he prudently opted to drive away.

When the boss was informed of the nasty incident outside his front door, he was understandably upset. Boyd sheepishly but thoroughly explained the events as they had unfolded. Mr. Jackson seemed afraid … of his own younger brother. Who could blame him under these grim circumstances?

For the next several days, there were neither security details to run nor errands to complete for the boss. Mr. Jackson secluded himself in the house without any word heard from him. It was a quiet time for his security personnel; they barely spoke to each other or anyone else; and they waited for a welcome directive of some kind.

In a televised interview in early 2010, Boyd Williams, Baron James, and Michael Garcia confirmed that they never observed Mr. Jackson ingesting drugs in any form. They had heard allegations and rumors from media sources that their boss might be addicted to prescription drugs. They also knew well that Michael Jackson suffered from both physical and emotional pain.

At the age of twenty-five, Michael Jackson suffered second and third degree burns on his scalp during a frightening accident that occurred while he was filming a commercial for Pepsi-Cola. Airborne pyrotechnics, set off prematurely during his dance routine, cascaded onto his uncovered head and his hair caught on fire. A palm-sized area at the top of his head was severely burned; his hair in that spot was gone, exposing raw, red skin. Michael was rushed to the hospital on a stretcher and subsequently treated for the injury and for the severe pain, exacerbated by damage to nerve endings. Michael Jackson consented to taking prescribed painkillers and sleeping pills for the first time in his life.

In 1993, with the personal assistance and take-charge support of Elizabeth Taylor—who declared to the media that she loved Michael "like a son"—he checked into a drug rehabilitation program in England. In a press conference at the time, Michael Jackson explained that he had begun using painkillers seven months earlier, after having undergone reconstructive surgery for his scalp burns from the Pepsi commercial nine years before.

With his security personnel, Mr. Jackson was sometimes "focused elsewhere" and a few times seemingly absent. However, the men knew that he was certainly not accountable to them and could behave in any way that he wished. He was the boss; he was always functional; and he was also prone to engaging in creative thoughts, which made him appear preoccupied. Often, they discovered, he had not slept the night before; he had not turned off the designated lamp that signaled his going to bed, and it remained lit until after dawn.

When Michael Jackson and his three little ones celebrated birthdays and holidays together in Las Vegas, none of the members of his family attended. There may have been telephone calls made that his security team did not witness, but there were no Jacksons coming to visit with gifts or good wishes, not on their watch.

Michael Jackson generally withdrew from his father and siblings during the last few years of his life. Self-protection was his likely primary motivation. Michael had supported most of the members of his family both financially and in other ways that, with his vast and unique scope of influence, only he could do. He contributed the majority of the money that maintained Katherine and the Hayvenhurst household, which consisted of various Jacksons who came and went, and lived there for long periods of time.

He had given his name, talent, hard work, time, and commitment to the family in so many ways from the time of his childhood. As a boy, he created the choreography for himself and his brothers; he wrote songs; and he served as an example for the others of the skill level and dedication needed for their success.

"Do it like Michael," their father would admonish his brothers. Michael became the real draw for the crowds that attended their concerts, bought their records, and followed the group as die-hard fans.

It would take a skilled analyst to determine the exact age at which Michael Jackson became the breadwinner of his large family. He was no older than a young teenager when that happened, and his family had already become dependent upon him in many ways.

His mother and father discouraged his solo career for the sake of his other siblings. They needed Michael to continue as a member of The Jacksons, to sustain the feverish pitch of their followers and consumers, and to maintain their pinnacle level of fame.

Of course, Michael Jackson did eventually succumb to fate and the compelling pressures on him to take off into the stratosphere of stardom by himself. After The Jacksons *Victory Tour* in 1984—which set a record for gross sales and included fifty-five concerts, playing to two million people—Michael devoted his time and talents to creating and producing his own music. He became a solo artist. Unfortunately, his brothers seemed to languish, in terms of their shared musical career, in the wake of his leaving the group.

At one point, according to J. Randy Taraborrelli's biography, there was a one-million-dollar bounty offered by a wealthy group to anyone—family member, security personnel, manager, attorney, friend, *whomever*—who would convince Michael Jackson to contract to perform in South Korea. Automobiles were purchased for several of his "people" as inducements to get their boss to agree to the projected concerts. They never did materialize—although Michael, worn out by the badgering of those close to him, finally consented—because the negotiations process got messy and probably duplicitous on the part of the foreign promoters.

His parents and brothers continued, from time to time, to apply pressure on Michael to rejoin his brothers in performing concerts and touring. They also sought various kinds of financial support and endorsements from their famous son and brother. There were frequent rumors that The Jacksons would reunite for a new concert tour; every several years one of the brothers or "someone close to the family" would make the announcement. In June 2009, Jermaine was quoted as assuring the media that the brothers would soon reunite for a series of concerts.

In recent months, mother Katherine, sisters LaToya and Janet, and brother Jermaine have written their own books about themselves and Michael. They tell their own stories, reveal new information, and present the human side of Michael to the public. However, it is interesting to note that all of them cover and emphasize the earlier years of Michael Jackson and include relatively little about his last few years. There is a reason for that, of course, and it is because they had much less first-hand information and contact with him during that period of time. Michael became mysterious to his own family, with the possible exception of his mother, with whom he shared a larger part of himself. Even with her, though, he chose what to reveal. He did not want to worry her, for example, with serious problems related to his cash flow. The Hayvenhurst property was scheduled for imminent foreclosure when Michael passed away.

Even as early as 1993, during his interview with Oprah Winfrey, Michael revealed his lack of frequent contact with his siblings. He

said, "I love them very much and wish I could see them more."
Everyone in the family understood the infrequency of get-togethers,
he explained, because they are a show-business family. When they
did gather at one of his siblings' homes, Michael related, "We'll
fellowship, get caught up, talk...."

Janet Jackson, who is the most successful living member of
her family in terms of her economic worth, did not seek monetary
help from her more famous brother; she did not need help. Janet
maintained her feelings of closeness to her older brother throughout
his life. Their relationship was not encumbered by any likely request
by her for his economic support. Janet is a millionaire many times
over, in her own right, and her current career is soaring.

After their first and only collaboration—on the award-winning
song and short film *Scream* in 1995—Michael said:

> I've had so much fun working with my sister. I'm closest to
> Janet of all the family members. We laughed. We cried. We
> had a lot of fun.

In an interview with Piers Morgan in April 2011, Janet described
Michael as "sweet, gentle, very smart, [and] all about love." His
love for people, Janet explained, was pervasive, extending from
the downtrodden to royalty. She recalled for the viewing audience
her experiences with Michael as a young man, when together they
would often buy and hand out meals to the homeless. Janet spoke
about Michael's private relationship with Princess Diana, whom
he comforted and counseled. "Be determined," he had advised the
Princess, when she was facing great adversity and media onslaughts.

Michael Jackson's love and personal support reached far beyond
his nuclear family. He demonstrated his caring and affection for
nieces and nephews and other members of his extended family. Some
of them he helped financially, and some he assisted in their careers.
A good example is found in Michael's having produced the lovely
ballad "Why" for his nephews' musical group, 3T. He also sang it

with the three young men in the creative short film that boosted their career to a new level of success and public recognition. Unknown to many fans of Michael, he also helped his sister Rebbie in show business by composing and producing some of her music during her short-lived career. Rebbie chose to marry and raise a family rather than continue to pursue a professional path in the music industry.

His nephews revealed their intense feelings for their Uncle Michael in the printed Memorial program that was distributed to attendees in July 2009:

Uncle Michael, I can't even begin to express how important you have been in my life. You will always be a huge part of who I am now and what I will become in the future. I love you.... Taj

You have filled my life with knowledge, laughter, happiness and love. To the world 'Michael Jackson' is the greatest. To me, Uncle Michael is even better. I love you beyond life, Taryll

You taught me how to smile. You taught me how to dream. You taught me how to live. Uncle Michael, I will always cherish all of our special moments and blissful time together. I love you so much. TJ

    *   *   *   *   *   *   *   *   *

The Joseph Jackson nuclear family has been contentious in many ways across the years. The family members fight among themselves about all kinds of issues. The media seem to love to report on these conflicts and hassles. The Jacksons question each other's judgment and criticize each other's behaviors in a variety of circumstances. Ultimately, Katherine Jackson's decision seems to prevail in almost all important matters related to the family, according to several of her sons.

When he left the country in September 2005, Michael Jackson distanced himself from more than the place of his birth. He purposefully put distance between himself and most of the other people in his life, including his family. He was emotionally worn-out, drained of energy and motivation, and ill-equipped to maintain demanding relationships of any sort. He chose to focus on his three little children and, after a brief hiatus, on his music and potential plans for future involvements that would resuscitate his professional career and take him in new directions. He could not afford to be challenged or distracted by cloying or complicated interpersonal or family interactions.

He wanted to be left alone..., at least by those who were needy and seeking from him what he no longer had to give. He suffered from money problems, legal entanglements, and gnawing uncertainty as to where he stood in the world, in the music industry, and with his fans. He had to question everything about the life he had known, the life he had thought he understood ... until the tsunami of sexual molestation charges robbed him of his kingdom and any real possibility of attaining peace of mind.

Michael knew one thing above all else: he loved his children with his heart and soul. He would be the father to them that he felt he never had. Prince, Paris, and Blanket were his *family*, and he committed to them with renewed fierceness and passion.

One person who was critically important in the lives of Michael and his children was Grace Rwaramba. She became "like family" to Michael, Prince, Paris, and Blanket. She was nanny and friend, confidante and assistant. For the program at Michael's Memorial, Grace wrote:

Dear Michael, the last 17 years with you I will never forget. Thank you for your love[,] your understanding. Thank you for entrusting me with your precious children.... Through the peaks and the valleys, we laughed hard, and we cried but through it all you taught me to always rise above it. I miss you so much....

Oprah asked Michael Jackson in 1993, "What do you know for sure?" He humbly responded, "I'm still learning; I can't say that I know anything for sure."

Certainly during his last four years, Michael Jackson still felt that he "knew nothing for sure." Perhaps, he knew even less—or understood less—than he did in 1993, when he was unquestioningly "at the top of his game" with a soaring career and a newly-acquired sense of satisfaction, born of his "ability to give back" through works of charity.

Having distanced himself both geographically and emotionally from his family and most other people after his 2005 trial, Michael had few personal interactions with his siblings. For LaToya, not much changed because she did not see her brother Michael for years at a time.

As he wandered from place to place, being a father and working on his music, Michael spent his time and placed his focus on his immediate world. He could no longer allow himself the luxury and pain of functioning as a fully active member of a contentious, complicated fame-based family. In his 2011 book, *You Are Not Alone: Michael, Through a Brother's Eyes,* Jermaine confirmed that Michael did indeed have only infrequent contact with his family members.

Although his family relationships had become more tenuous, Michael attended the sixtieth wedding anniversary of his parents in May 2009. With his three children by his side, he celebrated the triumph of the roller-coaster marriage of Joseph and Katherine Jackson, six decades of love, conflict, child-rearing, joy, heartbreak, betrayal, accommodation, and forgiveness. All of his siblings were there to celebrate with their parents and each other. That was the last family event that Michael Jackson attended.

Jermaine recounts that Michael invited all of his family members to attend his upcoming *This Is It* concert in London. They were all looking forward to seeing him and each other at that time....

Bottom line, they were a family. All of the Jacksons share the basic philosophy that, when the vicissitudes of life demand a united front, they need to be there for each other. And they will be....

"Second Family"

There are always surprises for anyone who delves into the fascinating private life of Michael Jackson....

One of the biggest of those is the Dominic Cascio family, who virtually came out of the woodwork to confess to having been Michael Jackson's "second family" for twenty-five years! Through an interview on *The Oprah Winfrey Show* in December 2010, Dominic, wife Connie, sons Frank and Eddie ("Angel"), and daughter Nicole emerged as the secret, adopted family of superstar Michael Jackson.

Dominic met Michael when he was manager of the Helmsley Palace Hotel in New York City. Michael Jackson stayed in suites there and began visiting Dominic's family at their suburban Franklin Lakes, New Jersey home.

Sometimes he would just show up at their house unannounced, knocking on their door in the middle of the night, according to the Cascios. Michael loved feeling like part of the family. He would stay in the basement, which was fixed up into comfortable, makeshift sleeping quarters; a recording studio; and a wooden dance floor just for Michael.

He would bring his children and sometimes leave them for short periods of time, while he went out with one or more of the Cascio family members. This was unusual for Michael, who was so protective of his children, and the family interpreted this behavior as showing a special level of trust in them. They would all pray, "say grace," at the dining table together—Michael, his kids, and the five Cascios—and they would often share stories about what they were grateful for in their lives.

The Cascios speak about exchanging Christmas presents with Michael every year and how he loved art, books, and Disney paraphernalia. Michael even helped with some of the housework from time to time, such as sweeping the floor and taking out the trash!

He was his usual humble self and always "down-to-earth" with the Cascio family; he could relax there. They would often "hang out" and talk across the kitchen counter. Connie made Michael's favorite foods, which included homemade pizza, turkey, mashed potatoes, and stuffing. The family even created a movie-theater-style candy counter for the times when Michael would visit.

Michael traveled with members of the Cascio family across the years, and members of the family would often visit him at

Neverland. Michael was a mentor to Eddie, teaching him about music and recording. Frank "Tyson," who changed his name from Frank Cascio, became Michael's personal assistant for nearly a decade, from the nineties into the 2000's; he started to work for Michael when he was eighteen. Frank, as both employee and friend, was involved in Michael's trial as a key witness for the defense.

The Cascios claim that Michael Jackson, with his children, showed up at their Franklin Lakes home and stayed for nearly three months, from mid-August to approximately November 7, 2007. He was accompanied by a tutor for the children and security personnel, none of whom moved into their house.

The basement recording studio was used by Michael and Eddie Cascio to write and record a number of songs, three of which were later included in the posthumous album *Michael*. These songs became the subject of heated controversy, when some members of Michael Jackson's family and many of his colleagues and fans challenged the authenticity of "Breaking News," "Keep Your Head Up," and "Monster." *Is it really Michael's voice in these tracks?* Forensic musicologists were hired to conduct studies of the vocals. The representatives of Michael Jackson's Estate, having received confirmation from the experts, then issued a statement that verifies the lead vocal on the controversial songs as Michael Jackson's.

Avoiding controversy for many years, the Cascios remained loyal to Michael by keeping their close relationship with him a secret. They said, in late 2010, that they were approached many times in past years by the tabloids to sell stories, but they declined and eschewed publicity in order to honor Michael's desire for privacy. They offered Michael a sense of normalcy within a family and in a world otherwise bereft of those experiences for him.

The Cascios' last conversation was with Michael on Father's Day, June 21, 2009, when he called their home. Michael passed away four days later. The entire family mourns his death as if he were indeed a member of their family unit.

"It's an everyday battle that we all have," Connie explains; "... at least once a day we mention him—because we actually can feel him in our home."

In the official program at Michael's Memorial, the Cascios are referred to as "The First Family of Love." They wrote:

> ... It is only once in a lifetime where you meet a true Angel sent from the Heavens above.... The wisdom, guidance, and knowledge will always be remembered and put into action.... Our friendship will ... always be treasured. WE THANK YOU and will love you FOREVER and ALWAYS.

**I love family life ...
everything about it.
I want [my children] to grow up
being surrounded by love and by family.**
— Michael Jackson

**The Jacksons are a family
who are a legend in the history
of the United States and
the history of the world.
They started from nothing ...
and they reached tremendous heights.**
— Thomas Mesereau

Michael Jackson's TSUNAMI: The Trial

**I know in my heart of hearts
that Michael Jackson was not guilty
of any of these grisly charges.**

— Thomas Mesereau

**... Michael seemed to have the appearance
of an ancient king. There was something
imperial about him. So absolutely
commanding with his presence....**

— Aphrodite Jones

If anyone could get used to extortion attempts and legal jockeying of the heinous sort, it would be Michael Jackson. *But is that possible?*

Suffice it to say that his "people" had to deal with threats of various kinds of legal action against their boss on a regular and routine basis. He had big money and he gave it out to get rid of nuisance lawsuits and frivolous challenges. It was the quick and easy way out. Michael did not have the stomach to fight. The anxiety and ambiguity in these situations were too big a price for him to pay; he would rather pay money and move along. He wouldn't miss the money anyway; he had plenty. *He would rather have fewer sleepless nights than a few more million dollars.*

Unfortunately, however, such expedient behavior just invites more problems—more lawsuits and threats. It becomes a vicious cycle.

*   *   *   *   *   *   *   *   *

In 2002, Martin Bashir came onto the scene. He was a British journalist with few credentials except for a piece called "Satanic Lovers" and his one big splash in the pool of fame—an exclusive, intimate interview with Princess Diana during a turbulent period of her marriage to Prince Charles. He made a name for himself in the media world overnight. Michael Jackson was impressed. Michael greatly admired the Princess, had gotten to know her to the point of having telephone conversations with her, and deeply mourned her untimely death.

Using his professional relationship with Diana as a type of calling card, Bashir schmoozed his way into Michael Jackson's life. He penetrated the long-standing barriers that protected Michael from incursions into his private space by savage media. He praised and complimented him; he guaranteed that he would present Michael to the world in an honorable, honest, and new way; he promised to be trustworthy. Bashir claimed that he would allow the world to see Michael Jackson the real man, the loving father and humanitarian, for the first time ever.

Maybe it was time, Michael reasoned; he hadn't given an interview of international scope for nearly a decade.

Michael didn't know that Martin Bashir had been censured for "unfair journalistic practices" in the United Kingdom. He found that out during Bashir's testimony at his criminal trial several years later—*after* he had been done in by the slick, conniving, and unscrupulous opportunist.

Bashir promised to help Michael advance his dream of establishing an International Children's Day, which would join Mother's and Father's Days on the calendar; it would specifically honor and benefit children. For Michael, that was the clincher for the deal with the journalist. He fondly envisioned the creation of a stipulated day every year, on which all parents would spend quality time with their children. Michael said that, if he had enjoyed such a day—even if only once a year—with his own father during the years of his childhood, he would have had a better relationship with the man. Michael had never played a game with his father in his life; he missed out on the playing-and-bonding component of a father-son relationship. His "dream" was poignant and ingenuous. Michael wanted to spare the children of the world the pain of familial alienation that he endured.

Michael Jackson agreed to do the proposed documentary with no financial benefit to himself. He was satisfied with his negotiated remuneration to be directed to specific charities. Perhaps more astoundingly, he asked for no conditions whatsoever.

Michael obviously trusted Bashir … to the incredible extent that he allowed him eight months of full access to his Neverland home and to other sites where Michael visited and worked, in cities from Miami to Berlin. This was terrain that had never been breached by a person of the media. Bashir followed Michael around, interviewed him numerous times, and filmed him everywhere. Bashir was even allowed to interact with Michael's young children. Michael Jackson bared his soul to this man, who would turn into a Judas.

To his face, the manipulative reporter would say things to Michael like, "You have a spectacular relationship with your children; when I see you with them, it almost makes me weep." He was addressing Michael's obvious tenderness and loving behaviors with his little ones.

In the final, gerrymandered version of the documentary "Living with Michael Jackson," Bashir omitted the accolades and, instead, expressed "grave concerns" about Michael's parenting. It was like an episode of *The Twilight Zone*—the discrepancies were so great between Bashir's ingratiating words to Michael Jackson in private quarters and his nasty comments and cruel innuendo in the telecast program. Bashir was self-righteous and judgmental throughout the aired program. He successfully sucker-punched his guileless victim by sinister editing of the footage.

Unfortunately but unsurprisingly, "Living with Michael Jackson" attracted a huge international viewing audience. The shocking experience turned into a ghastly nightmare for Michael Jackson....

Bashir had told his trusting "mark" that he wanted to film him with one of the many children whom he befriended and helped. Michael complied by inviting Gavin Arvizo to an interview session with himself and Bashir.

In this segment, Bashir captured Michael and Gavin holding hands, while Gavin sang the praises of Michael Jackson for having saved his life. Bashir skillfully asked questions that turned into a trap for Michael, who admitted that he sometimes shared his bed with children, that it was innocent and caring. Gavin echoed the sentiment. Michael was like a father to Gavin and his two siblings, a brother and a sister, who also spent overnights at Neverland, along with their mother. It was all clearly unrehearsed, impromptu conversation. *It was a bombshell.*

Martin Bashir ensured for himself an immortal niche in television history. He all but put the nails into the coffin of Michael Jackson.

A tornado of events occurred after Michael's telecast self-disclosures. He was accused of pedophilia by many in the media world. The State of California child protection agency began an investigation of Michael Jackson, and a whirlwind of suspicion and outrage spun out of control.

Some thinking people asked, "Why would a man guilty of *anything* improper permit an investigative reporter *full and complete access* to his residences, life, and family, across the span of eight months?" "Would any pedophile admit on international television that he 'slept' with children?"

Michael had displayed poor judgment, of course. He revealed both his naivety and his generalized trust in a world that would undoubtedly understand the innocence—and even the superlatively caring behavior—that he was describing. In third-world countries, he would probably be right, but not in twenty-first-century America.

In the program, Michael clarified that his friend Frank Cascio was also present and that he and Frank slept on the floor, while the two young boys, Gavin and his brother, took the bed. It was "not sexual," Michael protested, and Gavin earnestly agreed, on camera. However, any and all details were considered superfluous; everyone stopped listening after the statement about sharing a bed.

To complicate matters, Bashir and his producers had neither sought nor received the permission of Gavin's parents to film the minor for a television program. These were not amateurs, but the prize was worth the price, the risk. They had captured Michael Jackson in footage that would either kill him or, at the least, maim him. *What a coup!*

Michael was horrified when he watched "Living with Michael Jackson" on television in February 2003, ... and things only got worse.

Some of his "people" jumped into action in attempts to salvage Michael's image and to protect him from what seemed to be nuclear-level fallout. They commissioned a rebuttal program, "Michael Jackson: The Footage You Were Never Meant to See," which was designed to include interviews with various people, including Gavin Arvizo, his mother Janet, and two siblings. All of the Arvizos confirmed enthusiastically—and at times tearfully—that Michael was always and only "father-like" to the children (Gavin, at this time twelve; brother Star, fourteen; and sister Davellin, eighteen). Janet insisted that "no one had ever been there" for her or her children, except for Michael Jackson.

The Arvizo story—which would play out in full detail at the subsequent trial—was that, in 2000, Michael was told about Gavin when the child was suffering from Stage Four cancer. The boy, then ten years old, lost organs to the disease; he lost his hair and ability to walk; and he was undergoing a series of chemotherapy treatments and using a wheelchair to get around. According to his mother, Gavin lost his left kidney, left adrenal gland, spleen, the tip of his pancreas, and multiple lymph nodes; "he had a sixteen-pound tumor removed"; and cancer was found in both of his lungs. He had numerous blood transfusions of both white and red blood cells. Gavin's doctor told his parents to prepare for a funeral for their son.

Michael Jackson heard that this terminally-ill child desperately wanted to meet him. He discovered much later that Jay Leno, George Lopez, and Chris Tucker had also been approached to reach out to the boy. Gavin's father, David Arvizo, and mother were lobbying the celebrities to give money and to sponsor fund-raising events for their son, even though—undisclosed by them—medical insurance covered the cost of the boy's hospitalization and treatments. [Jay Leno, George Lopez, and Chris Tucker had all walked away from the Arvizos when they came to realize their manipulative and dishonest ways of using celebrities to their financial advantage. Tucker went so far as to warn Michael Jackson to be very wary of them.]

Not knowing anything about the Gavin family's history, Michael Jackson opened his heart, his wallet, and his home to them. He telephoned Gavin twenty times from various places around the world, while the boy was in the hospital and undergoing chemotherapy. Gavin could call Michael "any time." Michael invited Gavin and his family to visit him at Neverland. Gavin said that he thought about the prospect of such a visit all of the time during his cancer treatments. Once there, they were hosted with the same level of privilege that was extended to famous visitors such as Marlon Brando; they stayed in the Elizabeth Taylor Guesthouse.

Gavin, his mother, and siblings were treated like celebrities, including being transported by Michael's private limousine and Rolls Royce to and from their one-room apartment in East Los Angeles. Their own living quarters were so small that all of the Arvizos shared the same bed. At Neverland, the family had full access to the main house—Michael's residence—in addition to their beautiful, assigned guesthouse.

Janet charged to Michael's accounts thousands of dollars in luxuries and personal services, including body waxes, to which she was driven in his dispatched vehicle. He bought for the children a computer, toys, and clothes; gave Gavin one of his jackets and an expensive watch; and paid for their dental work. He provided the family with a car and vacations by private jet. The Arvizos were welcome to visit Neverland even when Michael was absent; they were given the run of the Ranch and all of its facilities; the boys found out the alarm codes. The family stayed for three weeks at a time, and a number of times when Michael was not on the property.

These people joined the long list of those whom Michael Jackson hosted and helped. There were thousands of children—a great many of them dying, ill, or disadvantaged from the inner city—who were brought in, by the dozens, every few weeks whether or not Michael himself was present. Often he was touring and not in residence. The children were given cotton candy, popcorn, their choice of every kind of treat in the candy store, access to all of the amusement rides and zoo, and all at Michael Jackson's expense. When he was on site, he would perform for them, putting on a private show in his theater. He staffed the Ranch with dozens of security personnel and other attendants so that the children would have a safe, fun-filled, and memorable day like none other.

Michael Jackson's philosophy was to give the children "something to live for and something to look forward to." For those with terminal illness, if he was able to effect a few more days of life for them, it was worth it all. If he could provide them with fun, escape, and happiness for a day—these children whose lives were bereft of joy and hope—he wanted to do it.

"Without exaggeration, it would be impossible to count the number of disadvantaged families with whom Michael has formed emotional attachments ... and equally impossible to fathom the number of boys he has known, befriended and taken into his home and his confidence," wrote his biographer Taraborrelli. "There have been so many. He's fortunate that only two out of what must surely be hundreds have presented a problem for him." It is especially "fortunate" and surprising—it should be added—when betrayal of Michael Jackson's trust and love could become so lucrative for the ungrateful, greedy, and morally corrupt.

Not only did young Gavin recover from his cancer, but he thrived! He and his siblings called their benefactor "Daddy Michael," with their mother's full support and encouragement. They attributed Gavin's miraculous recovery to Michael Jackson, who had refused to accept the doctor's terminal prognosis and had insisted that, at Neverland, they would "blanket him with love."

Michael prayed for Gavin, explaining to him the power of faith and prayer, and he sponsored a blood drive for him. He played games with Gavin, even allowing him to win, according to his grateful mother. He encouraged the boy continually to envision a Pac-Man character eating up all of his cancer cells, destroying them. Michael Jackson believed in "mind over body"; he wanted Gavin to believe also, and to be cured.

When the boy's health dramatically improved and his prognosis changed to recovery, the family started behaving as if they were entitled to Michael's wealth; the Neverland staff saw major problems. Michael started spending less time with the family. The Arvizo parents then paid a visit to Larry Feldman, the same attorney who had negotiated a settlement with Michael Jackson in 1993 on behalf of a boy who alleged improprieties by the superstar. At that time, Michael agreed to pay approximately $20 million to resolve this matter. The actual settlement was reportedly close to $16 million, while $1.5 million went to each of the two parents, and "up to $5 million" to the attorney. Michael was advised to "settle it" to continue with his spiraling career and his touring, uninterrupted. That was the *better* alternative, his people urged, to halting the incoming flow of millions of dollars and engaging in long, drawn-out legal travail and bad publicity.

Bottom line, the 1993 matter apparently turned into a successful extortion attempt. The boy, his father, stepfather, and mother all reaped the benefits, as did their attorney. Many reporters have since emphasized that Michael Jackson's insurance carrier was actually responsible for the settlement, but there is little doubt that Michael Jackson wanted the painful matter to end ... at almost any cost.

Unknown to many people, even those who followed the 2005 trial, if the Arvizos prevailed in criminal court against Michael Jackson for any charges against him, they would have years within which to file civil charges against the mega-wealthy celebrity. The only question, in that event, would not be "Will Michael Jackson pay damages?" but simply *"How much* will he pay?" Everyone knew by then that Michael Jackson would settle with huge money rather than endure another trial.

It was discovered during the preparations for the trial that the Arvizos were upset over money. They did not get paid for either

Bashir's "Living with Michael Jackson" or the filming of them for the rebuttal documentary that was produced by Michael's people.

So, after they had gushed on camera about all of Michael Jackson's kindnesses to them and volunteered that he had saved Gavin's life, they experienced a change of heart. They "decided" that Michael was guilty of sexual molestation, "lewd acts," and serving alcohol to a minor. Count One was "conspiracy involving child abduction, false imprisonment, and extortion."

*   *   *   *   *   *   *   *   *

More than seventy Santa Barbara sheriffs raided and ransacked Neverland, with a search warrant, in Michael Jackson's absence on November 18, 2003. They executed the fourteen-hour surprise raid while Michael was staying at the Mirage Hotel in Las Vegas and working on the short film *One More Chance*. "I don't think I'll be able to get through it," Michael reportedly told an aide when he heard the news.

The authorities tossed his bedroom, tore apart his bed, and emptied the boxes that held his personal mementos. They went through every book and video in his libraries, checked every inch of his bathroom, and rifled through his closets and drawers. They drilled open his safes, in one of which they found a large pile of cash. They inspected his laundry and looked for non-existent secret rooms.

This was likely the biggest raid in U.S. history on a suspected perpetrator for any crime, including serial murder. Everyone wanted in on the act. The authorities could boast to their friends and colleagues that they had tossed *Michael Jackson's private home*.

It is interesting to note that, for years surrounding 2003, a series of clergymen in a variety of U.S. cities were accused of sexual molestation of children, and some were convicted. *None* of them experienced the invasive, all-encompassing raid on their homes that Michael Jackson endured, nothing that even came close.

The authorities were looking for any incriminating evidence that would convict Michael Jackson. They were seeking child pornography or similar damning material. The FBI later searched Michael's computer files, confiscated by the sheriffs. No child pornography was found.

Their macho behavior during the raid was theatrical and rapacious; their intentionality seemed like that of a lynch mob. Some of the sheriffs jerked their hands to their guns as they climbed stairs and rounded corners in the house, whose owner was not even in residence. Some seemed to be having fun. It was all captured on film by the Sheriff's Department camera crew; the District Attorney supervised.

At the Trial of the Century, Michael Jackson was facing a total of ten felony charges against him (which the judge turned into ten felonies and four misdemeanors for the jury's deliberation). If convicted, he could be sentenced to a maximum of *fifty-six years* in prison, or nearly nineteen years if given concurrent sentences. He knew that a terrible outcome would kill him. *What would become of his children?*

To many observers, the charges against Michael Jackson of extortion and conspiracy to kidnap would have been laughable if they were not so serious.

A staggering number of credentialed media—2,200 individuals—registered to cover Michael Jackson's trial in the quiet town of Santa Maria, California, with a population of only 82,000. It was like an invasion. Every day for the duration of the proceedings, nearly five months, bomb squads and arsenals of ammunition were stationed by the authorities near the courthouse.

Jury selection was difficult because nearly every potential juror knew about the case from the media. Of the pool of 240 prospective jurors, only six were African Americans. The final twelve jurors consisted of eight women, four men, and not a single African American.

Every weekday the trial was conducted by Judge Rodney Melville. Cameras and recorders were not allowed in the courtroom. There were 135 witnesses and 600 exhibits. Twelve years of Michael Jackson's private life were revealed, scrutinized, and dissected. Nothing was off limits.

"Living with Michael Jackson" was shown in the courtroom in its entirety. At Thomas Mesereau's request, the judge also allowed the outtake footage to be played. District Attorney Thomas Sneddon vigorously objected to the jury seeing this outtake footage, but to no avail. Michael had assigned his own personal videographer to film all of his interactions with Bashir, which was a wise and fortuitous decision, because the edited-out material showed his gentleness and gullibility in contrast to the interviewer's shrewd skills at manipulation and deceit.

The judge ruled that the jurors would not visit Neverland during the trial, though Mesereau had requested that as necessary. Instead, a video of Michael's expansive home and spectacular grounds was played in court. It was commissioned by Thomas Mesereau and produced by Larry Nimmer, a professional legal-video filmer, who said years later that this project opened his eyes to the dangerous side of celebrity and the media. Nimmer was deeply affected by the plight of Michael Jackson, who was so vulnerable a target. He visited Neverland half a dozen times; took extensive footage of its twenty-two buildings and 2,700 acres of grounds; and then, for two days, testified to every setting and significant item that played on the courtroom screen.

Neverland was a magical place that reflected fantasy and represented fun. Zoo animals roamed in spacious, separate habitats; the many amusement rides were colorful and inviting; the grounds were covered with flowers; white swans swam in a four-acre shimmering lake. Three private trains traveled across the property; life-sized statues of children were scattered all around; and a gold crown sparkled in the sun atop the large black, gilt-covered Neverland interior gate. There were video libraries, in which the titles were arranged by category, many of them family entertainment; a movie theater that was outfitted to accommodate the handicapped; and a separate arcade building with a variety of games. There was a mail room that stored the thousands of letters, cards, and gifts sent to Michael Jackson from around the world.

Mannequins, in the likeness of both young and old persons, were placed in various rooms throughout the sprawling house. There were huge collections of art and sculpture, photos and memorabilia of all kinds, and magnificent furniture and accessories.

Michael's two-story bedroom was vast. On its first floor were a large sitting area, imposing fireplace, oversized red-velvet throne-chair, and a grand piano. On the second floor there was "stuff" everywhere—furniture, artwork, four televisions, computers, CD's and DVD's, video games, books, collectibles, board games, cartoon characters, stuffed animals, action figures, stacks of files, and unwrapped gifts. To say that it looked "lived in" would be accurate—and even an understatement.

The huge king-size bed was covered by a shimmery silver-blue bedspread and matching stuffed pillows. Hanging on the wall over Michael's bed was a large painting that looked like "The Last Supper." Sitting at the center of the table was Michael Jackson; on his left and right were individuals whom Michael admired, including John F. Kennedy, Walt Disney, Elvis Presley, Albert Einstein, Abraham Lincoln, and Thomas Edison. Some people in the courtroom perceived this painting as apocryphal, with its theme reminiscent of the ultimate betrayal of Christ by Judas. Michael had chosen this particular artwork for a very special placement—as his headboard. [Bashir had praised Michael, in outtake footage, for his desire to take care of the world's children—calling it "the jewel in the crown"—but he callously betrayed him by editing the final program to make Michael look sinister and suspicious. It was Judas-like behavior.]

Michael's closets were filled with his things, ranging from Disney characters to elaborate, shiny collectibles of all types and sizes. The general clutter seemed in contrast to Michael's clothing, which was tidily arrayed by type of garment; his pants, shirts, and jackets were carefully arranged on hangers, by color. This made sense because Michael perceived his clothing as an extension of his *persona* and image. He was always methodical and perfectionistic when it came to his own appearance; his clothes needed to be readily available and impeccable.

Blanket's crib was next to Michael's bed, which served as a reminder to everyone that the man on trial for his life and freedom was the father of two young children and a baby. On his bedside table was a photo of Marilyn Monroe, and next to it was a biography of Pope John Paul II. Although there were photos and posters displayed throughout the room, not one of them was of Michael Jackson himself.

The overriding theme of the entire home was "children." Michael's bedroom looked like a fun place—like a college dormitory room—one where kids could feel comfortable and interact with all of its things.

"For Michael, kids were king; that was the thread in every fiber of his home," wrote Aphrodite Jones, who studied every piece of evidence from the trial for her 2007 book, *Michael Jackson Conspiracy.* Ms. Jones admitted to having been one of the hundreds of reporters and journalists who *wanted* Michael Jackson to be found guilty. Like nearly all of her media colleagues, she was disappointed, even angry, when the "not guilty" verdicts were announced. Then, however, she got curious. She sought and received Judge Melville's approval to review every transcript, article of evidence, and exhibit from the court proceedings.

Wow! Ms. Jones realized that Michael Jackson was indeed innocent, while she sat alone in the basement court records room. *Of course* he was declared *not guilty*! He was only guilty of being too childlike in his level of trust and correspondingly too generous in his behavior. Jones, a long-time true crime reporter, experienced the "St. Paul Syndrome"; she fell from her horse who was headed in one direction, so to speak, and converted to the opposite direction—a firm belief in Michael's complete innocence. *She had an epiphany!*

Aphrodite Jones wrote her manuscript and then self-published, because no one in the publishing industry was interested in a book that might exonerate Michael Jackson, not even one by a seasoned and successfully published author. *Sad but true.*

Ms. Jones revealed that the media industry had a *huge* investment in the outcome of this trial and that a guilty verdict was both coveted and expected. The media tried to help it along by continuously distorted and slanted coverage. Stories were already written and ready to go about the "guilty" verdicts, Michael's being hauled off to prison, his suicide attempts, and deep depression. The reports of his guilt and despair were fully fashioned and ready to be released at the tap of a laptop computer's "Send" signal. Photos of his likely prison cell had been taken and developed for prospective quick dispatch to news bureaus. Footage of dark, cramped prison cells was played on television channels throughout the week of the jury's deliberation.

Award-winning journalist Charles Thomson analyzed the coverage of Michael Jackson and his trial in "One of the Most Shameful Episodes in Journalistic History," wherein he stated:

> Allegations which were disproven in court went unchallenged in the press. Shaky testimony was presented as fact. The defense's case was all but ignored.... Anybody who had been paying attention to proceedings could see that the doubt was so far beyond reasonable it wasn't even funny. Almost every single prosecution witness either perjured themselves or wound up helping the defense. There wasn't a shred of evidence connecting Jackson to any crime and there wasn't a single credible witness connecting him to a crime either.

The waves of disappointment, after Michael Jackson's acquittal on all fourteen charges, from the hundreds of media people there were palpable. They packed up their computers, picked up their tents, and swiftly left with visible frowns and in silence. Some refused to give up and simply fashioned stories of how Michael Jackson had gotten away with horrible crimes.

The public did not hear anything about Michael's innumerable and continuous charitable acts on behalf of children and the needy. The media ignored the testimony of a series of witnesses who praised Michael for his good works. Those things did not make for good headlines; they did not sell newspapers.

The public did not hear the shaky details of the allegations, the rebuttals, and the testimony of dozens of witnesses who spoke on Michael's behalf and who denied his culpability.

Debbie Rowe, although called by the prosecution, testified that Michael was a good man and father, and she just wanted to be his friend. She surprised everyone, not only because of the positive content of her testimony, but because she was emotional and teary—obviously truthful and moved by Michael's horrible predicament, which brought out her feelings for him.

The mother of Michael's accuser in 1993, June Chandler, testified that her son Jordie had not spoken to her in more than eleven years. This timeline would set the date of her last conversation with Jordie not long after Michael agreed to the approximately $20 million settlement that made them rich—herself, her two husbands, and her young son. To the surprise of everyone, she also testified that she "never" had an issue with Michael being around her son! She said that Michael seemed lonely and that he had wanted to be part of their family.

A series of young men who had visited Michael and stayed with him when they were children appeared in court to validate that his behavior was always appropriate, innocent, and caring.

Twenty-two-year-old Wade Robson testified that he had known Michael Jackson from the time he was seven. He and his family moved to Los Angeles from Australia in 1991. They visited Michael at Neverland twenty-some times. Nothing inappropriate happened, Robson said, and he remained friends with Michael Jackson, who also helped him with his career across the years.

Brett Barnes had flown from Australia, at his own initiation, to testify on behalf of his friend Michael. He had known the superstar since he was five and had visited Neverland at least ten times with his family. Mr. Barnes described his times in Michael's room as "mini-parties," with boys and girls there, including sometimes Michael's cousins.

Barnes was "very mad" about the allegations against Michael Jackson, and he testified to the good, healthy fun that he had enjoyed with his friend. He was "really, really, really not happy" that people were trying to establish that he and Michael Jackson had been involved in inappropriate sexual activity. Mr. Barnes testified that he had to quit his job in Australia, which he gladly did, in order to come to these trial proceedings for the sake of his friend.

Macaulay Culkin, whom Michael chose to become the godfather of Prince and Paris, was one of the best and most compelling witnesses. Twenty-three years old, Culkin testified that he and Michael shared an understanding of the loneliness of child stars, who are "pigeonholed" and misunderstood by people. The *Home Alone* star testified that he first heard about "allegations of Michael's inappropriately touching [him] years before" on a news program on CNN. He was adamant that nothing inappropriate had ever happened, and he was angry that officials had not even contacted him. He had to hear shocking allegations on national television.

"I think they're absolutely ridiculous" was Culkin's response, under oath, to Mesereau's question of what he thought about these allegations of impropriety by Michael Jackson.

Jesus Salas, Michael's personal house manager for twenty years, testified that visiting children had access to all of his employer's prized possessions—including movie theater, rides, and zoo. All of Michael's invited guests were given the combination to the main house—his residence—and they were able to enter the main buildings freely. There were very few rules except that the children were not allowed in the wine cellar and specific safety regulations were enforced. The security guards were plentiful but unarmed, even though intruders had been caught at Neverland from time to time. Michael Jackson did not want any weapons on the property; the safety of children was his foremost consideration.

Mr. Salas told the jury that he had seen busloads of thousands of children arrive to visit Neverland, many from Los Angeles, but they were also from all around the globe. He estimated that he had seen *hundreds of thousands* of children visit, each having "the time of their lives."

Other Neverland employees testified that it was as if the Ranch had a "revolving door." Michael Jackson had so many guests, both when he was at home and in his absence—which was described as weeks and even months at a time—that it kept everyone very busy in their assignments of providing service.

Of special significance in all of the long weeks of testimony was the total lack of credibility of the accuser family. Janet Arvizo and her two sons had been involved in a "shoplifting incident" several years before they met Michael Jackson. Gavin had left a JC Penney store with some clothing that the Arvizos allegedly had not paid for; in the parking lot they were confronted by three Penney's security guards, two men and a woman. The police were called, and Janet was arrested. During the booking, Janet made no reference to any alleged sexual improprieties by the guards; she stated that she was "fine." Before long, however, she claimed to have been sexually molested by all three guards and also beaten. Her young sons Gavin and Star backed up their mother's story as her witnesses.

With the assistance of an attorney, the Arvizos brought legal action against JC Penney, which chose to settle with the family for $152,000. During Michael Jackson's trial, Gavin and Star admitted to having lied in the JC Penney matter to support their mother in her lawsuit. Janet also all but admitted to having lied. This indigent Latino family had learned to use charges of sexual molestation to obtain big money. The children had learned to work with lawyers and to lie about sexual misconduct for financial gain.

Janet also falsely filed for a variety of government-based programs to obtain significant financial help, including welfare, food stamps, unemployment, and disability. She was not eligible for these programs because of the many thousands of dollars from JC Penney in her bank account. She received money to which she was not entitled. These facts were exposed during the trial, but the judge allowed her to plead "The Fifth" to alleged welfare fraud and perjury and thereby avoid testifying against herself related to these matters.

Janet and the three Arvizo children testified that father David had physically abused all of the members of his family and on many occasions. Janet had gotten multiple restraining orders against her husband. It was *only* Michael Jackson who showed paternal kindness to all of the Arvizos. Janet had called Michael "a godsend." She had said, "We may be broken, but Michael fixed us."

They repaid him by alleging improprieties by him that they claimed occurred *after* the 2003 "Living with Michael Jackson" program aired and after they showered him with praise in the filming of the rebuttal program. This timeline did not make any sense from other established facts.

Michael had distanced himself from the boys at that time, at his advisers' urging. The relationships between Michael and the Arvizo family had become uncomfortable because of the media backlash and public furor. Neverland employees reported that the boys had become bold and destructive. They trashed their guesthouse, threw things at the zoo animals, started the amusement rides without the required employee supervision, defaced Michael's guest book, crashed a golf cart, and broke into the wine cellar and helped themselves to wine. Kiki Fournier, a Neverland housekeeper, testified that Star pulled a knife on her in the kitchen. She explained that she did not feel it had been intended as a joke but an assertion of some sort of authority. The Arvizos were behaving like they felt entitled to Michael Jackson's largesse and wealth.

The stories that Gavin and Star told in court regarding Michael Jackson's alleged inappropriate behavior—"lewd acts" in the legal jargon—conflicted with each other. They contradicted their own stories. The mother and all three children were caught telling lies.

One example occurred when Star took the stand early in the trial. He told two different stories about an act of alleged impropriety by Michael on two consecutive days in court. During cross-examination by Thomas Mesereau, the attorney showed Star an issue of the magazine *Barely Legal* and repeatedly asked the boy if this was the specific issue that Michael Jackson had shown him and his brother Gavin. Star insisted that it was the very same issue that Michael showed them. Mesereau then revealed for the court that this issue was in fact published in August 2003, five months after the Arvizo family had left Neverland for good. [Of course, the media reported the allegation that Michael Jackson had shown pornography to minors; they did not bother to report this charge as refuted and false in cross-examination. This serves as a good example of the typical coverage by media of the trial.]

All four of the Arvizos testified in court that they had "lied" when they made exuberant and glowing, positive comments about Michael Jackson during the filming of the proposed rebuttal program. When the jury watched the *entire* footage, however, including the time during which the family was not aware that the camera was rolling, it became clear that they were liars ..., not during that taping, in which they praised Michael over and over again, but during their trial testimony. *One way or the other, they were liars.*

A partial timeline of events is the following:

February 6, 2003 – "Living with Michael Jackson" is telecast in the U.S. There is immediate media and public furor over contents of the program.

February 7 – Michael allegedly *begins* sexually molesting Gavin Arvizo, shown in the documentary with Michael.

February 14 – The Department of Children and Family Services and the L.A. Police Department begin investigations into the relationship between Michael Jackson and Gavin Arvizo.

February 18 – The Santa Barbara County Sheriff's Department begins its own investigation.

February 24 – The DCFS and LAPD investigations end with the conclusions that any allegations are "unfounded."

April 16 – The Santa Barbara County Sheriff's Department closes its case against Michael.

June 13 – The Arvizo family members change their stories, alleging that Michael Jackson did wrongful things; the investigation is reopened by the Santa Barbara authorities. The "change of mind" occurred after the family visited attorney Larry Feldman, who had represented the Chandlers in 1993, obtaining for them an approximately $20 million settlement from Michael Jackson.

Janet Arvizo would ramble on when she was on the stand. She sometimes snapped her fingers at the jury while she was speaking. When she lamented that she feared that Michael Jackson would kidnap her family in a hot-air balloon, people in the courtroom looked at each other. She seemed like a bad joke.

Meanwhile, nothing was funny to Michael, who was learning more about this family with every passing day in court. They had presented themselves to him as guileless, innocent people who needed him desperately and had grown to love him deeply.

Michael never took the stand at his trial. He sat every day, with straight back and eyes fixed in front of him, at the defense table. The ever-present sketch artist, who daily released the only visual representations of the court proceedings, later said that, at times, Michael was unblinking. He had to hear sordid tales about himself—fabrications and lies—Monday through Friday; he had to sit there and keep silent.

In addition, Michael Jackson was bound by a gag order, issued by the judge, for more than a year, from the time of his arrest and ongoing through the months at trial. He was therefore powerless to respond to the vicious and inaccurate media publications and programs. The media pounced on this situation by fabricating stories, distorting facts, and sensationalizing every aspect of the charges against Michael. There could be no rebuttal or refutation from him; if he responded, he could—and probably would—be found in contempt of court.

From the sheer weight and volume of information and exhibits that were presented to the jury, it appeared to some that a guilty verdict on at least one or more counts was inevitable. Betting on the trial outcome took place, not just in Las Vegas but everywhere. Many wondered if a jury with its skewed racial composition— not one African American—would be biased against Michael and unduly influenced by the fiery Caucasian prosecutors, who were clearly on a mission—heavily funded by taxpayers' money—to get him.

On "Pajama Day" especially, Michael Jackson made global news, and it was made to look like a dreadful outcome would be in store for the superstar. Slowly and seemingly dazed, Michael— flanked by a small herd of security guards—walked from his vehicle into the courthouse; he was wearing pajama pants and a sport coat. His unusual and unconventional appearance—in stark contrast with the spiffy, custom-made outfits that he wore on every other day—generated a storm of media coverage. What a bonanza for the tabloids! Everything they could wish for … and more.

In truth, Michael had fallen at home in the early morning. He sustained an injury to his back and was taken to the hospital for treatment, undoubtedly including medication for pain, which would dull his senses. Thomas Mesereau requested of the judge a one-day reprieve from court appearance for his client. The judge not only denied his request but insisted that Michael Jackson appear by 9:30 A.M. or he would be subject to the loss of his $3 million bail and to jail for the rest of the trial for contempt of court. Mesereau telephoned Michael to tell him the bad news and to advise him to appear in whatever clothes he was wearing. He had better comply with the judge's ruling.

His driver broke the speed limits to get Michael to court. However, there was no time for him to change from his pajamas, which he had worn to the hospital. A sport coat was provided him by one of his people, and he arrived just minutes after the ordered time. Fortunately, the jurors were sequestered and kept unaware of the incident. In court, Michael sat behind the large defense table with only his upper body visible to the jury panel.

J. Randy Taraborrelli described that day as especially significant:

> Michael seemed to be dying in front of our very eyes. He was clearly in terrible pain, both physical and emotional. Anyone who cared about him would have been heartsick by the sight. It was horrible to watch as he slowly deteriorated to the point where he could barely walk into the courtroom.

Surely Michael Jackson will be convicted, thought the prosecution and media, in tacit cooperation with each other. The news experts, frowns on their faces, said it didn't look good for the King of Pop. Off camera, they smiled.

"It only takes one lie under oath to throw this case out of court by you," Thomas Mesereau told the jurors in his closing statement for Michael's defense. "And you can't count the lies here."

Not guilty of all charges! One by one, the verdicts were read by the jury foreman. They were broadcast by loud speaker outside of the courtroom for the thousands of people gathered there. Michael's fans, hundreds of them from around the country and the world, were there for him. Every day fans congregated at the wrought-iron gates of Neverland, through which his black sports utility vehicle drove Michael slowly and stoically, past the devout well-wishers. He always rewarded them with a wave of his hand or the peace sign. They surrounded the courthouse in support of him; they held huge signs declaring his innocence. To them this trial was an outrage.

A white dove was released from a cage into the air by a lovely, smiling blonde woman after each "not guilty" verdict was read. The fans exploded into wild cheers, fell into each other's arms in their joy, and they wept. Some of the jurors also wept openly.

"And then there was the real Michael, who was a well-dressed, highly poised man, who seemed to be a humble spirit. In person, he was a shy and quiet guy who had no relation to that tabloid character, whatsoever," Aphrodite Jones wrote. "On the day of the verdicts, looking at his face, his body language, and his aura, it was clear that the man known as the King of Pop—was a kindhearted soul who had become a victim of his own fame. There was nothing arrogant about him ... [or] weird...."

Simply put, this accuser family had been shopping for a wealthy celebrity sponsor to take care of them, to satisfy their evolving needs. One way or the other, they would get everything they could, any way they could. They hit the jackpot with Michael Jackson, whose heart broke for the poor, dying child and his struggling family, and whose financial resources were made readily available to them. He became "like a father" to the three Arvizo children, only more caring and gentle than their own. They described him as "unselfish and kind," with "unconditional love" for them.

Michael Jackson had to withstand a level of scrutiny into his private life that few people could survive. This was the *best*, the strongest case that the District Attorney could bring against Michael Jackson, and it was weak to the extreme. His accusers were just not credible, there was no evidence or collaborating witnesses, and the testimony was full of holes and contradictions. It was just "smoke and mirrors," and all at taxpayers' expense, at an astronomical cost for years of witch-hunt activity by government officials.

"I never expected Michael Jackson to be convicted on any count, felony or misdemeanor," Tom Mesereau states today. He tried to reassure his tortured, sleepless client during the months of the trial that he would be acquitted.

What the jury came to realize was that Michael Jackson was more childlike and caring than anyone could have guessed and that he opted for a fantasy-like life because of the harsh, unacceptable realities of his isolation and vulnerability. He was trusting to the extreme and generous to a fault.

"I see God in the face of every child," Michael had said many times. Although—and perhaps because—the *adults* in Michael Jackson's life had used and betrayed him since his earliest years, he trusted *children* with an absolute faith.

How ironic—and sad—that his downfall was caused by a child, and one whose life he had saved.

**I am bewildered at the length
to which people will go
to portray me so negatively....
They just go too far.**

— Michael Jackson

**I would slit my wrists
before I would hurt a child.**

— Michael Jackson

THE BACK STORY: SURPRISES

**This prosecution was a travesty
of justice and one of the most
mean-spirited attacks on
an innocent person in legal history.**
— Thomas Mesereau

**He didn't know that
they would torture him.**
— Thomas Mesereau

"**W**ith his head held high, the superstar remained motionless. Only those who could see him close up, could detect a slight tear running down Michael's face." The "not guilty" verdicts were announced slowly but forcefully, one by one, fourteen of them.

It was June 13, 2005, a sunny day in Santa Maria in more ways than the literal interpretation.

Aphrodite Jones wrote the succinct description of the Defendant's reaction months later, after she came to repent the part she had played as one of the hunters in pursuit of Michael Jackson's demise. They were like the hounds that follow and surround the terrified, trapped, worn-out fox before they tear him to shreds; she admittedly had been one of the blood-thirsty pack.

"... We confidently came to our decisions. It is our hope that this case is a testament to the belief in our justice system's integrity and truth." Judge Rodney Melville read the jury's statement for the world to hear.

"Mr. Jackson, your bail is exonerated and you are released," the judge concluded.

One can only imagine the surge of relief that overtook Michael Jackson, who was not only declared not guilty of horrific behaviors but once again a free man, released from crushing worry over an opposite outcome. If convicted, he would have been immediately whisked off to a detention facility and, soon afterward, led to prison to serve a maximum sentence of up to fifty-six years. In the worst case scenario, Michael Jackson would be one hundred and two years old if he lived to the end of a non-commuted maximum sentence!

No one close to Michael, including Thomas Mesereau, believed that he could survive even weeks in prison. He would die. Mesereau was convinced from the very start that he was indeed fighting for Michael Jackson's very life.

Locked up, Michael would be without his trademark clothing, without the make-up that camouflaged his skin disorder—he would be robbed of his dignity. He would lose himself, not just the King of Pop that he had worked so hard to create, but the gentle, private man that he truly was, underneath everything. His *persona* would be gone and so would his will to live. He would also undoubtedly become a target for the dangerous criminals imprisoned with him.

Although he did not know it at the time, some of Michael's "people" had been busy tagging hundreds of his possessions at Neverland for sale and auction. The media had designed a plan for spectacular coverage of the "Fall of the King," the various outlets secretly vying with each other for the most shocking and disturbing storyline. A bidding war raged over who would get the first leaked images of Michael Jackson in his prison cell before the jury even began their deliberation.

Michael Jackson—after he read a brief statement thanking God, his fans, and family for their love and support—went home. At Neverland he relocated to a guest cottage on his property. He could not return to the bedroom that had been violated by the dozens of sheriffs who tore apart his bed, tossed around his cherished memorabilia, and handled and inspected every item among his private possessions. They also bagged hundreds of items to take with them, including photos of his friends, personal videos, and diaries in which he had recorded his private thoughts about his life and about God. His bedroom—tossed and pillaged—would never feel right to him again.

He embraced each one of his children with special appreciation for his ability to do just that. *Everything had changed for Michael Jackson.*

Before, he had felt "invincible" and said so, upon the release of his 2001 album of that name. How ironic that seemed! Michael learned that his immense wealth and presidential-level of security protection meant nothing when he was captured by the legal system with warrants, charges, an indictment, and a nightmare trial. There was a total loss of control—devastating for anyone, but especially for this man, a consummate perfectionist who needed to feel in control of his life, work, environment, and destiny. Before this dreadful series of experiences, he assumed that he would always be able to find the means to protect himself, his children, and his future. *No more.*

Michael Jackson was overtaken by a tsunami of feelings. He was traumatized, shaken to the core, humiliated. He realized in full focus that he had been savaged. He suffered from anxiety, depression, sleeplessness, and a generalized sense of insecurity. Panic turned to pain.

"Why? Why?" he was overheard saying to himself repeatedly as he stomped his leg while sitting in his vehicle, only minutes before the verdicts were read. He had been reading from the Bible during the seemingly endless ride to the courthouse, where his fate—determined by twelve strangers—would be revealed.

Search the literature about Michael Jackson, the infinite Internet information, and reports from those who knew him. *No one* has claimed that Michael Jackson amazingly recovered or "popped back" unscathed from the horrendous ordeal of his trial. Thomas Mesereau says what other "knowers" have also revealed: *Michael Jackson never recovered from the torture of his trial.*

Although fully acquitted and at liberty to return to his life, Michael lost his emotional compass. He was a man who had done everything right; who had steadfastly avoided hurting the feelings of anyone; who was always gracious in his speech and generous to everyone, even strangers who were in need of help and love. How could anyone go after him with such malicious intentionality and try to destroy him absolutely? How could people that he unquestioningly trusted and helped so much in so many ways turn on him in such a callous, extreme way, showing their willingness to see him gutted and ruined? How could people actually enjoy inflicting such pain—inserting the knife and twisting it and twisting it? He could not get past these thoughts, these revelations, the pain and incomprehensibility of it all.

The man who had internalized a Peter Pan philosophy of refusing to "grow up"—if that meant becoming callous, jaded, or tarnished by a cruel world—had undergone a crash course in big-time ugliness … and evil.

*   *   *   *   *   *   *   *   *

It was Michael's lucky day in April 2004, when Thomas Mesereau agreed to take his case and represent him. Mesereau was favorably compared to Clarence Darrow, one of the greatest trial attorneys of all time, because of his integrity and his success rate in court. Mesereau insisted that his brilliant, hard-working partner, Susan Yu, be hired to join him as he assumed the leadership role on Michael Jackson's defense team. And lead he did....

Michael's attorneys who were in charge when Mesereau stepped in were having too good a time. They seemed to love the media spotlight, the glory of representing the most famous man on the planet at the biggest trial of their lifetime. Randy Jackson observed these people one night at a swanky restaurant—laughing, joking, and excitedly planning their roles in the impending drama. Michael's brother decided that a different approach was needed and fast.

Johnnie Cochran from the infamous O.J. Simpson trial recommended Thomas Mesereau to Randy, who urged Michael to retain him, but the attorney was not immediately available. He was representing actor Robert Blake for the alleged murder of his ex-wife, but later, during jury selection, Mesereau and his client had a difference of opinion that resulted in the attorney's departure from the case. Randy Jackson then telephoned Mesereau again to renew the earlier offer for him to become legal counsel for the defense in the criminal case against Michael Jackson. Mesereau accepted and he jumped into the preparations with force and fervor.

The four-member defense team that would appear in court consisted of Thomas Mesereau; Susan Yu; Robert Sanger, a local attorney; and Brian Oxman, who was later terminated by Mesereau. Other attorneys and assistants helped in the case, but they worked behind the scenes.

Mesereau avoided the media entirely. Although he could not control the circus outside, he committed himself to preventing one within Michael Jackson's legal camp. He and Susan Yu moved into neighboring units in a condo building that was located a good distance from media-saturated restaurants and hotels. They created a "war room," began a hermit-like existence, and worked every waking moment on behalf of Michael Jackson. They had his best interests at heart ... to the exclusion of all else; they avoided distractions; and they functioned with a missionary level of zeal and dedication.

Mesereau and Yu soon discovered, however, that their challenges were coming from multiple fronts. They had to deal with the resentment, jealousy, and efforts to sabotage them from Michael's "camp" and from other attorneys. They were deluged by efforts—some subtle, others overt and heavy-handed—by many people from the media to get to them for a coveted "sound bite" or any exclusive tidbit related to the case. "The media were like a cloud of locusts," Mesereau recalls; they were everywhere and they were relentless.

The scope of what was shaping up to become a "festive trial" for the media was alarming. Money was being offered in staggering amounts for leaks to the press and any "inside" information. After the trial, one alternate juror sold on eBay for $2,000 his personal notes, which he had taken while sitting in the courtroom. In them, he wrote that many of the prosecution's witnesses were strange and lacked credibility. He attracted a buyer who wanted a piece of Michael Jackson's history.

Mesereau and Yu worked tirelessly, reviewing approximately 4,000 binders of material prepared by their assistants for the trial. Mesereau went to bed by 7:00 or 8:00 P.M. every night and was up at 3:00 A.M. to continue the grueling work. He and Susan Yu sometimes ate their meals over the prospective exhibits and transcripts of depositions. Their only recreation was taking walks, during which they discussed the details of the case.

"The trial was a world event with twenty-four-hour coverage and non-stop stress for us," Mesereau reflected in June 2011. "I could barely get out of bed for two to three weeks after it was over. I was exhausted and drained."

While Thomas Mesereau was being forced to deal with the ongoing politics of Michael's people, who included the other attorneys and his manager, he learned about the maddening competing forces and complications of Michael Jackson's everyday life. "Adulation is a narcotic to celebrities," Mesereau explained; "these people ingratiated themselves to Michael Jackson for their own purposes. They only told him what they thought he wanted to hear.

"Success brings false friends and real enemies," Mesereau realized; and great success at the level of Michael Jackson's breeds both, to an alarming degree.

"The psychology of hangers-on is very interesting," he continued. "These people work hard to get the celebrity off balance, to frighten him, and to offer solutions to him that are beneficial to themselves. The goal is for them to be perceived as indispensable to the celebrity, as the answer to his problems."

Mesereau was summoned to Neverland on numerous occasions to handle disputes and a variety of "crises." There always seemed to be a new guru, adviser, or lawyer there, making promises to Michael. "They were a 'sea of fools,' and efforts to address this commotion were just wasted time.

"Michael Jackson was vulnerable, gullible, impressionable, and naïve," Mesereau discovered. "To Michael's great credit, he believed he could change the world with kindness, but, tragically, he was too generous to too many people." To many of those surrounding him—in contrast to his ingenuous spirit—Michael was just a commodity; he was the currency for their goals of self-advancement and financial gain.

"He was gentle, kind, compassionate, and easy as a client. Actually, I never had a better client to deal with than Michael. He listened well, sometimes asked questions, and accepted advice. He deferred to Susan and me; at times he didn't say much at all." Because Mesereau was not "Mr. Hollywood" but a down-to-earth, compassionate man, he connected with his tormented client in a special way.

For many years, Tom Mesereau worked regularly on a *pro bono* basis for indigent people, volunteering his time and expertise at various free legal clinics in Los Angeles. After Michael's death, he opened his own free clinic at an African-American church and accelerated his involvements to help people in need. He also accepts, on a no-fee basis, a death-penalty case every year in the Deep South on behalf of a destitute person who cannot afford to pay for his legal representation.

"You become a better person, a better lawyer," he explains, "from this work that is so important—and life-saving—for poor people." Mesereau, who calls himself "a private person, independent, and rebellious," has been a champion of the poverty-stricken and of African Americans throughout his adult life.

Minnie Fox, an African-American woman who was the girlfriend of Mesereau at the time, arranged for the very last group of disadvantaged children who visited Neverland for a day of fun. Michael Jackson spoke to the children, including Minnie's son Norvell. All of the kids had a great time enjoying the rides and animals. Although there was a long waiting list of children hoping to visit, Neverland Ranch was permanently closed to them at the end of 2003.

Mesereau and Yu seemed made to order for Michael Jackson at this most important and painful juncture of his supremely challenging life. Together, the law partners set the course, direction, and priorities of their case on behalf of Michael.

"We worked to *humanize* Michael Jackson to the jury; the prosecution worked to *demonize* him. We could not have been at more opposing positions."

Thomas Mesereau and Susan Yu focused on portraying the real person behind the fame for the judge and jury of twelve.

*   *   *   *   *   *   *   *   *

The very human Michael Jackson was working hard to sustain himself. He tried to act as if everything was okay for his kids at home. He would eat dinner with them, help with homework, read a story, watch a movie, make popcorn, and put them to bed. Then he would be on the telephone with his attorneys, out of the earshot of his children.

"They knew something scary was happening," Mesereau realized. "They are very smart children." The children appeared to be very solicitous of their father. They gave him bear hugs and were reluctant to release him from their arms. They raced into his embrace when he came home. All of the televisions at Neverland were permanently set to the Disney channel; the children's Internet use was closely supervised by a teacher or their nanny; and people did not speak about the trial in their presence. "Still, they knew," Mesereau believed, "and they worried about their dad."

Michael would be awake and out of bed around 3 A.M. He often walked through the rambling house, alone and silent. He usually went outside to be close to nature, to hear its sounds, and to try to create fleeting moments of peace for himself. He looked into the sky at the stars and moon.

He spoke to Thomas Mesereau and to Susan Yu by phone during these wee hours of the morning. Poignantly and pleadingly, Michael urged Mesereau and Yu not to give in to the temptations surrounding them. He begged for his attorneys to keep steady in their representation of him in court. He was afraid that people might attempt to pay them off—perhaps with an offer of millions of dollars—to betray him.

"Michael was so unaccustomed to honest, loyal support by his attorneys," Mesereau realized, "that he expected the usual perfidy or lapses in their work on his behalf." *How very sad,* thought Mesereau, who resolved to himself to stay on course with even more zeal.

Thomas Mesereau and Susan Yu did not so much as ask Michael Jackson for an autograph or a photograph, out of their commitment to represent him without self-serving action of any kind.

Michael Jackson also worked hard to maintain the King of Pop. Every day between 6 and 7 A.M., a new custom-made outfit was delivered to Neverland for him to wear to court. Michael Bush prepared a unique suit with a military jacket and vest for his long-standing client. He always incorporated a special touch just for Michael Jackson, such as gleaming gold buttons, an original lapel insignia, or an eye-grabbing gold medallion around his neck. On every jacket, in a contrasting color, there was an armband, Michael's unique symbol that was designed to remind people of the plight of children around the world. Michael Jackson looked original and spiffy.

"To look good is to feel good," some say, but with Michael Jackson this aphorism was only a futile goal. He was like a soldier who was fighting for his life. He wore the uniform for it ... except that his outfits looked incongruously regal and impressive.

Karen Faye, Michael's make-up artist and hairstylist, would arrive at Michael's room to help him with his final preparations. She would fix his hair and apply his make-up. First, however, they would hug each other and pray together; sometimes Michael wept softly.

He was ready to leave for the courthouse daily by 7 A.M., ready for the degradation ceremony that was awaiting him.

The day of his arraignment was "the worst of all days for Michael, ... he was scared out of his wits, and had not had a wink of sleep in any of the nights previous to it ... though one would never know it by looking at him," wrote J. Randy Taraborrelli. The back of his neck throbbed, his temples hurt, and his vision was blurry, Michael later confided. In spite of his aches and pains, Michael Jackson put on a strong front for the sea of cameras and for the horde of fans.

"They brutally attacked his sexuality," Mesereau laments. Was he asexual, homosexual, heterosexual, a pedophile? "They harped on this question and tried to make him look weird and strange. They attacked his make-up and attire." The prosecutors pulled out all of the stops.

From every nook and cranny of Neverland, all of Michael Jackson's possessions had been reviewed, inspected, and explored in preparation for this trial. The District Attorney's office was dedicated to the mission of getting him convicted. To their disappointment, little surfaced that could be used to fashion Michael as either criminal or deviant. His vast library of many thousands of books included two that contained some photographs of nude men; these had been sent, unsolicited, to Michael by a man from afar. The only other potentially problematic material for Michael Jackson's defense was some "girlie" magazines that were found; these included *Penthouse, Hustler,* and *Playboy*, which are generally perceived to be everyday, mainstream publications. These items were "the best" for their case that the prosecutors could come up with.

Larry Nimmer, who videotaped Neverland for the defense, said off-the-record that the "find" of "girlie" magazines only served to reveal Michael Jackson as "a red-blooded American male" and to confirm his sexual preference as heterosexual.

*   *   *   *   *   *   *   *   *

"Vendetta" is the word that the jury foreman, Paul Rodriguez, used in expressing the likely motive of District Attorney Thomas Sneddon in his case against Michael Jackson. Sneddon had presented "evidence" to a Grand Jury in Santa Barbara County against Michael Jackson during the early nineties. He also encouraged the County of Los Angeles to do the same, and a Grand Jury was convened there also. *Neither brought indictments against Michael Jackson.*

In 1995, Michael released an original song on his *HIStory* album that was called "D.S." Some of its words are "You know he really tried to take me down by surprise.... Dom Sheldon is a cold man.... I bet his mother never taught him right anyway...., a cold man." The song was a thinly disguised affront to Thomas Sneddon, who apparently took it personally.

Sneddon responded by accelerating his efforts to nail the mega-famous star. The Santa Barbara Sheriff's Department set up a website to invite information and complaints against Michael Jackson, and Sneddon followed up with a thorough investigation of every rumor. He traveled to Canada, Australia, and Europe, at taxpayers' expense, to ferret out any "victims" of Michael Jackson; he targeted any possible "sexual misconduct" in his investigations. Sneddon made telephone calls, interviewed people, and looked for leads and potential victims everywhere. He seemed doggedly determined.

"I felt he was a very vindictive person," Paul Rodriguez courageously said about D.A. Sneddon in the aftermath of the verdicts.

Across a decade of the District Attorney's focused efforts, both national and international, he could come up with no witnesses or professed victims to come forward to testify against Michael Jackson. When the Arvizo family seemed willing to fit the bill, Sneddon proceeded—in spite of their checkered history that included alleged perjury and welfare fraud by Janet ... and in spite of their videotaped praises of Michael Jackson and his kindnesses to them.

While the State of California was struggling with budgetary crises and warnings of school teacher cutbacks and potential bankruptcy, Sneddon waged his tax-funded campaign against the global superstar who lived in his jurisdiction. The D.A. hired a PR firm; nine fingerprint experts; and "every conceivable expert" in areas such as accident reconstruction, computer graphics, DNA, forensic accounting, finance, criminalistics, telephones, acoustics, security systems, child molestation, psychology, pathology, and jury consulting. Mock trials were reportedly conducted in anticipation of the Trial of the Century.

Of course, the cost of security alone, although undisclosed, was obviously astronomical. The level of protection provided for the defendant was equivalent to that of the president of the United States, and the thousands of people from other places created the need for round-the-clock assignment of police and sheriffs.

"The prosecution spent more money and time trying to convict Michael Jackson than any prosecution in history," wrote Thomas Mesereau for the book *Michael Jackson Conspiracy.*

Perhaps the D.A. and the other two prosecutors were intoxicated by the power they grabbed by pursuing the great Michael Jackson and dragging him into a court of law … in front of billions of world viewers. They got way more than their "fifteen minutes of fame"; they got hours upon hours of coverage, across nineteen months, from the Neverland raid to the fourteen verdicts at the criminal trial.

Since the 2005 trial, conspiracy theories have surfaced to proffer more sinister explanations for the seemingly fanatical behavior by the D.A. In a relatively small community, wherein the powerful and the moneyed interact regularly and form alliances for their mutual benefit, Michael Jackson might well have represented a wider target than would be readily apparent.

Michael Jackson was the only African American who lived in his geographical area, and he was the wealthiest individual. (To racists, Michael Jackson had the audacity to marry white women.) He owned and occupied the largest tract of land, Neverland Ranch, 2,700 acres in prime wine country. Michael had announced publicly, in self-disclosing pride, that he would "never ever" sell Neverland: "It represents the totality of who I am—it really does; I love it." During pleasant times, he also said, "It's like stepping into Oz; once you come in the gates, the outside world does not exist." Michael wasn't leaving, not by his own design.

If the only black guy around was eliminated somehow, the world might be a better place, some neighbors might reason. In fact, if he went away, his land could be turned into profitable vineyards. It could become available at a bargain-basement price—there, for the taking by some lucky entrepreneur with a little ready money.

Stranger things have happened than cooperation among opportunistic and powerful individuals—even a conspiracy—to effect a prime piece of real estate coming onto the market at a laughably low price. If Michael Jackson were out of the picture—and what better way than imprisonment?—there would be no one with an emotional attachment to the property to be dealt with. There would only be some executor looking to make a fast buck from a quick sale that brings a hefty commission.

Sneddon also appeared to be functioning from a policy that stacked up charges against the accused. If you throw enough charges against a person, the jury is bound to convict on something. With that same line of reasoning, more than seventy sheriffs raided Neverland, more than 100 search warrants were sought and issued, and the local authorities seized Michael's records that had nothing to do with child molestation—his financial, bank, land, and car rental records.

According to journalist Charles Thomson, Sneddon appeared to be tampering with fundamental elements of his case against Michael Jackson whenever evidence came to light which undermined the Arvizo family's claims. Thomson wrote:

> ... [W]hen the DA found out about two taped interviews in which the entire Arvizo family sang Jackson's praises and denied any abuse, he introduced a conspiracy charge and claimed they'd been forced to lie against their will.... [When] Jackson's lawyer ... announced that the singer had a 'concrete, iron-clad alibi' for the dates on the charge sheet, ... the molestation dates on the rap sheet had been shifted by almost two weeks. Sneddon was later caught seemingly trying to plant fingerprint evidence against Jackson, allowing accuser Gavin Arvizo to handle adult magazines during the grand jury hearings, then bagging them up and sending them away for fingerprint analysis.... [T]he media ... seemed perfectly content to perpetuate damning propaganda on the prosecution's behalf, despite a complete lack of corroborative evidence....

At the beginning of the investigatory interview of Gavin Arvizo—which was captured on film and played for the jury—the officers had said to him, "Michael Jackson has done wrong.... He's the bad person, not you.... We're going to try our best to make a ... criminal case...." They then led the boy through a series of questions that were more cajoling than straightforward questions. To many in the courtroom, it appeared to be an interview with two agendas against Michael Jackson—one by the authorities and the other by the young boy, who ultimately did not seem credible to the jury. [Although the prosecutors believed that this footage was the trump card of their case against Michael Jackson, it was this block of evidence—the authorities' interview of the accuser in its entirety—that had great weight with the jury in reaching their conclusions, the "not guilty" verdicts.]

*   *   *   *   *   *   *   *   *

"Intuition" is a word that is typically eschewed by attorneys. In their training and law practices, attorneys are schooled to use their reason, their cognition; to focus on the facts and, from those, to draw rational conclusions. They are cautioned not to allow their feelings to get in the way of their intellects.

Thomas Mesereau used his intuition very purposefully and skillfully in every step of Michael Jackson's trial. He and Susan Yu discarded the "rule book" that they had been taught in law school. They violated the major principles of "good defense attorneys." They took the risks; they followed their intuition....

With jurors, "you are not just dealing with their intellect; you are trying to reach their hearts, souls and spirits," Mesereau insists, and he follows this earnest belief. For the Jackson case, the attorney and his partner reviewed thousands of binders of material for the critical cross-examination of major prosecution witnesses. During his actual cross-examinations, however, he sized up each witness and then proceeded accordingly. Sometimes he was aggressive and confronting; sometimes he decided to converse "delicately and gently" in a non-hostile manner. With Debbie Rowe he did not use a single prepared binder! She looked over at Michael Jackson from the witness stand and visibly softened; she was sympathetic to her ex-husband and showed it. Mesereau pleasantly questioned her accordingly, and her testimony was very beneficial to Michael.

Like Ms. Rowe, many of the witnesses came across very differently than he expected. He decided quickly and spontaneously how to cross-examine each witness; he seized the moment. As the result, "some of the prosecution individuals turned more into my witnesses," for the defense.

The general consensus was that this case was unwinnable, Mesereau says as he recalls the biased, distorted coverage of every aspect of the trial, both before and during the proceedings. "I had to ignore the predictions of the media and focus only on the inside of the courtroom—the jury and judge—and nothing else. I think American juries tend to be at their most intuitive, most instinctive, most intellectual, and most intelligent level when they are deciding a criminal case."

Mesereau adopted—and announced to the jury—the gutsy position that he would *prove* Michael Jackson's *complete innocence.* His did this although theoretically all he needed to demonstrate in court was that there was "reasonable doubt" regarding the defendant's guilt in each charge against him. That is the law.

"I will prove that Michael Jackson is innocent and I ask you to hold me to this contract with you," he told the jury in his opening statement. This unexpected pledge from the attorney surprised everyone and got them to wondering. His high-risk behavior came from human intuition and emotion, not from anything he was ever taught. If the jury thought that he would get "not guilty" verdicts for Michael Jackson through some technicalities or special finesse, he wanted to change their expectations at the very start. He knew that Michael was innocent and he set about to *prove* it.

"Winning this case required unconventional, unorthodox, creative and risky strategies and tactics," Mesereau says, "but, of course, the pundits were wondering what was wrong with me." Why would I assume burdens that legally were not required to win this case?

"The heck with reasonable doubt, I won't raise it until my closing statement. These good, honest, hard-working people want to know the truth.... I have to approach them as the one most willing to present the truth and not as someone hiding behind legal concepts or burdens." Mesereau continued through nearly five months of daily trial sessions without mentioning "presumptions of innocence," "burdens of proof," or "reasonable doubt." This was shocking rule-breaking behavior for a defense attorney.

One of the principal themes of Michael Jackson's defense was that the mother of the accuser was a con artist, that the woman had schooled her children to target celebrities for money. Mesereau argued that "this family knew a criminal conviction would automatically lead to millions of dollars in damages in a parallel civil proceeding. You just take the judgment of criminal conviction and file it in civil court. All that is left is how much money will be awarded in damages." In fact, regardless of the outcome of the criminal trial, the Arvizos could file a lawsuit against Michael Jackson in civil court.

The Arvizos had already visited Larry Feldman, the attorney who achieved the great prize of an approximately $20 million settlement with Michael Jackson on behalf of the Chandler family in 1993.

To the total amazement of everyone, especially other attorneys, Mesereau made another rule-breaking decision. Attorneys are often taught not to allow opposing witnesses to "run off at the mouth." When the prosecutor put Janet Arvizo on the stand for direct examination, she talked on and on in answer to his questions. Mesereau refused to object and simply allowed her to talk on interminably. He believed that "the more she talked, the more fake, offensive, and ridiculous she appeared!"

The prosecutor kept looking over at Mesereau, expecting him to object. Then the most amazing thing happened: *the prosecutor began objecting to his own witness!* "Non-responsive!" and "move to strike!" he called out during Janet's ramblings. "It was a debacle for the prosecution," remembers Mesereau, with pleasure in his voice.

In addition to the content of the bizarre things Janet was saying, the prosecuting attorney's objections to stop her from continuing only served to make her look worse and less credible. She testified that she feared that Michael Jackson would carry off her family in a hot-air balloon as part of his conspiracy to abduct and kidnap them! She also admitted that sometimes she imagines things that did not really happen.

Fortunately, within all of her verbal wanderings during three days on the witness stand, Janet did admit that she *had never witnessed inappropriate behavior from Michael Jackson toward her sons.* She also all but admitted that she had lied under oath in the JC Penney case—in which she had alleged sexual misconduct by its security guards—which resulted in her windfall $152,000 settlement.

When her son Gavin, the alleged victim, took the stand, Mesereau sized him up as a thirteen-year-old "going on thirty." He had been taking acting lessons, wanted to become an actor, and liked being in the spotlight. The attorney perceived this major witness as "clever, dishonest, deceitful, cool and with an obvious agenda." He had lied in his deposition for the JC Penney case, in which his mother made false claims that she was sexually molested by the store's security guards.

By his answers to Mesereau's questions, the boy established that he wanted to stay at Neverland and to take the trips he and his family had enjoyed with Michael Jackson. Gavin testified that he went on amusement rides with Michael and that he met people and did things that he could only dream about before Michael's generosity opened these doors to him.

Then Mesereau did the unthinkable, especially for such a key witness. He asked one of the two "forbidden" questions for defense attorneys. *Never ask "How?" or "Why?"* says the rule book: *You relinquish witness control and you most often won't want to hear the answer. It can destroy your case.*

"And at some point you became very angry at Michael Jackson, didn't you? *Why?*" Mesereau and the others at the defense table braced themselves for the boy's response. This could be the most devastating answer in the five months of the trial.

Gavin started rambling about how Michael had abandoned him and his family. For example, one day when he was at Neverland, the staff informed him that Michael was not on site; soon after, however, he looked across the grounds and saw Michael walking there. Michael was avoiding him; he felt ignored!

"He never mentioned anything about child molestation!" Mesereau remembers with vivid clarity and with delight.

This may have won the case! The alleged victim of sexual molestation did not even mention any kind of inappropriate behavior when asked this key, probing question. Instead, he elaborated on the anger and disappointment he felt when his alleged abuser had in fact moved away from him, had "abandoned" him. He clearly was missing the relationship that he and his family had enjoyed with Michael Jackson.

The jury members listened intently to Gavin's testimony, many of them leaning forward in their seats. Many of them would say post-trial that Gavin was just not credible as "a victim."

It was unfortunate for Michael's defense that Mesereau was unable to get television news veteran Larry King to testify in front of the jury. Lawyers for King and his employer CNN argued that he could not be called upon to reveal in court any legally protected information from a source. Specifically, during pretrial preparations, Mesereau discovered that Larry King had held a conversation with the attorney whom the Arvizos were trying to employ at the time, Larry Feldman, who had gotten the approximately $20 million settlement for Michael Jackson's accuser in 1993. According to Larry King, Feldman had referred to Janet as "a wacko" who was "out for money" when the attorney spoke to the famous newscaster over lunch one day. That event was never presented to the jury because the judge ruled it inadmissible.

Of the sixty witnesses called for Michael's defense, one of the most helpful may well have been actor and comedian Chris Tucker of *Rush Hour* movie fame. Tucker testified that he had also tried to befriend and help the Arvizo family, but they became bold, grasping, and manipulative, taking advantage of his kindnesses, which included money and favors. In fact, Tucker had taken the Arvizos on numerous trips to Neverland, even at times when his friend Michael Jackson was not there. Later, after bad experiences with them, Tucker warned Michael to be wary of these people, as he had decided to discontinue his relationship with them when it became uncomfortable and unpleasant. Tragically, Michael did not heed his friend's warning.

       *   *   *   *   *   *   *   *   *

In his post-trial review, Mesereau luxuriated in the awareness that the risks he had taken on behalf of Michael Jackson in his defense were gutsy but effective.

Even in the jury selection process, Mesereau had opted to ignore the experts. "Sometimes your human soul gives you messages that your legally trained mind rebels against," he says, with the confidence of a successful man.

A jury consultant had been hired by Michael Jackson's defense. Most clients cannot afford the fee because the process employed by jury consultants is so elaborate and time-intensive. They are usually psychologists or social scientists who understand the use of statistics and analytical methods. They conduct telephone interviews to determine what influences people in a given community about the case at hand. They analyze the data according to race, income level, religion, politics, location, occupation, and gender. Then they develop a profile of an ideal juror for the prosecution and an ideal juror for the defense. They establish priorities for the potential selection of jurors by the respective sides of the case.

"I discarded most of the jury research data," explains Mesereau, who opted for his instincts, intuition, and a focus on his reading of human nature.

The jury consulting data discouraged the selection of women with children as jurors in this case. The belief was that the allegations would disturb mothers more than anyone else because of their natural instincts to protect children from predators. Mesereau decided, in contradiction to the scientific findings, that he wanted women, and in particular mothers, on this jury.

His rationale was that his client Michael was "being vilified and demonized as a weird, male predator." The prosecution was trying to demonize Michael Jackson by questioning the direction of his sexuality and by attacking any ambiguous and unconventional behaviors as somehow deviant or dangerous. The prosecutors were trying to prejudice the jury against him. To Mesereau, this was "bigoted, mean-spirited, unprofessional, and ultimately counter-productive."

Females are more open-minded to different lifestyles, he believed. Heterosexual females are far less threatened by attacks on a person's sexuality than heterosexual males. Also, mothers are more perceptive regarding the veracity and credibility of children. Mesereau believed that the women, and especially the mothers, would see through the lies of the Arvizo children and their mother. There were *eight women* on the empaneled jury.

One of the jurors who was welcomed by Mesereau was a young, white disabled man in a wheelchair. The attorney reasoned that such a man would probably not appreciate the vicious attacks by the prosecution on Michael Jackson's appearance, including his skin disorder.

To humanize Michael to the jury was one of the primary objectives. Mesereau emphasized the main characteristics of Michael Jackson. He was a man who never had a real childhood and did not trust adults. He could easily live a profligate life with his great wealth, but instead he devoted himself to the causes of children around the world. He wanted to create an international holiday for children, and he visited a hospital or an orphanage (or both) in every one of his concert cities. The jury saw videotapes of inner city children visiting Neverland and enjoying its zoo, amusement rides, and movie theater. Michael was a proven "protector of children rather than their enemy."

Because "I realized that he is a unique personality who brings all races together rather than divides them," Mesereau stressed this reality in court. He refused to use race as an issue. Mesereau could readily have pointed out that Michael Jackson was the only African-American man in his geographical area and also the wealthiest. He could have presented his client as a target of racism in general and, specifically, as the target of the three white prosecutors, their white male jury consultant, and the other white people in authority positions. Thomas Mesereau did none of this. Michael was color-blind; he loved people of all races and ethnicities; and Mesereau, on Michael's behalf, would not make race an issue.

In this conservative, largely blue-collar community of working people, the overwhelming majority of whom were Caucasian, with some Latinos, Mesereau decided to *ignore* the issue of race at the trial. He also did not request a change of venue to another area, as he could have done.

Thomas Mesereau had gone into the community himself to check out the feelings of the people; he chatted with them; and he asked questions. He discovered that the people seemed to like Michael Jackson. He had a reputation for being polite and friendly when he interacted with townspeople; he bought art and other items from local vendors; and he was the employer of a large number of individuals. To some, he was a "lovely guy." Some residents of the community described the sheriffs as overbearing, and others spoke about their suspicion of a vendetta by certain authorities against Michael Jackson.

Early on, Mesereau requested Michael's father Joseph and brother Jermaine to discontinue their television appearances and interviews, in which they were accusing the prosecutors of racism.

Also, to Mesereau's dismay, Michael's publicist Raymone Bain reportedly called in three of the country's top civil rights activists, during the time of jury deliberations, to support Michael Jackson publicly and to inject race as a factor. Reverend Jesse Jackson, a friend of the Joe Jackson family and of Michael, showed up immediately. Mesereau asked Reverend Jackson—who, in spite of the name, was not a relative of Michael—to turn around and leave; the attorney explained his rationale; and the clergyman angrily complied and left. Reverend Al Sharpton told Mesereau that he would appear only if asked by the attorney, who replied that his help was not needed. Louis Farrakhan of the Nation of Islam, who was engaged in a business relationship with Michael Jackson that included the provision of security personnel, did not show up on the public scene. Farrakhan appeared to sense that his presence would not be helpful to Michael Jackson.

At Thomas Mesereau's urging, Raymone Bain was fired. Michael's defense team and case could not be compromised by a representative of his who, Mesereau believed, was going her own way and "calling in troops" that would become counter-productive.

In private, however, Tom Mesereau knew that race is often a major consideration. He has written and presented on this topic at law schools.

On the personal level, Mesereau, who had earned Michael's trust, got an up-close view of his client's problem with a dual racial identity. One day Michael lifted his shirt to show his attorney his back, which was brown with white patches. "His skin looked like that of a cow," says Mesereau, with respect but also truthfulness. The attorney recognized that his client was self-conscious about his skin condition—his vitiligo—especially as it manifested on his face. This was the reason for Michael's very pale white face and for the make-up that he used to smooth out its appearance, Mesereau realized. His understanding of his unique client became deeper and fuller with every passing day.

*   *   *   *   *   *   *   *   *

Behind the scenes, Thomas Mesereau and Michael Jackson were both dealing with more than their share of pain.

Michael was undergoing the most dreadful episode of his life, with everything at stake for him. He also had other monumental legal and financial burdens. Worst of all for him, he feared the loss of his children if he would be sentenced to prison, if his ex-wife would succeed in obtaining custody of them, or if a government agency would force them away from him and into some foster home. His head was swimming and his heart was drowning.

"And the D.A. wanted to destroy Michael; he wanted to watch him splatter. That was a big part of it...." Thomas Mesereau gained special insight into the workings of the powers-that-be in this case. Michael Jackson could not fathom such a motive against a living human being; it was totally beyond his ability to comprehend.

He seemed to be very depressed at times and suffering from anxiety and serious sleep problems, recalls Mesereau. "I never saw him take any medication or prescription," the attorney says, "but it would not be surprising—in fact even expected—for someone who was going through what he was to be taking medication to help him through such trauma."

Sometimes Mesereau would visit with Michael at Neverland. He could understand why Michael so loved the fantasy-like home he had created.

"It was magical!" Mesereau reminisces; "with twinkling lights on the trees, the beauty of nature all around, and the wonderful animals. I loved being there.... One day while I was visiting, a baby alpaca was born. It was the most beautiful animal I've seen in my life!

"Michael was someone who ... loved to see a child from the inner city who was growing up in poverty and violence come to Neverland and look at a giraffe and smile and look at an elephant and smile. Get some free ice cream and just be happy. It just meant a lot to Michael because he was a very good person...."

Mesereau visited with Michael in his bedroom on a number of occasions. "Michael was lying in bed, exhausted," the attorney recalls with sadness. "He was petrified, and it was heartbreaking to see him losing weight and looking worse and worse across those weeks."

Thomas Mesereau was also dealing with his own deep personal pain. During trial preparations for Michael, he discovered that his only sister was diagnosed with terminal cancer. She had a tumor in her brain and in her lung. She died in early 2005, during Michael's trial.

"When she came home from the hospital," Mesereau recalls sadly, "there was a delivery of a huge bouquet of flowers, so large that they had trouble getting it through her door. The flowers were from Michael, and with them was an original poem that he composed for her. In spite of his own anguish at the time, he reached out to her in this special and personal way. That was Michael Jackson."

As Michael's attorney, Mesereau suffered the same harsh treatment directed at his client's other advocates. He learned that members of the media were investigating him, tracking down former girlfriends for any "dirt" they could find. They also continued to try clever ruses of all kinds to get to him, to find out something personally damaging or embarrassing to him, or to trick him into revealing some juicy tidbit about Michael Jackson. He was offered business deals and special favors by media for exclusive disclosures. Thomas Mesereau rejected every one of them.

The feeding frenzy of media, from the tabloids to reputable mainstream outlets, was very disturbing to Mesereau. From the channel-surfing he did during short breaks from his trial preparations, he saw that the coverage was shockingly destructive and biased. Daily, allegations were reported, but not the subsequent testimony and evidence that contradicted and refuted them. The sordid allegations were left dangling in viewers' minds without the follow-up that should have blown them away.

"We would destroy the credibility of the prosecution's witnesses on cross-examination, but that never made it to the telecasts and newsprint," Mesereau explains. "It was like a parallel universe. It was both incredible and awful. I'd see coverage and wonder 'what was that?' It had no connection to the truth of what happened in court."

Charles Thomson, on June 14, 2010, described the media as "out of control":

The sheer amount of propaganda, bias, distortion and misinformation is almost beyond comprehension.... [T]he newspaper cuttings, the trial that was relayed to us didn't even resemble the trial that was going on inside the courtroom.

The transcripts show an endless parade of seedy prosecution witnesses perjuring themselves on an almost hourly basis and crumbling under cross examination.

The media detailed, day after day, the "heinous accusations and lurid innuendo." Thomson reminded us that when news of the raid on Neverland Ranch broke, news channels abandoned their schedules and switched to 24-hour coverage of the unfolding "scandal." Michael Jackson's image was doomed by the melodrama created by the Santa Barbara District Attorney and Sheriff's Office and by the sensationalized coverage that exploded onto television and computer screens from media, interested only in ratings and revenue.

In addition, millions of viewers watched late-night talk-show hosts, like Jay Leno, make cruel and damning jokes about Michael Jackson. They were usually raw and fierce, and they could be repeated over office water coolers the next morning by "wise guys" who loved a joke at someone else's expense. Mesereau was mortified over the media coverage, whether it was cloaked as "the news" or delivered as humor. "Ninety-nine percent of it was negative," he remembers with a visible wince; "it was awful."

The *extent* to which the media would go to snatch relevant people for appearances on their sometimes lurid programs was shocking to Tom Mesereau. After the verdict, he discovered that he was being sought aggressively by the "bookies," attractive young women whose job it is to entice key people to agree to an interview with their employer media outlet. The attorney hid out to avoid them and their clever ploys to get to him.

"Michael Jackson, bottom line, was a delicate, sensitive soul in a harsh, mean-spirited, cruel world," Mesereau says. "And the way he was tortured by people that wanted to make him controversial and profit off of his eccentricity was one of the great tragedies of our time."

*   *   *   *   *   *   *   *   *

Perhaps the most terrible, soul-shattering charges that Michael Jackson faced were that, in addition to allegedly harming the Arvizo children, he was the mastermind of a *conspiracy* to imprison a family, to abduct children, and to extort. Mesereau describes his client's reactions:

> ... It was painful, it was horrifying [to Michael].... These are things that *Michael was not capable of even imagining* and to formally charge him with this and then to call witnesses who clearly were not telling the truth, to try and build a case against him, was frightening and very disheartening for him. [Emphasis added]

What the D.A. tried to prove was that Michael held the Arvizos at Neverland against their will and that he extorted them—not for money, but for their testimony on his behalf in a proposed television rebuttal to Bashir's destructive documentary. While the Arvizos stayed at Neverland, during the period of their alleged captivity, they were driven by Michael's staff into the local town for toys shopping, dental work, and a variety of beauty treatments for the mother. They were charging thousands of dollars to Michael Jackson.

"How many times did you go to Neverland to have to try to escape from there?" Mesereau asked the tongue-in-cheek question at trial.

In truth—which was proven by log books and receipts—the Arvizos were driven to and from Neverland by Michael's employees *at least three times* during the period of their alleged "captivity"! There was ample testimony by staff members at Neverland Ranch to prove that Michael's luxury vehicles transported the family, returning them to their Los Angeles apartment when they wanted. In addition, the Ranch is fenced off by only simple, easily-breached wood fences; there are no secured fences around the property; and the Arvizos could therefore have left at any time.

"We were not even allowed to know the time of day," Janet testified in an attempt to emphasize the level of trauma that she and her children suffered. In reality, she and her children were staying in the Elizabeth Taylor Guesthouse, the most lavish on the property; through its windows, across the grounds, a large, tall clock was clearly visible. Larry Nimmer testified that working clocks were distributed in profusion throughout Neverland. In addition, many of the clocks would light up throughout the night. Nimmer showed video footage of all kinds and shapes of clocks on the grounds and in the main house, to which the Arvizos had full access. In fact—any time at their request—they were served special-order meals in Michael Jackson's kitchen, prepared by his chefs and cooks. On a kitchen wall, a large clock was prominently displayed.

Gavin told the authorities, in his official taped statements, that he was afraid at Neverland, specifically scared "that they might kill us." The boy was on a roll. His allegations grew more bizarre as the investigators encouraged him: Michael Jackson is the bad person; we're trying to get him; and we need your help.

Because Michael Jackson did not even own a cell phone, it was difficult to convince the jury that he had planned an abduction of this family across days and weeks. He went out and about, including to Miami, Florida, during this time period. There were no phone records that the prosecutors could use to connect him to any communications that would have planned a kidnapping.

Also, the Arvizos visited Michael Jackson in Miami! They were flown to and from that city in the private jet provided by him.

It is interesting—even shocking—that the D.A. never bothered to bring charges against any of the other alleged co-conspirators, all of them associates of Michael Jackson. One might ask the appropriate question, "How can there be a conspiracy by only one person?" And who, in his wildest imaginings, could envision Michael Jackson personally abducting a family of four ambulatory individuals? Or even *wanting* to do such a thing?

*   *   *   *   *   *   *   *   *

Michael Jackson made clear that he was heterosexual; he was *not* gay, as erroneously reported by some tabloids. He was not a child molester or a pedophile. Of these realities, Thomas Mesereau is certain. No one explored the private life of Michael more than his lead defense attorney. Mesereau had to get to know as much as he possibly could so that he could properly defend his client.

Michael did share his two-story bedroom with children, boys and girls, and also women. It was like a college dorm at times. Michael perceived his room as a place to entertain, interact, and "crash." People there would talk, laugh, play games, watch movies, and fall asleep. Some people do that kind of thing in high school or college. Michael—who could not regularly attend secondary school or college because of his career explosion during those years of his life—created a kind of dormitory setting for himself in his home. He was unconventional in his viewpoint, yes, but he was also an innocent; it was all non-sexual.

When he was growing up in a tiny two-bedroom home in Indiana, its eleven occupants—two parents and nine children— used their beds as furniture; they had to. Not only did the family members share their beds, but they used them for playing games, studying, eating, listening to music, and other everyday activities. When on tour, Michael had to use his hotel room bed as his base of operations; he often entertained people who sat on his bed with him.

"The most loving thing you can do is share your bed with someone," he said in the "Living with Michael Jackson" documentary. "Always give the beds to the company, you know?" he continued, reminiscent of the hospitality lessons he had learned from his mother, who was known as a consummate hostess.

Many individuals at his trial testified in support of Michael's childlike innocence. Some were young men who had maintained a mutually caring relationship with him for years, from the days of their childhood. Michael cherished that innocent, guileless part of himself.

*   *   *   *   *   *   *   *   *

By the time the trial was conducted in 2005, Janet Arvizo had become "Janet Jackson" by marrying a man named Jay Jackson—no relation to Michael. She had recently divorced David after years of alleged abuse at his hands. She asked Judge Melville to allow her to use her new name, but the judge refused, citing the confusion that would be caused. Janet also had an eight-month-old child by her new husband.

Janet Arvizo pled guilty to welfare fraud and was convicted in February 2006. She was required to serve 150 hours in community service and to pay $8,600 in restitution. She served no jail time.

Evan Chandler, at 65, committed suicide on November 5, 2009, less than five months after Michael Jackson's death. He was found dead in bed in his luxury New Jersey apartment; he had shot himself in the head; the gun was still in his hand, according to police. Evan Chandler left no note or other written communication.

In 1993, Evan Chandler allegedly had attempted to extort $20 million from Michael Jackson. When seemingly unsuccessful, he appears to have instigated the sexual molestation accusations by his son Jordie against the superstar. Soon thereafter, the Chandlers obtained a settlement for approximately $20 million. In the settlement agreement, it was stipulated that "neither side admits wrongdoing to the other." (The Chandlers denied any wrongdoing at any time.)

In 2006, Jordie Chandler filed charges against his father, Evan Chandler, for alleged physical abuse. He accused his father of life-threatening behavior that included trying to choke him, spraying him in the eyes with Mace or pepper spray, and striking him on the head with a dumbbell weight.

His mother, June Chandler, testified at Michael's 2005 trial that her son Jordie had not spoken to her in more than eleven years. June was also divorced from her second husband, David Schwartz.

Jordie Chandler made himself unavailable for Michael Jackson's trial. He would not testify, although he could have chosen to do so. He had reportedly left the country at the time. Thomas Mesereau disclosed, at a Harvard lecture after the trial, that he had witnesses who were going to say that Jordie told them that molestation by Michael Jackson never happened and that he would not speak to his parents again for what they made him say. Jordie sought and got legal emancipation from his parents in a court of law and then disassociated from them.

Regarding the Jordie Chandler matter, Geraldine Hughes came forward and wrote a compelling book, *Redemption* (1997, 2004), in which she states unequivocally that she witnessed the "set-up" of Michael Jackson by Evan Chandler and his attorney, Barry Rothman. Ms. Hughes was the sole legal secretary who worked for Rothman in the summer of 1993. She reveals the "truth about the Michael Jackson child molestation allegations as I witnessed from inside the walls of the accuser's camp." She comes forward as a "witness who can attest to his innocence." She never met Michael Jackson nor did she receive any compensation or support for her disclosures from him or any of his people.

Ms. Hughes affirms:

There were a lot of things about Michael Jackson being reported on the news and in the tabloids that were simply not true and, likewise, there were a lot of factual events that went unreported that were crucial in this case....
It is time to set the record straight.

Among her many disclosures about the sordid matter, including the alleged extortion attempt, the author presents excerpts from the recorded telephone conversation between Evan Chandler and Dave Schwartz, the stepfather of Jordie. In that conversation, Evan Chandler, father of Jordie, says:

I am prepared to move against Michael Jackson. It's already set. There are other people involved that are waiting for my phone call that are in certain positions. I've paid them to do it. Everything's going according to a certain plan that isn't just mine. Once I make that phone call, this guy is going to destroy everybody in sight in any devious, nasty, cruel way that he can do it. And I've given him full authority to do that.

Hughes describes the authorities who got involved in the matter: "It appears that many of them got caught up in the frenzy and did not want to let go when no evidence to support the allegations could be found." Michael Jackson was never charged with any crime related to Jordie or his family, but he was "put through the wringer" by these calculating, unsavory people for their financial gain.

* * * * * * * * *

Thomas Mesereau learned, in the aftermath of Michael Jackson's full acquittal in 2005, that "notoriety trumps credibility." A literary agent approached Mesereau with an offer to represent him to the publishing industry for a book that she encouraged him to write about Michael Jackson and his notorious trial. *Nine* publishing companies rejected the prospect of a book by Mesereau, who got the distinct impression that, unless he would reveal some sinister material about Michael Jackson, none of the publishers would pick up his story. They were simply "not interested" in an honest, forthright account of the real situation. They were not interested in Michael Jackson's innocence. *"Have a nice day."*

"Generally speaking, there was no strong public backlash that we had to deal with after Michael's acquittal," Mesereau explains in 2011. Most people liked Michael; many intuited that something was very wrong with the over-the-top prosecution and nasty media coverage. Michael came across as meek, mild-mannered, and malleable in the on-camera footage of his trial comings and goings.

Although his fans were ecstatic over the verdicts, the general population was mostly *"blasé." "Oh well"* seemed to be the prevailing response, if not in so many words, in the spirit. Also, most people didn't even really know what he was "exactly" charged with, except "bad" behaviors with children.

"We saw nothing like the public outcry and outrage in the aftermath of the O.J. Simpson and Casey Anthony acquittals," Mesereau elaborates in 2011. "In both of those cases, the reactions across the country were extreme; people were incredibly angry." Mesereau felt not only relief and elation on behalf of his innocent, vindicated client, but he appreciated the generalized sense of "okayness" with the legal outcome that he perceived from the public at large.

Financial advances had been offered for book deals to a number of individuals with the expectation that the thematic direction would be Michael Jackson's being sentenced to prison for the rest of his natural life. After he was acquitted, tabloids continued to offer significant monetary bounties for people who would come forward with reports of any improprieties by Michael Jackson. Some of his "friends" conspired against him, and some of his employees shopped the tabloids for the best deal for "secret information" of one kind or another. The more money on the table, the more sordid the allegations became.

It was the profiteers who lost from Michael Jackson's innocence, from his legal vindication. Literally *billions of dollars* would have been made by tabloids and mainstream media if Michael Jackson had gone to prison. Stories under their control—not his—would have been cranked out across many years in the future. Many relished the prospect of sheer enjoyment of a prospective triumph over the man— the mega-star—who had made himself so unavailable to them. On a slow news day, they could always design a story about the misery and sorry plight of Michael Jackson in prison. Topics would include brutality directed at him by other prisoners, mysterious pen-pals and secret marriages, furtive visitors, downward-spiraling health, jail-bred idiosyncrasies, and suicide watches. *When would he finally end it all?*

And just think—they would savor writing the words—*he once was King.*

To contribute to making Michael Jackson's situation as bad as possible—for his image, his reputation, and his feelings—*this was the most publicized trial in world history.*

"The media's irresponsible coverage of the trial made it impossible for Jackson to ever feel truly vindicated," even after 14 unanimous "not guilty" verdicts. Charles Thomson described the dynamics:

The story was over. There were no apologies and no retractions. There was no scrutiny—no inquiries or investigations. Nobody was held to account for what was done to Michael Jackson. The media was content to let people go on believing their heavily skewed and borderline fictitious account of the trial.... And those who refused to tell us [the truth] remain in their jobs unchecked, unpunished and free to do exactly the same thing to anybody they desire. Now that's what I call injustice.

Well, Michael Jackson triumphed and transcended. Ultimately, he was a survivor. He was made of strong fiber; he could trace his family history to his roots, to a slave in the Deep South. He studied—in history books and the Bible—the great men who overcame the worst of circumstances. Now he was one of them. Severely wounded but alive and free, he would move on....

> ... The epitome of western celebrity obsession[,]...
> a 21st century lynching....
> I think [this trial] will be remembered
> as one of the most shameful episodes
> in journalistic history.
> — Charles Thomson

[Michael's] wistful desire to heal the world with love, music and artistry clashed horribly with the barbaric way he was exploited. The world is a far better place because of him.
— Thomas Mesereau

The Morass of Michael Jackson's Finances

**If you enter this world
knowing you are loved
and you leave this world
knowing the same,
then everything that happens
in between can be dealt with.**
— Michael Jackson

**When you're a show business child
people make a lot of decisions
concerning your life
when you're out of the room.**
— Michael Jackson,
Word Up! Magazine

*F*ive million dollars. That is the amount of cash—give or take a few thousand—that Michael Jackson kept with him, locked in the most secure safe in his home or hotel suite.

News media reported, after Michael's passing, that $5 million in cash "disappeared from his Holmby Hills home." Shortly thereafter, it was returned to authorities.

Why did Michael Jackson ensure that he had this astronomical sum of money within arm's reach?

Michael wanted to have immediately available a reasonable sum that could be used to ransom his children in the event that one or more of them would be kidnapped! His security teams across time came to understand their boss's motivation. Michael Jackson lived in constant fear that his kids would be snatched away by a clever, nefarious individual or team of professionals. During the months of his representation of Michael, attorney Thomas Mesereau learned early on that his troubled client worried that his children might be kidnapped.

Anyone who knew anything about Michael Jackson knew that he would pay a king's ransom to reclaim his child or children if taken from him.

"I almost lost my children," Mr. Jackson said more than once to his security personnel, the fear audible in his voice. If Mr. Jackson had been sentenced to prison time after his nasty trial, his children would probably have been placed by a state agency with ... *who knows?* He didn't know, of course, but the thought made him shiver.

"It would kill me to lose them," he would say, and the refrain echoed in the minds of his listeners....

As the biological mother of Prince and Paris, Debbie Rowe had taken advantage of the 2003 charges against Michael Jackson by filing a petition in domestic court to restore her parental rights. In addition to that serious legal assault on Michael, the California Department of Children Services launched a full investigation into his fitness as a father; their eventual determination was that he was indeed a good parent; but he endured months of agony and maddening ambiguity. Along with all that he suffered from the devastatingly serious charges against him in criminal court, Michael Jackson worried constantly about the potential loss of his three little ones. *Would he lose the most precious gifts in his life?*

Fortunately, after his full acquittal at trial came an acceptable outcome of Ms. Rowe's legal machinations. She accepted a large financial settlement; Michael kept his children; and she obtained the right to visit them, which she exercised rarely across subsequent years. To the surprise of the prosecutors at Michael Jackson's trial, when they called her as a witness for their case, Ms. Rowe came across as deeply sympathetic to Michael Jackson. On the stand, she made it clear that she wanted to be his *"friend"*—a helpful sentiment for his defense but an unlikely outcome of any legal proceedings that she brought against him.

As rationale for the at-hand five million dollars, Michael Jackson could not trust the people who controlled his purse strings. If one of his children were kidnapped and held for ransom, he could not rely upon them promptly to produce the requisite money to effect their release and return.

In addition, because Michael Jackson could travel often, readily, and immediately, as he wished, to other states and countries abroad for various reasons, he could not count on the availability of quick money from a banking institution. The hours of operation alone could be a complicating factor if he needed money fast.

Therefore, across many years Michael Jackson and his security teams guarded his stash of millions, kept within arm's reach of his sleeping quarters.

When Mr. Jackson traveled by plane, he carried a suitcase full of cash with him. The vigilance, focus, and anxiety of his guards increased accordingly. The saying "Cash is king" had real meaning to Mr. Jackson. He knew that he could exercise some real control by having ready cash—not directed by others in his employ—available to him at a minute's notice.

Early on, it became apparent to his Vegas security personnel that their boss did not understand the status of his financial affairs. He had "people" who managed his assets and holdings, which included extensive publishing rights to songs by *dozens* of recording artists at the caliber of the Beatles, Bob Dylan, Neil Diamond, Taylor Swift, Elvis Presley, Madonna, and the Jonas Brothers. In 1985, Michael Jackson had bought the rights to the ATV catalog of thousands of songs, including the majority of the Beatles works, for $47.5 million, which turned out to be a great deal for him. His share of this publishing catalog has since been valued at as much as one billion dollars or more—depending upon the complex factors used for making such estimates.

It is interesting to note that Michael signed over his "power of attorney" to John Branca, his manager at the time, who finalized the deal in England. It was Branca—not Michael—who actually signed the historical documents for the purchase of the ATV catalog, the most valuable in the annals of recorded music. Michael Jackson obtained a spectacular outcome that time with a trusted representative who negotiated the transaction on his behalf and appropriately exercised his power of attorney. In later years, unfortunately, Michael continued the dangerous practice with others in his employ who were not so trustworthy.

Michael Jackson was in fact a shrewd entrepreneur with excellent instincts and a studied approach to investing, but with the accumulation of so much wealth and the opportunity to increase it came a horde of other people to oversee and manage it. From the time when he was a child star, Michael always had his monetary matters handled by designated accountants, lawyers, and management personnel.

It seemed consummately ironic to Boyd Williams, Baron James, and Michael Garcia that, although millions of dollars flowed to and from Michael Jackson's accounts, the security guards themselves went unpaid for weeks at a time. The boss's managers neglected to execute the simple procedures that would get them paid in a timely manner.

The men did not blame their boss for this incongruous, bizarre, and frustrating situation. Michael Jackson had neither a checkbook of his own nor did he receive financial statements. He was not directly accessing the myriad accounts in his name; his designated "people" did everything for him ... or did not do it, as the case might be. From what the security team could tell, it had always been this way for Michael Jackson.

Thomas Mesereau knew that Raymone Bain signed the checks for Michael Jackson while she was his manager. He and Susan Yu went unpaid for their services for long periods of time, while Ms. Bain made excuses and actually used the cliché, "The check is in the mail," when it was not. The attorneys did not blame Michael; they knew that he was "out of the loop" regarding his own accounts and bills payable.

Since Michael Jackson's earliest days of earning big money, his father Joe, as the manager of his sons' musical group, controlled their income and expenditures. Michael would be given a modest allowance by Joseph, from which he would typically buy art supplies or, to his father's chagrin, purchase candy for the entire neighborhood of kids. Later, starting when he was a young man in his early twenties, he replaced his father with others in his employ who managed his business affairs and finances, including attorney John Branca, who in 2009 also became one of the two trustees of Michael's Estate. There were not only a series of managers and proxies across time, there were many different people, among them attorneys and accountants, who held sway over the flow of Michael Jackson's moneys.

In the transition from one manager to another, sometimes huge amounts of Michael Jackson's money remained in an account, overlooked or ignored. Other accounts would be opened, with the new manager having oversight and power over them.

When Michael Jackson wanted a new Cadillac Escalade, it simply appeared one day in front of his home. Someone somewhere made the necessary arrangements, including the delivery of the registered vehicle to the front door. Michael Jackson did not need to sign a title, apply for a license, or ensure appropriate registration. All of these tasks were performed invisibly for him.

It was all he ever knew. Michael Jackson lived in a charmed world, on the one hand, but in the dark on the other. It was a dark world in more ways than one....

Many weeks passed during which the members of the security team went without getting paychecks. Because both Williams and James needed timely money for themselves and their families, this serious lapse in appropriate pay cycles caused them great hardship, worry, and embarrassment. They faced serious threats of their own personal vehicles being repossessed and cancellations of their home utilities; they became accustomed to hostile responses from their creditors.

When they sheepishly informed Mr. Jackson every so often, he expressed genuine concern.

"Listen, I am the machine that keeps everything going, and these men take care of me and my children," Mr. Jackson said on the telephone in their hearing. "Pay them!" he insisted.

"You'll be paid on Thursday," the boss informed his security guards after he hung up the phone. "I'm really sorry about this."

Thursday would come and go; then another and another. At its worst, the team endured four months in a row without getting a paycheck.

It is reasonable to assume that these breaches of payment responsibility were, at least at times, attributable to the boss's manager's purposeful forgetfulness. After all, the assignment of his security team members to Michael Jackson was not the decision of this manager, who would have preferred in these strategic positions certain hand-picked individuals that were more malleable to her. Maybe these men would just quit, allowing the manager to put into place individuals who would do her bidding. Williams and James were loyal to Mr. Jackson and him alone, and they prided themselves on their consistency of trustworthiness and genuine dedication to his welfare.

Imagine a probable scenario.... Two of Mr. Jackson's "people" would be vying for the same loan on his behalf. Let's say that the loan was in the staggering amount of $30 million. Both would obtain bank-approved loan documents that were prepared by their respective lending agencies to secure the loan. All that would be needed was Mr. Jackson's signature. The victor would receive, let's say, an 8% finder's fee, resulting in $2.4 million—not bad for a few strokes of Michael Jackson's pen. To get to Mr. Jackson, each of the loan "finders" would need to go through his security people.

It was more than obvious that individuals connived their way into Michael Jackson's circle by belittling and criticizing others whom Mr. Jackson had come to trust. His security team members witnessed "a constant war of words" among the boss's attorneys and manager. Obtaining and maintaining financial control of Michael Jackson was the dogged goal of many of his people, some of whom appeared to be "like modern-day pirates." They would often try to use his bodyguards to their own personal advantage.

"Have him sign *my* papers, Boyd," would come the directive by phone from the boss's manager, who wanted Michael Jackson to execute a particular document or contract. "When will Mr. Jackson sign the papers I sent over?" another voice would inquire. These were often competing transactions, urged by different individuals for execution, to the exclusion of the others.

Feeling desperate about their own personal finances, the members of the security team grew to resent especially the attorneys who were on the receiving end of multimillion-dollar fees on Mr. Jackson's payroll.

Michael Jackson was not the culprit in this ongoing drama. He seemed to believe that these attorneys and his manager had his best interests at heart, but as so many others had done, they used him and his resources for their own gain.

Bottom line, the off-site, invisible representatives of Michael Jackson applied all of the incoming funds first to their own fees. The team went unpaid when there was reportedly "insufficient funds" for their payroll. Mr. Jackson believed that the men who protected and took care of him and his children every day should be the priority of his representatives who were controlling the money spigot. However, he seemed helpless in getting them paid, and he was obviously frustrated and noticeably upset over the entire "dreadful situation."

His management people paid the royal sum of *one million dollars* to lease the Summerlin home in Las Vegas *for only six months*. Mr. Jackson never saw the house until he arrived in the U.S. on that first night during Christmas week of 2006. It had been on the real estate market for years with an eventual asking price of $1.5 million. Someone was getting a hefty commission in this more-than-sweet deal for the owner and whomever else, the middleman.

Toward the end of the lease period, with the help of his security personnel, Michael Jackson and his little family moved out of the Summerlin house. He had no intention of returning, and its management company was not happy about the non-renewal of a one-million-dollar rental agreement.

Raymone Bain, as Michael's spokesperson, issued a statement that said, in part, "Mr. Jackson has not 'left' Las Vegas nor is he being 'evicted' from his residence in Las Vegas. He decided not to exercise the option to purchase the house. Period." Rumors found their way into print and newscasts about Michael Jackson's prompt departure from the house as if there were some unsavory reasons for it. In reality, the house was a security nightmare for Michael and for his security team.

Just as in the days when he was a child but earning millions for his record company and family, Michael Jackson exercised little control over his finances. He was not directly managing any part of his vast financial empire, and it was probably impossible for any one individual to oversee the magnitude of his affairs. With no financial statements provided him, an accurate picture of his economic position was totally lacking. Mr. Jackson didn't even know which banks and other institutions held his money or how much he had or didn't have. This deplorable situation continued through his last months, as he confided to Reverent June Gatlin that he was kept clueless as to his money affairs.

With regular verbal assurances by his "people" that everything was "fine," Mr. Jackson signed his name wherever he was directed to do so. It was understandable that these employees could easily take advantage of him. *Everything was not fine.*

An analysis of Michael Jackson's life during these years reveals that his financial troubles did not stem from expensive shopping sprees or an excessively lavish lifestyle, as compared to celebrity circles. Massive mismanagement of his affairs and finances, exorbitant attorneys' fees, and high-rate interest paid on loans were the real reasons for his downward-spiraling economic condition. His assets were heavily leveraged, and his people were earning fees from the various serial transactions; the more transactions, the more fees. Michael Jackson's financial status became a messy quagmire of debt and asset leverage.

The situation was ripe with opportunities for skimming and inflating bills, hidden commissions, and mysterious fees from all around.

His security team soon discovered, via email communications, that incredible amounts of money—millions of dollars—were channeled through the pipeline of Mr. Jackson's maze of accounts on a regular basis, but their boss barely seemed to notice the flow, at least not the specifics of it. To the security men, who were impressed by "all of the zeroes" in the amounts of money, Mr. Jackson's apparent lack of notice appeared to be a combination of apathy and trust on his part, and probably more of the latter. It was also undoubtedly the result of years of conditioning.

On more than one occasion, his security team was threatened by hotel management with ejection of their client after an unpaid balance for the bill resulted from a credit card having been declined. "Just give them another credit card," Mr. Jackson would tell them. Reportedly, the Reverend Jesse Jackson paid for Michael Jackson's hotel bill when his visiting friend was unable to cover its cost with his own credit. His security guards would sometimes use their own credit cards for Mr. Jackson at hotels, for the dual purpose of disguising their boss's identity and paying his immediate bills without unpleasant complications. They would then apply for reimbursement as one of Michael Jackson's creditors.

Although Mr. Jackson was informed, from time to time, of certain financial setbacks, he was naïve regarding the urgency of some situations and he was protected in large measure by everyone around him. The boss was living in an entirely different realm from everyday people, and *he had never known anything else.*

The stark reality was that, if Michael Jackson had five million dollars in cash only steps away, his everyday needs were being met, and he and his children were comfortable in a lovely residential setting, he was content. When he wanted something, it would appear. When he wanted to go somewhere, the best transportation was immediately arranged and provided. When he traveled, it was by private jet and the best security vehicles, driven and escorted by trained, skilled people. It was like magic.

Money became like the props in a board game for Michael Jackson; it seemed, at times, not real. Or, it was like silly putty; it could be pulled and stretched in so many ways. His managers and accountants shuffled it around from place to place. They borrowed and leveraged; his assets were pawns in the game.

If his management personnel fulfilled Michael's immediate needs, they could otherwise do what they wanted. He was ostensibly happy and out of their way. They could juggle accounts, make deals, negotiate arrangements, and pay his bills or not pay them. Those bills included the payroll for his security guards, which was often a "back-burner" line item.

His security team members often ran errands for Mr. Jackson to pick up very costly items for him and/or his children. The irony of it all was not lost on the unpaid men, but they reminded themselves that Michael Jackson had never experienced any other "M.O." across the entire span of his life. He could not relate to their worry and sense of urgency over the paychecks that would buy their families' food, clothing, and shelter, and maintain their personal vehicles and necessary insurance policies.

Most of his on-site employees found it impossible to be angry with Michael Jackson, who was so disarming in his demeanor, childlike in his genuine naivety, and fragile in appearance. He was pale and thin; the bones in his chest protruded and were visible when he wore his V-neck T-shirts. At 5'9", he weighed approximately 140 pounds. He seemed so vulnerable....

His Vegas-based security team members were not the only people who were willing to work for Michael Jackson without timely payment. Many vendors and providers of various services to Michael were happy just to have an association with him. People who were so fortunate as to obtain employment with Michael Jackson were delighted on many levels. If things didn't work out—or if they decided to succumb to opportunism and throw principle to the wind—they could always just sue him. Litigation against Michael Jackson always seemed to work out well for the litigant, as he was generally willing to throw money at the problem for it to go away. Unfortunately for Michael, however, most of the lawsuits were for tens of millions of dollars, or at least started out at that level.

Michael Jackson was kept unaware of all of the moving parts of managing his household, his security, and his business empire. As a case in point, he never had his own credit card until he was nearly fifty years old. Michael's head of security helped his boss fill out the required forms, which the bodyguard then faxed to the credit agency. When Mr. Jackson first tried to use his card, it was declined; he had failed to telephone to authorize its use.

Sometimes the registrations for Michael Jackson's security vehicles expired; his manager had failed to renew them. Bills and invoices went unpaid and the interest due on them accrued.

Some people within Michael Jackson's professional network used scare tactics to intimidate him as a form of control. Michael was motivated by love but also occasionally by fear. When a person does not have direct power over his affairs, a sense of insecurity sets in, and those who do have power can manipulate and exploit him. Thomas Mesereau got an up-close view of these dynamics on several occasions when he was called to Neverland to help work out a solution to a conflict on behalf of Michael. He witnessed the opposing pulls and tugs on Michael from his various advisers and managers.

Even when he was a young celebrity in the eighties, Michael Jackson was subjected to rip-offs. "When the vendors saw him coming their way, they would triple the prices of all of their goods just because they knew Michael represented a windfall for them....

The fact that the prices were raised especially for him did not escape Michael," wrote J. Randy Taraborrelli, who discussed this matter with him.

"They see me coming," explained Michael; "they take advantage of me. That's not really fair, is it?" He would be accompanied by his bodyguard, who would pull out a wad of hundred-dollar bills to pay for the purchases of his usually masked boss. It was the *Michael Jackson factor*. It was the vendors who probably should have been wearing masks, based upon their rapacious behavior.

Michael Jackson's life was replete with "smooth criminals," con artists, profiteers, and sycophants.

Michael Jackson's hobby in Vegas was making online bids and purchases of certain collector's items such as Peter Pan memorabilia, always a favorite of his. He also invested thousands of dollars in books for himself and his children. The boss perceived books as an important investment. He valued their staying power— the permanency of printed, bound books that conveyed knowledge, information, and inspiration.

He was also a devoted reader of *The Wall Street Journal* and *Robb Report;* he sustained an interest in financial matters even though he was not directly involved in his own. Michael Jackson had always demonstrated a good head for business. His purchase of the publishing rights to the ATV catalog and other savvy business decisions proved his excellent instincts and intimate knowledge of the workings of the entertainment industry. Donald Trump referred to Michael as "brilliant" and a good businessman, who "changed during the last decade of his life," to his financial detriment. Mr. Trump came to know Michael Jackson well when he and Lisa Marie Presley lived for months at the Trump Tower in New York.

Whom could Mr. Jackson trust? His Las Vegas security men worried over this question, on behalf of their troubled boss, especially when such vast amounts of money were at stake and so little information was provided to govern decisions, to authorize expenditures.

Apparently, from time to time, the boss's trust level seemed to plummet relative to those who worked for him, his various representatives, surrogates, and proxies. Mr. Jackson's concerns about trust generated to his security guards, at least until they proved themselves to him.

When the particular incident occurred, they didn't understand what they perceived as paranoia on his part. It was later, in the fullness of their discoveries about his finances, past betrayals, and some of his self-serving people, that the men realized why Mr. Jackson chose to test them....

One morning, while standing alone in a public place, Boyd Williams was approached by an unidentified man, who whispered to him, "Would you like to earn an easy $50,000?"

Shocked by so overt and stunning an offer from a stranger, Williams asked, "What do you mean?"

"If you will report to me the exact whereabouts of Michael Jackson at a specific time next week, the money is yours. Call me tomorrow if you want to know more," said the mystery man, thrusting a business card into the guard's hand.

Boyd did not telephone the man, nor did he speak about this incident to anyone. He wondered if Baron James had gotten this same offer, but he was afraid to ask. Williams was troubled over the brief, cryptic conversation, turning it around and around in his mind, but he decided that if he did nothing, all would be well.

Some days passed. Then, Mr. Jackson asked him, from the back seat of the SUV, "Boyd, did you get an unusual offer last week?" The guard froze at first; he knew what the boss meant by the question.

"Yes, sir," he confessed, turning around to look Mr. Jackson in the eye. Then he explained about the unknown man, the business card, and the $50,000 offer.

"I'm proud of you, Boyd," Mr. Jackson exclaimed. "If you had made that phone call, you would have been fired, of course." He continued, "But you did the right thing. You should have told me about it when it happened, though."

"Yes, sir, I know, and I'm sorry about that, but I didn't want to worry you," Williams replied.

Boyd Williams discovered that the boss had set up this experiment to test his loyalty. *A lesson learned.* He not only kept his job but he earned the trust of Mr. Jackson, which he vowed he would forever work to maintain.

Michael Jackson was dealing with post-trial travail on many levels. His public image was tarnished by the media's discoloration of every aspect and angle of the trial proceedings. They glossed over the legal establishment of his innocence, and many of them implied or opined that his acquittal of all charges by the jury was an erroneous decision. His music career appeared stalled; his albums were selling at a slowed pace; and his income declined significantly from previous years.

Michael adopted a makeshift lifestyle, different in nearly every way from the glorious days of Neverland, except that he still had his precious children.

  * * * * * * * * *

Many of his family members were experiencing similar financial pressures and distress. Michael Jackson had supported them in myriad ways for many years, but he became financially unable to continue at that level....

From the time when his solo career was soaring, he consented to detour from the path of creating his own music for his brothers' sake. Michael was blazing new territory both in global recognition and in the number of records sold; he had one blockbuster hit after another. His innovative album *Thriller*, which remains overwhelmingly the best-selling of all time, was flying off the store shelves "like a household item." Meanwhile, his brothers' careers floundered.

The Jackson 5, as the undisputed kings of Motown, were earning seven-figure paychecks for single performances in their heyday; they sold more than 100 million albums, second only to the Beatles. By 1983, however, his brothers had reportedly spent their respective shares of the take. His mother implored Michael to rejoin his struggling brothers in a shared lucrative opportunity in 1984 for a series of fifty-five stadium concerts, the *Victory Tour*. All of his brothers needed the money, Katherine reminded Michael. He finally succumbed to his mother's entreaties, and, as the main draw for the crowds, Michael Jackson toured again with his brothers, playing to sold-out auditoriums.

The *Victory Tour* turned out to be only a temporary fix for the financial woes of the Jackson brothers, except for Michael, who continued with his own music and became the top earner of all time. In fact, Michael donated to charity the entire $5 million that was his share from the *Victory* concerts.

By 2008-09, Michael's brothers were in economic trouble, as reported by *Michael Jackson Tribute—Exclusive Collector's Edition* (2009):

Jermaine Jackson, having been "slapped with $5 million in federal and state liens a few years ago," wasn't doing much and was often staying at the family home at Hayvenhurst.

Jackie Jackson, the oldest brother, was managing his son Siggy's aspiring career as a rap singer. The Internet-based clothing business that he started had failed.

Marlon Jackson was reportedly stocking shelves at a supermarket in San Diego. He was staying in a hotel for a period of time.

Tito Jackson was still in the music business as guitarist with a jazz and blues band that was playing at small venues, earning a fraction of the amount that was his draw from The Jackson 5 stadium performances.

Their father Joe Jackson was trying to maintain himself by promoting several girl singing groups in Las Vegas. [It was reported elsewhere that Joe insisted on payment for the interviews he gave during Michael's criminal trial.]

Mother Katherine, always a stay-at-home homemaker, managed and resided in the five-acre Hayvenhurst mansion. [It was reported elsewhere that the estate was in danger of foreclosure.]

Janet Jackson, in stark contrast, was worth more than $150 million (as one of the top-ten best-selling artists in contemporary music). Janet was successfully continuing her acting career and was regularly sending money to her parents; she was called "the family breadwinner" by the media. Janet bought a home for her parents in Las Vegas, which could become a blessing if the Hayvenhurst home would be lost to irreversible financial trouble.

La Toya was labeled a millionaire in the *New York Post*. She was earning a living primarily in Europe and the United Arab Emirates; she was judging beauty and singing contests. La Toya was living with a wealthy boyfriend in Beverly Hills and reportedly had little contact with her siblings.

Rebbie, the oldest of the Jackson children, left the music business soon after achieving a gold album, *Centipede*, followed by three less successful albums. She was still married to her childhood sweetheart, Nathaniel Brown, after thirty-five years. The couple had three children and they were residing in an exclusive neighborhood of Las Vegas.

Michael Jackson was reported—gleefully by some medialoid sources—"to be struggling."

During his last years, there was a short list of people who were real friends to Michael Jackson, who seemed sincerely to care about him. Most of those within his circle of regular contacts consisted of business associates. To many of them, it seemed, Michael Jackson was nothing more than a source of largesse or a "gravy train." Though there were frequent telephone calls to him from his mother, the majority of his other calls were related to business matters.

*   *   *   *   *   *   *   *   *

When he worked for Michael Jackson, Thomas Mesereau relates that the defense team had to cope with three primary challenges: the prosecution, the media, and *"the legion of mediocre advisers surrounding the vulnerable, innocent Michael Jackson."* [Emphasis added] Perhaps Mesereau was too kind in choosing the word "mediocre."

In 2003, Michael hired attorney David LeGrand to investigate the many people who surrounded him at the time. LeGrand delved into Michael's financial affairs. According to several sources, including michaeljacksonhoaxforum.com, "LeGrand maintained that those who were whispering in Jackson's ear, [Ronald] Konitzer and [Dieter] Wiesner, had also taken nearly $1 million from Michael Jackson without his knowledge."

Eye-opening testimony regarding the state of Michael Jackson's finances and his detachment from their management came from Ann Kite at his 2005 trial. Ms. Kite was hired in February 2003, for the purpose of working on the restoration of Michael's image after the disaster of "Living with Michael Jackson." She had little experience in public relations, but she was the ex-girlfriend of one of Michael's closest advisers. Although she had "zero experience" with high-profile celebrities or matters, she was paid an advance of $10,000 for her prospective work. Unfortunately for her, Ms. Kite was terminated after six days of employment.

However, Ann Kite testified at the trial that, although she never met Michael Jackson or finished a full week of work on his behalf, she discovered that one of his advisers had "power of attorney" and had embezzled $980,000 from him. Ms. Kite was so concerned about what was going on around Michael that she initiated a meeting with his brother Jermaine. After their conversation, the power of attorney was revoked. She said that she distrusted almost everyone who was on "Michael's team"; she didn't know where anyone's allegiance was; and she worried about his vulnerability. And, all within six days!

Debbie Rowe testified to the pattern of behavior that she had witnessed regarding Michael's "handlers." She was convinced that Michael was not aware of many of the activities of these people and that three of the men had plans for Jackson "enterprises" in America and in Europe and for the use of his name for profit.

"... He's removed from the handlers, the people who are taking care of business, and they make all the decisions, and there's [been] a number of times that they don't consult him," Ms. Rowe explained.

One of his "people" bragged to Ms. Rowe that he had personally made millions of dollars on her rebuttal tape interview, which she had freely done, without pay, to defend her ex-husband in the aftermath of the "Living with Michael Jackson" disaster. She said that there were "precious few" people he could trust, that his associates were "liars" and "opportunistic vultures." Michael Jackson could be easily manipulated by the people around him. Debbie was both vehement and disgusted when she testified about these people; she said that one of Michael's advisers was "full of s——-" and then apologized to the judge for her language.

Debbie was probably the biggest surprise of the entire trial. As his ex-wife, she was incongruously supportive of Michael Jackson, and she said that she wanted to be his friend once again. After his acquittal, according to J. Randy Taraborrelli, Michael and Debbie reached an agreement for her to give up rights to the children in exchange for approximately $6 million, to be paid in a ten-year deal.

A forensic accountant, hired by the prosecution, presented a review and analysis of Michael Jackson's financial affairs for the jury. This level of intrusion, usually not allowed into testimony or evidence, was ruled as permissible by the judge because the prosecution argued that Michael had engaged in "the conspiracy to abduct" and "extortion" out of a motive related to his financial troubles. "To Jackson and his family, the idea that the state was allowed to put on such evidence, ... [and] was permitted to expose Michael's personal finances, was outrageous. The prosecutors were able to make Michael look fiscally irresponsible," wrote Aphrodite Jones after she later reviewed all of the information at trial.

The "hired gun" accountant did not have the complete data, however, regarding Michael's finances, but that did not stop him from drawing conclusions. He talked about an ongoing "cash crisis," wherein Michael was allegedly spending twenty to thirty million dollars a year, while his earnings were $11.5 million. He estimated Michael Jackson's debt in 2003 as $224 million. Michael had "borrowed extensively against the properties he owned"; foremost was the Sony/ATV catalog, which was estimated at a value of one billion dollars, half of that Michael Jackson's asset. The accountant portrayed Michael's annual expenses as $5 million for legal and professional fees, $5 million for security and the operation of Neverland, $2.5 million for insurance, and $7.5 million for personal expenses.

Michael's primary assets were three: the Mijac catalog, which contained publishing rights to Michael's songs and performances; the Sony/ATV catalog, which contained the rights to a vast library of songs; and Neverland Valley Ranch, which was estimated at that time to be worth approximately $50 million.

A five-year history of Michael Jackson's financial condition was laid bare for the jury, with all of its entanglements and convoluted loans. It was confusing.

Thomas Mesereau was annoyed with the "nerve" of the state's "financial expert," who was basing his testimony on incomplete information. The attorney asked, in his cross-examination, if the accountant was aware that Michael Jackson had been offered $100 million to do a national tour in 2002. The "expert" had no such knowledge and seemed to be at a loss for words.

The defense attorney got the accountant to admit that, to his knowledge, Michael Jackson had never filed for bankruptcy and that "it was entirely possible that a worldwide entity like Michael Jackson could solve his 'liquidity problems' in just one day."

The state of Michael Jackson's finances was both controversial and confusing—complex and tangled. What can we say with relative certainty about what he was dealing with during his last years?

These conclusions are valid:

Michael Jackson did not understand his own financial condition, due to its fiscal management by others, its complexities, and the lack of information provided to him.

He had a cash flow problem, which caused some bills to go unpaid and/or be paid late.

He borrowed against his assets and paid high rates of interest for the loans he took out.

He had assets that were worth at least many hundreds of millions of dollars: two music catalogs, with publishing rights to many thousands of songs, and Neverland Ranch, which was assumed by Colony Capital in a joint agreement with Michael in 2008, in order to prevent its foreclosure.

He was himself an indisputable asset, potentially worth hundreds of millions of dollars for performing, endorsements, and business partnerships.

He lived well in terms of residential comfort, the ability to travel, and the wherewithal to satisfy his everyday needs and those of his children....

        *   *   *   *   *   *   *   *   *

Like everything else related to Michael Jackson, his Last Will & Testament became a controversial matter. Executed and signed in 2002, the Will was legally challenged soon after it was discovered in mid-2009. Joseph Jackson filed a legal challenge to the Will, contesting its validity. Katherine Jackson brought separate action, seeking to become the third executor of her son's will, but her effort was unsuccessful. The court of jurisdiction ruled that this 2002 Last Will & Testament, signed by Michael Jackson, was a properly-executed document and would be enforced.

In his Will, Michael left the guardianship of his three children to his mother Katherine. If she would become unavailable, Michael named Diana Ross as second in line. (Since the time when Michael lived with Ms. Ross when he was emerging as the boy-wonder of The Jackson 5 at Motown Records, he admired her greatly as a person and, years later, as a mother.)

Michael Jackson left 40% of his Estate to his mother, 40% to his three children, and 20% to charity. His named executors are his long-time friends and business associates John Branca and John McClain.

John Branca was rehired as Michael Jackson's lawyer just eight days before his death! The two men had an on-and-off relationship across three decades. Michael had been best man at Branca's first wedding in 1987; the superstar was accompanied by his chimpanzee Bubbles, who was also wearing a tuxedo for the gala event. Branca had cleverly negotiated the highest royalty rates in history for his client and the release of *Thriller* through a compromise disclaimer, intended for the elders in Michael's church, against its "demonology." He also arranged for the purchase of the ATV music catalog and the merger of Michael's ATV Music with Sony Music.

Known for combining business savvy with "show biz," Branca has influenced many facets of the entertainment industry from merchandising to the way concert tours are organized. He had left Michael's employ in 2006. Branca explained later that he "felt the singer was taking advice from people who didn't have Jackson's interests in mind."

John McClain was a successful songwriter and guitarist who then went into management at the executive level in the recording industry. He is also an entertainment lawyer whose list of successful clients is long and impressive. McClain was credited with making Janet Jackson, Michael's younger sister, a mega-star after he assumed full control as her manager. Impressed with his wildly effective make-over of young Janet, Michael employed McClain, whom he had first met during his high school years, as a valued and capable adviser. McClain, who also collaborated with Michael Jackson on a number of songs, continued as one of his closest advisers across decades.

In mid-2009, Branca and McClain immediately set about the business of sorting out the encumbrances and other complexities of Michael Jackson's financial matters, which include pending litigation of various kinds and other complications. They set as priorities their assumption of control of the financial situation and the retirement of debt.

Michael Jackson's Estate officially listed seventy-nine potential creditors with a claim to money possibly owed to them. Sixty-five creditors' claims were then filed as of February 2010, ranging from $1,420 to $300,000,000 (and more). It is interesting to note that one of Michael's recent former managers, Raymone Bain, filed for more than $44 million (pending litigation).

Soon after the executors' assumption of their responsibilities to the Estate, Katherine Jackson appropriately began receiving, on a monthly basis, large sums of money for her own needs and for Michael's children, who reside with her. Because Michael Jackson was financially supporting his mother through the years, his executors made a commitment to continue that responsibility.

As of February 2011, Michael's executors spent approximately $159 million paying back various debts, income taxes, and other expenses, including "uninterrupted support" for Mrs. Jackson and Michael's children, as he intended.

Michael Jackson knew exactly what he was doing when he fashioned his Will. He created a new nuclear family consisting of his beloved mother and precious three children, all living safely and comfortably on the money from his Estate. His children will be raised in ways he experienced and knew well.

He provided intelligently for his children both by naming his mother as their guardian and by leaving the three of them 40% of his Estate. They are surrounded by extended family, as his mother's home has always served as the temporary or transitional home for any family member in need and for others who chose to stay there. In late 2010, Jermaine's and Randy's children were living with her also.

Having contributed to charity every month of his life, according to *The Official Michael Jackson Opus,* Michael correspondingly left a substantial portion of his estate, one-fifth, to his favorite charities. He would be pleased to know that his incredible level of generosity for the benefit of others and the planet will continue in perpetuity.

Michael made no mention of his father or siblings in his Will. By these omissions, he left the exclusive decision-making to Katherine regarding other family members. She may choose to help them financially or not, including her husband Joseph. Katherine's ensured wealth and control make it even more unlikely that Joseph would ever choose to initiate a divorce from her.

Michael shifted the well-recognized moral power of his mother within his large family to a plateau that now includes monumental economic power. Mrs. Jackson, although shy, is a strong, formidable person, having successfully raised nine children and, for more than sixty years, survived what appears at times to be a supremely challenging marriage. Katherine is uniquely equipped to care for Michael's children and her new residential family.

$*$ $*$ $*$ $*$ $*$ $*$ $*$ $*$ $*$

"In 1989, Michael Jackson topped the *Forbes* list as the highest paid entertainer, with annual earnings of $125 million." According to *Guinness World Records 2011*, "this record is still unbroken 21 years later."

Headlines and news stories have virtually screamed out that Michael Jackson was pitifully in debt at the time of his death. Estimates ranged from $400 million to less than half that amount, still a daunting figure.

However, not only did his assets hold great value in the marketplace but his earning power was immense. Michael Jackson knew that he could earn millions of dollars in one weekend of performing in domestic venues and abroad. As an entertainer, *he was worth an inestimable fortune.*

To the date of the publication of this book, Michael Jackson remains the highest-earning musician in history. His Estate, which receives all earnings that would go to Michael if he were alive, took in "a whopping $400 million" in two years, effective June 2011.

"The continuing overwhelming worldwide interest in Michael confirms his status as the greatest entertainer of all time," said John

Branca, who added that the Estate has generated over $1 billion in retail sales during that time. The Michael Jackson Estate and Sony still share ownership of a music catalog that now contains *half a million* songs. Music experts now place its value "in the neighborhood of $1.5 billion, based on estimated proceeds of $50 million to $100 million per year." The Estate receives one-half of that money. (*forbes.com*, July 2011) John Branca estimated the gross value of the catalog at "upward of two billion dollars."

In addition, a "new report," as of July 2011, "reveals the unfathomable worth of Jackson's fine art collection," largely overlooked within the context of his assets and net worth. As an avid collector with a life-long interest in art, Michael Jackson invested large sums of money in artworks that included paintings, sculptures, and other artifacts. He reportedly owned a collection of art that is valued at more than $900 million and includes 182 works that he kept "in mint condition." To the surprise of many people, some of these works are by the King of Pop himself, who studied under David Nordahl, an artist based in Santa Fe, New Mexico, and Brett-Livingston Strong of Australia; the latter individual is the focal person in the new report.

David Nordahl, however, strongly believes that this report was issued in order to inflate the value of Michael Jackson's holdings along with the perception of Brett-Livingston Strong's market appeal.

The *Michael Jackson factor* is alive and well here, too, it appears. Controversy surrounded the ownership of the art collection when Mr. Strong claimed that he had "received Jackson's sketches and sculptures, free of charge," for his loyalty, continued friendship, and artistic partnership with Michael. His claim has been hotly contested, of course, and many "insiders" have insisted that Michael would never have given over his valuable artwork to an individual other than his children or mother, especially in light of his financial troubles during his last years.

Neverland Ranch remains another confusing asset in Michael Jackson's financial picture. Discrepant, contradictory reports have been issued for years regarding the status of this wonderful fantasy-like place that Michael created for himself and his loved ones.

In November 2008, Tom Barrack, a 63-year-old billionaire and owner of a private-equity firm called Colony Capital, took over Neverland, avoiding a scheduled foreclosure of the property. Barrack, who was described as "The World's Greatest Real Estate Investor" by *Fortune* magazine in 2005, has been so incredibly successful largely because of what has been described as his "maniacal stamina." He has been gutsy, unconventional in his business dealings, and uniquely enterprising. The "take-over" actually put Barrack and Michael Jackson in partnership, with each having claim to one-half of the property.

Barrack "gets it" when it comes to appreciating Neverland and empathizing with Michael Jackson's love for his idyllic home. There is a grandeur to the large expanse of rolling land, with 67,000 oaks and sycamores and a former Chumash Indian worship site overlooking a savannah-like plain. "You'll feel something," says Barrack, "which I think was what drove him [Michael Jackson].... You will actually feel it, I promise."

Michael had not been to Neverland since 2005, feeling that he and his home were violated beyond repair during the seventy-plus sheriffs' destructive raid on the property in 2003. The maximum count of employees at 275 at the peak of its operation had dwindled to four in 2008. The amusement park was dismantled, its rides sold off and removed; the zoo was emptied of animals through transfers to other facilities and sanctuaries; its snakes were released into the wild. Barrack's people have been working to rehabilitate the estate, refinishing the floors of the 13,000-square-foot main house and re-landscaping the grounds.

The elephant barn "now houses a labyrinth of walls filled with effusive notes penned by visitors from around the world." The reminders of Michael Jackson's "complicated legacy" are "the bronze statues of children at play that dot the estate."

Of special note is the dance studio, where "a solitary bulb lights a spot worn down by [Michael] Jackson's spinning." *Wow.*

Colony Capital also bought out the recording and performance rights that Michael Jackson had signed over to the son of the king of Bahrain in an ill-advised, and likely too hastily-made, business deal. Michael also agreed to return to work when he was advised that it had become necessary for him to do so. Barrack realized and recognized "the intrinsic preciousness of Jackson's talent and fan base."

"For sure, the guy [was] an absolute genius," Tom Barrack says of Michael Jackson, whom he met at the Palomino Lane home in Las Vegas. "He was remembering not just songs but every performance, every date, every script." When it came to business matters, though, Michael was not as adept.

Barrack remembers that, at their meeting, the 1,000-page Sony/ATV catalog was on the table between him and Michael Jackson. The billionaire was mightily impressed, and he was quickly won over for a deal with Michael.

Tom Barrack issued a formal letter to the local community in anticipation of the influx of Michael Jackson fans from around the world on the first anniversary of his death in June 2010. In the well-written communication, he urged a warm and respectful welcome for Michael's fans and admirers "because he deserved that," as did his fans. It was a classy gesture that honored Michael Jackson and his devoted admirers in a gracious and fitting way.

It is considered unlikely that Neverland will be converted into a museum or shrine to Michael Jackson's memory for the general public and his fans. The small, quiet communities nearby would probably not welcome the influx of many thousands of people throughout the year. The long ride from Los Angeles—three hours each way—would be difficult and discouraging for many people who otherwise would flock to the site.

Many fans keenly feel the loss of Neverland as a potential official place to remember, mourn, and celebrate Michael Jackson.

*   *   *   *   *   *   *   *   *

"Michael was a purist when it came to his creativity," Thomas Mesereau explains in an attempt to shed light on the discrepancy between Michael Jackson's brilliant mind and his apparent financial lapses. "He didn't want to get involved in the intricacies and headaches of fiscal management; he wanted to compose songs, produce them, and dance. He wanted to heal the world through his music and his love."

To give the reader an idea of the *enormity* of the undertaking that Michael Jackson delegated to others, the following is a list of the business entities that the "Michael Jackson Family Trust" was created to handle as part of his Estate at the time of his death:

100% Ownership
The Michael Jackson Company LLC
MJJ Productions Inc.
MJJ Ventures
MJJ Artistic Inc.
Nation Comics Inc.
Invincible Tours Inc.
Triumph International Inc.
Triumph Multimedia Inc.
Enchanted Kingdom LLC
MJ-ATV Publishing Trust
MJ Publishing LLC (a.k.a. Mijac Music)
New Horizon Trust I, II, & III
Go For Your Dreams Foundation

50% Partnerships
Sony/ATV Music Publishing LLC
Sycamore Valley Ranch Company LLC
SEE Virtual World MJ LLC

SEE Virtual World MJ Operations LLC
Cirque Jackson I.P. LLC
MJJ Records LLC
World Events LLC
MJ Licensing LLC

[Sony/ATV Music Publishing LLC alone owns the rights to more than 500,000 songs and manages them.]

Is it any wonder that Michael Jackson did not attempt personally to assume control of his vast empire of complex enterprises? It must have seemed like a virtual black hole to him, in a universe of seemingly infinite business constellations.

Across decades, Michael Jackson was at the apex of the music industry—and it was, in many ways, a curse.

Michael Jackson found it necessary to use his one-half share of the Sony/ATV music catalog as collateral to borrow $200 million some years ago. [He had bought the catalog in 1985 for $47.5 million; in 1995, he sold 50% of ATV to Sony for about $90 million.] Sony guaranteed the $200 million loan for Michael. If he would default on the loan, Sony could then move to claim his share of ATV. Michael Jackson lived in fear that he would default on the loan against his 50% share of the ATV catalog, which he wanted to become the inheritance of his three children.

Since 1979, when Michael was a young adult, he assigned all of his songwriting rights to his own publishing company, Mijac Music, which also owns other artists' publishing rights that Michael collected through his life. Since the middle of 2009, many lawsuits have been filed by his Estate for copyright infringements of Michael Jackson's music, trademarks, and image.

The Michael Jackson Estate signed a lucrative recording deal with Sony Music Entertainment on March 15, 2010, for the next seven years and ten new releases. It is *"the biggest deal ever in music*—worth up to $250 million with a guarantee of $200 million."* In addition to the new album *Michael*, there is reportedly enough material left by Michael Jackson for at least three more albums of new releases. [It is interesting to note that 2/3 of the sales of Michael Jackson records have traditionally been outside the United States.]

It's been said that, particularly for artists, "Death is an excellent career step." Although macabre and disrespectful, this saying does communicate a truth: Artists are worth more dead than alive; the works of deceased artists escalate in value.

Tragically, this is the case with Michael Jackson. This situation gives rise to even more grieving on his behalf by those who love him and to suspicions regarding the cause of his death. So many people have profited—and on a major scale—from his passing.

*   *   *   *   *   *   *   *   *

Conspiracy theories abound regarding Michael Jackson's death and its cause. Conrad Murray was found responsible for Michael's untimely and unnecessary death at a jury trial in September-November 2011, but a large number of people, including some members of the Jackson family, believe that others share in the blame.

AEG Live entered into an oral contract, based upon a written contract that was apparently never fully executed, on or about May 8, 2009. Effective at that time, Dr. Conrad Murray began work for Michael Jackson as his personal physician, in accordance with the agreement. The contract, by its written terms, was due to extend through the end of Michael Jackson's last performance for the London 02 concerts, a date that was expected to occur in 2010.

Reportedly AEG did not provide the written contract to Murray for signature until June 18, 2009. The company asserted that their legal department needed time to review the document and asked Murray for "patience" from May 8th onward. Because the actual contract on June 18th varied hardly at all from the version on May 8th—the name of Murray's company was simply added as party to the agreement—it appears that AEG was purposefully delaying the execution of the document. Dr. Murray signed the contract on June 24th; Michael Jackson never signed it; Michael died on June 25th.

According to the terms of the contract, AEG was required to provide a "cardiopulmonary resuscitation unit" (CPR machine) and a "qualified medical assistant" and "saline, catheters, needles and other mutually approved medical equipment, necessary for the services." AEG did not provide the equipment or the assistant. This lapse does not excuse Conrad Murray's administrations to Michael Jackson without such necessary precautions, but it gives rise to cries of culpability by AEG, from Michael's family and others.

Murray, it seems, was working for AEG, which had agreed to pay expenses—in addition to the $150,000 per month for his services—that were estimated at a total of $39,045 per month. The expenses included "airfare, transportation, housing rent and counsel tax, house utilities and maintenance, insurance, cell phones, furniture rental and equipment, and UK license expense." They also included "medical equipment, supplies, professional expenses" in the estimated amount of $8,000 monthly and "nursing staff" for $7,000 monthly (this $15,000 was part of the $39,045). [Reportedly Murray did not actually receive the exorbitant monthly payments because his patient's death intervened.]

It is argued by those who believe that AEG shares the blame for Michael Jackson's death that AEG knew or should have known that propofol was being administered to him by Murray; also, Murray appeared to be the doctor of their choice. Many believe that, because Murray was in financial trouble, he could and would be controlled by AEG. The contractual arrangement served to seriously compromise the doctor-patient relationship between Murray and Michael Jackson. This relationship should be inviolate in terms of the doctor's responsibility to do *solely* what is best for his patient. Period.

According to the lawsuit filed by Joseph Jackson against AEG, Murray was unable to pay his child support of $1,103 for one of his seven children; he did not have funds to support his other six children; his house in Las Vegas was under foreclosure; and, according to a financial declaration provided by Murray dated April 8, 2008, his gross monthly income was $3,300. In stark contrast, Murray's monthly income was due to be $150,000 with AEG—and more in terms of the liberal expenses that he was to be allowed and for which he was to be reimbursed.

It is also interesting to note that, in the contract between AEG and Conrad Murray, Michael Jackson was to pay Dr. Tohme Tohme "an amount not exceeding $100,000 per month." Tohme was supposed to be Michael's ongoing manager (from mid-2008), and it is considered strange at best that AEG would ensure the employment and/or payment of one of *Michael Jackson*'s employees.

*   *   *   *   *   *   *   *   *

Michael Jackson's fatal flaw was trust. In spite of flutters from time to time of understandable distrust of those around him, his behavior revealed that he *chose* to trust many of his financial managers and others whose jobs were to keep his affairs in order. He gave his "power of attorney" to various individuals across years, and his managers had control of his checking accounts and other finances.

Michael Jackson was so trusting that he and Lisa Marie Presley married without a prenuptial agreement. Because he followed his heart, Michael considered it inappropriate and uncomfortable to encumber his first marriage with a contractual agreement that stipulated division of property in the event of the dissolution of the union.

Fortunately for Michael, when the couple split up after less than two years, Lisa Marie took very little from him. Along with her mother Priscilla, she was heiress to her father Elvis Presley's fortune of hundreds of millions of dollars. She also had too much pride to demand a large sum of money from Michael. Many believe that they still loved each other. Reportedly, Lisa Marie received only ten percent of the royalties from Michael's *HIStory* album, which he produced during their marriage, and the rights to write a tell-all book about their marriage. She never took advantage of that authorship opportunity.

This entire scenario, however, reveals that Michael Jackson was consummately trusting of those whom he took to his heart.

With his contract with AEG Live also, Michael Jackson became vulnerable to disaster. Michael, courted by AEG across years for a contractual agreement to do concerts in partnership with the company, finally succumbed in January 2009. He agreed to ten concerts at the beautiful O2 Arena in London; after unprecedented ticket sales, AEG approached Michael to add forty more concerts, to which he agreed.

According to vindicatemj.wordpress.com, Michael Jackson's agreement with AEG is shockingly confusing and potentially very detrimental to Michael. Entitled "EVERYTHING HE HAD for a $6,2 mln. [sic.] PROMISSORY NOTE," the Internet article presents excerpts from the Michael Jackson-AEG agreement with editorial comments and critical analysis.

The opening page addresses "Dear Dr. Tohme Tohme," setting a personal tone, and then proceeds to middle pages that "are the epitome of legal demagogue[ry] the sole goal of which is to deliberately make easy things difficult for the reader...." There is a Letter of Intent, apparently signed by Michael Jackson (as an *individual*) on January 26, 2009, with attachments that were "most probably made later." The first pages appear to be a contract. The second paper is a Promissory Note saying that $6.2 million will be loaned to Michael Jackson *if he guarantees its repayment by the assets of his company.* The third part is the Inducement Letter, which states that Michael guarantees the performance by Artistco of all of its obligations to AEG Live LLC.

It appears that there was a "cut-and-paste" process that created these documents, and Michael Jackson was committing all or most of his assets as collateral for some advances paid him by AEG, in the amount of $5 million. With possibly all or most of his assets tied up in his company, Michael was risking nearly his entire net worth ... in the event of his default on payments to the company. In addition, the contract required Michael to pay $3 million to Two Seas Records LLC, in settlement of a dispute with that company.

The clauses in the Promissory Note are not numbered, Michael Jackson's signature appears on a separate page, and "all notices, approvals and consents required or permitted to be given hereunder" are to be sent by a fax machine. This last provision is a dangerous one indeed.

Much of the language in the documents is unclear and placed in unusual sections, and some of it is contradictory to other portions.

There are people who believe that AEG was after the assets of Michael Jackson, who seemingly became obligated to that company to the stunning point of "risking his entire fortune" for a short-term boost to his cash flow.

Michael was arguably much worse off, from a financial point of view, with his commitment to AEG and the fifty London concerts than he would have been without that responsibility. Furthermore, he ran the risk of losing nearly everything to the company. AEG would likely be better off financially if Michael Jackson *defaulted* on the agreement. Some people believe that was the real intention of the company—a default by Michael Jackson.

*   *   *   *   *   *   *   *   *

Dr. Tohme Ramez Tohme, a native of Lebanon who is not a licensed physician in the U.S., became Michael's business manager and spokesperson in the summer of 2008. It was Michael's brother Jermaine who introduced the men to each other. Tohme claimed that he was not receiving a salary from Michael Jackson; it was reported that he was getting $100,000 per month from AEG; but it appears that AEG was guaranteeing—or attempting to guarantee—$100,000 monthly from Michael Jackson.

Tohme has asserted that he began to work for Michael Jackson to help him save Neverland from foreclosure. Breaking his silence after pervasively being labeled as "mysterious," "unknown," and "elusive" by journalists, Tohme came forward in early July 2009, days after Michael Jackson's death. He reported that he was "inspired" to help Michael because he saw that he was "a wonderful human being" and a great father to his three children. Tohme claimed that he arranged for the deal with Colony Capital that resulted in a partnership between that company and Michael Jackson, with Colony paying off the approximately $23.5 million loan against Neverland Ranch. Tohme was reportedly a friend of the chairman/CEO of Colony Capital.

A relative stranger to the music business, Tohme said that one of the first things he did for Michael was to fire many of his staff, including security guards, "in order to build a fence around the singer" and protect him from nameless others who wanted to control him and his finances. He arranged for the confusing and ill-fated auction of Michael Jackson's possessions from Neverland, which was halted through legal action and then a settlement agreement between the auction house and Michael.

Perhaps the most astounding fact in the Tohme-Jackson scenario is the $5.5 million *in cash* that Tohme handed over to authorities and that rightfully went to Michael's Estate shortly after his death. He claimed to the Associated Press that this was a "secret stash" of cash that Michael kept near him; Tohme temporarily removed it; and then he "was honest" by returning it. He claimed that, because of his appropriate behavior, the Estate should return the favor by opening its books to him. He brought lawsuits against the Estate for $2.3 million for the Neverland deal and at least $39 million for the AEG deal for *This Is It*. Some have questioned Tohme's assertion that he negotiated the deal with AEG, which he calls the "crown jewel" of achievements; he may not have been employed by Michael when the arrangement was made. The apparent conflict of interest— with him working as an "unpaid adviser and manager" for Michael Jackson, while receiving (or being guaranteed) $100,000 per month by/through AEG—has been cited in various media outlets.

"There's a divide between me and my representatives and I don't talk to my lawyer, my accountant," Michael told his spiritual adviser Reverent June Gatlin in September 2008. "I talk to him [Tohme] and he talks to them," Michael continued, "and I don't like it. I wanna get someone in there with him that I know and trust. I don't know what's in my accounts." Reverent Gatlin played an audiotape of Michael saying these words, when she came forward via public interviews after Michael Jackson's death. Michael was disclosing his serious misgivings about this new manager to her.

Tohme claimed that he was working on other deals related to Michael's finances—his assets, loans, and business opportunities— which included a clothing line, a video game, and a Broadway play through Nederlander Productions. Michael's manager enjoyed the excitement of his client's life, accompanying him to London in spring 2009, when Michael was greeted by helicopters, paparazzi galore, and throngs of adoring fans. Tohme revealed that Michael had plans for more achievements, which included innovative music, movies, and even green-cities projects.

"I had never seen a better father," Tohme said of Michael Jackson; "I had never seen fans who loved anyone so much." Michael reportedly severed ties with Tohme in May 2009, after he learned that his manager had allegedly threatened the boss of the auction house over Michael's memorabilia going to a bid process for sale.

Reverent Gatlin explained that Tohme had completely taken over Michael Jackson's life; that Michael was "scared" of him; and that he consented to tape his feelings in a candid conversation with her. The aggressive manager succeeded in isolating Michael from people he loved. Michael complained that he had no access to his own money; Tohme reportedly exercised "power of attorney" for Michael Jackson.

Intrigue and confusion surrounded the issue of Michael Jackson's managers during 2009. Tohme presented himself as Michael's business manager since 2008. However, Frank Dileo claimed that Michael rehired him as manager in March 2009. In addition, Leonard Rowe—who formed an alliance with Michael's parents Katherine and Joseph—insisted that Michael hired him as his manager, and he has produced a letter, dated March 25, 2009, to substantiate his claim.

On April 2, 2009, *Celebrity Access* published an article titled "Will Michael Jackson's Real Manager Please Stand Up?"

There was a major power struggle going on. Leonard Rowe was connected to the AllGood Entertainment Jackson Family Show project, for which Michael was being pressured to perform with his siblings. Katherine and Joseph were supporting this project; Michael was seemingly not interested.

Randy Phillips of AEG reportedly brought in Frank Dileo, whose relationship with Michael had deep roots, in an attempt to control Michael in the direction of fulfilling his commitment to AEG and the London concerts. However, in November 2008, Dileo and AllGood Entertainment signed a binder agreement, in which Dileo promised that Michael, Janet, and The Jacksons would perform a concert in Texas in July 2010, to be taped and marketed as Internet pay-per-view. This agreement mandated that AllGood would pay Dileo $150,000 as a non-refundable commission for Dileo to get Michael to put his signature on the contract. AllGood offered to pay Dileo *after* he would obtain Michael Jackson's signature; Dileo declined to move forward *without* the $150,000.

AEG, reportedly fully aware of the power struggle, retained Frank Dileo as Michael's "manager" in order to prevent Leonard Rowe from meddling in the AEG deal that Michael had made. A press release, issued on March 26, 2009, announced that Leonard Rowe had been appointed as Michael's manager. Michael, however, had no knowledge of it, and he allegedly stopped taking calls from Rowe in response to the "maverick" public announcement that was released by those individuals who embraced the AllGood project.

To add to the confusion, AEG's Randy Phillips told *Celebrity Access* on April 2nd that they (at AEG) "have been working with

Dr. Tohme" in connection with all of Michael Jackson's concert dates.

Joe Jackson and Leonard Rowe went to Michael's home on April 14, 2009, to get Michael to sign a letter of direction that named Rowe as his manager. By writing on it, Michael changed the letter to stipulate that this applied only to "finances and the O2 Shows in London" and "This can be revoked at any time." Michael then signed the letter with Joseph looking over his shoulder. He did not appoint Rowe as his *business* manager; Rowe's role was strictly defined and limited. Leonard Rowe signed a contract with AllGood Entertainment on behalf of Michael Jackson in February 2009!

Michael, Katherine, Joseph, Leonard Rowe, Randy Phillips and Paul Gongaware (the last two on behalf of AEG) attended a meeting on May 15th at the Beverly Hills Hotel. Leonard Rowe was terminated by Michael on May 20, 2009.

After Tohme was also reportedly terminated in May 2009, Frank Dileo claimed that he assumed the position of Michael's manager; in fact, he dated his assumption of that role to March 2009. Dileo had served in that capacity from 1984 to 1989. Surprisingly, however, Tohme reportedly fired staff members at both Michael's Holmby Hills home and his Las Vegas home on the day that Michael died; he still claimed to be in charge of Michael Jackson's business affairs.

Frank Dileo attended a meeting with a small group of others at Michael's Holmby Hills home on June 21, 2009—four days before Michael's death. He was there as a friend concerned about Michael and as his manager.

Interestingly, attorney John Branca and Frank Dileo were back on Michael Jackson's team once again, after a long hiatus for each of the men. With their renewed active involvement on his behalf, one can only speculate as to the status of Michael's affairs, including his draconian contract with AEG, if Michael lived.... [Frank Dileo, 63, passed away on August 24, 2011, just weeks before the start of the Conrad Murray trial. Fondly called "Uncle Tookie" by Michael, Frank Dileo died from complications from heart surgery that he had undergone in March.]

       *   *   *   *   *   *   *   *   *

Is there any wonder why Michael Jackson's financial affairs were in such a mess or why he was the defendant in so many lawsuits? For many years, there were too many fingers in his financial pie … and some of them dirty fingers at that.

Perhaps Baron James summarized it best—and most succinctly: "Michael Jackson was in a snake pit!"

It has been said that there are "two things too awful for a person to see in the making"—sausage and the law. There may be a third thing—the totality of the people, the web of intrigue, and the sinister machinations involved in Michael Jackson's financial affairs during the years before his passing.

There were forces of evil around him.
— Thomas Mesereau

Living well is the best revenge.
— George Herbert

Flypaper:
Sticky Lawsuits & Such

**The bigger the star,
the bigger the target.**
— Thomas Mesereau

**Everybody['s] wanting a piece of
Michael Jackson.**
"Breaking News,"
Michael Jackson

The lawsuits never stopped coming; nor did the threat of lawsuits. Michael Jackson was an easy, moving target for every kind of legal challenge. He had big money and he would pay to avoid going to trial ever again.

An attorney who had represented Michael and some of his family members for more than a decade revealed that *Michael Jackson had given about 500 depositions in his lifetime and was involved in more than 1,500 lawsuits,* according to biographer J. Randy Taraborrelli. Michael was a plaintiff and a defendant, mostly the latter. Assuming that these spanned thirty years—from the time he was a big star at twenty to his last year, at fifty—that would be fifty a year on average, or four per month, or one a week!

David Nordahl reveals, in August 2011, that Norma Staikos, Michael's chief of staff at Neverland, had confessed to him that Michael Jackson—or his "people" on his behalf—had to deal with *"fifty to sixty extortion attempts every year."* Most of these were for spurious paternity claims against him, from women he did not know, and some related to the rights to his music, from individuals claiming that he had "stolen" their songs. No one has succeeded in striking it rich by prevailing in court with such a lawsuit against Michael Jackson.

He started signing entertainment contracts at the age of five or six. By the time he was a teenager, Michael Jackson had signed more than his share of legal documents, which other, older individuals presumably read and put in front of him. It is interesting to note, however, that Joe Jackson announced years later that he had never read the first Motown contract that launched his sons into the arena of great fame and success.

Sometimes, across the years, lawsuits were filed against Michael Jackson as a form of extortion. In other words, an attorney—on behalf of his client—would file a claim in court against Michael, fully hoping and planning for the offer of a quick settlement. By that filing, he or she would avoid being accused of extortion. It was legally "safe"—as extortion is a criminal offense—to bring a lawsuit rather than to say, "Give us x millions of dollars or we'll go after you in court and bring you to trial," or "We'll go to the media with this nasty story about you." Even if it was a spurious, fantastical claim, it was likely to be met with dollars from the "deep pockets" of Michael Jackson. And the mega-star could not reasonably accuse the lawsuit filer of an extortion attempt.

Michael hated giving depositions; as is the case with many people, they made him very nervous. It was during the deposition stage of a lawsuit when his personal participation would be required. It was not only the massive inconvenience that troubled him; it was the seemingly endless questions for a man who could express himself through lyrics much more easily and eloquently than through verbal explanations. Also, during depositions and the discovery process, his personal life would become exposed for public consumption.

Some of Michael's legal problems were caused by those in his employ to whom he gave his "power of attorney." These individuals could make deals and enter into contracts on his behalf. Michael Jackson was always ultimately responsible, from a legal standpoint, of course. This routine practice was both high-trust and high-risk, with dreadful potential ramifications.

During his last years, there were dozens of lawsuits for every kind of reason, alleged liability, and tort. In some cases, it appeared that the plaintiff just wanted to meet Michael Jackson! It became well known that Michael did not have the stomach or heart for conflict, especially as played out in a court of law. "Been there, done that!" was his understandable, sardonic response—followed by "Never again."

No wonder Michael Jackson agreed to a settlement with his accuser's family in 1993 rather than pursue exoneration in a court of law. His security team continually witnessed the conflict-avoidant behaviors of Mr. Jackson; by contrast, these men were conflict-tolerant, but in their line of work they had to be.

"Settle it! Just settle it!" were words often overheard by his security guards when their boss was discussing pending litigation or a recently-filed lawsuit against him. He did not want a fight; he desperately wanted just to be left alone; he wanted to be a father and a private citizen in pursuit of the closest that he could get to a normal life. *Not a chance....*

Michael hated having to spend so much time away from his children when he was required to appear at a law firm for a deposition. Sometimes he sensed that his appearance and participation in a deposition were unnecessary. On one such occasion, he said, "Michael Jackson showing up is more for P.R. purposes for my attorney than anything else."

This insight on Mr. Jackson's part really did make eminent sense. What better public relations for any law firm than representing a client with the mega-status and prestige of Michael Jackson? What a great reflection on the *"Michael Jackson* law firm"! What terrific publicity would undoubtedly be available for the firm and the individual attorneys handling the case. *The Michael Jackson factor.* Everyone wins … except Michael Jackson, of course.

Sometimes a deposition or legal meeting with the lawyers would take all day, from early morning to late at night. It would be a grueling experience for Mr. Jackson, who would be visibly tired out on the ride back to his residence. More than once his Vegas security team waited through the entire day, until nearly midnight, for their boss. Mr. Jackson, from the back seat of the vehicle, spoke openly to them on the way back. He had done a lot of obligatory talking at the proceeding, answering what seemed to be a string of often-foolish questions.

There were moments of laughter among the three men as the SUV rolled along. There were also moments of silent sadness in the back seat.

The boss is a man with seemingly unlimited opportunities ... coupled with infinite grief, his security guards knew.

Michael Jackson was considering many offers for his endorsements and performing opportunities while he lived in Las Vegas. Among them was an offer that would have used his image and music on slot machines in the Vegas casinos. Mr. Jackson had nixed the idea because of the teachings of his childhood religion, which prohibits gambling, and probably also because of the crassness of this kind of endorsement. After all, he was *Michael Jackson*!

With the face that he presented in public, Michael Jackson seemed unaffected by the multiple frivolous but taxing lawsuits, the hiatus in his music publishing and performing career, and the morass of his financial affairs. Those who were close enough to him, however, saw that these matters were taking their toll on him. He presented himself as generally happy, though sometimes he secluded himself in his private quarters; he would sing and dance in the privacy and safety of his own home; and he spent virtually all of his time with his little ones.

Maybe he was just trying to make lemonade with his lemons, and maybe his kids will one day own a grand lemonade stand....

In Las Vegas, his security men dreaded answering the phone when a call came from one of Mr. Jackson's attorneys. Most of the time it was bad news—someone suing their boss again for something of which he was unaware or something that seemed ridiculous. Understandably, Mr. Jackson did not receive the reports well. He was comfortable enough to vent his frustration to his security team.

Mr. Jackson was expressing real and deep feelings, his security team knew, and they also realized that few people ever saw him do that. They felt genuinely sorry for him ... and helpless. After all, they were responsible for protecting the world's most famous man and there was absolutely nothing they could do to defend him against the devastating emotional effects of his out-of-control legal and financial matters.

Once, while Mr. Jackson was using Boyd's cellular phone, something infuriated him to the point that he threw the phone across the room. After a few moments of silence, Mr. Jackson said softly, "I'm sorry, Boyd; you're going to need a new phone."

Michael Jackson could not get off the bizarre, interminable treadmill of his life. After all, he was human, worn out, and sick of the constant travail and drama, which were not within his control.

The lawsuits in which Michael Jackson found himself embroiled were amazing in both their number and their direction. It would take a pages-long scorecard to keep track of them all. The attorneys were numerous, and many billed Michael at a ridiculously high hourly rate or charged an astronomical retainer. Again, *it was the Michael Jackson factor.*

Although there are many attorneys who work on a *pro bono* basis for the needy and who save lives in the criminal court system, many of Michael Jackson's legal representatives seemed to be self-seeking and rapacious. They seemed to like to kick up the sand....

If only one attorney resides in a small town, he will starve. If, however, another attorney moves into town, the two will own the town by the end of five years. Michael Jackson's attorneys were making good progress toward owning his town. And, he was literally helpless. Once a lawsuit was filed against him, no matter how trivial or unfounded, his attorneys would be required to respond by filing motions and responses and by observing various legal protocols and procedures. These became self-perpetuating.

Other lawsuits came, and, all the while, the attorneys' meters were running …, some say "spinning like an electricity meter on a hot day."

Some of the litigation was for money allegedly owed to the plaintiffs by Michael Jackson, such as payments in arrears. Even the seemingly legitimate claims were inflated by interest, asserted damages, and additional attorneys' fees. The stark reality was that the worse it got for Michael Jackson, the better it got for his lawyers; the more work they got, the more money they made.

It would be futile for Michael Jackson to yell "Stop the train, I want to get off!" His attorneys were the conductors. Anyone who has been involved in a lawsuit of significant duration can attest to the level of stress that it creates. The ambiguity of the prospective outcome and the lack of control inherent in the process, especially for the defendant, are excruciatingly difficult to handle. *Imagine Michael Jackson's psychic turmoil while undergoing so many lawsuits at the same time. And with each one, he could potentially lose a fortune.*

*   *   *   *   *   *   *   *   *

Many of Michael Jackson's legal entanglements were really nasty business. For example, a man named Victor Gutierrez wrote a book for private publication about Michael and his 1993 accuser Jordie Chandler. In it he alleged that he found a videotape of Michael and the boy. Michael's attorneys brought a lawsuit against the man and challenged him to produce it. Of course, no such videotape existed. Victor lost the suit and wound up owing Michael Jackson nearly three million dollars. "He declared bankruptcy, moved to Chile, and hasn't been heard from since," according to J. Randy Taraborrelli.

Michael's approximately $20 million settlement with Jordie Chandler and his family was one of the worst mistakes of his life. It was the expedient thing to do at the time. His advisers urged him to take the easy way out so that he could continue to earn huge money for himself and thereby for them through uninterrupted performing.

But his image never recovered from that ill-advised decision, and he condemned himself to more accusations and exploiters, who hoped to achieve a similar lucrative outcome for themselves.

"That settlement was a tragic event for Michael," Thomas Mesereau explains in 2011. "He opened Pandora's box." Michael could never again close it. That approximately $20 million paved the way for the Arvizo family—and others—who would claim improprieties by Michael for what they hoped would be a fast buck, or rather, millions of them.

His legal problems typically created more media trouble for Michael. As public information, the lawsuits generally became known, and the alleged details provided juicy material about Michael Jackson, most of it untrue. He was embarrassed, of course, when his private life became public. In 2002, for example, one of Michael's former financial managers, Myung-Ho Lee, sued him for more than twelve million dollars. As part of this litigation, Michael Jackson's monthly budget was disclosed; it included regular payments to Debbie Rowe for $1.5 million. This information resulted in public questions about Ms. Rowe's claims that she gave Michael two children as special gifts to him and that his payments to her were also gifts.

Some of the legal entanglements and lawsuits that burdened Michael Jackson, during his last four years, are the following....

2005

In July 2005, Prescient Acquisition Group Inc., a financial company that specialized in asset acquisition, filed a lawsuit against Michael Jackson for $48 million in asserted fees for providing assistance to Michael in debt restructuring. That same month Judge Rodney Melville ruled that most of the items that were seized from Michael's Neverland Ranch should be returned to him.

London's *Daily Mail,* a tabloid, published a story about the allegations of a New Orleans man who claimed that Michael Jackson had physically assaulted him with a razor blade and had drugged him, among other things. A public hearing was scheduled for August 2005, by a Louisiana court that wanted Michael or a representative to appear. This accuser had a criminal record for harassment and was an admitted bigamist. The allegations were completely discredited, and the case was later dismissed in its entirety.

Michael Jackson's attorneys filed a civil lawsuit in London on his behalf against Granada TV, the producer of the documentary "Living with Michael Jackson." The suit was for "betrayal" of Michael Jackson by Martin Bashir and for violation of the agreement made before filming began. It also sought unused film footage of Michael's children, where they are recognizable. A settlement was reportedly reached between Michael Jackson and the television company after the 2005 trial ended with Michael's full acquittal. Ironically, Janet Arvizo joined Michael Jackson in this lawsuit for including her children, who were minors, and using images of them in that documentary program without her permission.

In September 2005, Ray Hultman, one of the jurors in Michael's criminal trial, filed a lawsuit to break a publishing contract that he had signed for a "tell-all" book about Michael Jackson and the world-renowned case. Michael was not directly involved in this lawsuit.

That same month, two men were indicted for secretly recording conversations between Michael Jackson and his former attorney during their flight on a private jet from Las Vegas to California in November 2003.

The next month, Michael Jackson and his MJ Company filed a lawsuit against concert promoter Marcel Avram and Mama Concerts, his German-based company. The suit was for "breach of contract" and "to prevent arbitration" over a 1999 concert contract in dispute between the parties.

Surprisingly, Michael was called for jury duty by the Santa Barbara authorities, but his attorneys filed for a deferment for him because he was living in Bahrain at the time.

That same month, October 2005, Michael's attorneys countersued his former aide, Marc Schaffel, for allegedly "concealing and misappropriating over one million dollars." Schaffel had filed a lawsuit against Michael Jackson in November 2004, for more than $3 million "in allegedly unpaid loans and other debts."

2006

In January 2006, Michael abandoned a lawsuit against Henry Vaccaro, a New Jersey man who had posted Michael Jackson memorabilia for sale on a pay-per-view website. The suit had been for $10 million.

Later that month, Michael Jackson was cleared of charges alleging animal cruelty that were brought against him by PETA, People for the Ethical Treatment of Animals. A government inspection at Neverland Ranch found that the animals were being cared for properly.

In April, a lawsuit against Michael Jackson by "a fan" who alleged that he "was lured into Michael's limousine and held for nine days" against his will, was dismissed—another spurious and vicious claim.

Also during April, Michael resolved matters at Neverland regarding alleged problems with insurance and staff payments. He paid outstanding wages and employed ten new workers to assist in the care of the animals in his private zoo.

In June, there were changes announced in Michael's management structure, and his attorneys were dealing with a number of lawsuits, which included one with Debbie Rowe over "maintenance" money and visitation rights with the children. The legal cases reportedly occupied his lawyers throughout the summer months.

In July, Judge A. Howard Matz sentenced one of the two men convicted of taping Michael's private conversations with his attorney Mark Geragos on a chartered jet plane in 2003. The judge stressed the seriousness of the crime by sentencing the man to eight months in federal prison, six months in a halfway house that offers drug and alcohol rehabilitation treatment, and a fine of $1,000.

The judge in Debbie Rowe's case involving visitation rights ordered Michael Jackson to pay his ex-wife $60,000 to go toward her attorneys' fees. "She has millions of dollars, so she should be able to contribute to her own fees," the judge announced, referring to a financial settlement of approximately $8 million from Michael. She had requested nearly $200,000 in attorneys' fees.

Michael was no longer working with the Bahrainian record label Two Seas, according to an announcement made in late September 2006. Legal troubles would ensue....

During October, Debbie Rowe and Michael settled their disagreement over child custody and visitation rights. Michael retained custody of their two children, and Ms. Rowe's rights to visit with the children were acknowledged.

A short time later, the second defendant in the illegal, on-plane taping of Michael Jackson and his attorney was sentenced to six months of home detention, three years of probation, and a fine of $10,000.

In December, Michael Jackson filed a lawsuit against his former financial managers, Bernstein, Fox, Whitman, Goldman and Sloan, LLP.

2007

To begin the new year 2007, two lawsuits were filed against Michael Jackson, according to the *LA Times*. They both related to his former accountants, Bernstein, Fox, Whitman, Goldman and Sloan, LLP. The first alleged unpaid bills of nearly $110,000 owed to a company that installed television equipment for Michael, and the second alleged that he owed the accountants an amount in excess of $950,000 for managing his accounts.

In February, a lawsuit was filed against Michael Jackson and Marian Medical Center in Santa Barbara County by the family of Manuela Gomez Ruiz. The suit alleged "abuse of celebrity status," because Ms. Ruiz was moved, in February 2005, from a two-bed trauma room at Marian so that Michael Jackson could have the room after he was admitted for flu-like symptoms. Ruiz, 73, who had suffered a heart attack, died.

In April, more than one thousand items were seized after a business venture of the Jackson family failed and ended in bankruptcy. Michael and Janet Jackson filed a lawsuit to prevent the auction of personal clothing of family members, artwork, and personal notes; the event was scheduled at the Hard Rock Hotel and Resort in Las Vegas at the end of May. Michael was upset over the prospect of his personal belongings being randomly auctioned off to the highest bidders.

Attorneys for Michael Jackson reached a settlement with regard to the personal items and memorabilia due to be sold off, and the auction was scheduled to proceed, as planned. Bids were forthcoming from all around the world. Ten percent of the proceeds went to five children's charities in America.

Michael Jackson and Sony/ATV announced that they had acquired Famous Music LLC, which added another 125,000 songs, from classics to contemporary hits, to their existing music publishing catalog.

In mid-June 2007, on the day that a court case was due to begin, an announcement was made that Michael Jackson and Prescient Acquisition Group settled their dispute. Michael denied having signed an agreement with the company to refinance his debts for a fee of 9% of the total, which, if the alleged amount was correct, would have been $48 million. It was believed that no documents were available to prove that Michael had made this agreement, and absent proof, the company accepted a settlement.

At the same time, Michael Jackson decided not to renew his one-million-dollar, six-month lease at the Summerlin home in Las Vegas. Raymone Bain issued a statement denying a number of rumors about Michael; it included a vehement denial that Michael believed that a member of his family had stolen money from him. The statement also said:

> While in his entire career, Mr. Jackson has never uttered a disparaging word to any reporter ..., there are those [who] ... write reports ... to try and destroy Mr. Jackson's image.... Mr. Jackson's attorneys will address [these matters].

In July 2007, a law firm that worked for Michael Jackson during 2003 won their case for payment of fees. He had to pay nearly $217,000 in fees and more than $39,000 in interest.

Roberto Hernandez filed a lawsuit in August for $50,000-plus in damages, claiming that he was hurt when he tried to take photos of Michael Jackson and his children in January. Hernandez alleged that one of Michael's bodyguards beat him and stole his camera outside the Monte Carlo Hotel and Casino.

In October, Michael was ordered to pay the same law firm (from the July 2007 decision) another $175,000 for billed services.

2008

Ola Ray, who played Michael's girlfriend in the *Thriller* short film, claimed that she was paid only £600 for her role. Although she admitted to having loved working with Michael and flirting with him, she filed a lawsuit against him in February 2008, for more money for her work in 1983.

Also in February, a legal notice was issued to Michael Jackson, stating that unless he paid off the approximately $24 million loan, Neverland would be auctioned off in March 2008. The proposed sale would include everything, including all fixtures and fittings, personal belongings, household goods, and recreational items, including the trains and tracks, and the trees and plants.

In March, the owner of Extrajet, the air charter company employed by Michael Jackson to transport him to Santa Barbara to submit to the authorities there in 2003, was ordered by a judge to pay more than $12 million in damages in a civil suit. The man pled guilty to planting a secret camera on the plane in order to tape Michael Jackson and his attorney discussing legal plans.

That month, one of Michael's lawyers announced that a confidentiality agreement had been worked out with the Fortress Investment Group; Neverland Ranch was spared from being sold. In May, the foreclosure sale of Neverland was canceled, according to court papers. Michael announced: "I am pleased with recent developments involving Neverland Ranch and I am in discussions with Colony [Capital] and Tom Barrack with regard to the Ranch and other matters that would allow me to focus on the future."

Michael hired Dr. Tohme Tohme as his new manager and president of MJJ Productions in June. As the result of the financial reorganization of Neverland Ranch, all of Michael's personal belongings "must be removed from the property."

Dr. Tohme signed an agreement with Julien's Auction House on behalf of Michael Jackson in order to arrange for an auction of certain items that Michael allegedly no longer wanted.

Michael's attorneys reached a settlement with Sheikh Abdullah bin Hamad Al Khalifa, who claimed that Michael owed him $7 million. The agreement—made in November 2008, just before Michael boarded a flight to England for an appearance in the London High Court scheduled on the next day—meant that he postponed his travels. It was a "close call" for Michael, who dreaded going to court. Al Khalifa, an amateur songwriter, alleged that he advanced Michael Jackson money for a joint album and an autobiography that were never completed. Michael claimed the money was a present. Al Khalifa had hoped to work with the superstar on their musical careers.

Billionaire Tom Barrack and his firm, Colony Capital, paid the loan due on Neverland, thus averting foreclosure on the property, in November 2008. Michael "filed a grant deed on the ranch that makes the new owner an entity called the Sycamore Valley Ranch Company LLC, a joint venture between Jackson and an affiliate of Colony Capital LLC."

The golden gates of Neverland were removed and put into storage. More than 2,000 items—ranging from personal effects and costumes to pieces from Michael's private art collection, as well as fittings and furnishings from Neverland—were due to be put up for sale at a four-day public auction at the Beverly Hilton Hotel in Los Angeles.

Billie Jean Jackson filed a lawsuit against Michael Jackson, claiming that she was secretly married to him and that she gave birth to his third child, Prince Michael II (Blanket). In December, she filed the suit at Los Angeles Superior Court "because she is always arrested at the home of her husband, Michael J. Jackson." She demanded a payout of nearly one billion dollars, joint custody of the six-year-old, visitation rights on weekends, and a say in the boy's education. This lawsuit was widely perceived and reported as "frivolous and without merit."

2009

During January 2009, filmmaker John Landis and his company Levitsky Productions brought a lawsuit against Michael Jackson over royalties for the short film *Thriller*, which Landis co-wrote and also directed. He filed a second suit, against Michael Jackson and Broadway producer James Nederlander, alleging that the two lacked the legal rights to adapt a stage production based on the short film *Thriller*.

In March, Michael filed a lawsuit against Julien's Auction House to stop the sale of his personal possessions. The suit claimed that many of the items were "priceless and irreplaceable" and alleged that the attempt to sell them was "malicious, fraudulent, extreme, outrageous...." It stated that Michael had authorized the auction house to remove the items from Neverland but not to sell them without his permission.

In mid-April, it was announced that the auction of Michael's property from the Neverland Ranch would not proceed as scheduled. The sale was canceled and his property was to be returned to Michael Jackson.

A settlement agreement was entered into between Michael and Julien's, which allowed the auction house to hold its planned exhibition of Michael Jackson's belongings, open to the public. The terms of the agreement were not disclosed, but a joint statement between the parties was released: "Arrangements [were made] that will allow the collection to be shared with and enjoyed by Jackson's fans for many years to come." The statement also said that both sides would be making a "substantial" donation to MusiCares to benefit artists in need.

On May 8th, Dr. Conrad Murray "officially" began working as Michael Jackson's personal physician.

Raymone Bain, Michael Jackson's former publicist and manager, filed a $44 million breach of contract lawsuit during the month of May, in a Washington, D.C. civil court; she alleged that Michael had failed to pay her for services rendered. Dr. Tohme was reportedly terminated as Michael's manager, and Frank Dileo was acting in that capacity after a hiatus of many years in his employment with Michael. [The question of who was really Michael's manager was argued by individuals and the media across many weeks.]

In May 2009, AllGood Entertainment sent a "cease and desist" letter to AEG, the promoters of Michael's imminent *This Is It* concerts. The company claimed that Frank Dileo, acting as Michael's manager, signed a deal in 2008, in which it was promised that the entertainer would perform with other members of his family, including Janet, in a Jackson family reunion show in Texas, scheduled for July 2010. This deal, for which Michael was due to be paid nearly $24 million, allegedly prevented him from setting up any other concert deals for one and one-half years.

At least four attorneys were retained by Michael in June to represent him in the $44 million lawsuit filed by Raymone Bain. A response to her suit must be filed before the ten-day default notice is up.

John Branca was re-hired on or about June 17th as Michael's lawyer after many years had passed since his last period of employment with Michael.

Michael's death was announced officially on June 25, 2009, at 2:26 P.M.

According to *USA Today* on September 21, 2011, Michael Jackson "was entangled in 38 lawsuits" at the time of his death.

Peter Lopez, Michael Jackson's entertainment attorney from 2006 to the date of his client's death, committed suicide at the end of April 2010. Mr. Lopez, 60, died of a self-inflicted gun-shot wound to his head. He was found at his house in Encino Hills, California, shortly after he drove his children to school.

Mr. Lopez had issued a formal statement after Michael's death. In it, he said that the media frenzy and sensationalized coverage of his client's death were "irresponsible." He added, "It's very hurtful and harmful to have this sort of talk out there...." He expressed special concern regarding Michael's children and the media speculations about them.

Peter Lopez took his own life ten months after the tragic death of his client Michael Jackson. Mr. Lopez left a note, asking his family for forgiveness, but he gave no reason for his suicide.

*   *   *   *   *   *   *   *   *

In the "Creditors' Claims Filed and Disposition of Claims" against Michael Jackson's Estate, effective February 2010, *sixty-five* claimants were listed. Along with dozens of other claims not involved in litigation, a number of ongoing lawsuits were listed in the official documents....

AllGood Entertainment, Inc., and AllGood Concerts, LLC, filed for $300,000,000; the claimants filed a lawsuit in U.S. District Court in New York prior to Michael Jackson's passing. This suit alleged that an agent of Michael Jackson had agreed that he would perform several Jackson family reunion concerts before going on the road with any other show. AllGood claimed that by agreeing to do the O2 Arena concerts in London, Michael Jackson breached their agreement. [In August 2010, a federal judge ruled that Michael's agent Frank Dileo merely struck the deal in principle; it couldn't become binding without the signatures of Michael and his brothers; and the deal was "too sketchy" to be enforceable. The lawsuit was dismissed, and it was called "frivolous" by the attorney of Michael's Estate, Howard Weitzman.]

Steven Echols filed a lawsuit in the amount of $261,169. Echols claimed that he and his company were contracted with Michael Jackson for bodyguards between February and December 2008. He said that invoices given to Mr. Jackson's "people" at the time were not paid and amounted to $300,000. [This case was settled out of court, as reported in May 2011.]

Helen M. Harris-Scott filed a lawsuit against the Estate for $50 million. In 2006, she sought $100 million, alleging that Michael Jackson wire-tapped her phone, placed tracking devices in her vehicle, hired "organized criminals" to watch her inside her Los Angeles house and to report to him, and tampered with her food and water. She had claimed that Michael Jackson also communicated with her personally through his music. She sought a public apology from him in her lawsuit. *TMZ* gave this their "Crazy Lawsuit of the Year" award. [Harris-Scott's lawsuit was dismissed on March 1, 2010.]

Aner Iglesias filed a lawsuit for $234,000-plus. Iglesias was the landlord of the Palomino Lane estate that Michael rented from March 2008, through August 2009, a date long after Michael and his family stopped living in the home. Iglesias alleged damages to the house that included the phone and alarm system. [This matter was settled out of court by the Estate for an undisclosed amount of money in March 2011.]

The lawsuit filed at the beginning of 2009 by filmmaker John Landis for $300,000-plus was reported as "settlement negotiations ongoing." Levitsky Productions, Inc., Landis's company, was reported in "settlement negotiations" also.

Richard LaPointe, a memorabilia collector, filed a lawsuit against Michael Jackson's Estate and Julien's Auction House for $5 million for an auction of Michael Jackson memorabilia that was canceled. He alleged that he was the highest bidder on dozens of MJ items and therefore entitled to the goods. [This case was settled out of court, as reported in May 2011.]

Ola Ray's lawsuit for royalties from *Thriller* was reported with the amount of claim as "to be determined," and with a status of "settlement negotiations ongoing."

Stinky Films, Inc., filed a lawsuit in the amount of $1 million-plus; status was "negotiations ongoing."

Raymone Bain's legal action against Michael Jackson shortly before his death listed two amounts allegedly due her for services rendered and profit-sharing in the amounts of $360,000 and $44 million-plus. The lawsuit was dismissed and was on appeal.

The theater production company Nederlander Presentations, Inc., filed a suit [in June 2010] against the Estate for breach of contract in an amount "to be determined." The lawsuit alleges that Michael Jackson signed a contract in October 2008, when plans were made to produce a Broadway musical based on *Thriller*. The plaintiff was also seeking to obtain new, previously-unheard songs and musical compositions by Michael Jackson for the show.

Jose Freddie Vallejos, as a private citizen, brought a lawsuit against the Estate, seeking $3.3 million. The suit alleges that the City of Los Angeles erred when it paid for the cost of security for Michael Jackson's Memorial in July 2009. The plaintiff claimed that, if successful in this lawsuit, he would reimburse the city for the expenditures.

*   *   *   *   *   *   *   *   *

In October 2009, as reported by *TMZ*, attorney Sidney Lanier filed a lawsuit against Michel Jackson's Estate, seeking $3 million and an apology. According to Lanier, he represented Michael Jackson in several cases. Lanier claimed that he represented Jackson confidante Marc Schaffel in a hotly-contested case in 2005, and after the case, Michael Jackson refused to pay the attorney's fee and filed a lawsuit against him for alleged fraud. Lanier claimed that his reputation was sullied all over town by this lawsuit, and he was put through "two years of expensive, stressful litigation and ridicule." He was sorry about Michael Jackson's death only because he "wanted him to apologize...."

An accounting firm, Cannon and Company, filed a claim with the Estate in October 2009, asserting that Michael owed them $56,582 for services rendered earlier in the year 2009. *TMZ* reported that one of their invoices was from July of that year, the month after Michael died.

An ex-choreographer for Michael Jackson, LaVelle Smith Jr., filed a lawsuit against the Estate in October 2009, claiming that he worked for Michael for several different stretches of time in 2008 and 2009, and that he was paid only part of what he was supposed to get, leaving $144,500 still owed to him.

According to *TMZ* on April 12, 2010, claims against Michael Jackson/his Estate included the following:

Claire McMillan was seeking $2.2 million for her tutoring services in the home-schooling of Michael Jackson's children.

Nona Paris Lola Ankhesenamun Jackson claimed to have been married to Michael Jackson and sought to obtain custody of "her" three children. She lost several lawsuits since 2006 over her claim. [This litigant joined a virtual parade of individuals with similar claims during Michael Jackson's lifetime.]

In October 2010, Billie Jean Jackson filed suit against the judge who threw out her paternity case against Michael Jackson. She was seeking $600 million from Judge Mitchell Beckloff for discrimination, emotional distress, and prejudice after he failed to order a DNA test to establish whether her child was the son of Michael Jackson, deceased (for sixteen months) at the time of her filing against the judge.

In Germany, litigation is proceeding against Dieter Wiesner, in which he is accused by a former business partner of "illegally acquiring rights to Michael Jackson's global brand name," purchased a decade ago by the German company MJ Net AG. In April 2011, it was disclosed for the first time that Michael Jackson and Wiesner settled a lawsuit through a confidentiality agreement in September 2007, in which Michael agreed to pay Wiesner a total of $3.48 million. [Wiesner had met Jackson in 1994, and he became Michael's personal manager in 2002.] After Michael Jackson fired Wiesner in 2003, the German brought a lawsuit against his former employer and "good friend" in a Los Angeles court. [Wiesner reportedly had been convicted of tax evasion and fraud in the past.] Jurgen Bachus, former chairman of the board at MJ Net AG, filed a claim for $5 million against Michael's Estate in March 2010.

Dr. Tohme Tohme, Michael's manager from June 2008 to May 2009, when he was reportedly fired, has filed two lawsuits against the Estate. In the first, he is seeking $2.3 million for having a role in the refinancing of Neverland. In the second, he is seeking 15% of the deal between AEG and Michael Jackson that resulted in the *This Is it* production. Not including the highly profitable DVD and album sales from *This Is It,* the gross theater profits alone were $260 million, which would garner $39 million for Tohme if he succeeds in this litigation. [According to the written contract that was not fully executed between AEG and Dr. Conrad Murray, Tohme was to receive—and/or was receiving—a salary of $100,000 per month for his employment as manager on behalf of Michael Jackson.]

Although the action was not directed at Michael Jackson, concert promoter Citadel Ltd. filed a lawsuit against Frank Dileo in August 2010. The company alleged that Dileo accepted $300,000 in fees, wired to him in April to June 2009, for performances that Michael Jackson was supposed to give in Trinidad and Tobago, scheduled for just months after Michael's June 2009 death. The judge in the case ruled a "default" because the defendant Dileo had not answered the complaint.

According to www.mjj2005.com, the researcher there concluded, in May 2010, that the total amount of potential payouts for lawsuits by the Estate of Michael Jackson was $432 million, and "the total payouts will not exceed 20 millions in my opinion." These figures are admittedly estimates, based upon this one researcher's "educated opinion," but they are only speculative and—according to many other people—are probably too conservative.

         *   *   *   *   *   *   *   *   *

This has been a peek into the litigious world of Michael Jackson, both in life and in death. *Is there any reasonable doubt that he was virtually drowning in legal actions from all around?*

**The worse things got for Michael Jackson,
the better they got for many in his employ,
including, of course, the lawyers.**

**A lawyer with his briefcase
can steal more
than a hundred men with guns.**

— Mario Puzo *(of The Godfather)*

Nothing But the Facts ...

I think the country that
treated Michael Jackson worst
was the United States.

— Thomas Mesereau

I just simply want to be loved
all over the world ...
wherever I go.

— Michael Jackson

"Get out of there!" Thomas Mesereau advised his weary, worn-out, but relieved client by telephone.

"Why? What have you heard, Tom?" Michael Jackson asked his attorney, with anxiety in his voice.

"No specific words, but the District Attorneys are humiliated and angry over your acquittal, Michael. They won't stop until they get you on something. You need to get out of their reach." Mesereau was advising his client and friend to "Get out of Dodge" for his own safety and peace of mind.

"You don't need a law degree to understand this verdict," announced CNN legal analyst Jeffrey Toobin. "It is an absolute ... victory for Michael Jackson, utter humiliation and defeat for Thomas Sneddon, ... who has been pursuing Michael Jackson for more than a decade, who brought a case that was not one that this jury bought at all." Sneddon and his fellow prosecutors felt humiliated on a personal level, Mesereau knew, and pressured on a professional level, because of their public failure and the untold millions of dollars of taxpayers' money that they squandered.

It had taken sixty-six days to get the case to the jury, forty-five for the prosecution to present its side, fifteen for the defense, and ten days for the jury's deliberation. Before the trial, more than a decade of attempts to nail Michael Jackson had failed; seventy-plus sheriffs raided Neverland; and more than 100 search warrants were issued. The costs for these extraordinary efforts—coupled with the exorbitant budget line-item for security for the trial—were staggering and, to some, alarming.

Thomas Mesereau was convinced that the Santa Barbara D.A. might use any future incident—such as a child or teenager who might be injured after having trespassed onto Neverland to explore the property—by jumping on it as evidence of some sinister or inappropriate behavior by Michael Jackson. A full, intrusive investigation would ensue, and on and on.

Certain individuals from the media had already been promised, by the D.A.'s office, the special privilege of immediate notice of any alleged infraction by Michael Jackson or one of his "people." They were guaranteed the opportunity for first coverage of such an event.

"At first, Michael Jackson was reluctant to leave Neverland; it meant so much to him," Mesereau explains. "But he realized the truth in what I was telling him ... and the danger."

Shell-shocked from the horrendous experience of twenty months of searches, investigations, an indictment, and a searing trial, Michael Jackson was hospitalized after his acquittal for dehydration, exhaustion, weight loss, and a stomach ailment. He had lost a noticeable amount of weight even though he was dancer-thin before the trial began in early 2005. He looked frail; he felt awful.

Michael was experiencing a tidal wave of stress after a tsunami of a trial. He suffered from symptoms of post-traumatic stress disorder for months—and arguably *forever*—after the ordeal legally ended. The emotional effects continued—nightmares, anxiety, depression, and the sleeplessness that had always plagued him, but became the norm for Michael.

He hoped to avoid further publicity; he desperately wanted anonymity; and he longed to live a life that might approach normalcy for himself and his young children.

Michael Jackson began what would become four years of a restless, nomadic existence. Always taking his beloved children with him, Michael would travel from one place to another, sometimes staying for a span of months and sometimes for only a handful of days or an overnight.

His wanderings seemed especially sad to those who knew him because he had always loved the idea of having roots. *Michael was a homebody.* He had lived at the Hayvenhurst family compound from the time he was a preteen until the year he turned thirty. In his mid-twenties, he was the biggest celebrity on earth, but he was still living at home with parents and several siblings! When asked about this curious decision, Michael responded that he feared that he would die of loneliness if he lived alone....

In 1988, he bought the 2,700-acre Sycamore Valley Ranch in the Santa Ynez Valley near Santa Barbara, after he had stayed there with "Beatle" Paul McCartney and his wife Linda, who were renting it at the time. Michael then set about changing its name—inspired by his favorite mythical character, Peter Pan—to Neverland Valley Ranch. He then installed a large-scale amusement park, zoo, and other thrilling amenities to transform it into a fantasy-like kingdom for himself and for needy children visitors. Later, he would have his own children to enjoy it with him.

"Evil to him who thinks evil" are the words, in Latin, that were incorporated into the intricate inner gate to Neverland Ranch. Sadly, it was evil-thinking people who caused Michael's necessary self-eviction from his beloved home.

Across thirty-five years, Michael Jackson lived in only two homes—extraordinarily large buildings that afforded privacy, security, comfort, and even creative inspiration. They both occupied enough verdant land to accommodate wild animals and to elicit and foster deep enjoyment of nature. They also had specially-designed facilities for entertainment and studios for Michael Jackson's recording of music and for dancing.

Following Thomas Mesereau's advice, Michael Jackson began a self-imposed exile. He and his three children fled to the Persian Kingdom of Bahrain. He had been invited by Sheikh Abdullah bin Hamad Al Khalifa, the son of the king; Michael and his children moved into the prince's palace. This move would begin an eighteen-month series of temporary residences, with Michael as a guest or renter, across a variety of countries. While overseas, he lived a mysterious life, out of public view except for very rare glimpses by paparazzi. He lived in lavish facilities, but they were not really "home." *A cage is still a cage no matter how well appointed, nicely decorated, or beautifully draped.*

Michael Jackson's fans and a large segment of mainstream media overseas showed continuous, loyal support for him. It was in his own country that Michael Jackson was mocked, harassed, and negatively represented by the media. In foreign countries, Michael Jackson was well known to visit iconic places in the cities of his concerts, such as statues of famous leaders and religious shrines. He would often place flowers there to show his respect for the culture, its history and heroes. Always, he visited a hospital or orphanage; personally handed out gifts, often numbering in the hundreds; shook hands and hugged the children; and posed for photos intended for the suffering and dying individuals, not for publicity.

Michael Jackson often sent one of his people to inquire about the cost of a medical treatment needed to save a life when he was told the family could not pay for a surgery or other intervention for their child. Then he would make arrangements, usually anonymously, to cover the cost of the life-saving measures. Some of these philanthropic activities leaked to the media abroad and they published the information. This was a very different brand of media from that in the United States, and it created a widespread appreciation for Michael Jackson by the general public that was lacking in his home country.

Desperate to flee from the accusations, innuendo, and lurid speculation about him that was filling American airwaves and newsprint, Michael Jackson sought refuge in foreign countries. He realized all too well that the mud, the stain, and the appearance of guilt—created and fostered by ruthless American media—persisted after his full acquittal of all charges. He carried that burden with him. *All of his life, he only wanted to be loved.* Now—even after the verdicts that should have vindicated him for once and for all—he was still being abused and vilified in his home country....

Happenings, Comings & Goings

In late June 2005, it was announced that the sales of Michael Jackson's records and DVD's had risen by over 300% since his acquittal. In July, Sony Music released "Live in Bucharest," featuring Michael's *Dangerous* concert—filmed live and showing audience reactions among 70,000 attendees—in Romania in 1992; sales soared.

Michael arrived in Dubai in August, with a Bahraini delegation; he checked into the Burj Al Arab Hotel. He was accompanied by Sheikh Abdullah Al Khalifa, his host in Bahrain. They stayed for a week, during which they toured the cosmopolitan city.

In mid-September, Michael rented out the entire "Wild Wadi" water park in Dubai for children and their parents to have fun, at his expense. Michael also visited the park that day.

Michael stayed at London's Dorchester Hotel, overlooking Hyde Park, during October. There he met with his fans, signed autographs, and posed for photographs. He climbed onto a car roof in the parking lot and waved to the fans. Michael attended the *Billy Elliot* musical, reportedly arriving fifteen minutes late to avoid a mob scene. However, in the melee outside the Victoria Palace Theater, Michael fell to the ground while trying to make his way through hundreds of gathered fans, in spite of his security personnel forcing a path for him through the boisterous crowd.

In October, Thomas Mesereau flew from California to meet with Michael and Grace Rwaramba at the Dorchester. Grace, his long-time nanny and friend, and Michael had telephoned Susan Yu numerous times to ask her advice about a variety of matters related to his departure from the U.S. and adjustment to a foreign environment. Michael felt emotionally close to both Mesereau and Yu, trusting of them, and desirous of getting their best advice related to his concerns.

Among other matters, Michael needed to address many issues related to the care of his Neverland animals and the transfer of many of them to other places, and to make decisions about dozens of his employees at the Ranch. He had retained lawyers in the Middle East to join the contingent of lawyers that was America-based.

"Michael was happy to see me, but he seemed shy and anxious," Mesereau reports. The attorney soon learned that "there was still a merry-go-round of would-be 'saviors' to take advantage of Michael Jackson while he was abroad."

Tom Mesereau and Susan Yu continued to advise and to represent Michael Jackson for many months, until the spring of 2006. At times, Michael telephoned Susan Yu "on a nearly daily basis" to seek her opinions.

During October 2005, with his children, Michael visited Madame Tussauds wax museum and the famous Harrods department store. He met Mohamed Al-Fayed, the owner of Harrods, while he was visiting. He went to see the Wallace and Gromit movie, *The Curse of the Were-Rabbit,* before leaving London for Bahrain.

In late October, Thomas Mesereau issued a statement on behalf of Michael Jackson:

> He's looking much better. He's with his children, and he's moving on in life. He's living permanently in Bahrain. He has friends there who have been very loyal and helpful to him in a difficult period of his life. He looks really well.

Michael Jackson presented awards at the Dubai Desert Rally Racing Tournament in mid-November. A spokesman for Michael "denied that he has put Neverland on the market for sale."

In response to comedian Richard Pryor's death in early December, Michael issued a statement that described his friend as "a trailblazer, whose extraordinary talent and genius provided the blueprint for others to follow. I send my love ... to the entire Pryor family."

At Christmastime, Michael issued a holiday greeting to his fans, wishing them and their families a wonderful holiday season and thanking them for their cards, letters, love, and support. "I love you all!" he concluded.

Some of Michael Jackson's friends visited him in Bahrain to celebrate Christmas with him and his children.

2006

During January 2006, Michael was seen shopping in a mall in Bahrain. He was wearing the disguise of a black veil and burka, a full-body cloak typically worn by Muslim women.

Michael Jackson and his children flew to Hamburg, Germany, in late January, to spend a few days; the trip was called a "private visit."

From Bahrain, at the end of January, Michael issued a statement that expressed his sadness over the passing of Mrs. Coretta Scott King, widow of Martin Luther King, Jr. "Mrs. King is an irreplaceable jewel, who will be greatly missed," he wrote; "I am deeply saddened...."

It was announced, during April 2006, that Michael had employed a new manager, English "music mogul" Guy Holmes. He was working on a new album for a proposed release in late 2007, on the label Two Seas Records, for which he had entered into a partnership with Abdullah Hamad Al Khalifa.

In May, Michael attended a concert by a famous Lebanese singer. He also gave an interview to a British newspaper, *The Mirror*, at the offices of Harrods. The reporter, who said that Michael hugged her in greeting, also stated that he looked "totally different from the gaunt, hunched figure ... at the end of his U.S. trial" and that he seemed relaxed. Michael was looking around London and in Scotland and Ireland for a place to live. "I've always liked the U.K.," Michael told her, "and I just love the fans here.... I'm feeling good." He was in London for "only a couple of days" and then left for Japan.

At the end of May 2006, Michael received *MTV Japan*'s Legend Award at the awards ceremony in Tokyo. The special award was for his record-breaking career in the music industry, having sold more than *100 million albums* in Japan! Michael was visibly moved by the ecstatic response from the audience. He told them:

> This is a great honor. I love you more.... I promised myself when I came up here that I wouldn't get emotional.... You're [referring to the Japanese people] very sweet, generous, kind people.... Thank you to all the people who believe in me....

He visited a Tokyo children's home the next day, interacted with 140 children, and watched a special performance for him of traditional music and dance.

While visiting Paris, France, in mid-June, and reportedly under the protection of "about ten bodyguards," Michael went to the Disneyland Resort, where he enjoyed a number of the rides.

Days later, Michael and his children arrived in Cork, Ireland. He was wearing a disguise of a black scarf, hooded sweatshirt, and a baseball cap.

In County Cork, Ireland, Michael and his family stayed at Blackwater Castle, built in the twelfth-century and located on a protected nature preserve of more than fifty acres of woodland. They also stayed at Ballinacurra House, a "luxury estate for exclusive hire," consisting of an elegant country mansion situated in a totally private environment.

Michael was hosted by Michael Flatley—known for his world-acclaimed *Lord of the Dance* shows—at his palatial, 150-acre estate CastleHyde, overlooking the Blackwater River in County Cork.

Thriller Live, an extravagant show with thirty dancers that celebrates the hit songs of Michael Jackson and The Jackson 5, premiered in London at the end of August. Adrian Grant, who began the Annual Michael Jackson Day for the fans, is the creator and producer of the show. He became a friend of Michael in the early nineties, visiting with him in the U.K. and at Neverland Ranch.

Also at the end of August, Michael received a long-distance telephone call from the States to inform him that 40 acres of Neverland had burned; the source of the brush-fire was unknown. Numerous water drops were made by helicopter, and nearly 100 firefighters responded to the wildfire to keep it from the main house. Fortunately, none of the animals was harmed; no buildings were destroyed; nor was the damage to the burnt acreage irreversible across time. [Michael never returned to Neverland to view the damage or for any other reason.]

Michael Jackson and children moved into the luxurious Luggala Castle in County Wicklow, Ireland, in early September 2006. Reportedly, the castle "came under a virtual siege" from Michael's fans during his stay. The famous Gothic Revival house is well known for royalty, inspired musicians, and the many celebrities who rent the seven-bedroom home, which is set on a "magical 6,000-acre estate" in its own private valley in the Wicklow Mountains. While staying there, Michael and his children toured the local area and visited a favorite bookstore together.

The Michael Jackson family also occupied the luxurious Grouse Lodge in County Westmeath during their Ireland stay. Grouse is known for being Ireland's first International Residential Recording Studio; it is located near the picturesque village of Rosemount, near Dublin. Its two world-class studios are continuously available for its residents, who also have access to a full array of amenities in a stunning natural setting. Michael worked on his music in the studio with state-of-the-art equipment in a huge control room.

Returning to London in mid-November, Michael took over two floors of the Hempel Hotel in Notting Hill. He was reported as accompanied by a group of twenty-five, which included his three children. He enjoyed a midnight shopping spree at Topshop after meeting and dining with its owner at a "trendy restaurant."

On November 14, 2006, Michael Jackson visited the *Guinness World Records* office in London. There he received eight World Record certificates for accomplishments across years of hard work, recording, and performing. The most recent of the eight was for the "Most Successful Entertainer of All Time."

The next day, Michael attended the 2006 World Music Awards in London. He was honored with the Diamond Award—given to artists who sell more than 100 million albums. It was presented to him by Beyonce Knowles, with these words:

Tonight we are celebrating 25 years of *Thriller*. If it wasn't for Michael Jackson I would never have ever performed. I love you, we all love you.

Michael accepted the award with words of gratitude:

There have been many people who have loved me and stood by me. I love all the fans from the bottom of my heart.

Michael threw his black jacket into the crowd as a souvenir for a lucky fan, and he left the stage to immense applause.

Days later, Michael granted a brief interview with *MTV UK News*, in which he confirmed that he was working on a new album and that he was "mainly writing it myself." He was also looking for a new house.

Michael and family visited Dublin, Ireland, for an undisclosed span of time—perhaps one month—until, on December 23, 2006, they flew to Las Vegas, Nevada, with their nanny Grace. From the airport there, they were driven to their new rental home in Summerlin. Michael's manager had arranged for a six-month lease for him without his having seen the property.

When Michael and his children arrived at the mansion at 2785 Monte Cristo Way, the exterior of the house and the trees were decorated in sparkling lights, and inside a large Christmas tree was set up with presents underneath. The decorations had been arranged by Jack Wishna, known in Las Vegas as a deal-maker of big projects, and his wife Donna.

*   *   *   *   *   *   *   *   *

The Home: 2785 S. Monte Cristo, Summerlin, Las Vegas

Set on one acre, the 16,400-square-foot home is located on a corner of intersecting streets. Surrounded by eight-foot walls, with a large wrought-iron gate in front of the house, it has six bedrooms, ten bathrooms, three office suites, an elevator, large formal rooms for entertaining, a theater room, and an orchestra loft. A special feature of the home is the 2,000 square-foot master bedroom with a large covered patio, huge closets, Jacuzzi tub, and a secret exit to a rooftop deck for sun bathing or relaxation. The fitness room features a dance floor and dry sauna. In the backyard are basketball and tennis courts and a large pool. [The home would later be sold for $3.1 million in January 2010. With Michael Jackson as its recent occupant, the sales price of the home exceeded its predicted market value.]

Because Michael Jackson and his children occupied this home for a six-month stretch, it is considered special to his fans. During the last four years of his life, Michael stayed in many places. This house, however, is characterized by not only a relatively long period of time of his residence, but by being the place that he occupied immediately after returning to the United States from abroad. It symbolizes his re-entry to the country and his return to his American fans and admirers.

*   *   *   *   *   *   *   *   *

At the end of December 2006, Michael Jackson attended the funeral of James Brown. He sat between Reverends Jesse Jackson and Al Sharpton. Michael said, "Words cannot adequately express the love and respect that I will always have for Mr. Brown...." Michael visibly wept for his mentor and friend.

2007

With the start of 2007, Michael was thinking more about his career direction and next move. During the first week of January, he dined out with Emmy Award director Kenny Ortega at the Wynn Restaurant in Las Vegas. Michael and Ortega had worked closely together on the *Dangerous* and *HIStory* world tours.

During his first weeks of living in Las Vegas, Michael took his children to see Lance Burton's magic show at the Monte Carlo. He left before the end of the show so that the audience would not be distracted from Lance's curtain calls. He also went to see the Beatles *LOVE* musical at the Mirage. Michael went backstage to meet the cast and crew to thank them for the spectacular show.

In early February, in an interview with Robin Leach, Michael disclosed that he would be utilizing the services of Simon Fuller, who created the hit show *American Idol*, to help him plan his future professional activities. That same week, *Rolling Stone* reported that Will.i.am and Michael Jackson had been collaborating on as many as eight songs together.

On February 14, 2007, Michael and his family enjoyed lunch at Wolfgang Puck's Chinois in a private room, after shopping for toys at Caesar's Palace Hotel. The occasion was Prince's tenth birthday, on the previous day.

Later that month, Raymone Bain issued a statement that denied certain rumors about Michael Jackson. In it she confirmed that "Mr. Jackson has been presented with numerous proposals which he has not solicited, several of which include performing in Las Vegas. Mr. Jackson is currently reviewing … each proposal...." She clarified that Michael moved to Vegas not to shop a show for himself, but because he found it a good location to record with other artists, songwriters, and producers, who were working with him in the studio.

Michael flew to Japan during the first week of March in order to attend two fan events. While there, he stopped at the huge electronics store Bic Camera, which gave him two hours of after-closing time to shop by himself. He met with fans who had bought $3,500 VIP tickets to a special dinner and show. At a Tokyo nightclub, Michael watched a show from a special private room upstairs, while 1,000 of his fans crowded onto the first floor.

Michael was flown by helicopter to Camp Zama, the U.S. base with several thousand American troops and their families. He shook hands and gave a brief speech, which included his praise and thanks:

> Those of you in here today are some of the most special people in the world. It is because of you ... and others who have given their lives to protect us that we enjoy our freedom.

Back in London in mid-March, Michael and children checked into the Jumeirah Carlton Towers Hotel in London, accompanied by "an army of bodyguards," according to hotel staff. He shopped for clothing at Topshop and visited with its owner, Philip Green. Michael was mobbed inside his hotel by zealous fans, and when he stopped to sign autographs, he was pushed against a wall and hit his head.

Several days later, Michael was seen at Heathrow Airport, leaving the U.K.; he was escorted by security guards and police officers. Raymone Bain confirmed that Michael was "a little under the weather" when he returned from Europe but that he was not hospitalized, as had been reported erroneously.

In mid-April, the magazine *Sister 2 Sister* reported that its publisher, Jamie Foster, had traveled as part of Michael's entourage on his trip to Japan the previous month. Photos of his children were taken without their scarves, a most unusual occurrence. She described Michael as just like "a regular dad" and "a good parent." The children "have a lot of fun with their dad," she wrote. Ms. Foster praised the kids for their intelligence, politeness, and love of laughter and jokes.

Michael and his children arrived in London during the third week of May. He was an honored guest at the twenty-fifth birthday party for Prince Azim, the son of the Sultan of Brunei, at one of the family's homes in England. Michael Jackson was a special guest among hundreds of celebrities at the lavish party.

Back in the United States in early June, Michael was seen in Los Angeles. He took his children to see *The Bodies—An Exhibition*, which displays the skeletons of real people who donated their bodies to science, and also *Titanic—An Artifact Exhibition*.

Raymone Bain issued a statement, on behalf of Michael Jackson, to clarify that he had decided not to renew his lease or to purchase the Summerlin home in Las Vegas. He was also "putting finishing touches" on his music in the studio. The official statement attempted to refute more rumors about Michael Jackson and included the following pointed words:

> While in his entire career, Mr. Jackson has never uttered a disparaging word to any reporter, nor has he ever used or instructed his security to use any force toward any reporter, there are those whose vehement hatred for Mr. Jackson has reached a level where all journalistic integrity has been lost, in order to write reports for which there is no substantiation, are untrue, written to create a frenzy, or used to try and destroy Mr. Jackson's image. They know who they are; and this is a sad commentary … which Mr. Jackson's attorneys will address.

After they vacated their Summerlin home, Michael and his family took up temporary residence at the Goodstone Inn and Estate in Middleburg, Virginia. With only a main carriage house and six luxury suites—each one set upon rolling, verdant acreage in a private setting—this seemed an ideal place for Michael Jackson. Its 640-acre plot of land had been a plantation during the time of the Civil War; it is still accessible from a small country road. Less than one hour from Washington, D.C., it served Michael Jackson's needs for quick access to that city.

At this special place, Michael was able to run around with his children on the expansive grounds, a rare treat for him and them because of the prohibitive security measures that governed his outdoor activities. The usual confidentiality agreement was executed between the management of Goodstone Inn and Michael's representatives. However, James Blount, the new manager as of March 2011, reveals that Michael had a large-screen television set brought in for himself and his children, one that met his specifications. When the family left, it was also left behind.

In mid-July, Michael and his family visited the Smithsonian Institute, where they were given a private tour before it opened to the public. It was reported that the Deputy Director, eighty-four years old, personally showed the family around. Of special significance was that this same man had toured Michael Jackson at the Institute twenty-five years before.

Dominic Cascio and his family disclosed, in December 2010, that Michael Jackson and his children lived with them for nearly three months at their Franklin Lakes, New Jersey home during the fall of 2007, from mid-August to early November. Eddie ("Angel") Cascio and Michael wrote and recorded songs in the home's basement studio during this time. Michael could enjoy the feeling of being part of a family with the Cascios, whom he had known for approximately twenty-five years in a relationship that was kept secret from the public.

Michael went to New York in mid-September; he stayed at a mid-town hotel. Michael participated in an elaborate photo shoot for the Italian *Vogue* magazine, for the October issue. These would be the first "official" photos of Michael Jackson in a long while.

While in the "Big Apple," Michael and his children went to see the *Lion King* musical and met the cast after the show.

Issued in late September, *Vogue for Men* fashion magazine featured Michael on the cover and included a twenty-page spread of his latest photographs. The magazine reported that Michael Jackson had "not been photographed in this way for sixteen years."

Michael issued a warm, effusive "thank you" to his fans for all of their beautiful cards, photos, messages, videos, and gifts that were sent to him for his birthday on August 29th. His official letter to all of his fans was released in early October; he mentioned in it that he would soon be sharing exciting news from his recent efforts.

Michael visited the Brooklyn Museum in New York at the end of October for a photo shoot staged there. Michael, who had brought his son Blanket with him, "grooved to his music while posing, and even danced a little." When the shoot was finished, Michael left to put his children to bed. In celebration of the twenty-fifth anniversary of *Thriller, Ebony* magazine published a 22-page spread on Michael from the photographs taken at the Brooklyn Museum.

On November 8, 2007, Michael Jackson attended the sixty-sixth birthday celebration for the Reverend Jesse Jackson at the Beverly Hills Hotel in Los Angeles. That same evening, Michael walked the red carpet at the 10ᵗʰ Annual Awards dinner for the Rainbow/PUSH Coalition, which was combined with Reverend Jackson's birthday event.

Michael and his children remained in L.A. for a while, during which time Michael was seen shopping on Melrose Drive with "just one lady for company." He reportedly wore a baseball cap and an outfit that made him look "like a homeless guy," according to one male fan, who was ecstatic to have the opportunity to interact with Michael Jackson. He told the man that he was "trying to be just like you"—wanting just to shop without a fuss—and asked the fan not to tell anyone that he was in the shop. Michael signed an autograph for his delighted fan, who later said, "Despite his appearance, there's still something magical about the guy. He was very gracious." Michael was swarmed by fans when he left, however, and they followed him through an alleyway to his waiting vehicle.

In December, *Rolling Stone Japan* featured Michael Jackson in an "extra" 44-page book dedicated to the King of Pop. Epic Records/Legacy Recordings released the 25ᵗʰ anniversary edition of *Thriller*, the biggest-selling album of all time. The new album features sixteen songs that include the original nine tracks and five new remixes.

Michael Jackson was staying in Los Angeles in early December. There he was spotted as he was leaving an electrical goods store in Beverly Hills.

At the end of December, the singer Usher revealed to the *Atlanta Journal* that he was working on a single "that includes Michael Jackson."

2008

In January 2008, rumors were published that Michael Jackson was planning a series of concerts at the O2 Arena in London and that he would be in residence there for one month. Michael's new single, "The Girl Is Mine 2008"—his collaboration with Will.i.am— became available as a digital download. That month, Michael sent a video message to the NRJ Music Awards show in Cannes, France; he accepted an award celebrating the twenty-fifth anniversary of *Thriller.*

In mid-January, the local media discovered that Michael and his children had "been camped out" in a suite atop the Palms Hotel in Las Vegas "for almost two months." Michael Jackson was using the hotel's studio for intense work on his new album. Michael was spotted "out in the public with regularity" and, specifically twice in one week, taking his kids to see the local sights. He and his children took an after-hours tour of the Venetian Hotel's Madame Tussauds wax museum and they attended the Tournament of Kings show at the Excalibur.

During the week of January 28th, a photo was taken and published of Prince and Paris in Las Vegas without veils. It was referred to as "the first picture of them unmasked."

At the end of February, Michael entered the *Billboard* chart at number 1 with *Thriller 25.* It sold more copies than any other album on the chart for over a decade.

Michael and his children had lunch together at Planet Hollywood inside the Miracle Mile Shops in Las Vegas.

Michael Amir Williams, his personal assistant, signed an agreement in Michael Jackson's name to lease the Palomino Lane home in Las Vegas from March 1, 2008, through August 31, 2008; the lease would later be extended to August 31, 2009.

*   *   *   *   *   *   *   *   *

The Home: 2710 Palomino Lane, Las Vegas

Dubbed "Palomino Hacienda," this expansive home—with 20,600 square feet of living space in the main house—has seven bedrooms, eleven bathrooms, a recording studio, an elevator leading to the master bedroom, a Spanish chapel, tunnels dug beneath so that residents may move about unnoticed, separate guest/maids quarters with separate kitchen, a huge family room, dining rooms, several living rooms, a cobblestone esplanade, vast outdoor barbecue areas and gardens. A fountain and large sculpture of a crescent moon being hugged by cherubs sit in the middle of the estate's center courtyard. On what looks to be a bell tower, but without the bell, four musical notes are placed on the high structure. "When Michael saw those," his realtor discloses, "he knew he had to live here; it was destiny."

The home also includes an 8,500-square-foot basement, which was used as Michael's storage area for his vast collection of memorabilia, books, and art. Among the stored items were two golden statuettes, Oscars for historic Academy Awards. One of them was the Oscar for the Best Picture from the 1939 epic film *Gone with the Wind,* which Michael bought at auction for a record $1.5 million, and the other was from *Chariots of Fire* in 1981. The basement was also used as his personal studio, "where he created some of his last works."

The property encompasses 1.7 acres and has several courtyards and trails that lead throughout the grounds.

[In July 2011, the estate was on the market with a listing price of $12 million. It has become a pilgrimage site for Michael Jackson's fans.

In recognition of Michael Jackson's birthday on August 29, 2011, a huge banner—with a photo of Michael in classic dance pose—was displayed inside the front wrought-iron gates; on it were the words "Happy Birthday! Michael." Fans from many parts of the world visited on the days surrounding his birthday to pay homage, to leave flowers and memorabilia, and to photograph various angles of the exterior of the huge home and its grounds. Posted on the high walls surrounding the estate were large signs—"24-Hour Video Surveillance/ARMED RESPONSE"—a stark reminder of the highly-guarded life of its most recent occupant, Michael Jackson the King of Pop.]

Interestingly, Michael and his children occupied the 3,982-square-foot separate guesthouse when they were in residence, for security reasons. The main house—huge and rambling—was believed to be situated too close to the road and too potentially vulnerable to a breach of security. Michael felt comfortable and safe, for himself and his children, only in the guest/maids quarters, which were more easily protected.

     *   *   *   *   *   *   *   *   *

In May 2008, *Thriller* joined a list of twenty-five recorded items to be preserved in the Library of Congress in Washington, D.C., "because of their cultural significance." The Library of Congress names such a list of items each year to be added to their archives.

During mid-May, Michael took his children to see *The Chronicles of Narnia: Prince Caspian* at the Brenden Theaters, located at the Palms in Las Vegas.

That month, Michael attended the fiftieth birthday party of fashion designer Christian Audigier in Los Angeles. He took the microphone to wish a "happy birthday" to his friend and prospective business partner; plans were under discussion for a Michael Jackson line of clothing to be issued by Audigier's company.

After returning to Las Vegas, Michael was seen at the MGM Grand, watching the Ultimate Fighting Championship Match, in which Tito Ortiz lost to Lyoto Machida. He was wearing a disguise of a burka and dark glasses, and he was seated in a wheelchair.

Michael had dinner with Thomas Barrack, Jr., the CEO of Colony Capital, LLC, in the Vegas Hilton's Verona Sky Villa during early June. Days later, he took Prince, Paris, and Blanket to see *Kung Fu Panda* at the Brenden Theaters.

In July, Michael was spotted in Las Vegas leaving a bookstore, pushed in a wheelchair by an assistant, with his three children walking along with him. Later that month, he and his children attended a performance of *Mystere* by Cirque du Soleil at the Treasure Island Hotel.

"Hold My Hand," a new song by Michael Jackson and Akon, was leaked on the Internet during July.

In August, *King of Pop*, Michael's new "greatest hits" album, was made available for purchase. The album differs significantly in each country in which it was released, because fans' voting was used to determine the songs for each country's version. The album was issued in 26 countries; the only song that appears on all versions of the album is "Billie Jean." The timing of *King of Pop* was planned to celebrate Michael's fiftieth birthday. [It is interesting to note that, although this album became available in more than two dozen countries—including culturally-different and distant nations like Taiwan, South Korea, Finland, Hungary, India, China, Brazil, Argentina, and Australia—it was not released at all in the U.S.]

That same month, Michael and his children attended a Cirque du Soleil performance at the MGM Grand Hotel. Shockingly, they were seated in the center of the theater—usually too vulnerable a placement—and Michael was wearing a hooded sweatshirt and mask.

Michael was seen at Planet Hollywood in Las Vegas and also at the 40-40 Club (Palazzo)—known for its live music, celebrity patrons, and sports memorabilia—on three occasions during August.

On August 28, 2008, Michael gave an exclusive interview to Chris Connolly and Michael S. James on *Good Morning America*, in which he spoke about his past, present, and future, as well as his dreams for his children. "I am writing [music] all the time; I love composing and the whole thing," he said. "But I am also raising my children and enjoying it and teaching them to ride bicycles and how to read. I love it."

Regarding his children, Michael explained, "I get pretty emotional when I see them having a wonderful time, when they are on a ride and they are screaming and they are happy." He was trying to give his kids the things that he didn't have as a child; he added that he just wanted to "fill them with a lot of enjoyment."

Michael also said that he needed to have "rhinoceros skin" when dealing with the pressures of fame and celebrity. "I am still looking forward to a lot of great things," he told his interviewers.

The next day, August 29th, Michael Jackson was at his Palomino Lane home when his fans showed up in full force and serenaded him for his fiftieth birthday. Michael rewarded them by sending pizzas to the group.

Michael and his children had dinner at Benihana Japanese Restaurant at the Las Vegas Hilton in September.

During early October, Michael and his children were seen shopping together in Los Angeles. They arrived at the Golden Apple Comic Books store, all wearing masks, which the children removed after entering the shop, while their father continued to wear his white mask. Later that month, Michael was spotted at an antique store and a cosmetics boutique.

The next day, Michael was seen arriving at Elizabeth Taylor's home to visit with his ailing friend.

During the fall of 2008, Michael and his children moved back to California, staying at the Bel Air Hotel in Los Angeles, with plans to live there until he would decide on a rental home for his family.

In late October, while visiting Australia, Jermaine Jackson announced that a Jacksons tour was being planned for 2009; he stated that Janet and Michael would perform and all of the Jackson brothers. Michael issued a statement about this matter:

My brothers and sisters have my full love and support, and we've certainly shared many great experiences, but at this time I have no plans to record or tour with them. I am now in the studio developing new and exciting projects that I look forward to sharing with my fans in concert soon.

On Halloween, Michael attended a party at the home of Natalie Maines of the Dixie Chicks. He arrived with Gregory Peck's widow Veronique and three children. Ms. Maines was quoted as saying, "A couple of people went up to him and told him he had the greatest Michael Jackson costume ever!"

At the end of October 2008, Michael met with Randy Phillips and others to set the parameters of his upcoming concerts for AEG. According to Kenny Ortega, Michael said, "I'm tired of being a vagabond. I just want a house for me and my kids." Michael expressed concern about being able to sell enough tickets for the shows!

"Michael has been seen out and about a lot in Los Angeles recently," according to the media reports. *TMZ* photographed Michael in his Cadillac Escalade, visiting the Kentucky Fried Chicken store in Brentwood. Earlier, he and Blanket paid a surprise visit to Off the Wall, one of Michael's favorite antique stores.

On November 7, 2008, *Thriller 25* reached Number 1 on the *Billboard* album charts.

Later that month, a spokesman for Michael, his New York lawyer, denied a British press report that stated that "Michael Jackson has become a Muslim." The statement, on behalf of Michael, was "That's rubbish...."

On November 27th, Michael reportedly celebrated Thanksgiving with his children in their new home, the $38 million Holmby Hills estate in the Bel Air area in California. Michael rented the home for $100,000 per month.

*   *   *   *   *   *   *   *   *

The Home: 100 North Carolwood Drive, Holmby Hills

Located in what is described as a "posh Los Angeles neighborhood" between Beverly Hills and Bel Air, California, this Holmby Hills three-story home, designed as a French chateau, has 17,171 square feet of space and sits on 1.25 acres of gated grounds, with a large swimming pool. Built in 2002, the estate has seven bedrooms, thirteen bathrooms, a theater and screening room, a wine cellar with a tasting room, an art studio, gym and spa facilities, twelve fireplaces, and a seven-car garage. Other special features include a state-of-the-art kitchen with an adjacent butler's pantry, a multistory grand entry, hardwood floors, a formal dining room, wood-paneled den and adjoining library with coffered ceilings. The guesthouse has stained-glass doors leading to the pool and gardens.

In 2004, the property sold for $18.5 million, and it was priced as high as $38 million in 2008. [In April 2010, it was on the real estate market for $28,995,000.]

[Fans and admirers of Michael Jackson regard this home with special reverence as the place where Michael Jackson drew his last breaths. They visit here in large numbers, with hushed voices; gentle, respectful demeanor; flowers, teddy bears, and written messages to show their devotion; and also tears of mourning.]

*   *   *   *   *   *   *   *   *

Michael was reported as being in Los Angeles in mid-December 2008, shopping in an antique store. His outfit consisted of a turquoise tunic over white pants, an eye mask, and a fedora. He stopped to sign many autographs for his fans.

Later, he was spotted wearing a Zorro mask while shopping in Los Angeles and visiting the office of his dermatologist.

During Christmas week, Dr. Tohme Tohme, Michael's "sole spokesperson," refuted allegations about Michael's failing health, especially as "fabricated" in an unauthorized biography. Tohme issued a statement that included, "Mr. Jackson is in fine health, and finalising [sic.] negotiations with a major entertainment company and television network for both a world tour and a series of specials and appearances."

Michael celebrated Christmas Eve with his three children, Dr. Arnold Klein, and actress Carrie Fisher in the family's new Bel Air/ Holmby Hills home. Ms. Fisher was invited because Prince, Paris, and Blanket wanted to meet Princess Leia from the *Star Wars* movie trilogy.

On the last day of 2008, Michael was seen at Hennessey & Ingalls Art and Architecture Bookstore in Santa Monica, California

2009

During January 2009, Michael met with an AEG delegation headed by billionaire founder Philip Anschutz at the MGM Grand in Las Vegas. Michael was accompanied by Blanket and his manager Dr. Tohme Tohme. Michael Jackson reportedly signed a deal for ten concerts in London for the summer months of 2009.

Michael's "Wanna Be Startin' Something" was played at the Mid-Atlantic Ball to honor President-Elect Barack Obama on the eve of his inauguration, January 20th. It was called "the perfect song for a new beginning."

The Grammy Museum in Los Angeles unveiled its *Michael Jackson Exhibit*, featuring many items from the elaborate clothing "that has come to define the King of Pop's uniquely personal style."

In late February, Michael and Christian Audigier went shopping together on Rodeo Drive in Los Angeles; they visited several upscale men's clothing stores.

On March 3rd, Michael arrived in the United Kingdom, landing at Luton Airport via the private jet of Mohamed Al-Fayed, owner of Harrods. From the airport, Michael, his children, and manager were driven in a white limousine to the Lanesborough Hotel in London. He was protected by a battery of security guards. Michael was there for a major press conference.

On March 5, 2009, Michael Jackson announced that he would perform ten concerts at the London O2 Arena, starting on July 8, 2009; the shows would be called *This Is It*. The King of Pop took the stage in front of hundreds of excited, screaming fans and media representatives. He said:

> Thank you all. This is it! These will be my final shows in London. And when I say "This is it," I mean it.... I will be performing the songs that my fans want to hear. This is the final curtain call. I will see you in July and ... I love you. I really do, you have to know that. I love you very much, from the bottom of my heart. This is it! See you in July!

Michael was visibly overcome by the hysterically enthusiastic response of the crowd. He giggled softly with delight and bowed his head, behind the podium. Then he gave the peace sign to his audience a number of times before exiting the stage.

Michael shared with his producer that he had decided to undertake these concerts because his children were now old enough to understand and appreciate what he does. He was also determined to highlight messages of urgency on behalf of the planet. *This Is It* would promote environmental awareness and the importance of love.

The next day, Michael attended a performance of *Oliver!,* the long-running London musical, at the Royal Theatre. He was accompanied by his children, actor and friend Mark Lester, and his four children. Large crowds of fans clamored for a glimpse of their idol; the scene was described as "chaos."

Michael published the following statement on his Internet website:

The Time Has Come! It is now I see and feel that calling once again, to be part of a music that will not just connect but make all feel one, one in joy, one in pain, one in love, one in service and in consciousness.

Michael Jackson took the time to telephone Jade Goody, the U.K. reality show television star, who was terminally ill with cancer. He sent her his warmest wishes.

On March 8th, Michael and his entourage returned to Los Angeles.

In mid-March, the wildly successful show *American Idol* featured all thirteen of its contestants performing the hits of Michael Jackson.

In response to the unprecedented pre-sales of tickets for Michael Jackson's *This Is It* concerts, the AEG Live organizers added forty more shows to help meet the overwhelming demand. *The first ten concerts were sold out within four hours on Ticketmaster!* When Randy Phillips of AEG asked Michael if he would agree to forty more shows, Michael said that he would, with two conditions. Michael wanted a house in the country—with at least sixteen acres and horses—for his kids and himself, and he wanted a representative from *Guinness World Records* to be present at the fiftieth concert in order to document his record achievement. AEG happily agreed, according to Phillips. With the additional shows, nearly one million people would be able to see the King of Pop perform at the 20,000-seat arena.

Randy Phillips, CEO of AEG Live, called Michael Jackson to tell him the incredible news of the stunningly quick "sold-out" fifty concerts. Phillips described Michael's reaction: "He was crying. I could hear it in his voice—he was choked up."

As the "hottest-selling on the planet," *This Is It* tickets were the fastest-selling in London's entire history. "Tickets sold at a rate of 11 per second, 657 per minute, and nearly 40,000 an hour." It was reported that 264,000 people were still in the queue waiting to buy tickets when the fifty concerts were sold out.

At the same time, a world preview exhibit of hundreds of items of Michael Jackson's attracted more than 25,000 visitors to County Kildare, Ireland.

In mid-March, the album *The Essential Michael Jackson* re-entered the *Billboard*'s Top Pop catalog chart and went straight to Number 1. According to the Recording Industry Association of America, *Thriller* was certified 28 times platinum in the United States alone.

Michael Jackson and Kenny Ortega attended the show *Le Reve* at the Wynn Resort in Las Vegas in early April.

Dancers from all over the world flew into Los Angeles to audition for Michael Jackson's *This Is It* concerts. Auditions were held in mid-April at the Kodak Theatre in Hollywood, and rehearsals were held in April, May, and June. AEG Live revealed that "the show will break new ground in both artistry and sheer cost"—with a production budget "north of $20 million," as many as twenty-two different sets, and an unprecedented 3-D film.

On April 16th, Michael met with his major collaborators for the London O2 Arena concerts. At that meeting, he announced, "I want to push it to its limit, all the way." The marching orders for everyone involved were to break the barriers, to push the boundaries of creativity, to put on a show like none other.

Michael started rehearsals for the concerts with Kenny Ortega and Travis Payne on April 20th. His long-time assistants—Michael Bush, costumer, and Karen Faye, make-up artist and hairstylist—were back on the MJ team.

On May 14th, with his three children, Michael attended his parents' sixtieth wedding anniversary celebration, held at Indian Restaurant Chakra in Beverly Hills. All of Michael's siblings were also present.

The next day, Michael attended a business meeting at the Beverly Hills Hotel with his parents Joseph and Katherine, Leonard Rowe, Randy Phillips and Paul Gongaware of AEG.

Michael Jackson and his children made time to attend the Beverly Hills Art Festival, where they viewed the paintings of local artists. Michael later visited *American Idol*'s rehearsals at the Nokia Theater.

On May 29th, Michael met with Kenny Ortega and others to plan a technologically dazzling pre-show for the concerts. The prelude to the concerts would include the unveiling of MJ's creation "Lightman," a huge futuristic figure, modeled from Shakespeare's Hamlet, who sees his own reflection in a dramatic scene.

From June 1st to 11th, Michael shot "The Dome Project" in Culver Studios in Culver City. This project consisted of seven works: "Smooth Criminal," "Thriller," "Earth Song," "They Don't Care About Us," "MJ Air," "The Final Message," and "The Way You Make Me Feel"—elaborate background films for his live performances on stage. Unprecedented 3-D effects were incorporated into the films. In fact, Michael created what he called "4-D": life-sized figures were designed to drop from the ceiling while the 3-D footage played on the massive screen at the back of the stage.

On June 3rd, Prince and Paris—as arranged by their father—logged in several hours in a Los Angeles recording studio.

In mid-June, Madame Tussauds Wax Museum in London announced that a brand new figure of Michael Jackson would soon be unveiled. This would be the tenth time that the world-renowned museum portrayed Michael Jackson, making him the most featured celebrity ever, with only the Queen of England having been portrayed more. That same week, it was announced that two-time "Mr. Universe" Lou Ferrigno—known for *The Incredible Hulk* TV program in the seventies—was working as Michael Jackson's physical trainer in preparation for his upcoming concerts.

During that month, everyone's efforts—most of all Michael's—accelerated in preparation for his grand concerts in London for one million eager fans.

On June 23rd, Michael's full rehearsals at the Staples Center were filmed (as they always were, so that he could study the footage and improve the show). The next day he rehearsed for the last time.

On June 25, 2009, the world gasped....

Michael Jackson, at the age of fifty, died suddenly of "cardiac arrest." He was in his bedroom at the rented Holmby Hills home that he and his children were occupying. A *911* call was made by one of his security guards at 12:20 P.M. Within minutes, an ambulance arrived and transported him to the UCLA Medical Center. There, doctors continued efforts to resuscitate Michael for more than an hour.

Jermaine Jackson appeared in front of dozens of media people and microphones to announce the death of "my brother, the legendary King of Pop Michael Jackson," officially set at 2:26 P.M.

Just as in his life, media all around the world placed Michael, in his death, in their lead headlines, on their front pages, and in their opening telecasts, via newsprint, airwaves, and cyberspace. *The King of Pop was gone.*

Two days later, the Jackson family issued a formal statement:

...We miss Michael endlessly, our pain cannot be described in words. But Michael would not want us to give up now. So we want to thank all of his faithful supporters and loyal fans worldwide, you who Michael loved so much. Please do not despair, because Michael will continue to live on in each and every one of you. Continue to spread his message, because that is what he would want you to do. Carry on, so his legacy will live forever.

* * * * * * * * *

From this admittedly incomplete review of Michael's activities—his comings and goings—it is obvious that *he was not a recluse.* Because of his fierce desire to remain private, paparazzi were able to capture *very few* photographs of Michael Jackson, and therefore we did not see him as he was moving around, interacting with select people, and living his amazing life.

* * * * * * * * *

Author's Note: Michael Jackson took his children with him whenever he could safely do so. References to his whereabouts in this chapter may not include specific mention of his children; such omissions do not necessarily mean that the children were not with their father.

> **Who *was* that masked man?**
> **I wanted to thank him.**
> — From *The Lone Ranger*

Wherever you go, in every country ...,
people yearn and hunger for
only one thing, to love and be loved.
Love transcends international boundaries
and heals the wounds of hatred,
racial prejudice, bigotry and ignorance.
It is the ultimate truth at the heart
of all creation.
— Michael Jackson

HEALER & HUMANITARIAN

**My mission is healing, pure and simple;
we have to heal our wounded planet.**
— Michael Jackson

**Where there is love,
I'll be there.**
— Michael Jackson

He was on fire! The six-year-old boy cried out in agony as his father fled the motel room where the two had been staying. Thankfully, little David Rothenberg did not die. He was rushed to the nearest hospital after people heard his screams and ran to his rescue.

The child had been asleep in bed, under the care of his father Charles, who had checked them into a motel in Buena Park, California, in 1983. During a phone call with the boy's mother, his ex-wife Marie, Charles became furious with rage. He doused his son's blankets with kerosene, lit them on fire, and raced from the scene.

At the hospital, doctors determined that the little boy suffered from third-degree burns over his entire body. They needed to amputate his fingers at the first joint; his ears and nose were gone. David endured indescribable pain that would continue unabated. Not only did he have to deal with the physical trauma but with the emotional pain of knowing that he was permanently disfigured.

David's ordeal continued through thirty-five painful, expensive surgeries that attempted the reconstruction of his face and body. Although Charles was sentenced for attempted murder and arson to thirteen years in state prison—the maximum allowable by law at that time—for the heinous crimes he committed against his son, David lived in constant fear that his father would come after him and hurt him again.

Michael Jackson reached out to David after he heard the news story about this reprehensible and, to Michael, *incomprehensible* crime. [He would also strongly empathize with the boy after the serious burns he suffered from the Pepsi commercial that went so wrong.]

Michael initiated contact with David; he invited the seven-year-old and his mother to visit him at his Hayvenhurst home. Michael encouraged David not to give up on his dream of becoming a singer, and he asked how he might help. Michael remained in David's life across the ensuing years....

"He was like a father I never had," David said of Michael Jackson, who did indeed become a surrogate father to the boy. Michael would always embrace him in greeting in spite of David's severe disfigurement. He communicated to David that he could and would be okay, that he could have a life. Years passed as David courageously progressed through grade school, high school, and college, and then continued on to law school in Utah.

"I need you to do something for me," Michael said to his security guard, who realized that this would be a special mission. "I want you to give this to a man for me," the boss continued.

"But I have to warn you that it might be difficult for you to look at him," Mr. Jackson went on. "He has been very badly burned...." The boss placed in the guard's hands a thick, bulging white envelope with white tape wrapped around it.

The security man dutifully carried out his orders. When he saw the young man, he understood what he had been told about David's appearance. He also discovered that Michael Jackson was sending cash to David for his college and graduate school expenses. Mr. Jackson had remained faithful—and generous—to David across all of these years, privately and quietly.

David Rothenberg—who has renamed himself "Dave Dave" to create maximum distance from his father and even the man's name—was one of a select group of people who attended Michael Jackson's funeral in September 2009. There, he brought tears to everyone by his eulogy for Michael, by his words of gratitude and love for the man who had given him more than money. Michael had given him dignity and hope.

People whom Michael trusted knew that he routinely reached out to the sick, the needy, and the dying. He gave the gift of his love through personal involvements as well as financial help of various kinds to those in need. He would telephone terminally-ill children whom he met in hospitals and orphanages to encourage them to fight their illnesses. He would tell them that he intended to see them when he returned to their city; he was giving them a reason to live. They were thrilled—*the King of Pop will come to visit me!*

Thomas Mesereau became aware of Michael's long-term, long-distance relationship with a little girl who was living in Chicago. She was paralyzed. Michael maintained telephone contact with her and regularly sent money to her family to pay for the intensive care that she needed.

"It's ... startling, actually, when one considers how easy it is to gain entree into the King of Pop's castle," wrote his biographer J. Randy Taraborrelli. Sick and dying children were always welcome at Neverland as guests; they would take field trips there for a day of glorious fun. Mothers could speak with Michael Jackson by telephone to tell him about their ailing children and to seek his intervention. Many children wanted to meet him as their dying wish. Michael Jackson provided and paid for facilities and resources of various kinds for handicapped children at his Neverland Ranch, including hospital beds in the movie theater, where the children would watch movies and cartoons.

Adrian Grant, founder of Michael Jackson's U.K fan club, was fortunate to be allowed to accompany Michael into hospitals, and he helped his friend and idol give gifts to the sick children. He describes how he was especially moved when "Michael brought a smile to the face of a dying girl who had lain motionless and silent for weeks. Her mother, at her side in constant vigil, broke down in tears as her daughter reached out and touched Michael's hand. Sounds like a miracle, but I saw it with my own eyes...."

"If you were hungry, he'd feed you!" says Eddie Jones in October 2011. "Michael Jackson was so sensitive to other people; he was passionate about them." Eddie was one of the dancers at the ill-fated Pepsi commercial during which Michael was badly burned. "I saw his hair catch on fire!" he recalls vividly. He has remained a friend of the Jackson family since that time. Today, Eddie Jones "fights for the civil, constitutional, and human rights of people" as the president and CEO of the Los Angeles Civil Rights Association.

Michael Jackson reached out to a teenager named Ryan White when he heard about the boy's expulsion from an Indiana middle school because he had been diagnosed with HIV/AIDS. Ryan became a poster child for the disease, as enlightened persons were starting to realize the genuine tragedy of its victims. Ryan was a hemophiliac who became infected with HIV from a contaminated blood treatment. Although his doctors confirmed that he did not pose a risk to other students, Ryan was banned from attending school; he became an outcast. AIDS was not only poorly understood at the time, but the stigma of homosexuality surrounded the national perception of the disease. Ryan was the victim of a fatal medical error. In 1984, he was given six months to live.

Michael spent time with Ryan, always trying to keep up his spirits; he kept in touch by telephone. He gave the boy a Mustang convertible so that he would have something special to motivate him to hang on to life. Ryan lived for five years more than expected, and some people attribute that "miracle" to Michael Jackson's influence and love. The boy succumbed to his predicted death in April 1990, one month before his graduation from high school.

Attending the emotion-filled funeral of Ryan White with First Lady Barbara Bush, Michael Jackson comforted the boy's mother and promised himself that he would do more. Michael dedicated his poignant song of mourning and loss, "Gone Too Soon," to Ryan White. The short film created for the song shows a panorama of the boy's life—photos of him at varying ages, his grandparents, and newspaper headlines that seem to cry out for human understanding. It is a significant artistic work that not only mourns and celebrates the courageous, mature young man, who refused to seek pity, but strongly promotes an important social cause. The film virtually begs for the reconsideration of AIDS as a *disease of victims* and for a national commitment to combat it.

During his concert tour in Budapest in 1994, Michael met a four-year-old Hungarian boy named Bela Farkas, who was dying from cancer. He needed a liver transplant, but there was little hope for him to have the necessary procedure. Michael directed his people immediately to search for a compatible liver for the child, which took them months, but when they succeeded, Michael paid for the surgery that successfully saved the little boy's life.

Children in wheelchairs and on stretchers were brought backstage by their parents, by the dozens, to meet Michael Jackson before or after his concert performances. He interacted with each one of these kids and encouraged photos to be taken so that they would have a lasting memory. During his *Bad* Tour, Michael allocated 400 free tickets at each concert to handicapped and disadvantaged children.

During his *Dangerous* World Tour, Michael visited a hospital or orphanage in every one of dozens of cities in which he performed. Instead of spending his time in hedonistic pleasures, he would fill up his security vehicles with toys and treats and then personally deliver them to ailing children. His team of assistants contacted the various facilities before his visits to determine their special needs. Michael arranged for the construction of playgrounds, the purchase of buses and special equipment, and the full payment of expensive operations needed by children whose parents could not afford them.

He purposefully, and with determination, brought a world spotlight to the miserable conditions of the orphans in Romania through his presence there and his telecast concert *Live In Bucharest.* He courageously dramatized the plight of the millions of slum-dwellers in Rio de Janeiro, Brazil, and of American prison inmates in two versions of his controversial short film *They Don't Care About Us*. He performed concerts in Seoul, Korea, and Germany, at the request of Nelson Mandela, for the benefit of specific charities in South Africa.

Michael Jackson sat at the bedsides of terminally-ill children of all shades of color, ethnic backgrounds, religions, and ages throughout the world. Michael believed that his primary job was as a global humanitarian.

*   *   *   *   *   *   *   *   *

When he was performing, Michael Jackson was famous for the precision and wondrous predictability of his perfectly-executed song-and-dance routines on stage. One night, however, he shocked the audience, his dancers, and crew by deviating from the planned program. Stopping in the middle of an uncharacteristically slow walk across the stage, Michael was looking down.

"Security!" he called out. Immediately a burly man in a dark suit ran onto the stage and to Michael's side. He looked puzzled and worried.

"I don't want anyone to step on this bug," Michael declared, still staring at the floor.

The security guard bent over and picked up the endangered insect with his fingers.

"Don't kill it!" Michael directed in a loud voice. The man obediently held up the bug, over his head, to demonstrate to Michael that the little creature was all right, as he and the bug exited the stage.

Michael Jackson couldn't hurt a fly, as the saying goes, *or a bug either.*

"If E.T. hadn't come to Elliot, he would have come to Michael's house," Steven Spielberg said after he had worked closely with Michael Jackson in producing the *E.T. [Extra-Terrestrial] Storybook.*

Michael was chosen to narrate the storybook about the lovable alien—far away from his home planet and lost on earth—because of his gentle, soothing voice that transmitted genuine caring. [Michael won a Grammy Award that year for Best Children's Album for his performance.]

Spielberg later disclosed that Michael Jackson wept during every take of the death scene of the endearing alien creature. His breaking voice was left in the final version for artistic authenticity.

*   *   *   *   *   *   *   *   *

Michael Jackson's "wallet" was as open as his heart....

Michael contributed the astronomical amount of more than $300 million to at least thirty-nine named charities. He earned inclusion in the 2000 edition of the *Guinness Book of World Records* as the pop star who supported the most charities. He gave more to humanitarian and charitable causes than any other celebrity.

"During every month of every year, decade after decade, Michael either gave to or helped the world's needy in some significant way," according to *The Official Michael Jackson Opus*. Most of his philanthropy was done anonymously.

Drought-stricken Ethiopia, in 1985, suffered one of the worst famines ever recorded throughout the world. One million people died from starvation and related illnesses. In response to this tragedy, which played out on televisions across the globe, people rallied to help. Perhaps most noteworthy were Michael Jackson and Lionel Richie, who set about composing a stirring ballad that they named "We Are the World." The two men worked tirelessly to complete the song within one week, hoping to ensure a fast release of the single. Forty-five hand-picked, popular vocal artists donated their services for this worthy and urgent cause. All profits from the song went to the United Support of Artists for Africa, better known as *USA for Africa*, which sent money and supplies to Ethiopia to save innumerable lives.

"We Are the World" became the fastest-selling pop song in U.S. history and a global hit. The song was simulcast on 8,000 stations around the world, and it sold 20 million copies, raising more than $63 million for Ethiopia and other African aid organizations. [The song won a number of awards, including Grammys for Song of the Year and Record of the Year.] From the raised funds, not only were food and water supplied to the suffering masses, but vitally important water wells were dug and classes for self-sustenance were taught on a large scale. Royalties from "We Are the World" continue to generate life-saving projects.

Also in the mid-eighties, Michael Jackson donated to charity all of his earnings from the *Victory Tour*, which was his last series of concerts with his brothers. For eight months of arduous rehearsing, touring, and performing, his reward was seeing his money go to three worthy causes, the first of which was the T.J. Martell-Foundation for leukemia and cancer research. He dedicated a portion of the funds to the Ronald McDonald House Charities, which enable thousands of sick children undergoing chemotherapy to attend Camp Good Times, a special facility for rest and relaxation. There, the Jackson Pond was established, where the children with cancer can play and fish. The third recipient of Michael's *Victory* profits was the United Negro College Fund.

In 1986, Michael established the "Michael Jackson UNCF Endowed Scholarship Fund" with a $1.5 million donation, which finances scholarships for performing arts students from the interest earned on that money. Year after year, worthy students benefit from this well-appropriated donation. More than 500 individuals, many of them the first in their family to attend college, have improved their lives and futures because of these scholarships.

Michael created "Heal the World," his own international foundation, in 1992. All of the proceeds from his globally-popular ballad of the same name went into the foundation. Amazingly, Michael also donated *all* of the profits from his worldwide *Dangerous* Tour to his "Heal the World" organization and other charities. The extent of his generosity can be measured in the exhausting sixty-nine concert performances of the tour to 3.5 million people; it spanned from June 1992 to November 1993.

In announcing this major undertaking, Michael said:

> I am looking forward to this tour because it will allow me to devote time to visiting children all around the world, as well as spread the message of global love, in the hope that others will be moved to do their share to help heal the world.

"Heal the World" sent money to causes that fight AIDS and juvenile diabetes; to the Make-A-Wish Foundation for terminally-ill children; and, after the Los Angeles riots, to create a program that provided immunizations, drug treatment, and mentorship to needy kids.

In Sarajevo, the capital of Bosnia, where tens of thousands were killed in the war, Michael jumped into action to oversee an international effort to assist those who were suffering and dying. Michael Jackson personally supervised the loading of 46 tons of supplies, including medications, blankets, clothes and shoes, into Sarajevo-bound aircraft in New York City.

In 1993, Super Bowl XXVII became one of the most-watched sports events in history, and never before did a half-time show attract more viewers than the game itself—nearly one billion people in seventy nations. Michael Jackson performed with—believe it or not—a 750-member choir. He did "Black or White" and "Billie Jean" and then ended with "Heal the World," during which 3,500 children of all ages and ethnicities marched around the stage and surrounded him. The 98,000 people in the audience also participated by holding up flashcards, on cue, which formed patterns of children, visible to the aerial cameras.

When Michael spoke during his performance, he issued this plea:

> We stand together all around the world to remake the planet into a haven of joy and understanding and goodness. No one should have to suffer, especially our children.... This is for the children of the world.

Michael Jackson donated his entire fee for this historical performance to charity.

In fact, Michael Jackson perfected the model of celebrities performing for charity. Following his example, numerous other entertainers have gotten personally involved in promoting charitable causes for victims of catastrophe, including Hurricane Katrina and earthquake-ravaged Haiti.

"We Are the World," performed by more than eighty artists, was reissued in 2010 for the people of Haiti. Released on the twenty-fifth anniversary of the original version, Michael Jackson's and Lionel Richie's song again raised huge amounts of money, this time for the needy in that tormented country. *Michael would be proud.*

He was the first major entertainer to offer a concert on behalf of the victims of 9/11, which he named *United We Stand: What More Can I Give.* He performed for a standing-room-only audience at RFK Memorial Stadium in Washington, D.C., in October 2001. Michael also dedicated his touching song "What More Can I Give" to the families of those who lost their lives in this American tragedy.

In addition to his being a significant personal contributor of money to the Make-A-Wish Foundation, which grants the specific wishes of dying children, Michael also made arrangements for regular and frequent visits to Neverland by these unfortunate kids of all ages. Whether he was in residence at the time or not, groups of these children were bused into his fantasy paradise, where his employees devoted themselves to providing a fun experience for everyone. The children were allowed to enjoy all of the outdoor facilities, which included amusement park rides, bumper cars, go-karts, train rides, and a zoo of exotic animals. The candy store and arcades were available at all times. The movie theater included a special second-floor viewing room equipped with a hospital bed for sick children who could not sit up by themselves. Michael Jackson absorbed the cost for everything, including the numerous additional security and service personnel who were needed to accommodate the children and their chaperones.

Michael also supported a small grassroots organization, run by only six employees, the Sickle Cell Disease Foundation of California, with contributions of his sequin-studded jackets, gloves, and other personal items. These were raffled off for undisclosed but significant amounts of cash for the cause. Other non-profit organizations, both in the U.S. and abroad, were recipients of Michael's personal clothing, such as his iconic jackets, which always fetched surprisingly hefty sums of money from the highest bidders at auction.

Always a risk-taker, Michael Jackson was one of the first American celebrities publicly to address the plight of the victims of AIDS. He both donated personal funds and urged others, by his example, to do likewise. His best friend Elizabeth Taylor joined him in championing this cause, which, at that time, was generally ignored in polite company and mainstream media. When he performed at President Bill Clinton's inauguration, Michael made a speech directed at the newly-elected leader, imploring him to support government funding for AIDS research.

Long before it became fashionable and politically correct to do so, Michael Jackson supported—by monetary contributions and through his music—a breadth of programs and efforts directed at environmental conservation and preservation of the Earth. From global warming to protection of forests, from anti-poaching to save-the-whales causes, Michael was there to shine a light, by his presence and songs, on these issues that were so vitally important to him and to the planet.

"Earth Song," visually brought to life through his creative and explosive short film, was the first major artistic work to draw sympathetic attention to a combination of man-made disasters that include war, poaching, seal slaughter, whale destruction, pollution, and deforestation. Using this disturbing but effective musical piece, Michael drew wide-scale focus onto our "crying earth" and "weeping shore."

In his marching-paced song "HIStory," Michael Jackson proved himself an ambassador of peace with his inspirational lyrics. He called upon all nations to sing and harmonize together around the world, for us all to live as brothers.

"Cry" is Michael's poignant song that beckons to people everywhere to come together to cry over our shared human losses and suffering. It is portrayed in an unforgettable, iconic short film showing men and women of all races and ages, holding hands in an unbroken line across savannahs, beaches, roads, bridges, hillsides, and forests. In *"Cry,"* Michael pleads for our help: "You can change the world; *I can't do it by myself....*"

Calling himself an "instrument of nature" in a self-disclosing, rare interview, Michael elaborated: "I feel that I was chosen as an instrument to give music and love and harmony to the world." He believed that it was his *job* to try to heal the world.

David Nordahl explains that "Michael—as a person who believed strongly in the importance of visualization—would take with him on tour my paintings of himself and children. He would hang them in his room to remind himself of his main mission, and they would help to keep him inspired."

The following is just a smattering of Michael Jackson's many charitable and philanthropic contributions....

The 1980's

Michael Jackson's benefit concert in Atlanta, Georgia, as part of his *Triumph* Tour, raised $100,000 for the Atlanta Children's Foundation, in response to a series of kidnappings and murders of children in that area.

Michael equipped a 19-bed unit at Mount Sinai New York Medical Center, part of the T. J. Martell-Foundation for leukemia and cancer research.

The Jacksons performed in Jacksonville, Florida, for 700 disadvantaged children, who were treated to the show. That same month, 1,200 tickets were donated to underprivileged children for The Jacksons concert in Dallas, Texas.

In 1984, Michael donated the entire $1.5 million that he received from Pepsi-Cola, as settlement for his serious burns in filming a commercial for the company, to the Brotman Memorial Hospital for the Michael Jackson Burn Center. Coincidentally, Michael had visited with burn patients at Brotman on the previous New Year's Eve, little knowing that, within a very short time, he himself would become a patient there.

The proceeds from Michael's song "Man in the Mirror" were donated by him to Camp Good Times for children who suffer from cancer.

In Japan, Michael dedicated the remaining dates of his Japanese tour to the memory of Yoshiaki Ogiwara, a five-year-old boy who was kidnapped and horrifically murdered; he donated $20,000 to the child's family.

He presented a check for $600,000 to the United Negro College Fund at a press conference held by his sponsor Pepsi-Cola.

In Rome, Michael visited children suffering from cancer at the Bambini-Gesu Children's Hospital, and he gave a check for £100,000 to the hospital.

Before his concert in Wembley Stadium, Michael handed to Prince Charles and Lady Diana a check in the amount of £150,000 to the Prince's Trust and a check in the amount of £100,000 to the children's hospital at Great Ormond Street.

At his thirtieth birthday, Michael Jackson performed a concert in Leeds, England for the charity organization "Give for Life," with a major goal of immunization of children. He presented the agency with a check for £65,000.

The National Urban Coalition Artist/Humanitarian of the Year Award was given to Michael in 1989. He was recognized for his efforts to encourage children to study natural sciences.

Michael donated the proceeds from a concert in Los Angeles to Childhelp USA, the largest charity organization against child abuse; the "Michael Jackson International Institute for Research on Child Abuse" was created.

Michael visited the Cleveland Elementary School in Stockton, California, in recognition and support of the children there. He spoke to the children to comfort them and help them to think positively again. Three weeks earlier, a 25-year-old gunman had a shooting spree on the school's playground, killing five children and wounding thirty-nine others, and then he turned the gun on himself.

The 1990's

President George Bush honored Michael Jackson by presenting him with the "Point of Light" award for his philanthropic activities and with the "Entertainer of the Decade" award.

The Council of the American Scouts gave Michael the first "Good Scout Humanitarian Award" for his activities supporting various charities, including the Make-A-Wish Foundation.

Michael presented the Youth Sports & Art Foundation of Los Angeles—an agency that supports families of gang members and those affected by drug abuse—with a wide-screen television set and a significant financial gift.

Several hundred turkey dinners, during the Christmas holidays, were donated to needy families in Los Angeles by Michael and his MJJ Productions.

In 1992, within eleven days, Michael covered *30,000 miles* in Africa, visiting hospitals, orphanages, schools, churches, and institutions for mentally handicapped children.

Michael presented the Mayor of Munich, Germany with a check for 40,000 DM for the needy people of his city.

Michael visited the Sophia Children's Hospital in Rotterdam and presented a check for £100,000.

When he heard that a boy named Ramon Sanchez was killed by a stray bullet during the Rodney King riots in Los Angeles and that his parents could not afford to bury him, Michael paid for the funeral costs.

He donated L. 821,477,296 to La Partita del Cuore in Rome and 120,000 DM to children's charities in Estonia and Latvia.

At his concert in Dublin, Ireland in 1992, Michael announced that he would give £400,000 of his tour earnings to various charities in Ireland.

Michael brought Mickey Mouse and Minnie Mouse from Euro-Disney with him when he visited the Queen Elizabeth Children's Hospital in London. Two days later, he presented Prince Charles with a check for £200,000 to the Prince's Trust.

Michael donated one million pesetas to charities headed by the Queen of Spain.

President Iliescu of Romania inaugurated a playground for 500 orphans which Michael financed. Michael chose Bucharest, Romania as his concert site for worldwide television broadcast because he wanted to bring attention to the numerous orphanages and their poor conditions in that country.

In November 1992, Michael Jackson personally oversaw the loading of 46 tons of medication, blankets, and winter clothes at Kennedy Airport in New York, bound for Sarajevo.

That same month, at Neverland, Michael hosted a mother and her young son, David Sonnet, who had suffered a brain aneurysm at the age of eight, leaving him unable to walk or talk. Later, David's mother credited Michael Jackson with helping her son to recover from a coma.

At the American Embassy in Tokyo, Michael received a check for $100,000 for his "Heal the World Foundation" by his tour sponsor Pepsi-Cola.

The National Football League and the Sponsors of the Super Bowl donated $200,000 and the BEST Foundation donated $500,000 to Michael's "Heal the World Foundation." At this time, "Heal L.A." was founded as a "sister" charitable organization.

More than $108,000 of computer games and equipment were distributed to children's hospitals, group homes, and children's charities throughout the U.K.; this initiative was sponsored by Michael Jackson and Sega.

Michael donated $1.25 million to children who suffered from the riots in Los Angeles.

Michael Jackson actively promoted the D.A.R.E. program, whose purpose is to educate children about the dangers of drug abuse.

New ambulances were provided Moscow, Russia and Buenos Aires, Argentina, through Michael's efforts; and 60,000 doses of children's vaccines were airlifted to Tbilisi, Georgia (with the Gorbachev Foundation).

With Pepsi-Cola Thailand, $40,000 was donated to Crown Princess Maha Chakri Sirindhorn's charity, the Rural School Children and Youth Development Fund, which provides school lunch programs in rural villages.

Michael donated $100,000 to the Children's Defense Fund, the Children's Diabetes Foundation, the Atlanta Project, and the Boys and Girls Clubs of Newark, New Jersey.

He paid for 5,000 underprivileged children to visit the Reino Adventure Park, where the famous whale Keiko from *Free Willy* was living.

In 1993, "Operation Christmas Child" airlifted more than 100,000 shoebox gifts of toys, sweets, and school items to needy children in Sarajevo through Michael's "Heal the World Foundation."

Michael donated $500,000 to Elizabeth Taylor's AIDS Foundation.

Through "Heal L.A.," $85,000 was provided to earthquake relief efforts in Los Angeles, California, in early 1994.

The "Caring for Kids" award was presented to Michael Jackson in New York; 100,000 children and young people, from 8 to 18, had voted for Michael to receive this award.

Michael worked to free dolphins that were locked up for years, and he promoted the creation of legal guidelines to govern the way dolphins live in zoos and parks.

In 1995, Michael made a private request to attend the funeral of Craig Fleming, a two-year-old boy whose mother threw him over the side of a bridge, along with his four-year-old brother, after which she jumped into the river to end her own life. Mother and four-year-old survived, however; Michael contributed toward the medical expenses of the boy and founded a special trust fund for his ongoing care.

In Hungary, four-year-old Bela Farkas, after months of waiting, received a new life-saving liver. Michael ensured the payment of the costs of the boy's transplant surgery and his medical care.

In April 1995, Michael sponsored 46 children from seventeen nations to gather at Neverland for the World Congress of Children, a three-day seminar to discuss drug abuse, homelessness, increasing violence, AIDS, and child abuse.

Michael received the 10th Genesis Award and the 1995 Doris Day Award for his efforts on behalf of animals; his far-reaching and poignant *Earth Song* short film draws public attention to the plight of animals.

In Kaohsiung, Taiwan, Michael visited a hospital for mentally challenged children and offered 2,000 free tickets to his sold-out performance in that city.

Michael donated the proceeds from his Tunisia concert to "The National Solidarity Fund," which is a charity dedicated to fighting poverty.

In Manila, Michael visited a children's hospital and donated a portion of his concert earnings to the renovation of the hospital.

Michael Jackson donated the majority of his earnings from his *HIStory* concert in Bombay, India to the poor people of that country. Three months later, Michael waived his fee for his Bombay appearance and donated $1.1 million to a local charity that helps to educate the children who are living in slums.

Michael visited a school for blind children and an orphanage, at which he passed out toys and gifts, and left a donation of $100,000. A spokeswoman at the facility said, "[The children] don't know him as a pop star; to them he is just a very nice man who came here to offer hope."

The British magazine *OK!* published exclusive photos of Michael's infant son Prince. The magazine paid Michael approximately £1,000,000 for the photos, all of which he donated to charity.

In November 1998, Michael arrived in Harare, Zimbabwe as a member of the American Delegation invited by the Minister of Defense. The delegation thanked the government of Zimbabwe for helping to keep the peace in this geographical area.

At the Bollywood Awards in New York, Michael was presented with an award for his humanitarian activities. On the award was written: "Though he comes from the young American tradition, Michael is the embodiment of an old Indian soul. His actions are an expression of the philosophy of Weda, which asked to work for the people—not for one's own interests."

Michael presented Nelson Mandela with a check for 1,000,000 South African rand for the "Nelson Mandela Children's Fund."

The 2000's

In 2000, Michael Jackson was honored—along with President Bill Clinton—at the Angel Ball in New York, for their work to fight cancer.

Michael Jackson was "one of the first people to donate money" to rebuild the storm-ravaged park of the Chateau de Versailles, where 10,000 trees were destroyed. French officials reported Michael's prompt financial response to their environmental crisis.

For various charities, Michael contributed his time and some of his personal possessions. He painted a plate to be auctioned for the "Carousel of Hope Ball" benefiting childhood diabetes research; donated the coat that he wore to Elizabeth Taylor's tribute concert in London for a cause that aids children and mothers with HIV; and donated a black hat, a personal "birthday phone call," and a jacket to an event given by UNICEF for efforts to prevent mother-to-child HIV transmission in Africa. He also donated an autographed teddy bear that raised $5,000 for a Las Vegas charity that enhances the lives of individuals with intellectual disabilities and their families.

Michael launched the Michael Jackson International Book Club in Newark, New Jersey, by personally handing out books to young people at a theater. As part of his "Heal the Kids" charity, this organization promoted childhood reading and encouraged parents to return to reading bedtime stories to their children.

Michael received the Humanitarian Award from The African Ambassadors' Spouses Association for his worldwide humanitarian activities, particularly in Africa. He financially supported programs in Africa to build and equip hospitals, orphanages, homes, and schools. He also financially supported programs directed at child immunization, HIV-AIDS, education, and apartheid.

At the Bambi Charity Event in Berlin in 2002, Michael donated and personally delivered one of his jackets, which raised $16,000 for the organization.

That same year, Michael performed at a fundraiser for the Democratic National Committee at the Apollo Theater in Harlem, which raised nearly $3 million.

Beyonce Knowles presented Michael with the Radio Music Awards' first Humanitarian Award in 2003.

Michael's "What More Can I Give" became his charity single, available for download, on behalf of Mr. Holland's Opus Foundation, Oneness, and the International Child Art Foundation.

In 2004, Michael Jackson went to Capitol Hill in Washington, D.C., to meet with African-American lawmakers to offer his support in the fight against AIDS and for help for African children.

The following is a partial list of the charities and philanthropic organizations to which Michael Jackson contributed:

AIDS Project L.A.
American Cancer Society
Angel Food
Big Brothers/Big Sisters of America
Big Brothers of Greater Los Angeles
BMI Foundation, Inc.
Brotherhood Crusade
Brotman Burn Center
Camp Ronald McDonald
Childhelp U.S.A.
Children's Institute International
Cities and Schools Scholarship Fund
Community Youth Sports & Arts Foundation
Congressional Black Caucus

Dakar Foundation
Dreamstreet Kids
Dreams Come True Charity
Elizabeth Taylor AIDS Foundation
Heal the World Foundation
Juvenile Diabetes Foundation
Love Match
Make-A-Wish Foundation
Minority Aids Project
Motown Museum
NAACP
National Rainbow Coalition
Rotary Club of Australia
Society of Singers
Starlight Foundation
The Carter Center's Atlanta Project
The Sickle Cell Research Foundation
Transafrica
United Negro College Fund
United Negro College Fund Ladders of Hope
Volunteers of America
Watts Summer Festival
Wish Granting
YMCA—28th Street/Crenshaw

Michael privately sent money to an unknown number of needy children. With few exceptions, only the children and their families know who they are.

He also gave cash to homeless individuals, via face-to-face interactions with them, on a regular basis. Michael would tell them to buy food for themselves, and, as was his style, he would look into their eyes while he spoke to them. He was giving them a sense of dignity, if only for brief minutes, as much as he was giving money. Only his security personnel know about these personal acts of love, compassion, and humanity by their boss Mr. Jackson.

If you and your friends sat around a blazing bonfire, swapping stories about Michael Jackson's humanitarian acts, you would still be talking, unfinished, when the last embers burned out—night after night, at that.

> **Child of innocence, messenger of joy**
> **You've touched my heart without a ploy**
> **My soul is ablaze with a flagrant fire**
> **To change this world is my deepest desire.**
>
> "Child of innocence,"
> *Dancing the Dream,*
> Michael Jackson

In a world made up of Givers and Takers,
Michael Jackson was a Giver.

ARTIST & ENTERTAINER

> **Michael Jackson set the bar**
> **and then he broke it.**
> — Berry Gordy

> **I'll never see this kind of talent again**
> **in my life.... There's something special**
> **in him that isn't of this world.**
> — Sheryl Crow [*Bad* Tour] about Michael Jackson

"Can you hear that, Mike? Can you *hear* that?" An excited Michael Jackson asked his musical director if he could detect a special nuance of a melody that delighted him. It was lost on Michael Bearden, who realized that the musical genius standing in front of his keyboard could hear things in the music that others did not. Bearden was himself a skilled musician, who beat out the stiff competition for his coveted job directing the music production for the eagerly-anticipated, sold-out *This Is It* concerts in London.

"We need *you*," Bearden responded without actually answering the question posed to him. "Can't nobody hear what you ... hear," he added—in awe—as his explanation to Michael Jackson. As he tried once again to perform the song to perfection, Bearden hoped that his ears would improve in their level of discrimination of the subtleties that Michael Jackson relished. He wanted to be able honestly to say, "Yeah! Isn't that great!" He wanted to experience that joy; he wanted to share it with the King of Pop, his boss and collaborator.

His colleagues behind the scenes and on the stage at the Staples Center in Los Angeles, in June 2009, realized that Michael Jackson was hard-wired as a genius. Most of them knew that he breathed rarefied air when it came to the mountaintop of musical ability. They got a peek, on a regular basis, into his brilliance. Everyone was working hard and long hours to bring to fruition Michael Jackson's vision for the greatest live show ever.

Everything in *This Is It* would be better than anything seen before. The technology of a three-story 3D screen, as backdrop to the live performances, was unprecedented in a concert auditorium. The sound technology was astoundingly brilliant; the twenty-some costumes for Michael Jackson were dazzling, with hundreds of thousands of Swarovski crystals; artists were working with engineers to create totally new visuals and outfits for the mega-star. Michael Jackson had his hand in everything. It was always his way to explain his total vision for the final product, to give specific recommendations, to oversee, and to motivate everyone to outdo themselves.

*   *   *   *   *   *   *   *   *

Michael Jackson "saw" music in colors and shapes. He told many of his professional colleagues that he could actually see the beat. Sometimes, too, he couldn't get the beat out of his head, especially at times when he was composing songs. The process took him over entirely; the music captured him. He spent sleepless nights struggling to bring quiet to his brimming mind.

"The breath of life to me is the music of life and it permeates every fiber of creation," Michael wrote in an attempt to express his feeling of being consumed by the music. "The same music governs the rhythm of the seasons, the pulse of our heartbeats, the migration of birds, the ebb and flow of ocean tides, the cycles of growth, evolution and dissolution." Music to him was primordial—the expression of the "ecstasy of divine union."

Singer/vocalist, dancer, songwriter/composer, lyricist, musician, arranger, producer, innovator, choreographer, mime, artist, designer, author, actor, director, short-film (video) pioneer, film and sound editor, music engineer, illusionist, entrepreneur, and celebrity, Michael Jackson did it all. And he brought his own unique creativity to everything.

With an insatiable hunger for knowledge about every aspect of the entertainment industry from an age when other children were learning to add and subtract numbers, Michael Jackson read, studied, observed, practiced, rehearsed, and asked questions of everyone who would listen to him. He was like a sponge absorbing everything.

A self-professed perfectionist, he would drill himself and everyone else who worked with him, over and over again, on songs and dance routines. Even when exhausted, his back-up singers and dancers said they considered it all important and amazing. No one worked harder than Michael Jackson himself, they would say, with obvious pride in themselves and in him. They were proud of "the magic."

Lou Ferrigno, who was working with Michael as his personal trainer in the spring of 2009, said that "Michael worked so hard ... until he dropped down [from fatigue]."

With admiration, his sister Janet had called Michael a workaholic, and she confessed that he worked much harder than she did on music and performing.

While in his service, Boyd Williams and Baron James observed Mr. Jackson at work; they also transported him to and from the studios where he practiced and recorded; and they conversed with him about his art and his plans. Early on, he told the men that he was offered opportunities to become a headliner in Las Vegas. A performing auditorium exclusively for Michael Jackson would be part of the deal if he agreed to a long-term contract.

Unwilling to commit to nightly performances, Michael Jackson could not bear the thought of forgoing this much precious time with his children. Fatherhood was now his first priority in life.

As compelling as his desire to spend time with his kids was the reality of Michael Jackson's having made himself into an incredible performing machine that had set a standard of expectation for himself and his audience that was difficult to maintain. If he were an entertainer who walked onto stage and sang into a microphone, he could have managed multitudinous performances. The harsh reality was that the level of energy he expended in singing and dancing, full-out and full-bodied for every number, took a toll that few entertainers could pay. Often he needed to be administered oxygen after a two-hour, non-stop live performance in concert.

Michael Jackson wanted to give every one of his shows the same electrifying enthusiasm. However, for Michael—who turned fifty in 2008—the wear and tear on his body would be significant and painful.

As a single parent of three children, Michael Jackson did double-duty as mother and father to his kids. From staying up all night with a feverish child to overseeing their home-schooling to ensuring the provision of their meals, he had a full-time job. In addition, he was dealing with litigation and financial matters that were extremely stressful, to say the least. Mr. Jackson had a financial empire and publishing kingdom that were managed by a long list of individuals, so many that he could not keep track of them himself. His was a complicated life on many levels. His security team articulated that "most people would jump off a cliff if they had to deal with what Mr. Jackson did."

Michael Jackson realized that he would have to consume 6,000 to 8,000 calories every day just to maintain himself while he was rehearsing and performing. He often admitted that, in general, he didn't eat very much. Michael lost at least five pounds during every performance, and he did not carry enough weight to sustain that kind of loss on a regular basis. He would need some number of days in between his performances to survive the grueling schedule. He would need to structure his eating habits in a carefully planned way and to ensure getting an adequate amount of sleep. These were big challenges for a man who ate sparingly and who suffered from a serious case of chronic insomnia.

The insomnia, Michael realized, would be a formidable impediment to his successful return to the stage on a demanding schedule. How could he perform at the exhausting level that he established for himself if he had been unable to sleep the night before? With this ongoing problem, it would be difficult—a constant struggle—for him to explode on stage night after night and wow the crowds with his "knock-them-dead" performances.

Even though the enticing offer of a Vegas-based run of shows represented an unprecedented level of remuneration in live entertainment history, Michael Jackson declined.

Having started at the tender age of five, Michael was at the point in his life where he had worked for *forty-five years*. That was the equivalent of a typical individual working from age twenty to sixty-five, a standard retirement age. Michael was once quoted as saying, "I've been performing for so long, I sometimes feel like I should be seventy by now." Michael Jackson had forfeited his childhood, unwillingly for the most part, to become a man who deserved a rest. He also deserved to give his kids the kind of childhood that he had only read about and observed in scattered glimpses.

Michael wanted to do things that he really liked and to experiment with new challenges. He hoped to become a director of movies, which he had always passionately enjoyed and studied. With no fanfare or publicity, Michael Jackson had lent his talents to the creation of a number of Vegas special attractions at some of the extravagant hotels because he relished the opportunity for a different kind of creative outlet. He worked as a consultant, lending his musical and artistic expertise to the projects.

Michael Jackson had mastered the diverse skills of his profession at an unparalleled level in the entertainment business. According to his long-time personal photographer, Matthew Rolston, who did Michael's last formal sitting in 2007, Michael was an expert in photography and always knew exactly what he wanted from a photo shoot. He was also remarkably skilled in lighting and costume design; he had personally supervised all of these preparations for his concert tours. And, his security team was well aware, from dozens of conversations and directions from their boss, that he knew all about security. Little wonder that Mr. Jackson understood security; he had needed it since he and his brothers made the big time as international stars when he was younger than Prince and Paris.

Michael Jackson provided direction to everything that he did, including song-recording, concert shows, and short films. He had his personal videographer tape his rehearsals, interviews, and practice sessions. For example, the videographer followed him around Neverland Ranch while he tried out different dance moves for his *Smooth Criminal* short film, in which he first intended to incorporate a cowboy theme but later decided on the unforgettable gangster theme. On stage, always employing multiple cameras— often six or more—Michael could ensure capturing the best angles of every dance move and special effect. He learned to do the film editing and cutting himself; the final product had to be exquisite and memorable. "Every shot you see is my shot," he explained to an interviewer. He focused on "what juxtaposition you want [people] to see" to "capture it properly." "Live in Bucharest" is an excellent example of Michael's flair for the dramatic and the effectiveness of his skillful editing.

His perfectionism, coupled with his goal to push and move societal boundaries, extended to clothing design. Across decades he was a trend-setter, known for his unique style. People wanted to see what he would be wearing next. It was always something that incorporated a new design element or combination, such as fabric with metal. Buckles, belts, beads, medals, chains, zippers, hoops, and studs became design elements that were incorporated into his clothing. The fedora hat, with a brim of exact, prescribed dimension, became universally identified with Michael Jackson, particularly in his performances of "Billie Jean" and "Smooth Criminal." Wearing a fedora both on and off stage, Michael Jackson launched this style of hat into mass appeal in America and countries abroad.

The armband, which became his signature look, was ubiquitously worn by Michael as a symbol to remind people of the plight of ailing, hurting children around the world. It was always made of a color that contrasted with the sleeve of his shirt or jacket so that it would be noticed.

White bandages wrapped around three of his finger tips became the standard accompaniment of his costuming for certain songs. A leg brace or arm brace, worn during his performance of certain songs, aroused the curiosity of his audience. It was incongruous to see him dance wildly while he was wearing what looked like a supportive medical device. He combined a unique style with mystery.

His most iconic symbol, however, is the single sequined glove, white and sparkling. He first wore it while performing "Billie Jean," which was described as "Michael's coronation into the international realm of fame and acclaim."

Michael Jackson popularized the military style in clothing. Fitted Napoleonic jackets with epaulets, shiny buttons, and various ornate insignia became the norm for his fearless approach to couture. These created a regal attitude that was communicated by his appearance and bearing; they accompanied Michael's entry into music royalty. After all, he was the *King* of Pop.

The red leather jacket became one of the most iconic fashion items during the eighties because of Michael Jackson. It was identified with "Thriller" and "Beat It," the symbol of those rousing songs, and a bold statement of "belonging" and "being cool" by those people who proudly wore one.

"Liberace gone to war" is the description used by his thirty-year costumer, Michael Bush, when he was asked to describe Michael Jackson's style. The most recognized entertainer of all time loved bling. Michael wore sequins and rhinestones on his apparel unabashedly and often; he also liked other gems and crystals on his clothing. These elements would converge with the military look—a type of glorious uniform—that seemed to bestow a high level of status on the wearer, Michael Jackson.

Always a man of contrasts, Michael also wore a plain, old-fashioned, white, V-neck T-shirt, visible under a jacket or heavier shirt, as part of his image. He also wore cropped trousers (usually black), which served to highlight his socks. According to some sources, Michael first adopted this style so that even those people at the back of his huge auditorium audiences could see and appreciate his dance moves. His above-the-ankle black pants with black loafers and white socks, sometimes sequined, were recognized around the globe as Michael Jackson's.

Certain postures and stances, frozen in time and repeated with precision, became identified only with him. His curved body in profile—head down, standing on the tips of his toes—represents Michael Jackson. When you see it, you think "Billie Jean." The pointed finger, his arm outstretched in exactly the same way every time, came to remind everyone of Michael Jackson.

Typically, performing artists seek to establish *one symbol* that is identified exclusively with them, as a trademark that promotes them and titillates the public. Some succeed; many do not. Michael Jackson established so many symbols unique to him that he outperformed *all* other entertainers in this arena. No other performer has ever come close to claiming the number of unforgettable symbols of their unique *persona* and presence that Michael Jackson created and projected.

In his music, Michael Jackson was not only a visionary and a pioneer but also a prophet. Until he revolutionized the genre of the music video, which he appropriately insisted on naming the "short film," these productions were quite simple, many of them not much more than an individual singing into a microphone. Michael Jackson was the first entertainer to incorporate a unique theme and a beginning, middle, and end to every short film that he created to convey his songs with visual representation. These short films were multi-dimensional with verve and color. They incorporated special effects that had never been tried before, such as the controversial face morphing used in *Black or White* and the full-body, straight-backed, forward tilt of the dancers in *Smooth Criminal*. Michael Jackson took out a patent on the anti-gravity shoes that he created for *Smooth Criminal*; it was the shoes that enabled the dancers to perform the astounding move that looked a lot like magic.

If you watched two dozen dancers, all similarly dressed, performing on stage, your eye would always go to Michael Jackson. His professional colleagues would describe how he stood out from the others. Dancers who trained for years marveled at Michael's abilities, at his fluid moves, precision, and innovation. Creating the choreography for The Jackson 5 from a young age, Michael Jackson *never took a dance lesson* either then or later; *he was a natural dancer.* Michael created and/or perfected the robot moves, the moonwalk, the toe stand, gang moves, synchronized group dance, Egyptian moves, the anti-gravity lean, and the controversial crotch grab. He incorporated influences from other cultures, as clearly evidenced in *Black or White,* with dance borrowings from the American Indian, Russia, and India.

Michael Jackson's voice was clear, strong, and distinctive. His touring voice coach Seth Riggs was in awe of him:

> He's a high tenor with a three-and-a-half octave range. He goes from basso low E up to G and A-flat above high C. A lot of people think it's a falsetto, but it's not. It's all connected, which is remarkable. During his vocal exercises he would put his arms up in the air and start spinning while holding a note. I asked him why he was doing that, and he said, "I may have to do it onstage, so I want to make sure it's possible." I'd never seen anything like that before.
> (J. Randy Taraborrelli)

In composing and recording music, Michael Jackson zealously worked toward a combination of perfection and uniqueness. He originated the use of multiple tracks of his own voice; he changed the tone and/or cadence of the music by adding a second track onto the first one; and often he blended in various unusual sounds on a third. His songs incorporated yips, yelps, whoops, gasps, tics, trills, and "hee hee"s, the last of which was unerringly identified as Michael Jackson's. He was the master of the "hee hee," delivered in a high voice. He also worked into various songs the chirps of birds; cricket sounds; shattering glass; cowbells; fog horns; chiming clocks; coin clinks; camera clicking; news broadcasts; car horns; sirens; music-box winding; door slamming; demonic laughter; crypt door squeaking; heartbeats; baby crying; children talking, whispering, and shouting; and rapper jive and taunts.

Michael Jackson also sometimes created his own words for his songs. One recurring word, "shamone," is a popular example; his fans wonder what it means. Regardless of his intended meaning, it just sounds good.

Michael's music is readily identifiable as his. He often used "fooler" or "teaser" beginnings, for example lovely symphonic introductions that led into the faster beat of the body of the song. His rich song endings seem to linger on; they are unforgettable. The listener finds himself humming the song in his mind endlessly throughout the day. Michael Jackson wanted melodies that would "stay with people"; that was his design. The songs have drama, with almost always a unique crescendo. It was as if he *built* his songs.

The richness of his music is even more impressive in light of the fact that Michael Jackson could not read or write musical notation. He would capture his original songs by singing them into a tape recorder. He would sing them to other people, including his producers, engineers, and the various musicians who ultimately performed on the recordings. Sometimes, he explained, a complete song would just come to him—melody, words, and instrumental parts. He became amazingly adept at simulating the sounds of instruments with his voice; this skill helped him translate to his musicians the sounds that he wanted to create. On the posthumous album *Michael*, the beginning of "(I Like) The Way You Love Me" includes snippets of Michael Jackson doing just that—using his voice to sound like specific musical instruments.

In his own words, Michael described his process of composing:

I hear the whole entire song and arrangements in my head[,] what each instrument is suppose[d] to do, I put them down orally on tape[,] then I go out and find that instrument. I don't give in until I get exactly what I want. I sing every part with my mouth. [From a hand-written statement published in the album *Michael*]

"One day he was walking around the house in his pajamas [as my family's houseguest], singing some new pieces that he was working on," explained Al Malnik, a friend of Michael, in *Haute Living* magazine. "He was walking up one set of stairs, and then down another. I asked him, 'What are you doing?' He said, 'I'm doing two songs at once! I am walking up … doing one song, and when I walk down … I do the other song.'" Malnik and his family marveled at "such talent"—"he could write a song in five minutes; it was unbelievable."

Michael practiced his steps in the Malnik home on a portable dance floor that they brought in for their fascinating guest. He dazzled them with his "amazing energy" and skill. It is also interesting to note that Michael Jackson met the Malniks in the late nineties, after he asked if he could see their stunning home on the ocean in Palm Beach, Florida. As it turns out, included among his vast creative involvements was that of architecture buff; Michael studied and appreciated the beauty and innovation incorporated in buildings.

Oprah Winfrey referred to Michael Jackson as the "King of Entertainment" when she interviewed him in 1993. It was reported by professionals in show business that "no one wanted to follow Michael Jackson on stage." He was a hard act to follow. Other entertainers did not want the audience to feel let down in the aftermath of his electrifying, hysteria-producing performances; they simply could not compete. They could not perform at his level, combining the singing, dancing, choreography, and passion that were uniquely his.

In his recording patterns, Michael was also different from others. As he explained in his "Private Home Movies," he would

begin assembling a new album by reviewing "over 100 songs" to
begin "to select down" to the best ten or so. Many artists produce
one excellent, stand-out song or two and then build an album for
release to the public by adding other cuts that are remakes or fillers.
Not Michael Jackson. He wanted every song to be a "killer" song;
to make the hair stand up at the back of the listener's neck; to be a
"thriller."

Michael's practice of packing his albums with spectacular songs
had commercial implications, of course. Each album was more
likely to become a big hit, but—had he taken the more conventional
route—he could have released many more albums and theoretically
made significant more money. What was most important to Michael
Jackson was the quality of his work, not the dollars generated.

Unknown even to many of his fans, Michael Jackson played a
number of instruments, including the piano. He did not talk about this
ability, perhaps because he was genuinely humble, and also he may
not have felt that he played them flawlessly, as he would require of
himself as a perfectionist. On his *HIStory* album, Michael Jackson
is credited with playing guitar, drums, percussion, keyboard, and
piano. He played many instruments on the single "Scream," his only
duet with his famous sister Janet. The *Scream* short film, featuring
both of them in jaw-dropping dance moves, garnered numerous
MTV Video Music Awards and a Grammy.

Through his music, Michael artistically conveyed his core
personal values and burning desire for a better world. He sang of
love, brotherhood, racial unity, environmental responsibility, peace,
and the need to heal our children and our shared planet.

"Black or White" resonated with people around the world.
It was a huge global hit because of its compelling messages: "It
doesn't matter if you're black or white" and "I don't want to live my
life being a color."

Always embracing peace over conflict, Michael Jackson
eschewed violence, which he demonstrated through both the

words and choreography of his songs. Even when violence appears imminent between people in the dance, there is a reversal of direction, a coming together at the end, such as in *Beat It, Bad,* and *Earth Song.* This was a strong message from Michael Jackson— it's always better to choose peaceful coexistence and brotherly love. "We are all one," he would remind us.

In his public life, too, he became identified with the peace sign, two fingers extended in the well-known universal gesture. Michael used it wherever he went, to communicate his appreciation of his fans and to remind them of his heartfelt message.

Always a spiritual man, Michael Jackson wanted his artistic works to serve as the channel through which the Divine flowed on earth. To *Ebony* magazine, Michael elaborated on his personal philosophy:

... I believe that all art has as its ultimate goal the union between the material and the spiritual, the human and the divine. And I believe that is the very reason for the existence of art and what I do. And I feel fortunate in being that instrument through which music flows.

He provided a further glimpse into his worldview and artistic vision:

Deep inside, I feel that this world we live in is really a big, huge, monumental symphonic orchestra. I believe that in its primordial form, all of creation is sound and that it's not just random sound, that it's music.

Michael Jackson sang stirringly about global issues in his popular song "HIStory"—victims "slaughtered in vain," soldiers and children dying, mothers crying, brotherhood, healing, and "the prophet's plan." When he performed "HIStory" on stage in dozens of countries, the flags of every nation in the world were displayed, one at a time, on a huge back-up screen. What other performer has done anything like this proud acknowledgment of all nations, even the tiniest and most overlooked?

Michael Jackson's artistic works reflect not only his personal values but his deepest feelings and most transforming life experiences. He left us a whole body of artistic work in which he reveals himself … in contrast to the mere footprint of his private life that he left in other ways. He wrote his autobiography *Moonwalk* (1988) and his creative *Dancing the Dream (1992)* poems and reflections when he was a young man; he chose not to provide us with significant written disclosures during his last seventeen years. *Moonwalk* is as understated as Michael was soft-spoken; he describes his life experiences with wonderful simplicity and humility. *Dancing the Dream* gives us glimpses into Michael Jackson's heart and soul, into his worldview, his sense of the divine, and his profound humanity. Many of his admirers wish for more, for writings and messages from Michael from more recent years; but we can feel grateful for what he gave. "What More Can I Give" is the name of Michael's song that is dedicated to the 9/11 victims and survivors. Perhaps it is an appropriate specific message from him to us....

*   *   *   *   *   *   *   *   *

Michael Jackson ensured that he worked with the best people, equipment, and resources in all of his musical endeavors. He combined the use of state-of-the-art equipment with world-class musicians and performers whom he admired. Even his short films featured the most prominent celebrities, including Marlon Brando, Iman, Eddie Murphy, John Travolta, Chris Tucker, Whoopi Goldberg, Paula Abdul, Naomi Campbell, Janet Jackson, Magic Johnson, and basketball superstar Michael Jordan.

"Michael Jackson always shared the credit with the others of us who worked with him," Siedah Garrett told the audience at the *Genius Without Borders: Michael Jackson* Symposium held at Columbia College in Chicago, Illinois, in September 2010. Ms. Garrett was one member of the panel of presenters who had worked closely with Michael across many years. She recorded "I Just Can't Stop Loving You" with him; co-wrote his favorite anthem "Man in the Mirror"; and performed with him on the *Dangerous* Tour.

"Michael made everyone feel as if he could learn as much from them as they could from him, and we all loved him for that," she related. He was humble and supportive of all who worked on his projects; he encouraged them and publicly gave them credit for their contributions. Because of his frequent, gracious acknowledgments, many individuals who worked for the King of Pop went on to major careers in their own right.

"They would have done anything for him," Siedah concluded, "because he was so generous to them."

Michael Jackson would have been guaranteed immortal status in the annals of music history from his early achievements with his brothers in The Jackson 5 and then The Jacksons. An unprecedented four consecutive #1 hits propelled the group into world orbit. Dozens of more hit records, sold by the millions, and tours of standing-room-only concerts earned the Jackson brothers an immutable legacy. They produced nineteen albums together and sold one hundred million records. Then, Michael surpassed all of that on his own as a solo artist.

Early in his solo career, after Michael Jackson read *The Greatest Show on Earth,* he committed himself to becoming the greatest entertainer of all. He saw himself as a totality in terms of his professional self; even when venturing out in public, he believed that he was on stage for the world's view. He was exquisitely aware of the image that he created and projected; he perceived it as an important part of his art. To Michael, even his face was an integral segment of the canvas of his artistic expression; he transformed it, in spite of controversy and criticism; and his facial appearance did noticeably change across time.

Michael Jackson did become the greatest entertainer of all time. Sheer numbers bear that out.... Thirteen Grammy Awards, eight of them in one record-breaking night; 750 million records sold before his death, a number that is rapidly climbing toward one billion; thirteen singles that reached the Number 1 spot on the *Billboard* charts; induction into the Rock 'n' Roll Hall of Fame twice. *Thriller* remains the best-selling album of all time, with approximately 110 million copies sold. *Thriller* is considered the watershed event that forever changed the face of music and the way its business is conducted.

Astoundingly, many of his albums spent months on the *Billboard Hot 100* list—*Thriller*, 108 weeks; *Dangerous*, 117 weeks; *Bad*, 85 weeks; *Off the Wall*, 73 weeks; and 98 weeks for the rest of his studio albums. End to end, that's more than nine years!

Michael's *HIStory* World Tour in 1997 included 82 concerts in thirty-five countries on five continents, with 4.5 million tickets sold, the most ever. His *Dangerous* World Tour, 1992-93, included 69 concerts in dozens of countries, to a total audience of 3.5 million people. His previous *Bad* Tour, 1987-89 (spanning 16 months), consisted of 123 concerts in fifteen countries, to 4.4 million people. These tours were record-breaking in terms of earnings and audience numbers.

Michael received 23 *Guinness World Records,* including one for the "Most Successful Entertainer of All Time." He holds more *Guinness World Records* than any other artist. He is also one of the longest-standing recipients, having achieved his first *Guinness World Record* at the age of eleven, when he was honored for being the "Youngest Vocalist to Top the U.S. Singles Chart."

Michael Jackson is the most award-winning artist of all time. He has been named the Artist of the "Decade," "Generation," "Century," and "Millennium." He was inducted into the prestigious Songwriters Hall of Fame in 2002. Of 392 "major awards" received by Michael Jackson, some of the most noteworthy, by category, are 56 Recording Industry Association of America Awards, 40 *Billboard* Awards, 26 American Music Awards, 23 *Guinness World Records,* 14 NAACP Image Awards, 13 Grammy Awards, 13 MTV

Awards, 13 World Music Awards, 10 Soul Train Awards, 7 BRIT Awards, 4 American Video Awards, and one Music of Black Origin (MOBO) Award. Michael won hundreds of other awards; they are too numerous to list. In fact, he won so many awards in so many countries throughout the world and broke so many global records that you would need an official music historian, with a lot of time available, to compile a complete list.

Of special significance, however, is Michael Jackson's *MTV* Japan's Legend Award, which he received in 2006 for having sold more than *one hundred million* albums in that country.

"No album has spent longer at number one in the U.K. this century than *The Essential Michael Jackson*, which held the position for seven straight weeks in 2009." Michael was hugely popular in the United Kingdom, and he holds many records of achievement in that country.

Dangerous was the fastest-selling number one album of all time in the United Kingdom, where it remained on the charts for ninety-six weeks, an achievement only exceeded in America. The albums *Bad*, *Dangerous*, and *HIStory* all debuted at #1 in America. The single "Bad" went to number one in America, the U.K., and countries around the world. In the U.K., *Bad* remained on the charts for an amazing 109 weeks. Michael Jackson was the first person in the thirty-seven-year history of the *Billboard* chart to enter straight in at #1 with his single "You Are Not Alone." Still, all of these hits did not approach the overall success of *Thriller*.

Michael Jackson's *HIStory* was the best-selling multiple-disc album by a solo artist in music history.

Time magazine wrote about Michael Jackson as the man who ruled the world of pop music during the 1980's:

> Star of records, radio, and rock video. A one-man rescue team for the music business. A songwriter who sets the beat for a decade. A dancer with the fanciest feet on the street. A singer who cuts across all boundaries of taste and style and color.

After those accolades, Michael continued on and surpassed himself again and again, through the nineties and into the beginning of the twenty-first century, when he turned his attention more toward fatherhood than his musical career. However, Michael continued to compose music through these years, archiving dozens of songs. He chose not to tour or perform at concerts because of his full-time commitment to his young children.

"Hollywood Tonight," one of the songs on his posthumous album *Michael,* rose to the Number 1 spot on the *Billboard Dance/ Club Play* charts in May 2011. With this achievement, Michael tied (with Enrique Iglesias) for the most *solo* chart toppers among men—*eight*—in the chart's thirty-five-year history.

Michael Jackson is the world's best-selling male solo pop artist.

In addition, he was named the highest-earning dead celebrity between October 2010 and October 2011, on the Forbes' annual list, for the second consecutive year. Michael Jackson's Estate brought in $170 million, well ahead of the second deceased earner, Elvis Presley, at $55 million.

*   *   *   *   *   *   *   *   *

To his own surprise and delight, Michael Jackson's comeback concerts at the O2 Arena in London, set to begin in July 2009, sold out in *four hours*! No one had seen anything like this volume of ticket sales before. To the original ten concerts, forty more were added, and they sold out, to one million eager attendees, within four days. Many thousands of people were still applying online for tickets but none were available.

This astounding response—far and away greater than anything seen before—meant more to Michael Jackson than the tens of millions of dollars that he was due to earn. Years before, when Oprah had showed him a video of himself on stage—the massive audience hysterical with joy—and asked him how that felt to him, Michael responded with alacrity, it felt like "Love." He then nodded solemnly and embellished, "Lots of love."

This Is It, referring to the final curtain call, was the title Michael conferred on his imminent concert series. He intended his performances to cap his career with an amazing last chapter, although some of his confidantes—including brother Jermaine—have confirmed that he planned to tour the world.

After his passing, his dear friend and the director of the concerts, Kenny Ortega, working with Michael Jackson's Estate, produced a movie by the same name. Michael Jackson never lived to fulfill his dream of a comeback for his welcoming fans and his own beloved children. Fortunately for the world, Kenny Ortega did it for him through this movie, which was gerrymandered from more than 100 hours of footage taken by Michael's own cameramen for his personal use.

This Is It quickly became the highest-grossing concert movie and the highest-grossing documentary in history, having shown in *ninety-nine countries* to appreciative audiences and millions of grateful fans, old and new. According to the *Guinness World Records 2011*, *This Is It* opened simultaneously in 250,000 movie theaters around the world and took in $200 million in its first two weeks alone. In the U.S. and Canada, it showed in 3,400 theaters. People slept on sidewalks overnight in dozens of countries to get tickets to the film when box offices opened on the first morning of sales.

For many, *This Is It* was the best way to experience Michael Jackson, to try to understand him, and to mourn him. "The man you never knew"—as the advertisement reminded you—was the star of this documentary concert film. Although you didn't know him, *he was the man who probably loved you.*

Michael Jackson—if he still walked among us—would no doubt say that this overwhelming, around-the-globe response to him and to his *This Is It* concert film is "Like love. Lots of love."

*   *   *   *   *   *   *   *   *

When God was giving out talent,
He gave all of it to Michael Jackson.
— Kenny "Babyface" Edmonds

The man who created the soundtrack
to so many of our lives
gave us such wonderful gifts,
and we can no longer thank him.

"BIZARRE BEHAVIOR"

Michael is the least strange man I know.
— Elizabeth Taylor to Oprah Winfrey

**Show me a creative genius
who isn't a little off-center!**
— David Nordahl

Bizarre behavior is normal in bizarre circumstances.

In fact, "normal" behavior doesn't work in bizarre circumstances! People need to adjust how they act and how they respond to the vicissitudes of life in order to survive. To thrive, people sometimes need to get really creative in their life decisions and everyday behaviors. To be happy, individuals need to find their own way.

And, of course, what is "normal" behavior anyway? It varies by person, by gender, age, environment, genetic background, ethnicity, geography, cultural influences, sexual orientation, and circumstances. Timing is an important variable, too; "smart" adaptive behavior at one time might not "work" at another time.

Michael Jackson, from his toddler years, had to learn how to adjust in a large, aggressive, ambitious family of entertainers. As the seventh of nine children, he learned important lessons from his siblings, but he had to make his own way.

"You are born with a pen and paper in hand, but you have to write your own story," stated the authors of *Living with Our Genes*. Michael Jackson wrote for himself one of the most fascinating, inspiring, and yet tragic stories of our times.

Michael used "creative coping" in his *unique* world. As a genius and a man apart from all others, he fashioned his own path....

Michael Jackson was more than the sum of his parts. We can analyze him by individual characteristics and dissect both his everyday behaviors and his most controversial actions, and we still do not come close to fully understanding the man. Yet, we can arrive at a distillation of the credible information to a point where we have a real visceral feeling of the child-man who was Michael Jackson. Many people come to feel a "soul connection" with him that is undeniable and deep.

Abused Child

Michael was undoubtedly a child who experienced corporal punishment and physical force at the hands of his stern, driven father. Joe Jackson admitted on national television, months after Michael's passing, that he did give him "whippings." Michael had revealed that he was so terrified of his father that he sometimes regurgitated at the sight of the man. He would run away from him to avoid being struck; often, he would not be so lucky as to escape from his father's acting out his anger.

"Joseph," who insisted that his children call him that instead of "dad," disciplined and controlled his sons by striking them with a strap, belt, or clothes-iron cord. Sometimes he inflicted the whipping when there was a lapse in their performing; maybe they missed a step or two in the dancing or sang out of key. Some people will say, "Well, that's how African-American parents raised their children in those days; they didn't 'spare the rod and spoil the child.'" Even if a person accepts that explanation, the "whipped" child feels abused, powerless, fearful, and angry.

His father also resorted to physical punishment with Michael and the other boys *when he was angry*. This situation is entirely different from a light slap delivered by a parent who is trying to teach something important without manifest anger. Physical assaults are an abuse of power by an older and stronger human being over a younger and weaker human being. When it's a father-son situation, the feelings are complex and disturbing. The child has to make some emotional decisions.

For Michael, *he chose to be loving.* From his physical abuse, Michael derived the decision to love others. He did not want to be like his father; he wanted to be the opposite. He could easily have become violent himself; a sullen, angry boy and man; an abuser. Instead, he fled to the opposite end of that continuum—he chose gentleness, exuberance, and nurturance of others. How amazing is that!

Many say that he internalized the gentle, compassionate nature of his mother Katherine, who modeled caring behaviors. As a polio victim, a social outcast during her teens, Katherine learned to feel deeply for other people who suffered from adversity. She loved babies and children. When she referred to eight-year-old Blanket as "the baby," grandmother Katherine revealed her strong maternal instincts and her perception of children as needing adult understanding and compassion.

What diverse messages Michael got from his parents! He learned about fear and the ugliness of power. He learned about the beauty of love and the compelling desire to protect those in need, particularly the very young.

Lost Childhood

Yes, Michael Jackson lost his childhood. Some people will say, "He was having fun, though, singing and dancing, and enjoying fame and celebrity." Child labor laws have been passed and enforced in this country for valid reasons. Among them is the recognition that children deserve a childhood without compulsory work demanded from them for remuneration, or otherwise. It may have looked like all fun for Michael from the outside, but it was grueling work and long days with no real breaks. Part of his job was to make it look like fun.

Even though he was not working on a sewing machine or in a cotton field, Michael Jackson was still required to *work* on at least a "full-time basis" from the time that he was seven! Of special significance perhaps is the reality that Michael was not able to *think* like a child or to succumb to the feelings of childhood. His work was all-consuming—he was singing, dancing, rehearsing, recording, giving interviews, traveling and touring. He often worked until 3 A.M. What he was doing required complete focus and the self-discipline that is typical of adulthood, not childhood. He was described as a man in a child's body; he was jokingly referred to as a "midget"—there had to be an adult in that little, exquisitely-performing body.

Michael not only had to forgo the daydreams, thoughts, and fantasies of a child, he did not celebrate holidays or birthdays. This deprivation was due to the religion of his mother, which prohibited these celebrations. Michael did not celebrate Christmas, for example, until he was thirty-five! He also was prevented, for long stretches of time, from playing active sports, such as basketball with his brothers. If Michael was injured, the show could not go on; if one of his brothers was injured, the others could keep going, with Michael center-stage, the major attraction for the crowds.

He recognized that he was the family meal ticket, from the time that he was eight or nine, even before The Jackson 5 made it big. Performing in modest venues, the family of brothers earned a decent living, but Michael was the most important entertainer and biggest attraction in the group. He carried a huge burden of responsibility for a little boy; he had to be good at what he did; he had to be consistent. If he stopped for any reason, his entire family would suffer. The Jackson 5 would likely be shut down or at least reduced to performing at sleazy nightclubs and second-class arenas; the family income would plummet. They had come from a tiny house in Gary, Indiana; the family struggled and lived paycheck-to-paycheck; and both father and mother worked from morning to night to get by— he in the steel mills, she at home. With little Michael as the big draw of the crowds to the family's shows, all of the Jacksons profited, and their quality of life improved tenfold.

It was indisputably Michael who brought fame and fortune to his family. They learned to depend upon it, to expect it, and to control him. After all, he was the little one. In family decision-making, his vote was overtaken by older brothers, whose votes were for *their* advancement. Michael needed to work to support his family and their aspirations ... and before he was even old enough to be able to form aspirations of his own.

What all this means is that Michael Jackson never had the opportunity to behave, think, feel, celebrate, or act like a child. He was a full-time worker in the service of his family and of the career that was thrust upon him. He was the income producer, the hope and dream for more and better, the pawn in the path of ambition and striving for a family that loved him, but also used him.

Michael was a commodity as much as—and maybe more than—he was a son and a brother.

Love of Children & Animals

As a young boy, Michael turned to animals for companionship and affection. He would talk to them and care for them with gentleness and warmth. He filled his bedroom with rats, and later he adopted a huge snake and a baby chimpanzee, whom he named "Bubbles."

Bubbles became Michael's constant companion from the time he saved the chimp from a research facility, where his fate would have been grim at best. Bubbles lived at Hayvenhurst as a member of the Jackson family. He ate at the family table; slept in Michael's room; and enjoyed the run of the house, including access to the refrigerator for an evening snack. Bubbles wore custom-made clothes, including pajamas; he learned to kneel to say his nighttime prayers; and he learned to do the moonwalk. Michael traveled the world with Bubbles; when he worked on the short film *Bad*, the chimp observed all of the dance rehearsals; and in Japan Bubbles participated with Michael in a formal tea ceremony, also attended by a mob of reporters.

When he went out and about, Michael was often accompanied by Muscles, his boa constrictor. The snake would twist, wind, and curl around tables and chairs while his master recorded music in the sound studio.

At Neverland, Michael's own exotic menagerie of animals lived well and freely roamed, overseen by a staff of veterinarians and caretakers. David Nordahl reveals that most of the animals at Neverland had been rescued from situations of abuse. Once there, at special facilities isolated from visitors, these animals were given the best available medical treatment until they were well enough to be released onto the grounds in natural habitats. Michael insisted on the most attentive care for his animals.

Michael Jackson formed a special relationship with his animals, whom he considered his friends. He didn't even have other, *human* friends until he was in his early twenties, and he had to work on those relationships. In contrast, his interactions with animals came naturally to him.

When he grew to realize what he had missed as a child, Michael explained, he began to feel strong love for children and deep appreciation of them. He marveled at their lack of inhibition, their honesty, their ability to show joy and to play with abandon. He felt like an alien soul with adults, but he felt within himself the stirrings of a child; he felt wonder at their innocence; he was awed by their charm; he realized their vulnerability.

It has been said that "a person can only feel his own pain." When we look at a suffering being or witness a death, we feel not as much for that person or animal as our own pain, which is awakened and magnified by our exposure to that stimulus, that reminder. Individuals cry at different things; we are moved by those events that touch our own experience and trigger our own "unfinished business."

Michael Jackson was emotionally affected by children in a pervasive way. He could not even watch television news or read certain sections of a newspaper out of fear of coming too close to the suffering and pain felt by a *helpless* child, whether homeless, sick, abused, disabled, or disadvantaged. He felt their pain; he felt it deeply.

Michael was moved to do something about it when he did see the pain; in fact, he felt compelled. Partially, perhaps, his reaching out to these children helped him work through his own pain, fill what felt like holes in his heart, bridge the huge gaps in his own experience. When he helped children, he felt right; he felt complete; and, in time, he felt compelled to keep doing that.

As a young adult, he discovered that he could be a child himself … with kids and with animals. They did not judge him; they interacted with Michael Jackson, not the King of Pop; they were neither "impressed" nor did they seek their own advancement at his expense or from his work. They were so unlike all of the adults in his life!

"Adults have let me down; adults have let the world down," Michael asserted in a 2003 interview. "It's time for the children now. It's time for us to give them a chance. Like the Bible says, 'A child shall be leader of them all.'"

With children, there was trust, fun, joy, happiness ..., the things that he missed during his own early years as a "performer-worker." Yes, he experienced some fun, laughter, and joking around with his brothers, especially when they were "on the road" together, sharing their meals and their beds with each other. In their small Indiana house, they would stand in line together, waiting to take a bath in the only tiny bathroom; they would dance together as they did their chores. Except for these pieces of childhood, Michael was without; he had to be "nose to the grindstone."

During adulthood, when he could make his own decisions, he preferred the company of children. With them he likely could forget the abuse he had suffered in his own childhood. It was almost as if it hadn't happened when he could romp with visiting kids, have water balloon fights, and laugh together on trains and amusement rides. He could forget the outside world from which craziness came— extortion attempts, lawsuits, nasty media coverage, and people who always wanted something from him.

Michael chose to be "child-like, not child*ish*," as he explained. He cherished the fantasy-world he created, the creativity that literally flowed from him when he indulged "the child within," and the beautiful outcomes, the songs that seemed to come to him without effort, especially when he was up in his "Giving Tree." Escapism was important to Michael. Isolation from the outside world brought him some relief from the pain, from the bad memories of abuse and alienation, and from the oppressive atmosphere in which his every move was structured, regulated, monitored, and often criticized and ridiculed.

Loneliness

Michael experienced emotional isolation throughout his life. Feeling abjectly lonely in hotels, even when there were thousands of fans chanting their love for him from the street below, Michael described it as an occasion that made him cry. "There's all that love out there," he explained, "but still, you really do feel trapped and lonely. And you can't get out." He composed the moving ballad "Stranger in Moscow" during such a time of excruciating loneliness.

Describing himself as one of the loneliest people on the planet, Michael Jackson *felt* alienated from others. He saw things through a different lens, and he processed what he saw within the mind of a genius. "I'm not like other guys, I mean I'm different," he said in his *Thriller* short film. Although that was a work of fantasy, how prophetic and true his statement was!

Michael missed not only the typical experiences of childhood but also those of adolescence. He did not attend school dances, sleep-overs, proms, or athletic competitions such as football or basketball games; he did not have friends.

Like most successful child stars, he was ill-equipped to have a normal adulthood. There were big gaps in his experiences, his emotional foundation, and his learning. These experiential deficits, coupled with the need for seclusion because of security concerns, turned Michael into an isolate. This is not to say that he was a recluse; he was not. Michael was the kind of person who could be lonely in a crowded room. Because he loved people, it was a curse for him to feel so separate and different from other people.

"I just want to try to fit in, you know?" Michael poignantly said to his interviewer in 2003 in the outtake portion.

Because he was *Michael Jackson!*, even those in his inner circles would behave differently with him. They "were not themselves," he knew, because they were in awe of him and/or they wanted something from him.

"You can see it in their eyes," Michael said. "You're being judged. People are looking through you—not even at you, but through you." With these words, Michael Jackson described the people he would occasionally encounter in a social context. He knew that they were thinking about the media portrayals of him as bizarre and weird. "It's so far from the truth," he stated. "That hurts."

It was only when he was behind closed doors, away from public scrutiny, as a father with his children that he could feel normal. Michael Jackson was a "normal father," as everyone who observed him up-close has affirmed. No wonder he loved being a father. On so many levels, it was his best thing, his best role in life. And, it made him happy; it brought him real joy.

Other than in his interactions with his children as their loving father, Michael Jackson got only rare glimpses and artful snatches of "normal" existence. He was a man apart, physically and psychologically.

Physical Isolation

Paired with Michael's pervasive feelings of loneliness was his physical isolation from others. He never socialized with neighbors, for example, nor could he mingle at parties or get-togethers like other people. Even among celebrities, everything came to a halt when Michael Jackson entered the room. Nearly everyone was star-struck when it came to the King of Pop.

His personal protection services were at the level of a world leader. His security details were typically comprised of many highly-trained individuals, armed and ready to protect him with physical force if necessary.

Michael Jackson was always running when he went out in public—away from the adoring and the curious, from the camera-crazy and the grabbers. This behavior was not only normal but it was necessary for his safety.

"Michael became like Houdini, a master at getting out of his clothing fast," David Nordahl recalls as he describes his outings with Michael. "It can get really scary—the mobs running at him. He had chunks taken out of his scalp in the fray, and he was especially afraid for his eyes. I saw him when he was frightened to hell, running to his car to get away. It was weird."

Michael's Las Vegas security people echo these words. They were often "very afraid" for their boss when he was recognized in a public place and the inevitable reactions occurred. "Mr. Jackson was always running," they explain, and his bodyguards would be running with him.

From an unknowing outside world, Michael Jackson's behavior sometimes seemed paranoid. But insiders know that his behavior was appropriate to the circumstances....

"Billie Jean," his breakout song in 1983, was written by Michael from real and frightening experiences with a woman who today would be labeled a "stalker." The words "Billie Jean is not my lover" and "the kid is not my son" are autobiographical denials of Michael aimed at this bizarre situation.

Although he never met her, a young African-American woman named Billie Jean claimed that Michael was the father of her son. She sent him photographs of herself and impassioned letters; in one of them she threatened to kill the child if she could not raise him with Michael and "become a family." She was later caught in the hospital where Michael was being treated for an ailment. Billie Jean wound up in an insane asylum, and her brother took in her children.

Michael was very aware of the fate of John Lennon, one of his heroes, who was assassinated at the age of forty, in front of his New York home. He also knew about the murder of Italian fashion designer Gianni Versace, who was a friend to many celebrities and Princess Diana. Versace, at the age of fifty, was killed outside of his Miami Beach home by a spree killer.

Selena, a top-selling Latin artist, singer, and songwriter, was shot and killed in 1995, by the former president of her fan club, when she was only twenty-three years old. Michael Jackson's music attorney, Peter Lopez, was the co-producer of the movie *Selena* about the life and death of the trailblazing entertainer; it starred Jennifer Lopez and came out in 1997. Selena had been called "the next Janet Jackson" by promoters, but she died before reaching that level of success, and at the hands of one of her "biggest fans."

Michael Jackson, at the pinnacle of worldwide fame and fandom, had myriad experiences with "crazies" throughout his life. In fact, this topic could serve as a worthy and interesting one for a book on its own merits.

Michael Jackson and his security people were ever-vigilant with crowds and individuals, and they could never let down their guard. This situation, of course, led to the isolation of the King of Pop from the general public and even from those who appeared to be admirers and fans. Wisdom dictated hypersensitivity to all potential threats to Michael Jackson's safety, and the net result was a restricted existence and the loss of personal freedom.

The Moving Cage

When worldwide fame was visited upon Michael Jackson, it came overnight. On one day, he could go outside and be unmolested by frenzied fans; the next day, he could go nowhere without creating a mob scene. Suzanne de Passe from Motown oversaw the Jackson brothers and taught them the survival skills needed by entertainers. She described the incredible phenomenon of their sudden, stratospheric success as "cataclysmic." Before he was a teenager, Michael was a star on the global stage.

With his celebrity came the need to be shielded, literally, from the outside world. It was dangerous for him to leave his hotel room without bodyguards. There was no such thing as an impulsive decision to go to a park or a playground. He didn't know what it was like to cavort in a public area, to walk the street, or to shop in a store ... without being accompanied and protected by hired security personnel.

Although he toured and traveled, he was always controlled and/or managed by the adults around him. They also provided for his needs; he got used to having things done for him. He stayed indoors unless his bodyguards led the way for him to the outside world. They stood as a barrier between him and the strangers who would run toward him, screaming and grabbing at him, every time that he was recognized. He learned to run from the mobs, flanked by his guards, for his own protection.

It was as if Michael Jackson was living in a moving cage. He might be in Japan or Great Britain, but he was in a hotel room with "protection" at his door until a prescribed time when he might venture out, always with security guards both preceding and following him. He could go only to certain places, those where his security team could protect him from physical harm.

Michael never shopped in a grocery store, for example, until his friend Al Malnik—a lawyer, businessman, and celebrated restaurateur—arranged for a simulated experience for his forty-five-year-old celebrity friend by having the store closed to everyone but Michael and a handful of people who pretended to be clerks. Wearing a baseball cap, jeans and jacket, Michael ran up and down the aisles with a shopping cart, putting mysterious selected items into it, and pausing to throw a Frisbee to a "clerk" across the otherwise empty aisle. He looked like he was having the time of his life, as the experience was filmed and later shown in his "Private Home Movies."

King of Betrayal

Michael was the victim of betrayal by others over and over again.

Employees would turn on him for a fast buck from a tabloid. Not just one or two, but dozens of his employees sought compensation for the sale of some artifact of Michael Jackson's or for some sordid tale—imagined or exaggerated—about Michael.

During the nineties, Ralph Chacon, one of Michael's former bodyguards, and Adrian McManus, a former chambermaid, and several other ex-employees joined forces to sue Michael in civil court; they lost. They were ordered to pay Michael Jackson $1.4 million for his legal fees and also damages in the amount of $40,000. The finding in court was that they had acted "with fraud, oppression, and malice" against Michael Jackson. These individuals had also hired a "media broker" to try to sell Michael Jackson stories to the tabloids, to shop for the best deal.

There were many others who plotted against their wealthy employer for financial gain at his expense by setting their sights on court action or, for much quicker results, the tabloids.

Michael's financial manager from 1998 to 2001, Myung-Ho Lee, sued his former employer for $12-plus million in 2002, and Michael, in characteristic fashion, settled the matter by giving Lee money. The man went on to bad-mouth Michael to the media, alleging that he hired a witch doctor to sacrifice cows to place a curse on specific people. What part of that bizarre story—about a gentle man who held a special reverence for the great religions and for animals—is even remotely believable?

Neverland maid Blanca Francia extracted $20,000 from *Hard Copy* for an interview with Diane Dimond and another $2.4 million in a settlement from Michael Jackson. Getting this kind of money for a few minutes of talking trash is "better than working" to some unprincipled people who decided to turn on Michael for cash. It was easy.

Michael's own sister LaToya could be easily numbered in the long list of betrayers. In 1993, she traveled around Europe, being paid to say on television programs that she feared her brother was a pedophile. For a sliding-scale fee of $50,000, LaToya would speak about family secrets, "and for a half-million she would throw caution to the wind and just come out and admit that Michael was a paedophile [sic.]," according to J. Randy Taraborrelli. Her husband Jack Gordon made these quick deals for LaToya's interviews for big bucks. The TV shows would pay *only* for such salacious comments, not anything for claims of brotherly innocence. Years later, LaToya explained that her allegations were all Jack's fabrications, which she was forced to repeat against her will. Michael forgave her in 2003; she apologized to the rest of her family members also; and they accepted her back into the fold.

Martin Bashir ingratiated himself to Michael Jackson by praising him and reminding him of the documentary he had made of Lady Diana—during a time of media bashing over her troubled marriage to Prince Charles—to uplift her image with the United Kingdom public. He then led Michael down a path of destruction, across eight months of total access to the celebrity and his residences, by portraying him in the most unfavorable light possible and by trapping him into statements that would cause his downfall.

Countless individuals among the inner circle of Michael Jackson savagely used him for their own purposes. One such person was Bob Jones, who had known Michael since he was a young boy at Motown and who later worked for Michael as his publicist for seventeen years. After the termination of his employment in 2004, he joined up with long-time journalist Stacy Brown to write a scathing book, an exposé, about Michael Jackson, filled with innuendo and the worst interpretations of his behaviors. Jones attacked his former employer's liaisons with "only white women"—drawing merely speculative racist conclusions—and stated that Michael wanted to distance himself from his black family. There is a tone of "sour grapes" throughout the book, as Jones's anger over his termination from a plum of a job is not even thinly veiled. He obviously hoped to get money from his affiliation with Michael Jackson in one way or the other. After his firing, he would get it by a flat-footed betrayal of Michael through a book based exclusively upon the superficial and the authors' idiosyncratic inferences.

From time to time, Michael Jackson found it necessary to fight back. Michael sued Victor Gutierrez, author of a book about him and Jordie Chandler, in which the writer claimed that there was a videotape of the two. In the legal challenge for Gutierrez to produce the alleged videotape, it turned out that no such tape existed. The maverick author lost the lawsuit and ended up owing Michael Jackson nearly three million dollars. The man declared bankruptcy, moved to Chile, and "hasn't been heard from since," according to J. Randy Taraborrelli.

"People don't know what it's like for me," Michael told Taraborrelli many years ago. "No one knows, really. No one should judge what I've done with my life, not unless they've been in my shoes every horrible day and *every sleepless night*." [Emphasis added.]

Michael Jackson was the King of Victims. People he didn't even know would try to "turn him in" for something or another. People he liked—even loved—and trusted would readily betray him for a chance at monetary gain and/or their "fifteen minutes of fame" with a media outlet.

The worst of all was that Michael Jackson was betrayed by a child. Before that, he did not even think that a child could be capable of treachery. And his genuine, to-his-core, pervasive love for children was twisted and turned into something that was made to appear sordid by blood-thirsty and ratings-lusty media. Michael Jackson deserved much better from us.

Many Faces

Michael Jackson admitted to two cosmetic surgeries on his nose and to having a cleft created in his chin. Across many years, he probably had more work done, as his appearance changed noticeably. A chronological series of photos, placed side by side, reveal the different looks of Michael Jackson.

Karen Faye, his cosmetologist, would tell Michael that he was beautiful. He saw himself as unattractive, however, and, as a perfectionist, he wanted to look as good as he possibly could. "I'm never pleased with myself," he confessed in an interview.

In the far distant future, it may well become commonplace for people of sufficient means—average incomes—to undergo cosmetic surgery easily and frequently. Even today millions of people use "plastic surgery" to improve their appearance—faces, noses, and breasts are tightened, slimmed, and accentuated to produce the desired results. As procedures become safer, easier, and less costly, more and more people are likely to obtain cosmetic surgery as a routine step in creating their desired personal image for the world-at-large.

Michael asserted that if everyone who had cosmetic surgery in Hollywood would leave town on vacation, the place would be empty.

Future generations are likely to consider Michael Jackson's changing faces as an integral part of his expression of artistic creativity. In truth, he perceived his face as part of the expansive canvas upon which he painted his *persona*. He changed his attire, his hair style, his face. At every stage of his evolving career, he looked different. Michael Jackson loved different.

"The Many Faces of Michael Jackson," an impressive amalgam of photography and original student art, greets visitors upon their entrance into Gardner Street Elementary School in Los Angeles, where Michael attended for a short time before he undertook full-time touring and schooling by a tutor. The students at Gardner School have embraced the black and the white Michael Jackson by displaying in their creative artwork, on the entry walls of their school, the different faces of the King of Pop from his childhood to his full maturity. Already, these young students recognize and celebrate the many faces of the consummately creative artist who was Michael Jackson. It is the young, as Michael would remind us, who will lead the way to our future....

Masks & Disguises

Often, when he ventured out from the privacy of his residence, Michael Jackson wore masks, veils, and a variety of disguises. From the time when he co-starred with Diana Ross in the movie *The Wiz*, at the age of nineteen, Michael loved assuming another identity. Playing the Scarecrow—to positive critical reviews for his performance—he thoroughly enjoyed both the costume and the make-up. Michael reluctantly returned to his own clothes and face after his film takes.

Although he admittedly had a flair for whimsy, most of his transformations were for the purpose of attempting to participate in a "normal" experience. Michael longed to see the world as an everyday person, to enjoy the kinds of experiences that non-celebrities take for granted. He wanted to try out public transportation, browse in a big-box store, and bask in the green environment of a park. Michael said that he regularly read graffiti on the walls of buildings to get an idea of what "real people" were thinking and doing.

Michael Jackson could not have what most people consider everyday experiences. His security teams could not protect him in public settings, wherein access to him by members of the public could not be controlled. He was always mobbed when he was recognized as Michael Jackson; he required medical treatment for injuries on a number of such occasions. He was nearly choked to death by people pulling the ends of a scarf around his neck; he was scratched and torn by people grabbing at him; and he sustained bruises when pushed against a wall or onto the ground by overly zealous, out-of-control fans. He had to run away and dash into waiting vehicles time and time again. *No one was more endangered by a frenzied public than Michael Jackson.*

What is unknown to most people, fans included, is that Michael Jackson was asked to leave shops by their managers on many occasions. David Nordahl recalls a number of times when he accompanied Michael, who was "thrown out" by a manager, expressing fear that his store or its contents would be destroyed by a mob reaction.

"One time, when we were shopping for supplies for Michael's art room for the children visitors at Neverland, we were pushing two carts heaped with craft items through a Toys-R-Us store," recalls Nordahl in 2011. "Michael wore a disguise—a hat with a pony tail, buck teeth, a rubber nose, Levis, and tennis shoes—in what turned out to be a futile attempt to avoid detection. At the register, a price check was needed on an unmarked item. It was then that the other shoppers recognized Michael, even in spite of his disguise, and this started a stampede of people running toward him. The manager rushed up to Michael and said, 'You need to leave *right now*!'" Of course he did leave; he returned to his vehicle. "Michael was humiliated," Nordahl explains sadly.

David Nordahl recalls when Michael Jackson and Lisa Marie Presley were stormed by a mob of fans in a store; the result was $100,000 in damages to the property.

Few people realized, however, that a big reason for Michael's donning masks and disguises was his understandable desire to avoid the humiliation of being evicted from a shop or other public place because of the very real danger that his mere presence created.

According to his security personnel, Michael Jackson was often detected—even when disguised—by his "swagger." "It's Michael Jackson!" someone would scream out, and the group of bodyguards and Michael would turn and run, in self-defense.

Michael Jackson's life was filled with aborted experiences, accompanied by the embarrassment of being told to leave public buildings and stores because he was a perceived threat to the premises, through no fault of his own. Just by being himself, he was in constant danger of physical injury and emotional harassment wherever he went.

It is little wonder—after one considers the facts of his existence—that he donned disguises of various kinds in his attempts to experience life as an everyday person. In exasperation or desperation, Michael even took to a wheelchair or swathed his face in bandages—his "burn-victim look"—in order to avoid the onslaught of people who would ruin for him an outing to a public place. From the outside, his behavior may have appeared strange indeed, but from Michael Jackson's shoes, he just wanted to be anonymous and to be like you and me.

Michael did abnormal things to try to sample normalcy.

Special Bond

Michael's closest friends shared with him the experience of having been a child star. He felt that only these people could have a chance of understanding him. Elizabeth Taylor, Brooke Shields, Liza Minnelli, Macaulay Culkin, Corey Feldman, and Mark Lester (of *Oliver!* fame) were individuals with whom he shared that special connection of knowing and feeling the pressures of early fame and lost childhood. He idolized child-star Shirley Temple and made it his business to meet her when they were both well into adulthood; he thanked her for having been an inspiration to him.

With people who were experientially ignorant of these deficits, Michael felt less comfortable. He could not be understood by someone who had a childhood, who did not know the continuous pain of being "different" and alone. He felt an emptiness inside him and gravitated toward others who could empathize. Michael spoke openly about his having walked the streets near his Hayvenhurst home during the height of his career, approaching strangers to ask them to be his friend. They would exclaim *"Michael Jackson!"* and, with that, all hopes by Michael for a real friendship were dashed. He so wanted to be loved for himself, not for the *persona* that he had so skillfully created.

When he and Lisa Marie Presley got together in 1993, he felt "at home" with her. Michael had never felt such a strong romantic connection with a woman before; he surprised himself. He had met Lisa Marie with her father Elvis when she was just seven years old—Michael was seventeen—and they were welcomed backstage after a performance of The Jackson 5. Michael knew that Lisa had seen first-hand the complicated life, pressures, and burdens of super-stardom, that she had been somewhat spoiled and very protected within that milieu. She knew what it was like to be the child of a major celebrity, Elvis Presley; what it was like for him to live in a "fish bowl"; what it was like to be bereft of privacy and anonymity. At the same time, she was isolated from the outside world for her own protection. Michael didn't have to do much explaining to Lisa Marie; she understood.

Strong Women

Michael Jackson was attracted to strong women. Only those who were very much "their own person," with strong egos and the proclivity to speak their minds, became his friends or intimates.

Starting with his mother, who raised a family of nine children and survived a challenging marriage that required work and forgiveness, Michael bonded with the strong, determined woman who had a kind heart. Her children were her life, and she showed them kindness and understanding. In their adulthood, her children admitted that she was the "real boss" of the family in her quiet, dignified, but subtly forceful way. Michael loved and trusted his mother with a passion. She was his salvation, helping him through difficult times and sometimes penetrating his consuming loneliness. At least he had his mother....

Elizabeth Taylor, with whom he forged a platonic relationship that ignored their age difference and made them intimate friends, loved Michael with special fervor. She had seven husbands and other lovers and suitors, but her bond with Michael transcended sex and romance; it was built on mutual understanding and unconditional love. Michael said that Elizabeth was "a child in her heart." With him she could be a different person from the glamorous, globe-trotting, heartbreaking icon; she could be Elizabeth the girl. Elizabeth Taylor was there for Michael when he needed someone, when he needed her. She personally assisted him into a drug rehabilitation program in 1993, when she fiercely and proudly announced to the media, "I love him like a son."

Lisa Marie Presley had grown up an indulged, privileged daughter of a mega-famous, wealthy father and celebrity mother. She admitted to a serious drug problem during her teen years, but she entered a detoxification program at the Scientology Center in Hollywood. By the age of nineteen, she was a new woman, "clean" and determined to stay that way. "It saved my life," she explained; she knew that she "was going to die" if she didn't get help. Lisa had lived a lot of life by the time she married Michael Jackson in 1994. She left her first husband, taking with her their two young children, and she leaped into a new whirlwind life as the wife of the complex and troubled Michael.

Lisa Marie was the daughter of the "King of Rock-n-Roll" and she became the wife of the "King of Pop." She was a princess; she could speak up for herself and she did; she could stand up to anyone. Her religion gave her the value system and determination to take responsibility for her life and to believe that she could take care of her husband.

Although Michael and Lisa Marie shared a special bond across their courtship months, during their marriage, unfortunately, they were not "on the same page." Among other problems, he desperately wanted children, while Lisa Marie had a change of heart after their wedding and refused to bear Michael's children.

Debbie Rowe, who became Michael's second wife, also had a strong personality; she was described as a "tomboy." She reportedly rode a motorcycle with the speed and abandon of a seasoned biker; she could swear like one of the guys. Debbie could take care of herself. She also helped take care of Michael when he was treating for his vitiligo under the care of her employer, dermatologist Dr. Arnold Klein.

She and Michael became good friends; she adored him and decorated her apartment with posters and pictures of Michael Jackson; and they spoke together frequently on the phone, often during late-night and early-morning hours. They commiserated with each other on the deficits of their respective marriages. When Michael confided to Debbie that Lisa Marie had changed her mind about bearing his children, she volunteered to have a child for her friend. What strength of character Debbie Rowe demonstrated in her unconventional, unselfish behavior! She birthed his first two children for Michael—"so that he could be a father," which she felt he deserved. Michael bought her a $1.3 million home in Beverly Hills in 1997, and they rarely saw each other after that. They divorced after Debbie discovered that she could not have more children.

Even Michael's spiritual adviser during his last months is a formidable, straight-speaking, confrontational person, who prides herself on imparting strength to others. Reverent June Gatlin helps people get in touch with their inner core, their inherent strength and goodness. Michael sought her consultation and advice in his spiritual quest, in his personal journey toward the attainment of peace of mind. Reverent Gatlin is a "fire-and-brimstone" preacher who works toward healing the soul; she speaks forcefully and unequivocally; and she welcomed Michael's confidences.

Fatherhood

"There is no miracle in life that compares with watching your child come into the world," Michael explained. "I love family life … everything about it. I want [my children] to grow up being surrounded by love and by family."

As talented as he was in the world of music, Michael Jackson was considered "best" as a father by those who really knew him. He adored his children and said that he would gladly give his life for them.

His two wives, friends, family members, and round-the-clock security people observed Michael as the most thoughtful and patient of fathers. He looked his children in the eyes when he spoke to them or told them, "I love you" or "I love you more." He sat on the floor with them in play; he frolicked around, playing tag and running for sheer joy with them when he could; he teased, joked, and laughed with them. He taught them to ride bicycles. He taught them to be polite and to consider the feelings of other people.

When one of the children would ask him a question, no matter how mundane it was, he would research the answer so that it would be the best that he could give. He taught Prince, Paris, and Blanket to see life and living things with wonder and awe; to appreciate what they had; and to empathize with others.

Michael and his children prayed together before meals. He read them bedtime stories. He taught them to search for deeper meaning in life's events and in nature's bounty. He visited hospitals with his children, instilling in them feelings of empathy for the pain and suffering of others and encouraging them to want to lend a helping hand.

For Michael Jackson, his carefully fashioned approach to fatherhood was probably a type of "undoing" for him. If he could be the best father possible, this accomplishment would somehow atone for the deficits in the parenting that he received. He could give to his children that which he lacked.

He so much wanted them to have a childhood. Michael got choked up when he spoke about them having fun. He wanted to keep them away from prying eyes, from potentially harsh judgment by strangers and the ill-intentioned.

"Honestly, I never saw those children begging, throwing a fit, or crying—not ever," says David Nordahl, who observed and interacted with Michael and his kids on numerous occasions, across weeks at a time. "They were the most polite and nicest children you could ever meet."

Michael was both father and mother to his children. He put them to bed at night; he sat with them when they were ill; he took them wherever he went. He was rarely gone for an overnight without them. He was nurturing and gentle; he spoke softly and rarely raised his voice; but "no" meant "no" when he had to say it. Michael would never lay a hand on his children for the purpose of discipline. He used time-outs or the loss of privileges when necessary, but, because the kids were well-behaved, even these measures were seldom used.

Insisting that they study hard, make their own beds, and clean up after themselves, Michael did not want his children to take for granted the life of privilege that he was able to provide them. He preferred to hide that reality from them, and they were required to earn rewards for good behavior rather than receiving everything just for the asking. He even tried to hide from his children the fact that they had a famous-celebrity father, "but that didn't last long," Paris explained in later years.

In 2001, Michael Jackson delivered a speech about raising children at Oxford University as he launched his "Heal the

Kids" charity. In it, he revealed his concerns about his own children:

> What if they grow older and resent me, and how my choices impacted their youth? ... I pray that my children will give me the benefit of the doubt. That they will say to themselves: Our daddy did the best he could, given the unique circumstances he faced. I hope that they will always focus on the positive things, on the sacrifices I willingly made for them, and not criticize the things they had to give up, or the errors I've made, and will certainly continue to make in raising them. We all have been someone's child, and we know that despite the very best of plans and efforts, mistakes will always occur. That's just being human.

Those who love Michael Jackson can draw comfort from the knowledge that he experienced real joy with and from his children. He never took them for granted. Especially when he fully and clearly realized that he might have lost them, during the terrible years of his trial and its incumbent travails, he cherished them with passion and ferocity. After he experienced that crash course in ugliness, cruelty, and terror, he came out the other end with an even deeper love and all-consuming devotion to his three children.

Michael Jackson continuously feared that one or more of his children would be kidnapped. His fears were born of self-awareness of his own vulnerability; without a second thought, he would do anything or give any amount of money to retrieve them if they were taken away.

As a great admirer of Frank Sinatra, Michael Jackson was undoubtedly familiar with the kidnapping of Sinatra's nineteen-year-old son Frank, Jr., in Nevada in 1963. Although the young man was released unharmed after the singer paid $240,000 in ransom to the kidnappers, the major point was that he was successfully abducted by dangerous miscreants.

Michael knew about the tragic fate of Charles Lindbergh's baby, as he explained to his sinister, conniving interviewer in 2003. The eighteen-month-old toddler, son of the famous aviator and his wife, was abducted for potential ransom from his home in New Jersey in 1932. His body was found two months later; cause of death was a massive skull fracture. (The man convicted of first-degree murder of the baby was sentenced to death and killed by electrocution.)

"I don't want that to happen to my children, so I put veils over them; I don't want people seeing them...," Michael said. He was admittedly fiercely protective of his kids.

Brilliance & Humor

Professional colleagues and friends of Michael Jackson have spoken frequently about his brilliance and intelligence. Michael was a sponge for knowledge with an incredible memory for anything that interested him.

Michael was asked in his Oprah interview, "What do you know for sure?" His immediate response was "Nothing, I am learning something new every day." He was not only humble with this reply, but he revealed once again his capacity for higher-level abstract thinking. Michael recognized that as human beings, we really know very little, as we glimpse the world from our tiny, individual perspectives. From his ruminations in *Dancing the Dream,* the reader gets a real feel of the mind of this man, who perceived the world as wonderfully complex.

According to Thomas Mesereau, Michael Jackson owned one of the largest private libraries in the world. Larry Nimmer, who videotaped Neverland, confirms that Michael had more than 10,000 books in his home; among them were hundreds of leather-bound classics. His close friends and security personnel attest to Michael's voracious level of reading, which was his quest for understanding and knowledge.

Michael Jackson strove to learn as much as he possibly could; he longed to be able to reconcile the contradictions in our world, to come to grips with the reality of pain and suffering of the innocent. He wanted to know what made people tick, and he wanted to indulge his expansive imagination for what *could be*, for future possibilities. Michael referred to himself as a "fanatic for knowledge"; he also said that he loved to do research into subjects of his interest.

On average, Michael read a book every day. He especially loved history, art, science fiction, and biographies, according to reports by his security guards, with whom he sometimes shared some kernels of recently-acquired knowledge.

As a young man, Michael would reportedly sit in a corner during a break in the filming of *The Wiz*, and write down anything "intelligent" that he heard spoken around him. He was mostly silent himself, as a shy person, but he recorded good ideas and words of wisdom on paper so that he could remember and use them later.

Michael Jackson's heightened sense of curiosity about people sometimes ran into conflict with what psychologists call "boundaries." In his "Private Home Movies," Michael confessed: "I go through drawers, I go through everybody's closets. I don't steal [anything], I'm just curious." Lacking the kinds of intimate relationships with friends that most people enjoy, Michael found himself exploring people's private possessions to obtain some understanding of what they were like and what they considered important.

With people to whom he felt close, Michael "put himself right out there—no walls of defence [sic.], no safety zone," especially with kids. Biographer Taraborrelli opined that Michael assumed that the children and their parents would have the same good, reciprocal intentions toward him, which was not always the case, of course. Michael's naivety was "refreshing," especially in a celebrity, but it was also worrisome because it left him so open to trouble from the ill-intentioned.

Michael's sense of humor, a notable personality characteristic that was enjoyed by his family and colleagues, was never aimed at another person. He used humor as a bridge to other people; he used it to put them at ease upon meeting, as people often did not know how to act in his presence. They were usually awed and speechless. Although he was shy, he had to learn to put other people at ease out of self-defense. If others were silent or stammering in front of him, he needed to say something to avoid mutual embarrassment.

Michael also enjoyed childlike humor and pranks. At the end of his short films, he and the crew would engage in silliness, such as pie-throwing or covering each other in whipped cream. He loved the laughter and the running around. He even enjoyed being the victim of the fun, such as when he was hoisted by wires to the ceiling by his playful director John Landis and when the man picked up Michael and turned him upside down. Michael said that his favorite things to do were climbing trees and having water fights, with squirt guns or water balloons.

His laughter was unforgettable, high-pitched and joyful. Michael's sister Janet revealed that it is his laughter that she misses most of all.

Impulsiveness

"I always do things through force and feeling, and I always follow my instincts," Michael Jackson said about himself when he was a young man. He listened to his heart; he made decisions based on his gut feelings.

Once in awhile, Michael got himself into trouble, at least in terms of the watching world, when he was impulsive. The famous "baby dangling" event in Germany is a classic example. In 2002, Michael was in Berlin with his three children. For days, hundreds of his fans were gathered on the street under his windows at the Hotel Adlon.

"Show us your baby! Show us your baby!" they chanted in unison. In response, Michael walked onto his balcony, holding his infant Blanket in his arms, a veil covering the baby's face. With his arm wrapped around the baby, he held him over the railing for a split second ... to show the fans below.

In America, the footage of this incident was played *in slow motion*, creating the impression that Michael Jackson was dangling his new baby and seriously endangering him. To Michael, his was a harmless act, as he was holding the baby "very tight" while he lifted him for *a moment* to receive the fans' joy directed at him. He later compared his action to a parent who tosses his baby into the air and then catches him; Michael said he would *never* do that. He apologized later for his behavior, explaining that he would never harm his child.

Unforgiving, the media played this scene over and over again; it went around the world. Interestingly, no one seemed even to know the reason why Michael was in Germany; the media generally didn't bother to publish it. He was there to receive the Bambi Award as the "greatest living pop icon"; he was there for its humanitarian activity. Of course, the *Michael Jackson factor* was in play—the media focused on literally *one second* for which they could choose to condemn Michael Jackson rather than on *years* of his continuous charitable activities for children and the needy.

Similarly, years before the Berlin event, Michael was photographed lying in a hyperbaric chamber, with the story line that he slept in this large glass tube because of his desire to live to be 150 years old. In fact, Michael had donated this life-saving device to a treatment facility for burn victims. When he later visited there, he tried out the chamber by climbing inside and reclining in it. A photo of him was taken and distributed widely, with the bizarre interpretation that he was seeking an incredibly long life through such strange means.

In 2004, Michael jumped on top of his SUV on the day of his arraignment so that he could acknowledge and wave to the hundreds of fans who had come to show support for him. His well-intentioned, unselfish act was portrayed as disrespectful and cavalier, as flaunting his arrogance in the face of heinous charges against him. Nothing could have been further from the truth. Michael was expressing his deepest regard and unspeakable gratitude to the people that he knew loved him and that he loved back, with force and fervor. He knew that those who were standing in the back of this horde of supporters were not able to see him, and they had come so far and waited so long. He gifted these people with the sight of him on the roof of his vehicle, showing his love through arm waves and the sign of peace.

His Humanity

Michael Jackson was always in touch with his own humanity. Songs like "Human Nature" and "Stranger in Moscow" reveal the surprising level of intimacy and self-disclosure that he shared with his listeners and fans. He sang out his deep sense of humanity, and even those who did not understand the words—non-English speakers—understood the feelings.

He openly wept and spoke about crying without shame. He choked up when he said "I feel your pain" to those in need throughout the world. He held his hand to his heart when he said these things. Michael was not afraid to show his feelings, his humanity. He was modeling these behaviors for the rest of us.

"Michael Jackson wanted to change the world," Thomas Mesereau proclaims as he vividly recalls the zeal of his childlike client. The attorney wanted to know Michael inside and out so that he could mount the best defense possible. He was stunned to realize that Michael Jackson had assumed for himself the mission of healing a troubled and hurting world. Michael felt that pain and wanted to do something about it.

Regardless of skin color, age, nationality, gender, place or circumstance of birth, every person was of equal value to Michael Jackson. He prayed with the sick and diseased; he flew to sit at the bedside of the dying; and he did these things without fanfare or public acclaim.

David Nordahl remembers his friend Michael accepting telephone calls from desperate mothers. When told that a dying child's greatest wish was to meet Michael Jackson the King of Pop, he would immediately make arrangements to visit that child with the gift of his presence.

"Why are you doing that?" Nordahl asked Michael, in disbelief when he realized that everything else was to be set aside in his friend's life while he went on a mission of mercy … and love.

"How can I *not*?" Michael responded. "Michael Jackson is not really important to this dying child, but the King of Pop is, so *he* is going." Michael dressed up as the King of Pop and hurried to the sickbed of the little girl or boy whose hours were limited.

"I'll be back in a couple of weeks to see you again," he would pointedly tell the child, who would have the gift of something to look forward to. He would also give the child a personal memento to keep.

"Even if I can give that child a few more hours or days of life, it is worth it," he explained to Nordahl, who was awed by Michael's generosity of spirit, time, and energy, and by his selflessness.

"He was a sucker for a sick kid," says Nordahl, who admired Michael for his open heart.

"Michael never changed across the twenty-one years that I knew him," Nordahl reports. "He was the same person always. Michael cared more about others than himself. He really did."

We are all one, Michael Jackson believed. "You and I were never separate, It's just an illusion.... There is only one Wholeness, Only one mind," he wrote in *Dancing the Dream*. He brought his pervasive sense of humanity to everything he did.

Anger & Therapy

The public Michael Jackson did not show anger. The private Michael Jackson learned that it was wrong to be angry at people.

Michael was described as "repressed" by his first wife, Lisa Marie. Others who were close to him expressed similar perceptions. Michael rarely got angry, but his security personnel, who were ever-present throughout his life and became almost like the wallpaper to him, witnessed an occasional expression of anger. He was human after all. He wanted to be left alone, but that was never going to happen. He was bombarded with lawsuits, threats, media blasts, and economic turmoil. There was never a respite. And, of course, there were those terrible charges against him from a family whom he helped beyond reasonableness; the gut-wrenching trial itself; and the acquittals, tidily dismissed by vicious media that used them as fodder for lurid "rehash" stories about the allegations.

After the trial, Michael reportedly began psychotherapy. No doubt a good decision, he could obtain assistance in working through the anger and rage that he justifiably felt. His friend Al Malnik revealed that Michael shared with him some of the anger he experienced. This was a healthy development, and it showed emotional growth. Gone were the psychological denial and avoidance of painful feelings from previous years. It is difficult for anyone to risk bringing forth the powerful feelings within; to feel the heretofore unacknowledged pain; to unleash the suffering and agony that have been packed away in the psyche.

Michael never spoke about the trial, according to his friends and family members. It is likely that he spoke about it in therapy. Hopefully he did.

According to his spiritual adviser, Reverent June Gatlin, Michael even used the four-letter "h" word. He had learned to *love* everyone, to forgive everything; he tried to live up to these teachings throughout his life. During his last years, however, Michael likely internalized the harsh realities that the ideal is not always possible—or even mentally healthy—and that anger felt in response to wrongs done to us is normal and a first step toward healing.

It is better for many people who admire him to think of Michael Jackson as an angry soul rather than a broken spirit. What appears indisputable, however, is that he was not *consumed* by anger; he was not embittered; and he was—in spite of it all—still able to love and to express that love.

Compartmentalization

A seven-syllable word that applies to Michael Jackson's coping mechanisms, compartmentalization means that he learned to build walls around certain experiences and feelings, within his own mind and in his behavior. For example, Michael shared only small parts of himself with others. He was selective in what he disclosed to each person. He was loving, affectionate, and warm to those within his chosen circles, but he withheld information at the same time. He was very selective about his self-disclosures, revealing his inner self rarely and to few people.

Michael's life and relationships can be compared to an intricate wheel. He was the hub and there were numerous spokes that never touched each other. He liked it that way, and it gave him a large measure of control and some privacy. For a man who wanted to be in control but found himself in indescribably complex life circumstances, his structuring the "spokes" of his life as he did was adaptive behavior.

Both of his wives found him to be mysterious, often difficult to understand. They loved him, but they both knew—for different reasons—that he did not really let them into the private places of his psyche.

Lisa Marie tried to "save" Michael, to change him, to make him less repressive. Michael did not want to open up all of his deep feelings to anyone. Her probing was probably scary to him because he had learned, from very early on, not to let himself feel too much. There was not much time for feelings and there were no outlets for their expression. Michael was a more-than-full-time worker and part of his job was to be consistently perky and focused. He was a public person from the time that he was a youngster. Output is what his family and his fans wanted from Michael Jackson the King of Pop, not feelings.

So, Michael bonded with Lisa Marie for the purposes of having children, the trappings of "normalcy," and his very own family for the first time. Sadly, none of that came to fruition for him. The marriage ended after twenty-two months. Lisa Marie referred to Michael's life as a "roller coaster," one onto which she jumped for a wildly exciting ride, and then leaped off again.

Debbie Rowe was then chosen by Michael to fulfill his life-long desire to have his own children. He compartmentalized that relationship to a specific goal.

"Debbie and I love each other for all the reasons you will never see on stage or in pictures," Michael explained. "I fell for the beautiful, unpretentious, giving person that she is and she fell for me just being me."

Calling Michael's life his "world of wonder," Debbie knew that she was allowed only small, limited connections to his psychological self and to the fabric of his life. He probably distanced himself from her after their divorce in the hope that she would not lay claim to their children sometime in the future and attempt to take them from him.

After she gave birth to Prince and Paris for him, they separated for good. Having seen each other seldom during their marriage, they reportedly saw each other not at all after their divorce. Michael took their children, as they had planned all along, and he seemed afraid of any further contact with her.

Ironically, he was emotionally closer to Debbie Rowe *before he married her.* They had been real friends for many years. Their wedding and marriage, however, were about children.

Even with his mother, whom he loved unconditionally, Michael revealed only those parts of himself that he carefully chose. She did not meet Lisa Marie until after Michael married her, and his mother and wife rarely interacted after that. Debbie Rowe never met Katherine Jackson until after Michael's death! His second wife and the grandmother of the children were never in the same room together ... until they met to discuss the future of the children in 2009, the important issues of their custody and residence.

With his father, Michael was guarded and reserved. He revealed very little of his real self. All of the conditioning, throughout his life, caused him to distance himself from his father. They could talk music or money, but since he fired his father as his manager when he was in his mid-twenties, Michael had less to discuss with Joseph, the man whom he longed to understand but couldn't.

Michael had a unique relationship, of course, with each of his siblings. During his adulthood, some of them hardly knew him, like LaToya, who didn't see him for years at a stretch. Others saw him more often and knew him somewhat better, but—during the post-trial years—he rarely interacted with them. He kept from all of his siblings a great deal of information about himself that pertained to his personal life and his finances.

No one seemed to know the *extent* of Michael Jackson's philanthropy. He spoke of it hardly at all. Very likely, his motivation for secrecy about his frequent, admirable acts of charity was related to a realistic fear that others would expect the same level of largesse that he bequeathed to strangers in need. If he gave millions of dollars to charitable causes, why could he not give millions to his family members, some of whom found themselves in financial trouble? He did regularly make contributions to the support of his various family members, but he most likely received messages from them that it was not enough.

Michael seemed to have developed the ability to put his financial problems in a mental compartment and simply not deal with them; he employed a gang of people to do that; and he paid them more than well. He put the extortion attempts, threats of litigation, and lawsuits into another compartment. There was a horde of people, whose meters were constantly running, who were retained to worry about them and to engage in the byzantine workings of the legal machinery.

Michael Jackson allowed the people in his life into his immediate space and consciousness only when he wanted to do so, only when he felt up to it. This is adaptive behavior, and when one discovers the many layers and complexities of his personal and business affairs, it is not surprising that he chose this route.

Business people, entrepreneurs, and some con artists were always seeking to get close to Michael Jackson, to engage him in some deal, in some way to advance themselves on his coattails. They often succeeded by burrowing their way into his trust, until such time that they overtly turned on him, or he realized that he had made a hasty decision to commit to them. Everyone wanted a piece of Michael Jackson. Even the international elite wanted to rub elbows with Michael Jackson, to meet him, to be photographed with him, and often to elicit some special favor or connection.

He had paid people to protect and isolate him for as long as he could remember. He liked it that way. His security personnel allowed in only those whom he directly approved. Ironically, he welcomed strangers in large groups to his home at Neverland Ranch; it was amazingly accessible to those who were ailing and disadvantaged. His personal interactions, however, were limited to those whom he specifically authorized, and that policy extended to his family members.

Michael learned successfully to use avoidance in his life. His security personnel helped protect him from those he did not wish to encounter. He changed his cell phone number frequently so that he could readily limit the individuals who were able to contact him directly. He used his vast number of employees to conduct his business for him and to keep the wolves at bay, at least far enough to prevent them from tearing flesh.

Michael Jackson needed to compartmentalize and to avoid in order to survive. He would make a telephone call when he wanted to connect with someone from one of the compartments. He had so many friends and so few friends. In his "Private Home Movies," Michael asserted that he could count his true friends as maybe five—"I can probably count my real friends on one hand." To hear *them* tell it, however, he had hundreds of people who claimed him as their friend, not so much after his humiliating trial, but before that awful event and especially after his death. Everyone was Michael's friend during the times of his Memorial and funeral, when the moving spotlights were everywhere, seeking people to jump in and claim some special relationship with the King of Pop. It was a ratings bonanza for the media.

Where were these people in his time of need, during his restless, lonely nomadic years?

Michael Jackson needed lots of mental compartments into which he could lock away the big pieces of unpleasantness, the affronts that kept coming. He needed to deny the ugliness by putting the nasty items into a mental attic, from which he would pull out specific items only when he really had to deal with them. He wanted to avoid the shocking realization that people could be so greedy, self-seeking, malicious, and, yes, evil. These traits were so unlike him; he was a gentle soul. How overwhelming to know that people who don't even know you are really out to get you! ...To do you in.

When he got the biggest lesson of his life, learning the cruelty of the outside world that he had tried so hard to avoid, having his nose rubbed in it—at his criminal trial for heinous acts—Michael nearly disintegrated. "There is no justice in the world" is an ancient saying, and, for Michael Jackson, it was accurate.

Bottom line, he had to cope in the best way he knew how. Michael's seemingly maladaptive behaviors are remarkably adaptive when one seriously considers and comes to understand the ocean in which he found himself. Any wave could potentially kill him—an especially successful lawsuit brought by a lucky and greedy person, a charge of sexually inappropriate behavior leveled against him by people who smelled blood and money, an insider's betrayal that could wound him, perhaps mortally. He was so very vulnerable.

Who among us would not want to sequester himself/herself in a way that would offer some relief, some respite? Michael Jackson may have been running out of the necessary mental compartments to store away all of the onslaughts to his dignity and to his chances for some peace of mind.

Scripting

Some psychologists believe in the theory that we subconsciously "write," or formulate, our life scripts during our early childhood. We internalize the strongest behavioral messages from our parents to decide the future course of our lives. We spend the rest of our years playing out that script, usually unaware of the blueprint that we have chosen for ourselves and our destiny.

Within this framework, we can determine Michael Jackson's script. As a young boy, working full-time to lead and support his family, Michael learned hard work, driving ambition, and self-discipline from his father. From his mother, he learned love of family and love for children and the importance of growing up to become a good father to his own children. From both parents, Michael learned to be responsible for the welfare of other people, primally for his own family members and then, by extension, for others.

From a young age, Michael Jackson believed that it was his responsibility in life to take care of others, to provide for their healing.

Even his name helped set the stage for Michael's life course. Meaning "Who is like God" from a Hebrew root word, "Michael" was also the name of the leader of the heavenly host in Christian theology, an archangel and the patron saint of soldiers. Michael Jackson knew the import of his name and he took it seriously.

"One who's most like God" are the words that Michael used to inform his *This Is It* musical director, Michael Bearden, of the meaning of their shared name. "We gotta be humble," he continued, with gravity in his voice. "We have to use our gifts together to help others figure out what their gifts are...." Bearden, impressed and sobered by the exchange, realized, "He had the humanity. He ... [really] cared about people."

"Our parents taught us to always be respectful and, no matter what you do, to give it everything you have," Michael explained about his childhood lessons. "Be the best, not the second best." And he was.

Michael internalized all of these early messages in the "writing" of his own life script. It is little wonder that he chose to return to the stage at the age of fifty, after a full life that included four decades of penultimate achievement in his chosen career. His script dictated the continuation of the ethic of hard work, ambition, and self-discipline in the advancement of his music. It also dictated his behavioral expressions of love for his children and his fans by delivering more of the songs and dance that bound him to that love. Unsurprisingly, he professed that his primary motivation for a return to the stage was for his children, who were old enough to understand what he did and to appreciate it. Prince, Paris, and Blanket had never seen their daddy perform on a public stage; he was anxious to provide them with that gift. Michael intended to deliver love. That was his scripted mission, and he was compelled by it.

Ninety-Ninth Percentile

Let us consider another tenable, and likely, theory about Michael Jackson that helps to understand him....

Human beings possess a variety of characteristics and traits, each of which can presumably be measured, comparing one individual to all others. Most people are familiar with the concept of percentile, for example, when receiving a test score of their child in an academic field, such as reading ability. If that child scored at the 99th percentile, she performed better than 99% of the others in the comparison pool. If he scored at the 50th percentile, he performed better than one-half of the population; he placed in the middle of the tested group.

Michael Jackson would most likely place at the 99th percentile, or very close to it, on a number of variables. These would include his musical ability in both singing and dancing; personal sensitivity; achievement in the entertainment industry; perseverance; hard work; and love for the planet, animals, mankind, and children. When viewed within this conceptual framework, Michael Jackson is more understandable on so many levels.

He was a man apart, among the "most" sensitive, caring, and talented of people. These qualities were undoubtedly both a curse and a blessing for him.

Michael virtually vibrated with sensitivity to music and nature. He saw the beauty in everything. His original poem "Planet Earth" is a moving, intimate, and self-revealing portrait of the man's worldview. Michael unabashedly disclosed his deepest feelings through his art:

In my veins I've felt the mystery
Of corridors of time, books of history[,]
Life songs of ages throbbing in my blood
Have danced the rhythm of the tide and flood....
Tender with breezes, caressing and whole[,]
Alive with music, haunting my soul.
Planet Earth, gentle and blue
With all my heart, I love you.
(*Dancing the Dream*)

Ninety-ninth-percentile Michael loved at that level. He also lived and struggled there.

His Three Biggest Mistakes
Michael Jackson created a world of trouble for himself three times in his adult life....

"He opened Pandora's box!" Thomas Mesereau exclaims when referring to Michael's having agreed to a settlement in 1993 with Jordie Chandler and his parents, the "accuser family." Michael became physically ill over this matter; he entered a drug rehab program in London, with the help of his best friend Elizabeth Taylor; and he suffered shock, humiliation, and despair to the point of being overwhelmed by his feelings. His advisers urged Michael to settle and move on; his career was bubbling over with success; money was pouring into his coffers—and those of his advisers.

Although at first he resisted a settlement, because of his innocence and the inherent injustice in it, Michael finally succumbed. The matter was resolved with approximately $20 million, and he could move along without fighting out the ugly situation in the media or in the court system. Along with many others who are staunchly on Michael's side, Tom Mesereau believes that he made the biggest mistake of his life to that point by agreeing to a settlement that made him look guilty to a large segment of the public. [Although his insurance company may have made the payments, Michael agreed to a conflict-avoidant end to this matter.]

Michael Jackson chose the *expedient path*, the easy way out of this unhappy mess, which was [allegedly] an extortion attempt that became successful for the conniving opportunists. He would learn to deeply regret his decision across time....

Michael's second biggest mistake was actually a two-fold error in judgment. The first part was his amazing generosity and unlimited trust related to the Arvizo family, whose young son Gavin suffered from Stage 4 cancer when Michael responded to their initial reaching out to him. He showered the family with love, attention, gifts, and unlimited hospitality. The boy recovered, thrived, and grew bold, along with his other family members, attempting to grab onto Michael Jackson's wealth and lifestyle.

Enter Martin Bashir onto that scene. The unscrupulous reporter cajoled Michael into agreeing to an unrehearsed interview of him with Gavin—without the producer's obtaining approval of the young boy's mother and without paying her. Bashir turned that television footage into a nightmare for Michael Jackson, one from which he would never fully awaken, or recover. This was the second deadly part of Michael's huge error in judgment; it was born of a combination of innocence and trust; and it unwittingly brought together two sources of assassins.

That interview, aired on "Living with Michael Jackson," metamorphosed into the 2003 sheriffs' raid on Neverland and the subsequent criminal trial that nearly destroyed Michael. It robbed him of his belief in the goodness of humankind and in the innocence of children.

Michael Jackson could never recover from the trauma of that trial, from the mortal wounds to his heart that were inflicted by the Arvizo family and Bashir. His unfettered, unconditional trust in these people turned into a fatal flaw.

Those with a good heart, like Michael, trust other people. They project their own goodness onto the people in their life who present themselves as loving and trustworthy. The Arvizo family chose greed and callous opportunism over loyalty to their champion and benefactor Michael, while Bashir chose raw ambition and sinister machinations over honesty and integrity. They combined their various ingredients into a toxic recipe to be administered Michael Jackson. It was a poisonous concoction, and it nearly killed him.

This whole sorry episode ruined his life.

Michael Jackson's trusting heart paved the way for his broken heart.

Michael's third biggest mistake—and his last—was his selection of Conrad Murray to serve as his personal physician through his *This Is It* "comeback" concert preparations. Murray's administration of the deadly anesthetic propofol to Michael in his home—without the proper, required medical facilities, monitoring devices, resuscitation equipment, and rescue procedures—caused his untimely and sudden death. Michael was simply *desperate for sleep*. Conrad Murray put Michael into an eternal sleep....

The common thread among all three of Michael's biggest mistakes was his childlike level and degree of trust ... of people who were not worthy of his love and generosity.

It was the child in Michael Jackson that ultimately killed the man.

Bottom Line

Michael Jackson is perhaps the most controversial entertainer of our times. Millions of people love(d) him with full, overflowing hearts to the point of obsession and total devotion; some people despise(d) and dishonor(ed) him.

As we evaluate the man, there are *indisputable* facts about him that, for some, tell the whole story ..., at least the important story.

Michael Jackson was *never convicted of any crime* in spite of herculean attempts and a "witch hunt," which spanned more than a decade, to bring charges against him in the legal system and to convict him. (Both the California authorities and the FBI investigated him thoroughly.)

Michael *never said an unkind word in public* about any of the individual members of the media who excoriated and defamed him or about his ex-wives or his family members. He never retaliated against those who attacked him ... in spite of his vast resources and the continuous opportunity to do so.

Michael *gave of himself and his resources*—in the record-breaking amount of *more than $300 million*—to dozens of charities, for children, the ill and dying, disadvantaged, poor, needy, and downtrodden, in dozens of countries across the entire span of his life.

Michael *broke more records* for artistic achievement and for philanthropy than any other celebrity of his and our times.

Michael *devoted himself full-time to raising his three children* from the day of their respective births until his death.

Michael *lost his childhood* to work; his *middle-aged years were cut short* by his needless and untimely death at the hands of a person he trusted; and he *was robbed of the opportunity to enjoy senior-citizen years*, to see his children grow into adults, and to know his grandchildren.

Michael is actively mourned throughout the world, in at least 180 countries.

Michael Jackson had to do abnormal things to enjoy some normalcy.

Don't judge a man
until you have walked
two moons in his moccasins.
— Michael Jackson

The Paragon of Paradox

Michael is the wisest
and at the same time
most naive person I know.
— Quincy Jones

Michael Jackson was the little boy from Gary, Indiana, who refused to grow up, in his heart. He was the dazzling, elusive King of Pop, who ruled the music world and exercised moral power over minds and hearts around the world.

Fascinating and mysterious, Michael Jackson was arguably the greatest paradox and enigma of our times. He felt lonely and misunderstood throughout his life, although he appeared to have friends everywhere. His genius set him apart. He lived in a wholly different world from others, both in the extraordinary breadth and depth of his creativity and in his physical domain.

Michael Jackson lived an epic life, akin to a Greek tragedy. He also led a rigidly confined life in the realm of his personal freedom. As a boy wonder, he traveled a meteoric path to stardom, wealth, and international recognition, all at unprecedented speed.

According to his mentor and father figure, Berry Gordy, Michael had a wonderful life, but he was a tortured soul. These are not incompatible.

He was forced to fight his "demons," both in the legal system, within which he was persecuted, and in his own emotional turmoil. He rose to heights unknown by others; he plummeted to rock bottom.

Michael Jackson was robbed of his childhood by fame and all-consuming work. His youth was compromised by the ravages

of celebrity. His middle-aged years were cut short by disaster—
an untimely death at the hands of another, a man he trusted. His
inalienable right to live into senior-citizen comfort was denied him
forever … at a time when he stood on the threshold of personal
redemption and renewed professional glory.

Black & White. Michael Jackson was black and he was white,
both at the same time! Born African-American, Michael Jackson
proudly embraced his roots and racial heritage. To his horror, his
skin started losing its pigment noticeably when he reached his mid-
twenties. Michael discovered he had vitiligo, an irreversible skin
condition. He underwent treatments for it and began engaging in
systematic attempts to even out the appearance of the blotchy,
chalk-white and brown skin on his face and body. Before long, he
looked like a Caucasian, a light-skinned one at that. The parts of
his body that were covered by clothes retained what he privately
called his "leopard spots," which understandably embarrassed him.
Still claiming and clinging to his blackness on an emotional level,
Michael indeed became a black man in a (mostly) white body.

The media tried to turn Michael Jackson into a caricature across
the span of years. The *paradigm* was set of an eccentric, weird man.
Into this model, the stories were molded about Michael, many of
them entirely fabricated because there was no firsthand information
available from him.

"Black folks never turned their backs on Michael," according
to *Ebony* magazine, because they knew that he was grappling with
the politics of being a black man in the American entertainment
industry, which was dominated by white decision-makers and power
brokers. Michael Jackson was a trailblazer in the music industry and
a symbol. He single-handedly broke down racial barriers and paved
the way for others.

The fledgling *MTV* music video channel at first refused to show
his short films, until his record company threatened to pull all of their
white singers' videos from the play list. After the wildly enthusiastic
response by viewers to *Billie Jean*, *MTV*'s first short film by a black

performer, the outlet wanted more and more of Michael Jackson. He catapulted *MTV* to a global identity, proved that music could be color-free, and established himself as acceptable to everyone.

"We loved him," *Ebony* concluded, "because we knew that America rarely forgives a Black man his genius, and our greatest artists often pay the price for the acceptance of their gifts with tortured psyches, haunted spirits and troubled minds." Michael never turned his back on the African-American music and culture that shaped him, and he proved that his roots were portable: "They can be planted in soil the world over ... and ... produce the sustaining fruits of joy and love."

During his infamous trial, a large segment of White America acted much like people who cannot drive by a bad auto accident without stopping to stare. Many, including Michael's competitors, relished his "fall from grace." It seemed like a fitting follow-up to a general *"How dare he?"* attitude that played out after he had exploded the invisible barriers and set astounding new records for achievement—new milestones unlikely to be reached by any others.

In the final analysis, Michael Jackson combined not only the music and cultural influences of his blackness but those of pluralistic modern society with his own unique creations of sound and soulfulness.

Male/Female Characteristics & Appeal. Michael Jackson's sexual appeal was a unique blend of male and female characteristics. "He animated and mythologized his own brand of mystery and sexuality," wrote *Ebony* magazine. His bearing and dancing were masculine and forceful; his elegance, gracefulness, and face itself reminded of feminine beauty. Michael was androgynous to some....

Referring to himself as a "gentleman," Michael demurred when Oprah asked him if he was a virgin, during her probing 1993 interview. His major long-term relationships with women, including Brooke Shields, Jane Fonda, and Elizabeth Taylor, were intimate but platonic. His two marriages, the first to Lisa Marie Presley and the second to Debbie Rowe, were short-lived. Cohabitation with

Ms. Rowe never occurred and with Ms. Presley was limited by his required absences for career reasons. However, after Michael's death, Lisa Marie Presley reaffirmed that she and Michael truly loved each other and enjoyed husband-wife sexual relations.

Still, Michael was perceived as sexually ambiguous. He strongly rejected all of the artificial barriers that divide people—gender, sexual preference, race, ethnicity, economic status, politics, and geography. According to Karen Faye—who became his friend through serving as his make-up artist across nearly three decades—Michael believed that standards for men and women should be equal. He wore make-up both on and off stage; he wore lots of bling; and he loved all of his fans—and all people in general—male and female, gay and straight.

In his personal life, Michael evidenced the strength and determination that are perceived as "male" and the nurturing behaviors and comfortable verbal expressions of love that are perceived as "female." He said "I love you" to his friends and admirers wherever he went. Those who really knew him, including his children, were aware that he was speaking with deep sincerity and gentleness of spirit. What other man do you know who says "I love you" with such frequency and genuine affection?

Rich & Poor. Michael Jackson was poor and then became immensely rich, and, at the end of his life, *he was both concurrently*! In the 2000's, Michael was cash poor and deeply in debt, but his assets—perhaps the foremost of which was himself as the planet's highest-earning entertainer—were worth a fortune.

As a young boy, he lived with his eleven-person family in a small house in Gary, Indiana—not much bigger than a conventional two-car garage. His father worked as a laborer in a local steel mill. When Michael was not yet a teenager, he became world-famous as the lead singer-dancer of The Jackson 5, and along with that achievement came commensurate wealth.

From his subsequent solo career as a young man, he broke all records of music industry earnings. During the last decade of his life, Michael's financial empire became a Sisyphus-like burden, overtaken by an army of attorneys, managers, and others who assumed control. His 2005 criminal trial, at which he was fully acquitted, generated a kingly level of debt in attorneys' fees and stalled the career that had produced such enormous wealth.

Yet, Michael Jackson's publishing catalogs, against which he took out necessary loans, were valued at hundreds of millions of dollars, up to $1.5 billion or more. He retained these assets to the end of his life. With them, although cash strapped, Michael Jackson was still a wealthy man.

In addition, his talent was his best asset. Michael Jackson could earn millions of dollars in one weekend of performing in venues around the world.

Man as a Child/Child as a Man. Michael Jackson had the work ethic, determination, and schedule of a grown man from the time he was seven years old, "the age of reason." As an adult, he said, "I was so little when I began to work on our music that I don't remember much about it." He amazed everyone around him with his seriousness of purpose, ambition, and perfectionism—traits typically neither associated with children nor observed in them.

Michael had to forgo his childhood; he could not enjoy the personal freedom or opportunity to play like children his age; and, because of his religion, he celebrated no holidays or birthdays at all. Each day for him was like any other, filled with work— rehearsing, recording, performing, touring, giving interviews, and similar activities required to maintain a successful, frenetic, family-based career.

As a child, he was described on various occasions as "like a thirty-year-old man." When his brothers were playing ball, Michael was practicing his choreography or observing other performers to learn from them. He demonstrated a level of zeal and dedication as a young boy that was unique and amazing to those who interacted with him.

Singer Smokey Robinson, who got up-close views of Michael as a youngster, while they were both recording for Motown, said that Michael was "like an old soul in a young body."

"All work and no play" became the standard for young Michael in his daily life. He often longed to join the children on the playground across from his recording studio, but he realized that he never would.

Even playing basketball with his brothers was discouraged by their father. If one of his brothers was injured, the show could continue without him. If Michael was injured, the show would come to an end until he was well again. Joseph did not want to risk the significant loss of income and momentum; Michael could only watch, with a sense of longing.

When he became a man, Michael experienced a metamorphosis. He was childlike, a condition that he embraced in himself. "It has been my fate to compensate for the childhood I've never known," he sang in his poignant autobiographical ballad "Childhood"; "... people say I'm strange that way 'cause I love such elementary things."

Michael attributed his creative side to the child within him; he took his inspiration from children; and he gave tirelessly to children's causes throughout his life. He loved play, pranks, and practical jokes. He identified strongly with Peter Pan, the mythical boy who lived without growing older in a never-never land. "I *am* Peter Pan," Michael insisted, "in my heart." At his Neverland Ranch, the standard activity for all of his personal guests was fights with squirt guns or water balloons; everyone got wet.

"Children are drawn to him, like a magnet," explained Karen Faye. "They recognized a kindred spirit, ... his unconditional love, and related to him because he was a child at heart. Children look at the world through fresh, unjaded eyes. Michael had the ability to see the wonderment of the world like they did."

When Jane Goodall visited him at Neverland, the two sat and talked on Michael's bed, across a big pile of pillows. She was seeking his support in her ongoing efforts on behalf of the chimpanzees in Africa. Before she left, Michael showed Ms. Goodall a girl's bedroom, filled with dolls and party dresses, and a boy's room, containing science equipment and toys.

"These are for the children I will have one day," he told her. Surprised and touched by his childlike ingenuousness and his dream of fatherhood, Ms. Goodall would remember Michael as "very sweet, brilliant and lonely."

When Jacqueline Kennedy Onassis, then editor at Doubleday Publishing Company, extracted a reluctant commitment from the very private Michael Jackson to write his autobiography, Shaye Areheart was assigned as co-editor of the book to assist him. It became a #1 *New York Times* best-seller soon after its release in 1988. To complete the writing of *Moonwalk*, Ms. Areheart met with Michael on his off-nights from Australian concerts in a variety of hotel rooms. They sat on his king-size bed, Shaye at one end in jeans and him on the other in Chinese red silk pajamas.

Michael became accustomed to spending most of his off-stage, leisure time on a bed, in sleazy motel rooms during the early years and at world-class hotels later. Because he was unable to go out and about freely, he stayed in—with his brothers at times, alone during his solo touring—and used his bed as home base for talking to visitors, eating meals, reading, and other routine activities. Michael's childlike worldview on the macrocosmic level generated to the microcosm of his personal life and bedroom. In other words, he perceived his bed as a perfectly acceptable place for entertaining, when he was a child and later as an adult.

Kenny Ortega marveled at Michael's sense of wonder. He described his reaction after every interaction with Michael Jackson: "I came out the other side looking at the world differently, looking at myself differently.... He was an angel walking the planet."

Private & Public. As a public figure, known in every corner of the world and designated "the most recognized person on the planet," Michael Jackson was astonishingly private in his personal life. Many years passed between the rare interviews he granted a few fortunate media people.

Michael made herculean attempts to avoid detection when he ventured out from the safety and security of his home or hotel. The frequently-worn masks and disguises of various kinds were usually futile attempts to remain undetected. Unfortunately for his image, paparazzi photos of many of these attempts sped their way onto tabloid pages, along with sensational articles designed to make him appear weird and bizarre. That's what sold—"Wacko Jacko."

"Jacko," the media-perpetuated nickname for Michael, was not only disrespectful and dismissive, but it is also a term with a racist history. Michael hated it.

According to the *Oxford English Dictionary*, the word "jacko" dates back to the mid-1600's, as a Flemish approximation of the Bantu word for "monkey." By the early 1800's, Jacko Maccacco, a famous fighting monkey, could be found on display in Westminster Pit, a notorious London arena for dog fights. The word has become part of the common vernacular, and it eventually became a racist shorthand for blacks.

The tabloids successfully wrestled away the spotlight from his gargantuan talent and soul-reaching music to move its focus to what he understandably deplored as "nonsense." The shape of Michael Jackson's nose became a pervasive, adolescent-like fixation for the media.

This most public man tried so hard to remain private. He was simply attempting to experience pieces of a normal life.

In triumphant mode, however, and on his own terms, Michael Jackson skillfully combined his public and private selves in his stirring music. So many of his songs are autobiographical revelations—intimate, personal, and self-disclosing. Some examples are "Childhood," "Stranger in Moscow," "Scream," "Black or White," "Will You Be There," and "You Are My Life."

American & Global. Michael Jackson was the unofficial ambassador of America to myriad countries on six continents. People of all colors and ethnic backgrounds perceived him as the ultimate American. Many people abroad learned English from the words of his songs, which inspired them to continue in the study of his language. The multitudes admired him as the epitome of

American freedom of expression and success. Whether his listeners were black or white, or something else, Michael's messages resonated with them, and their admiration for him often generated to his country of origin.

He was a global icon of unprecedented popularity. No one else came close to the international reach of Michael Jackson in the arenas of artistic recognition, musical impact, record sales, and numbers of zealous fans. No one else toured and held standing-room-only concerts in so many countries.

To audiences in nations that were tiny in size and world influence, he was a hero. *Michael Jackson has come to us!* He cared about them ... and they loved him for it.

Across the span of many years, he came a long but victorious way. During the days of the Iron Curtain, the Soviet Union officially censured Michael Jackson as the symbol of all that was bad and wrong about America, and banned the sales of his records. Their "black market" soon became saturated with Michael Jackson music.

Imagine the cultural infiltration of Michael Jackson to the extent that the Soviet Union considered him a serious threat to the minds and hearts of their youth! Years later, however, after the Curtain lifted, and he performed in Moscow to a grateful, excited audience, he was warmly welcomed by some of the government officials.

Father & Mother. Michael Jackson was both father and mother to Prince, Paris, and Blanket from their infancy. By design, he raised them by himself. The mother of the two older children, Debbie Rowe self-professed to feeling no desire to be a mother. She birthed the children so that Michael, who always longed to be a father, could achieve his fondest wish. Blanket was born to an unidentified surrogate mother, with whom Michael secretly made formal arrangements for his third child.

Michael Jackson embraced his role as single parent with enthusiasm and remarkable devotion. He committed himself to providing his children with the nurturance and support that would be typical from two parents. Michael postponed his pursuit of opportunities to tour and curtailed his involvements outside of the home for the purpose of parenting his three children. They were always with him; even when he traveled, they accompanied him.

With a pervasively nurturing personality—coupled with a predisposition for structure and loving discipline—Michael possessed the combination of traits required for effective parenting. His well-adjusted children described their father as both "very loving" and "a strict disciplinarian" during an exclusive television interview that was conducted with them months after his death.

Adored & Vilified. It would be redundant to describe Michael Jackson's immense popularity, which rose to the level of veneration in some quarters. Michael was revered throughout Japan, where his fans were considered the most enthusiastic and devoted from anywhere. He was sometimes understandably afraid there because of the frenzied behaviors of the people who thronged to see him. He was crowned a king and provided a gold throne in the Republic of Gabon in Africa; there he was awarded the National Honor of Merit, making him the first entertainer to receive the honor.

Michael Jackson was considered by a large contingent of his followers as a divine messenger from God. He was followed, from concert to concert, by hordes of zealous fans in Europe, who slept under bridges, in hallways, and in automobiles on their Michael Jackson pilgrimage.

On the other hand, there were many who hated him. Anyone at the pinnacle of any profession is subject to jaundiced scrutiny, harsh criticism, and oppositional forces. Michael Jackson was no exception. And the media fueled the perception that he was "different" to the point of moral corruption. They treated Michael Jackson's cosmetic surgery as outrageous and even sinful; his color change as traitorous and disgusting; and his other unique characteristics as inexcusably eccentric.

In the media, there was a double standard for Michael Jackson. For example, cosmetic surgery is commonplace, especially in

Hollywood, the home of the stars. It was generally acceptable, sometimes laudatory, for certain celebrities to partake of these readily-obtained, elective medical procedures—but shockingly wrong for Michael Jackson.

Michael was misinterpreted all around. His ubiquitous umbrella, treated as a laughable affectation in the tabloids, in reality was necessary because of his medical conditions, vitiligo and lupus, which caused his toxic level of sensitivity to the sun. His masks and disguises were desperate attempts to experience normal life within the context of an ever-present threat of mob reaction. The veils for his children were intended to shield them from the painful loss of anonymity that he had experienced at a young age. Michael ardently hoped that Prince, Paris, and Blanket could live a normal life.

Tragically, there were also people who believed that Michael Jackson was guilty of wrongdoing. Again, the media were guilty of perpetuating this horrible perception, even after his full acquittal by a jury at trial. And, *some people just loved to hate Michael Jackson.*

Spiritual & Earthy. From his earliest years, Michael Jackson was deeply spiritual, believing strongly in a higher power. He practiced his boyhood religion with his mother Katherine. As Jehovah's Witnesses, they attended the Kingdom Hall for worship and also went door to door to spread their beliefs in the hope of saving souls. Even during his *Thriller* days, when catapulted to fame and wealth, Michael knocked on doors, usually in disguise, to proselytize in accordance with the tenets of the Witnesses. The elders of the Kingdom Hall were severely critical of the ghostly theme of *Thriller* and threatened Michael's ex-communication. When he incorporated a disclaimer at the beginning of the *Thriller* short film, assuring viewers that he did not believe in the occult, the elders were temporarily appeased. Later, however, other prohibitions imposed by them caused Michael to opt for his career. The conflict between his art and his religion became too extreme and limiting. However, he remained spiritual and dedicated to a higher purpose throughout his entire life. He studied religions and read the Bible regularly.

Michael perceived the spiritual and the divine everywhere. In *Dancing the Dream*—his 1992 book of original poetry, prose, and parables—he wrote "Heaven Is Here":

> You and I were never separate
> It's just an illusion
> Wrought by the magical lens of
> Perception
>
> There is only one Wholeness
> Only one Mind
> We are like ripples
> In the vast Ocean of Consciousness

Michael Jackson was also irrefutably "earthy." In every performance, his dance moves and vocals revealed a sensual, profoundly intense individual, in touch with his own humanity.

Michael's passionate delivery of the rousing song "Human Nature" conveys his unapologetic decision to live and love in his own way. In *This Is It*, Michael's conversations with co-workers are laced with tactile allusions such as "sizzle," "simmer," "let it burn," and "making a tapestry" of music and visuals for the audience. "You have to be nourished by it," he tells his musical director in order to communicate the importance of getting the music to that special level that he sought. "Like dragging yourself out of bed," he says at another point to emphasize the laziness of the rhythm.

In his dancing, Michael used his entire body. He set himself apart from other dancers with his truly unique moves. Even the best professional dancers watched him in awe. His *This Is It* back-up dancers were "enthralled" and watched him rehearse every possible minute, according to Kenny Ortega.

Humble & Explosive. Michael Jackson was always described as humble and soft-spoken by those who knew him. He was never boastful or arrogant in his demeanor; he was unassuming and a good listener. Michael wanted to learn as much from other people as he possibly could. He frequently asked them about themselves and their childhood, and he absorbed all that he could about what made them tick and about their craft.

He walked and talked with gentleness of manner and spirit. Michael Jackson was known for gracefully bowing to his colleagues, often with his hands folded as if in prayer, in front of him. "God bless you," he would say in his feathery voice.

On stage, however, Michael presented a dramatically different *persona*. He was electric, bold, and flamboyant. He performed with all-out energy and radiating passion every song, every time. His tour musicians revealed that he rehearsed at the same level of energy, tirelessly repeating the performance toward the goal of perfection. According to Quincy Jones, his producer, collaborator and friend, Michael even danced as he sang in the recording booth—unusual behavior for singers because most would become breathless and unable to deliver a flawless vocal. Not Michael. It was as if he couldn't help himself from dancing; the music took him over entirely.

Jones also described the behind-the-scenes Michael as too shy to try out a new song in front of him, even in the privacy of the producer's home. With his back to Michael and no eye contact possible between them, Jones would sit on his couch, while Michael delivered his new song in its entirety. Yet, this same man could leap onto a stage in front of 70,000 people and feel "most at home there than anywhere else in the world."

High-Risk & Low-Risk. One of the hallmarks of Michael's genius was his breaking all of the boundaries and taking risks with his music, dance, staging, short films, and fashion. He found out what the norm was, and then he transcended it. He gently pushed everyone with whom he worked to excel, to surpass themselves, to soar to greater heights. He "set the bar" higher than it had ever been set, and then he wanted to go even further. That was Michael's professional self ... always.

In sharp contrast, in his private life he was very low-risk. Unassuming, reticent, and shy, Michael did not push in any direction in his personal life. In 2011, Larry King called Michael the "shyest person" he had ever met.

Michael Jackson did not run after Lisa Marie Presley, probably the only woman he ever truly loved, when she proposed divorce. She secretly hoped that he would court her again. He let her go, as he did Debbie Rowe, his second wife, after she bore him two children and discovered that she could have no more. He was neither aggressive nor assertive in his interpersonal relationships. In fact, he was generally passive, avoiding confrontation and unpleasantness whenever possible.

When it became necessary to terminate one of his employees, Michael always had someone else do it for him. He could not bear to fire someone himself. What is surprising, also, is the fact that so many people who had left his employ later re-entered his circle of employees, managers, and lawyers. Michael typically remained on good terms with them all the while.

With his children, Michael was consummately protective. He kept them private and veiled in public; he limited their exposure to the outside world via television and the Internet; and he personally guided their learning experiences. Michael was very careful and cautious regarding whom he would allow to interact with them or assist in their care. He employed the same nanny, Grace Rwaramba, as the children's decision-making caregiver, second only to himself, across the span of many years. He protected his little ones with the fierceness of a lioness with her cubs.

Joyful & Tormented. No one who has seen Michael Jackson perform or has observed him in the service of others could deny that he emanated joy. It was almost palpable. He conveyed his joyfulness with such energy and passion that it became contagious. Watch Michael Jackson's performance of "Man in the Mirror" at his Bucharest concert and you will marvel at the audience succumbing to his outpouring of love—tens of thousands of men and women, young and old, weeping and reaching out their hands toward him.

In his off-stage life, Michael Jackson was unsurprisingly a tortured man. He carried the burden of genius, the cross of having been unjustly accused of heinous acts, and the loneliness that haunted him during his entire life. During his last years, he was also burdened with a financial empire that spun out of control and with upsetting ambiguity regarding the directions of his future....

Victim of Fame & Contradictions. As a prisoner of his celebrity, Michael Jackson uncomfortably wore the cloak of fame, one that he could never remove.

Michael was appropriately described as a "loving singer" and an "angry dancer." The latter assessment was provided admiringly by Fred Astaire, who identified with Michael's powerful, forceful style.

Michael hated touring—it was a fatiguing and lonely job—while he loved performing. He said that he felt so "at home on stage" that he hated the show to end.

Seemingly asexual and yet so visibly passionate, he stirred powerful feelings in men and women.

He was both paternal and maternal in his manifestations of caring, not only with his own three children but with suffering individuals around the world.

Painfully shy, Michael still managed to get what he wanted in his music and artistic productions. He could and did make things happen, big things.

His private life was so constricted because of his level of fame, and yet he was a "man of the world" in his expansive public life, having experienced so much in his travels to countless countries on six continents.

Michael Jackson remained too trusting of people throughout his lifetime. This personality trait ultimately caused his demise, which arguably began with his 2005 trial and culminated in his untimely death at the hands of another. Yet he told his mother, in a post-trial conversation, that he trusted no one but her. *If only that were true in June 2009....*

Michael Jackson's peaks and valleys were like no one else's on Earth. Who else has reached the mountain-top of global adulation? Who else has so inspired and permanently affected so many millions?

Who else has been so publicly and pervasively humiliated and traumatized by vicious, unfounded accusations of moral wrongdoing? Who else has soared to such heights and then fallen so far?

His incredible life was both a blessing to him and a curse.

Michael felt invincible—and called himself that years ago—and yet he was so vulnerable. He became the victim of many—the jealous, self-serving, greedy, and unscrupulous.

He was the most powerful force in the worldwide music industry, but he was powerless over his fate.

He was strong-willed and accomplished lofty goals, but he was also a fragile soul.

Although Michael Jackson was followed by multitudes of people, both figuratively and literally, he remained so enigmatic and misunderstood.

The shy, unassuming little boy from a tiny house in Gary, Indiana, and the magnificent King of Pop all around the globe: *Both were Michael Jackson.*

He was a man of gentle strength with an unforgettably warm and radiant smile.

And we miss him, the man who was Michael, in all of his paradoxical glory.

Michael Jackson was bigger than life.
And yet, his life was too big for him.
It would have been too big for anyone.

*   *   *   *   *   *   *   *   *

MICHAEL JACKSON & HIS FANS

**While he was singing, dancing, inspiring,
and walking among us on Earth,
Michael Jackson
belonged only to himself.
Now that he has passed from this dimension,
Michael belongs to all of us
who love and embrace him.**

**From the abyss of my soul and heart
I love you.**

— Michael Jackson to his fans

**Asking me what [is] my favorite
Michael Jackson song is almost asking
me like ... what's my favorite breath
I ever took.**

— Ahmir Khalib Thompson
(?uestlove of the Roots)

The Internet nearly crashed on the day Michael Jackson died. With 5,000 hits per minute, the Web was overcome with cyber-traffic by people from everywhere who wanted to know what had happened to the King of Pop.

"How many people does it take to break the Internet?" *CNN Tech* asked. "On June 25, we found out it's just one—if that one is Michael Jackson." Service on the Internet was inaccessible for a time, and *Google Trends* called the Jackson story "volcanic."

Cell phone usage surged from the fervent and the far-flung, from the genuinely grief-stricken to the curious. Then there was a virtual, cyber "wailing wall" for Michael Jackson; people posted their passionate, primal feelings of despair and pain for this special man. Twitter outages were reported due to the sheer volume of activity.

Michael's fans cried a river, many of them inconsolable. People by the thousands undertook a pilgrimage to their city center or other special place of commemoration. They took flowers, candles, teddy bears, photos, banners, cards, and letters. They sang and danced to his songs. They held vigils; they fled to temples, shrines, churches, cathedrals, chapels, mosques, and synagogues to pray and to grapple with the enormity of this loss. They consoled each other, wept, and comforted their children.

Some people seemed to be "strangers to themselves"; they were surprised and startled at the depth of their grief over Michael Jackson's sudden death. Hundreds of thousands of people—that soon became millions—realized, for the first time, that they were ... *fans*. They loved this man; they had loved him as a boy; and now they would miss him....

     *   *   *   *   *   *   *   *   *

"I'm married to my fans," Michael told several of his interviewers across the years.

The only continuous, real love affair of Michael's life was with his fans. He cared deeply for them; he wanted to please them; he appreciated their love. He never lost sight of his importance to them, and it was a reciprocal relationship. They meant as much to him as he did to them, maybe more.

In his personal life that was almost devoid of genuine nurturance of him by others, Michael fed on his fans' love and passion.

Saturday mornings became special occasions for Michael Jackson and his security team when he would decide to take long circuitous drives throughout Las Vegas. These excursions were not sightseeing events; Mr. Jackson hardly looked out his window as his bodyguard drove the SUV down quiet streets, with his head of security "riding shot-gun" in the front passenger seat, as always.

Every so often the boss seemed to want to immerse himself in his fan mail and, like a restless child, he enjoyed the motion of the vehicle while he opened cards and letters. They came from the United Kingdom, Egypt, Japan, India, Ireland, Spain, Iran, and dozens of other countries; they flowed into the house from every state in the Union.

When the Michael Jackson family moved into their Vegas rented mansion, one of the bedrooms was converted into the Gift Room, which accepted the daily offerings and entreaties from his fans and admirers. Teddy bears and other cuddly animals covered in colorful faux fur made this room their new home. Hand-made and store-bought cards streamed in; typed and hand-written letters were stacked in piles.

Mr. Jackson would carry an armful of his fan mail into the vehicle and then set about reading it, thoughtfully, one by one. "I try to read as many as possible," he explained to his security team. He told the men that he got a lot of the inspiration to write his songs from these fans.

His security guards silently enjoyed Mr. Jackson's reactions to his cards and letters, some of which contained photos of their transmitters, and others held mementos of special significance. Some made him laugh out loud; some made him angry; and some made him very emotional. His front-seat protectors could tell that their boss was choked up or shedding tears over a heartfelt message to him from far away. Mr. Jackson realized that so many of his admirers wanted to establish a connection with him; longed for him to know of their respect and love; or desired him to know of their unconditional support. He was visibly moved by these people's expressions of deep feelings for him.

It was during these leisurely times, their vehicle ambling along, that his security team felt a notch less sorry for the boss. Mr. Jackson had permanently lost the quality of personal space and freedom enjoyed by the general population because of his fame. What was taken for granted by most people was futilely sought and cherished from afar by their boss. But on these days, he could feel loved.

Not only did Mr. Jackson continually remind all of his security personnel to be kind to his fans at all times, he occasionally would send water and soft drinks to his admirers when they kept vigil in front of his homes. The guards at Neverland and his other residences would carry out the bottles and cans, as directed, and distribute them to the thrilled recipients. *These came from him!* they knew, and these thoughtful gestures by their hero caused them to admire him even more.

When on tour, Michael Jackson was known for sending out autographed items, including pillowcases, to his patiently waiting fans, some of whom slept overnight in autos and hallways to catch a glimpse of him at his hotel window during the day. When it was cold outside, he sent out blankets. He often sent his faithful fans a written message, delivered by a bodyguard, telling them that he was going to bed for the night so that they could seek a place to sleep before renewing their watch in the morning. In the cities of Europe, there were often hundreds of people who stood for long hours below Michael Jackson's hotel suite windows. With smaller groups, such as those that gathered outside the main gate of Neverland, Mr. Jackson would send out snacks, pizzas, and cold bottled drinks.

Michael recognized his core fans, the ones who would follow him around from concert to concert or stake out their places in front of his hotel or house. He would point to one at a time and tell his security personnel, "That girl was at the last house for days," and "She was at my last concert," and other similar things. To the guards, these comments were astounding examples of their boss's memory and concern.

On the other side of that coin, some fans were manipulative and scary. These individuals would come up with some ploy to use in an attempt to gain access to Michael Jackson. For example, a young man would nonchalantly saunter to the gate of the Summerlin home and announce that he wanted to see Michael immediately, that he was expected by him. Some people would pretend that they were making deliveries to Michael or his family and would insist that they be allowed entry into the house. Of course, these bold people were summarily turned away by security, but some of them persisted and tried again later.

In small numbers, Michael Jackson accepted his fans' approach when he was in his vehicle and he signed as many autographs for them as he could manage. When he was with his children, however, he usually preferred that people respect him enough to allow him and his kids their undisturbed family time.

When he toured the world, Michael always instructed his security guards to allow children to approach him. Emerging from the massive crowds, flanked by Michael's bodyguards, the little children would be permitted to see their idol up-close. He would pat them on their heads, shake hands, sign autographs, and always gift them with his warmest smiles.

He took his fans seriously, as real people with real feelings. Sometimes he directed his security men to accept banners, posters, or original artwork from fans and admirers, who came to a concert or stood outside his hotel, holding their special gift for Michael. He posed for photos when it was safe for him to do so.

From his earliest years, Michael Jackson gave articles of his clothing to fans along the way. He realized how much these personal mementos meant to their recipients. He gave away many of his jackets, and he threw some of them into the audience during his performances or awards ceremonies. He also regularly flung his fedora into the crowd after dancing and singing his iconic "Billie Jean."

On one occasion, when a new Cadillac Escalade was delivered to his home, he beckoned a few of the fans who were gathered outside the front gates. They got to ride in the vehicle "for the first time" with Michael Jackson, as his driver slowly guided it around the circular driveway and then onto the quiet street. At times like this, Michael was shy but friendly. He asked people about themselves: "Where are you from?" "For how long are you staying in the area?"

His most ardent, committed fans had showed up in large numbers during his frightening trial. Every day across five months, people from all over had come, bearing printed signs and banners ... and love. Many had borrowed money and taken leaves of absence from their jobs to show their support for Michael Jackson during his darkest hours. Their hand-made posters lined the streets, and their boom boxes blared out his music.

No other entertainer could have drawn people from so many walks of life: every creed, race, and nationality was represented. People of all ages and religious denominations had flown in and had dedicated themselves to Michael. The fans who were there created a synergy that was undeniable.... (Aphrodite Jones)

"R.C." and her family were among the huge throng of people near the courthouse on the day of Michael's arraignment. They had traveled from Las Vegas, Nevada, to be in Santa Maria, California, hopefully to catch a glimpse of their idol and to show fiercely-felt support for him.

"My mother threw me under the bus for Michael Jackson!" says R.C.'s lovely daughter in 2011; she was sixteen at the time. She is good-natured in her tone when she tells the story—simply making the point that Michael was so important to her mother that it was like he was a member of their family. The girl explains that she had to last for fourteen hours without using a restroom so that she could keep her place, with her family, at their vantage point. They didn't come all this way to be confined to the fringe of the crowd and thereby reduce their chances to actually see Michael Jackson for a fleeting moment. She had to "hold it" and patiently stand in place with her family members, among the other dedicated fans.

Later, she and her mother went to Neverland as part of a group of honored fans. They did not see Michael there, but they used the restroom, went on the rides, and walked the grounds in awe. "It was the happiest place on earth," R.C. recalls, with a wince of joy; "like Disneyland, with songs playing, but it was also so very peaceful."

[R.C., her husband, and two children attained their fondest wish when they shook hands with Michael through his vehicle window in front of his Holmby Hills home in April 2009.]

Every day his fans were there at Neverland's gates and at the court building. They supported and encouraged one another; they tried to convince themselves and each other that Michael Jackson would be acquitted of all charges. Like his attorney Thomas Mesereau, they were convinced of his complete innocence. *They were hurting for him.*

"As Michael approached the court, … the wails of screaming and tears of emotion from everyone around him—made it seem like the whole earth stood still," wrote Aphrodite Jones. "For the people behind the gates and cyclone fences who were screaming and cheering, there seemed to be a communion. Something about Michael made hearts pound. Everyone in his presence could feel the music. They could feel the dance."

On June 13, 2005, Michael thanked his fans in a brief, emotional public speech after his full acquittal was announced in the courtroom and on loud speakers outside. He could not have survived this ordeal without them, he said, and he assured them that he was grateful from his very soul.

Michael Jackson would never forget his soldiers of love and what they had done for him. They helped save his life.

At his forty-fifth birthday celebration, a gala event, Michael Jackson thanked his fans—as he often did—in a heartfelt speech:

> I would like to thank my wonderful fans so very much for this event.... Thank you for putting together this fabulous party and for traveling from over 30 countries. I am deeply moved and touched by your love. I want you to know that I appreciate my fans not just on occasions like this – but every day of my life. It is your presence, your faith and your loyalty that has given me great strength during difficult

times, … I owe you. Over the years we became a family. You are all my family. My children are your children and all children of the world are our children and our responsibility. (September 3, 2003)

*   *   *   *   *   *   *   *   *

The aura and charisma of Michael Jackson were unique. His level of passion for his music and charitable causes was inspirational; his enthusiasm and ebullience were infectious. He was described as the only entertainer who regularly made his fans, of all ages, weak-kneed. He caused mob scenes and chaos wherever he went.

Also special is the connection the fans feel to each other. People from foreign countries freely embrace and hold hands with each other and with their American "friends in Michael." Strangers hug each other, exchange their contact numbers, and continue these relationships. It is lovely to see and experience.

Sometimes there is a bit of good-natured in-fighting among his fans. There are the "old" fans, those who have followed him since his childhood, throughout his roller-coaster ride of a life; they pride themselves in being as loyal as the family dog. Then there are the "new" fans, who fell in love with Michael Jackson after his passing; they were stunned, numbed, and dismayed by the gut-wrenching grief they suffered and the soul connection they experienced with this special man. Who are the *most* loyal, *most* dedicated to Michael Jackson? His old and new fans will occasionally argue the point, but they are united in their unequivocal admiration of him.

Michael's fans felt his joy; they felt his pain. They felt anguish over his cruel treatment by authorities in Santa Barbara and the savagery of self-serving, jaded media. Today, his fans want and seek full vindication for Michael Jackson—something he deserves and never got during his lifetime.

There are many fans who feel guilty that they were not there for Michael in his time of need. They didn't write that letter; they didn't stand outside the courtroom to show their ardent belief in his innocence; they didn't speak up to their friends on his behalf. Many of these people are attempting to atone for their having failed Michael Jackson through various acts that include clamoring for justice now that he is gone and getting involved in charitable works of all kinds in his name and in his memory.

*   *   *   *   *   *   *   *   *

Not surprisingly, some of his most ardent fans are today celebrities themselves. They were taught and inspired by Michael, who was known for his willingness to share the credit, mentor others, and help them when he could. He was known for being unselfish and caring; so many of his fellow artists remember him for these qualities. Michael amazed his colleagues with his unparalleled talent, tireless efforts, perfectionism, and mind-blowing creativity.

Here is a small sampling of people's reactions to Michael Jackson and their feelings for him....

Dearest Michael, how do we even begin to tell you what you meant to us?

What a beautiful journey we had with you. You touched so many lives and we are honored to have been one of them. How blessed are we to have been given an opportunity to see your dream of Neverland grow and flourish. What a lesson we learned in compassion, generosity and love from you. Because of you, the sound of children's laughter, the whistle of a steam train or the whirl of a carousel, will always bring a smile to our hearts. You will forever be felt in the gentle breezes rustling through the trees, in the trickling of the streams and in the stillness of the valley of Neverland.... The enormity of what you gave and created leaves us speechless. May you sing with the Angels above, our love forever, Your Neverland Family.

(From Michael Jackson's Memorial Program)

He has been an inspiration throughout my entire life and I'm devastated he's gone. (Britney Spears to *People*)

... Let us remember him for his unparalleled contributions to the world of music, his generosity of spirit in his quest to heal the world, and the joy he brought to millions of devoted fans. (Mariah Carey to *The Associated Press*)

... The incomparable Michael Jackson has made a bigger impact on music than any other artist in the history of music. He was magic. He was what we all strive to be. He will always be the King of Pop! Life is not about how many breaths you take, but about how many moments in life that take your breath away. For anyone who has ever seen, felt or heard his art, we are all honored to have been alive in this generation to experience the magic of Michael Jackson. (Beyonce to *Rolling Stone*)

A major strand of our cultural DNA has left us.... I think we'll mourn his loss as well as the loss of ourselves as children listening to "Thriller" on the record player. I truly hope he is memorialized as the ... moonwalking, *MTV* owning, mesmerizing, unstoppable, invincible Michael Jackson. (John Mayer on *Twitter)*

We have lost a genius and a true ambassador of not only Pop music but of all music. He has been an inspiration to multiple generations. I will always cherish the moments I shared with him on stage and all of the things I learned about music from him and the time we spent together.... (Justin Timberlake, *Michael Jackson Tribute* magazine)

Michael has the quality that separates the merely sentimental from the truly heartfelt; it's rooted in the blues, and no matter what Michael is singing, that boy's got the blues. (Marvin Gaye, *Rolling Stone*)

... That magical moment of Motown 25 has been unmatched on television. Name another moment that's effected [sic.] the world, not America, not the continent of Africa, ... Not the continent of Eurasia, I'm saying the world. He changed the world. And so for us, we only aspire to make music that affects people like that. (Pharrell Williams, *The Source*)

Michael Jackson was my Music God. He made me believe that all things are possible.... I love Michael Jackson. (Wyclef Jean)

He could have 80 people onstage all doing the same dance move, but he was the one guy who had that natural flow that nobody could match. (Slash, *Rolling Stone*)

All that I know comes from Michael Jackson. (Ricky Martin, *Iconic*, *#3*)

Michael Jackson is still the King of Pop. He has not abdicated the throne, nor has he been usurped. (Stephen Colbert, *MJFC,* Internet)

I'm so thankful I had the opportunity to meet and perform with such a great entertainer [who] in so many ways ... transcended ... culture. He broke barriers, he changed radio formats. With music, he made it possible for people like Oprah Winfrey and Barack Obama to impact the mainstream world. His legacy is unparalleled. (Usher, *Right On!*)

I don't think there's anyone who could approach Michael Jackson for sheer brilliance. Every song is perfect, every performance magnificent. (Sir Cliff Richard, *MJFC,* Internet)

I knew Michael as a child and watched him grow over the years. Of all the thousands of entertainers I have worked with, Michael was THE most outstanding. Many have tried and will try to copy him, but his talent will never be matched. (Dick Clark, USA Today *Michael Jackson* magazine)

He's incredible. He's a genius. Just to be in the same room [with him], I felt everything I wanted to accomplish in life has been achieved.... That aura ... that's how incredible that aura is.... The way he thinks.... Some artists think regional, some think national, I was thinking international. He thinks planets! It's on another level! (Akon, *MJFC*, Internet)

Not only that but he was an incredible father, a great dad. He treated his kids like kings and queens. He ... always wanted to find new ways to change the world.... I wish the world could have ... just seen Mike the person. (Akon, *Right On!*)

He was a kind, genuine, and wonderful man.... I loved him very much and I will miss him every remaining day of my life. (Liza Minnelli, *Right On!*)

Michael Jackson showed me that you can actually see the beat.... He made me believe in magic. (P. Diddy, *Michael Jackson Tribute* magazine)

MJ is not just the King of Pop but the "king" of our entire industry, ... no one can ever compete again ... game over.... (Will.i.am, *The Source*)

... [His] music ... is played in every corner of the world and the reason for that is because he had it all, ... talent, grace, professionalism and dedication. He was the consummate entertainer and his contributions and legacy will be felt upon the world forever.... I've lost my little brother ... and part of my soul has gone with him. (Quincy Jones, *Beckett Presents: A Tribute to Michael Jackson*)

Michael is a genius, a creative being in a whole other reality. (Chris Tucker, *Iconic, #3*)

The only male singer who I've seen besides myself and who's better than me—that is Michael Jackson. (Frank Sinatra, *Michael Jackson for the Soul*)

Oh, God! That boy moves in a very exceptional way. That's the greatest dancer of the century. (Fred Astaire, *Michael Jackson for the Soul*)

There is no one in the world like MJ! ... We all know him in one way or another. In some way he has touched us, been the voice of one of our sweetest memories. And what a wonderful, genuine, compassionate, soft spoken giant so full of love. He gave us love, excitement, one of a kind moments in a mundane world. (Alicia Keys, *Michael Jackson for the Soul*)

Every step he took was absolutely precise and fluid at the same time. It was like watching quicksilver in motion. He was wonderful to work with, an absolute professional at all times, and ... a true artist. (Martin Scorsese, *Michael Jackson for the Soul*)

From the beginning of my career, he was my idol in show business. He was a genius and an incredible artist! (Celine Dion, *Michael Jackson for the Soul*)

He was one of my childhood idols. I salute you, King of Pop. You made the whole world moonwalk together. (LL Cool J, USA Today *Michael Jackson* magazine)

I'll always remember how he wasn't a man of many words but he didn't have to be because his energy and spirit would totally light up a room. (Patti LaBelle, *Michael Jackson for the Soul*)

He had something so intoxicating about him, and when he was ready to share with you and be himself—I don't know if I've ever been that intoxicated by anything. (Lisa Marie Presley, *Michael Jackson for the Soul*)

When you were with him, you really felt like God was within him.... I know that people looked at Michael and thought he was strange, but to me, he was fascinating. He was the most inspirational person in my life. His one dream was to cure all the sick children in the world. And when I'd say, "Isn't that impossible?" Michael would just start to cry. He was very emotional about things that moved him. I guess you'd have to say he was a pure innocent in a world that wasn't so innocent anymore. (Brett Ratner, *Michael Jackson for the Soul*)

[Michael] Jackson breaks through to my spirit way beyond my skeptical side, beyond my rationality. And I'm not alone in feeling it. It's pervasive.... Few people have inspired this kind of phenomenon. Michael Jackson's life and work and spirit have somehow touched and ignited millions of souls. (Lorette C. Luzajic, *Michael Jackson for the Soul*)

He's the most thoughtful, respectful person I've ever met.... The last time I was at the [Neverland] ranch, they put up a big Sony Jumbo Tron across from a condo building for sick children, so if kids woke up at night, cartoons would be on. (David Nordahl, *Michael Jackson for the Soul*)

He's not afraid to look into the worst suffering and find the smallest part that's positive and beautiful. (Frank Dileo, *Michael Jackson for the Soul*)

Michael was one of the kindest, nicest people I ever met. His wistful desire to heal the world with love, music and artistry clashed horribly with the barbaric way he was exploited. The world is a far better place because of him. (Thomas Mesereau, "Defending Michael," mesereauyu.com)

People simply didn't understand him just like they didn't understand Beethoven and Mozart.... He was very shy.... He was simply magic. He was the most noble person in the world. No man on Earth can compare to his inner and outer beauty.... No one was even close to Michael's charisma.... He was the gentlest person on the planet. (Ruska Bergman, Stylist to Celebrities)

All I could think about him in that one moment was, 'I had abandoned him,' that we had abandoned him, ... we had allowed this magnificent creature that once set the world on fire somehow slip through the cracks.... [W]e were all busy passing judgment. Most of us had turned our backs on him.... Sometimes, we have to lose things before we can truly appreciate them.... (Madonna, *Michael Jackson for the Soul*)

Crucified by the circumstances of his life, it was as if poor Michael Jackson had no chance at all.... I began to feel at one with the sheer humanity of Michael Jackson, and all its complexity, fallibility and grace.... I began to feel such empathy for him, such pity for him ... and such great love for him as well. But more than anything, I felt immeasurable sorrow for him and for what his life should have been like.... (J. Randy Taraborrelli, *Michael Jackson* Biography)

*   *   *   *   *   *   *   *   *

Michael Jackson's last collaboration, the magnificent *This Is It* concert series, was captured in a documentary film. His collaborators and musician colleagues, all of whom were fans of Michael, shared their feelings and viewpoints in the additional footage released in the DVD. Here is some of what they said....

Within seconds of meeting him, he was ... an absolute sweetheart and just a good guy, ... a very approachable man. (John Meglen, Producer)

He was an innocent person ..., he came from a very innocent place. (Paul Gongaware, Producer)

Michael's vision knows no limit. (Randy Phillips)

He was so unashamedly bold [in his creativity]. He wanted to break every barrier.... He always wanted to do something no one's ever done before.... He was [also] very, very funny. (Michael Cotten, Production Designer)

He puts his whole body into a song. (Michael Durham Prince)

His moves are like words and he's like an encyclopedia.... [And] he was such a loving, caring creature. (Travis Payne, Choreographer)

The most special thing about Michael Jackson [as an entertainer] is his timing [the dramatic pause]; it sets him apart from everyone else.... There aren't too many people who can drop my jaw anymore; Michael Jackson was one of those people.... His hugs were the deepest and the most sincere, heartfelt hugs ever.... He was an angel walking the planet.... No matter how hard the world came down on him, he only reacted back with more love.... Michael was the loveliest soul.... (Kenny Ortega)

He draws from deeper emotion than anyone I've ever worked with.... Once every several centuries of mankind, God sends somebody special—a wake-up call—to enlighten the people ..., to excite ...; to show people how to be, how to love. That was MJ. (Jonathan "Sugarfoot" Moffett, Drummer)

*   *   *   *   *   *   *   *   *

"No star was more generous to fans (every member of the core group of Jackson fans that I met had, at some point, been invited into his house to have dinner or to watch movies and hang out), and no group of fans treated one another with more generosity than these women." So wrote Michael Joseph Gross, the author of *Starstruck*, a book about the relationships between celebrities and their fans.

National Photo Group, from early times, wanted to be the "Michael Jackson agency," the one with the scoop on the superstar and the hard-to-get photos. Christopher Weiss and another photographer were assigned to be "soldiers of the sit," the ones who would position themselves outside of his front gate. They became friendly with the core group of fans—described as mostly young, attractive European women—that followed Michael "from pillar to post." These fans would camp outside his homes and would huddle outside the hotel gate that was closest to Michael's room or bungalow, sitting quietly so that security would not detect them and push them away.

According to Weiss, who witnessed occasional interactions:

… Sometimes Michael would come out and say hello. One time he handed out five handwritten letters that said things like "I can feel your energy through the walls. You inspire me so much. I love you all. Thank you for being there. Thank you for being my friend. Thank you for loving me. With all the love in my heart, Michael Jackson"

"I was always impressed by that, how deeply he seemed to care for these girls," Weiss disclosed. "When he hugged one of them, he would put one hand on her neck, behind her head, that extra-comforting move like you would do to a person you know."

These women would draw straws to determine which of them would keep the written letters from Michael. They would make photocopies and give them out to all of the others.

In November 2008, Michael sent out two notes to fans outside of his Los Angeles hotel. In them, in his large, distinctive handwriting, he wrote:

I truly love all of you[.] I am recording tonight, for all of you, you are my true inspiration forever. I am living for you, and the children....

You make me sooo happy.... The sky is the limit. Higher consciousness always.... I love you. Michael Jackson

On the morning of June 25, 2009, a National Photo Group paparazzo named Alfred Ibanez was stationed outside of Michael's Holmby Hills residence, standing with five of Michael's fans, when an ambulance arrived. He telephoned his colleagues, Ben Evenstad and Weiss, who arrived on the scene in minutes. It was Christopher

Weiss who took the last picture of Michael Jackson; he jumped onto the ambulance and snapped a photo through the window. Michael was strapped to a gurney, his face shown in profile. [That photo—with its permanent place in history—has earned hundreds of thousands of dollars for the agency and its paparazzi from publications of it around the world. It is predicted to earn one million dollars.]

Weiss explains that "we had, as much as a photographer could for the last six months of his life, a relationship with Michael. There were days ... when we would just put our cameras down and visit with him. It's weird to say this, as paparazzi, ... but there was a closeness that our photographers had with Michael."

Michael Jackson was "the only celebrity that, if you were devoted enough, he would let you into his house." Other celebrities would call the police on the fans. "That's what all of them would do," he offers; "all but Michael. If you said 'I love you, I love you' to Michael, he would assume you meant you loved him, and he would let you in."

These paparazzi mourn Michael Jackson. They miss him and "the rare complexity of relationships that surrounded the King of Pop." *No one* is like him. Not even close.

      *   *   *   *   *   *   *   *   *

During the time when celebrities were hiring publicists to hide their personal lives, behavioral failings, and peccadilloes, Michael Jackson was revealing himself. He spoke about his painful and lonely childhood, the abuse he endured, and his heartfelt suffering over the plight of needy children everywhere. He incorporated these themes into his writings, as in *Moonwalk*, and his songs, as in "Childhood," which, Michael explained, was "the most honest song" he had written. "If you really want to know about me, ... you should listen to it." In his interview with Oprah, he disclosed that he "always cried from loneliness," from the time he was eight or nine years old. In the stirring "Give In To Me," Michael sings "I've spent a lifetime looking for someone who'll try to understand me."

Michael's rarity as a celebrity—a human being who wore his heart on his sleeve—was and is understood and appreciated by his fans. They feel a real connection to his core being.

It's All About L.O.V.E. and *Michael Jackson for the Soul—A Fanthology* are books written by Michael Jackson's fans and admirers. In these books, the contributors reveal the inspiration and special meanings brought to their individual lives by Michael Jackson.

Marjorie De-Faria journeyed to Neverland on the first anniversary of Michael Jackson's death. There she spoke to this author and others who had made the pilgrimage from foreign countries and from the fifty states—to anyone who cared to listen—about her unforgettable, transforming personal experiences with Michael. In spite of serious illness, Marjorie put herself together to try to see Michael Jackson when he was performing in concert:

> [In the crowd] suddenly he was in front of me.... Like a silly girl I began to cry, tears rolling down my cheek, as I reached over and gave him my artwork I had made especially for him. He gladly took it.... I reached out my hand to shake his hand, ... as if addressing a Royal King.... I wasn't prepared for what was to come next. He pulled me over to him, and he hugged me, and through more tears, I whispered, thank you. He held me tight, and whispered to me: "You should have stayed home, you look very sick".... I was overwhelmed.... Me ... a silly girl from Boston, who has been dreaming of meeting Michael for eons ... and he held me. Cry ... oh my ... the water gates were wide open by now.

What moved and impacted Marjorie so greatly was that Michael Jackson expressed concern for her, a stranger in a huge throng of people. He extended himself, as if he wanted to make her feel special, and he took the time to say kind words to her, while frenzied and screaming people were surrounding him. What Michael did not know—but perhaps sensed—was that she was receiving chemotherapy at the time; her face was swollen and discolored; she was very sick.

"I mourned Michael Jackson more than my own mother when she passed," Marjorie confesses, through a flood of tears that flow still.

In the fall of 2011, Paula Katsikas sent an unsolicited email to this author regarding her personal experience with Michael Jackson. She had dinner with Michael at an event organized by *MTV*. She describes the life-changing impact it had on her:

> It actually was a private dinner event and I was the winner from Australia. It will remain as my most precious memory. I am also going back to the States this December for MJ Cirque du Soleil in Vegas. Going to three shows. Michael is my passion.... I am by no means an impressionable teenager. I am a grown woman with no real issues in her life who has been touched so much by the man they call Michael Jackson. Even I can't explain it.

"Michael Jackson is crazy-insanely popular in Europe," explains Murat Tastan, 36, who came to the United States from Turkey fifteen years ago and has become an American citizen. "I came to New York in 1997, and not everybody is talking about Michael Jackson," Tastan marvels. "In Turkey, he occupied our lives; he was a huge, huge deal."

Tastan, who now lives in Florida, relates that he "watched a Michael Jackson *Dangerous* concert in Istanbul on September 23, 1993"—he remembers the exact date. "I watched it from a hill near the stadium with a group of friends. There were more than 40,000 in the auditorium, but the sound quality was good and we were so happy to be able to see him from the hillside. We loved 'Jam' and 'Heal the World,' which he sang, surrounded by kids. For the second half, they opened the doors and people streamed in.

"We skipped school to see his *Moonwalker* film in the movie theater. My friends gave me *The Making of Thriller* as a gift. Michael Jackson was pictured on our Pepsi-Cola cans. We watched him on Oprah in 1993. I was in grammar school when he got a Grammy Award. I've loved him since I was ten years old."

*   *   *   *   *   *   *   *   *

"What they often don't understand is how and why their grief is so gritty and so deep," Reverend Barbara Kaufmann wrote about Michael Jackson's admirers and fans, as she attempted to explain the pain. On her website, www.innermichael.com, Reverend Kaufmann—who is a minister and meta-physician—celebrates Michael and attempts to decipher his messages and meanings to the world. Claiming that Michael Jackson has 250 million admirers today, she attempts to comfort and inspire them in "Michael" directions.

"Many of them [MJ fans] have told me that they are surprised by the impact Michael's passing had on them—equivalent to a magnitude 7 or 8 on the Richter Scale," she wrote. This cataclysmic reaction is experienced by "old" fans, who followed and loved Michael across many years, and by newly-converted fans alike. "Some didn't know how deeply they could hurt. Some feel as if his leaving awakened something in them. It did. Many embarked on a personal spiritual journey....

"Michael was the lifeline of many. He was the one voice of sanity in a world gripped by so much insanity. For many, he was their hope, their confidante, their role model, their leader or guru."

Reverend Kaufmann points out that there is *no closure* with the death of Michael Jackson. The normal grieving process—usually following the path of initial shock, denial, pain, guilt, anger, bargaining, depression, reflection, loneliness, working through, reconstruction, acceptance, and hope—is not possible because the hype and media slant, by those who didn't know Michael, interrupt and taint the process.

"The man who was the world's greatest cheerleader, humanitarian and philanthropist was turned into a dark figure in the collective memory of the twentieth century and *that* hurts," the

Reverend explains. "It is especially vile when the realization hits that the dismembering of this gentle man was perpetrated only for profit. The manufactured books and stories about Michael Jackson sold and billions of dollars were made from siphoning the life from the man." She continues, "Michael did not have to die."

"If the real story were actually released into the culture ..., the fans would have some hope. If the whole sorry mess were exposed for what it was and the world was truly informed about the truth of this story [of Michael], and an acknowledgment was made of the damage, the fans could begin normal grieving. And eventually they would heal."

Michael Jackson fans "are trying to prevent another human being from dismemberment for sport and for profit," Reverend Kaufmann asserts, and she encourages that people simply listen....

Today, Michael Jackson's staunchest fans and admirers are contributing their time, talents, and money to worthy causes everywhere—in his name and in his memory. Disciples of the "King," they continue to spread his love throughout the world in concerted efforts to heal it. "I can't do it by myself," he sang out in the poignant song "Cry." His fans, old and new alike, have heard and internalized his greatest message.

Michael Jackson did the job he set out to do.

**It's the same wherever we go.
It really is. The love and appreciation ...
—so wonderful. The fans are so happy
and animated and it just touches my heart.
It's love. I pray is what I do. I thank God.**
— Michael Jackson
(October 30, 2003)

The Unwanted Chapter: Conrad Murray

**Before you judge me,
try hard to love me.**
"Childhood,"
Michael Jackson

**Lies run sprints,
but the truth runs marathons.
The truth will win this marathon in court.**
— Michael Jackson

It was 1:00 A.M. on Thursday, June 25, 2009, when his security guards brought Michael Jackson home from the Staples Center. Even at that hour, fans were standing in front of the imposing gate to Michael's leased home at 100 North Carolwood in Holmby Hills, California. No one could have any idea that Michael would be dead before his regularly-scheduled lunch with his beloved children, Prince, Paris, and Blanket, at 12:30 P.M. that same day.

Michael Jackson stopped to smile and wave at the excited group of fans. His driver paused the Escalade, at his direction, and he accepted the gifts that his admirers had brought for him. This happy ritual was the norm for Michael Jackson, whose ardent fans knew that he would usually acknowledge them, thank them for their devotion, and say "I love you." When that would happen, any amount of waiting for him seemed worthwhile to these people, who had come hoping for some tidbit of interaction or affirmation from Michael. He was always gracious and rewarded them with warmth and gratitude.

His security guards carried the gifts inside the home and placed them on the stairs. They said "good night" and left their tired boss to what would be his last night—and it would not be good.

Dr. Conrad Murray, who had driven to the home just minutes before Michael Jackson arrived, was waiting for his patient. Murray had been working for Michael, as his personal physician since an official date of May 8, 2009. Murray had actually started treating Michael regularly in April; reportedly, Michael Jackson asked the doctor to accompany him to London. Before that, Conrad Murray had occasionally treated Michael and his children for minor ailments, such as colds and flu.

Specifically, Murray, a cardiologist who owned and operated a clinic in Las Vegas, started treating the Michael Jackson family when they returned from Dublin, Ireland, in 2006, to settle into their rental home in Summerlin, only minutes away from the doctor's facility. During the spring of 2009, Murray was asked to become Michael Jackson's personal physician from that time through the superstar's last prospective concert, which was due to take place in mid-2010. AEG Live, the sponsor of Michael Jackson's *This Is It* concert series, was offering Murray a contract for his services.

Conrad Murray considered himself indeed fortunate to be able to become the doctor of *Michael Jackson.* He had been recommended by one of Michael's bodyguards in Las Vegas, a man whose father had been treated by Murray and then who himself became a patient.

Conrad Murray, an African American, was born on February 19, 1953, in St. Andrews, Grenada. He grew up in a poor "fractured family," in which he lived for years with maternal grandparents, who were farmers; later rejoined his mother at a young age; and did not meet his father until he was twenty-five. He moved to the United States in 1980; graduated from Meharry Medical College in Nashville, Tennessee; and completed his residency at Loma Linda University Medical Center in California. Murray opened a private practice in 1999.

"Unpaid debts, lawsuits, and tax liens have followed Dr. Murray's life," according to *Netflix* biography.com. "More than $400,000 in court judgments alone were issued against his Las Vegas practice, and in December 2008[,] Dr. Murray ... was ordered to cough up $3,700 in unpaid child support."

In 2009, Conrad Murray was married to a woman—since 1989—who was living with their two children in Las Vegas. He had a total of seven children with five women.

In the negotiations process between Murray and AEG, the doctor asked for $5 million, but the company agreed to $150,000 per month plus liberal expenses that included transportation, lodging, and other costs. Dr. Murray promptly sent out a letter to his patients, basically informing them that he had accepted a good opportunity for himself and that he would no longer be serving their medical needs. Michael Jackson became his only patient.

Michael wanted Dr. Murray to help him sleep. Suffering from profound chronic insomnia, Michael struggled night after night to sleep. While he was living elsewhere, such as in Las Vegas, he could function without sleep, if necessary, because his responsibilities were primarily those of an at-home father to his children. With his new mega-responsibility of preparing for a "comeback" that would exceed anything he had ever done before—to a record-breaking one million people across fifty shows—Michael felt *desperate* for sleep. How could he function unless he got the necessary rest and recuperative benefits of sleep?

[This author is married to a man who has suffered from a chronic sleep disorder, narcolepsy, for decades. After days of little to no sleep, an individual does become truly desperate for a night of undisturbed sleep.]

As was his style, Michael was not only singing and dancing in rehearsals, but he was overseeing every aspect of the incredibly elaborate, over-the-top show that included 3-D with a live audience, more than twenty songs, numerous costume changes, and mind-blowing choreography. Maintaining his energy level and general health was the *sin qua non* of the daunting imminent project that he had named *"This Is It,"* as his potentially last curtain call.

Just minutes before he arrived home in the wee hours of June 25, Michael had finished up that day's preparations for *This Is It.* The elaborate staging for the show had been moved to the Staples Center a few days previous. There, Michael had meetings related to various aspects of the upcoming show, and he did a full-out rehearsal with his dancers. "Earth Song," the most important message to Michael for his audience, was the last number he performed, and it capped the night of rehearsal. This performance was captured in the film *This Is It*, which was put together posthumously from more than 100 hours of footage that Michael's cameramen took across the weeks of practice and preparation. [His grateful fans are awed by his wisdom in filming all of his activities, a practice that he adopted many years ago. He would review parts of the footage to learn from it toward his goal of perfection.]

Exhausted and dehydrated, Michael Jackson took a shower and then set about the business of trying to sleep. As always, his mind was racing, his adrenaline flowing, and his tired body just not cooperating....

Dr. Murray started administering powerful medications to Michael Jackson as the slow hours of the night went by. Murray just kept giving his weary but emotionally "wired" patient one sedative after another. Finally, according to Murray, he gave his patient propofol at 10:40 A.M. Michael was dead before the paramedics arrived at 12:26 P.M., the time when he was supposed to be sitting down to enjoy his lunch with his three children in their dining room.

Dr. Murray claims that he came upon Michael, who had a "faint pulse" but was not breathing, at about 11:50 A.M. He told police that he had left the room for about two minutes to go to the bathroom. He left his patient unattended, unobserved ... while Michael's body was filling up with propofol....

Murray did not call 911 when he came upon Michael Jackson ... in fatal distress. Instead, at 12:12 P.M., Murray telephoned Michael Jackson's personal assistant, Michael Amir Williams, who was in his home in Los Angeles. He told Williams, "Get here right away; Michael had a bad reaction." He did not tell the man to call 911, and critical minutes were passing. Williams phoned Michael's on-site security men and told them to run to Michael's bedroom on the second floor.

Murray ran down a secondary stairway into the kitchen between 12:05 – 12:10 P.M., where he encountered the chef Kai Chase, preparing the lunch for the day. He appeared "in a panic," according to Ms. Chase, and he yelled for "security" and for Prince, Michael's twelve-year-old son. He never told the chef to call 911, and his failure to do so was inexcusable and probably served to ensure Michael's death. As would be discovered later, Murray was astoundingly without any monitoring devices, an audible alarm, or resuscitation equipment during his high-risk administration of powerful drugs, including propofol, to Michael Jackson.

Alberto Alvarez rushed into Michael Jackson's bedroom to see his boss on his bed, appearing to be dead. Murray was putting items into a bag, and he directed Alvarez to help him. The doctor started pushing on Michael Jackson's chest with one hand in what appeared to be some attempt to revive him. Alvarez made the telephone call, heard later around the world via media broadcasts, to 911 and the paramedics.

Dr. Conrad Murray did not tell either the paramedics or the emergency room doctors that he had administered propofol, the powerful, potentially lethal anesthetic that is used for surgery in a hospital setting or properly-equipped clinic. It is never used by medical personnel to treat insomnia—*not ever.*

Michael Jackson was rushed to the UCLA Medical Center, where emergency room doctors administered to him for more than one hour. These doctors would later testify in court that Michael Jackson had died at his home. They did their best to revive him, but he was already gone. He was pronounced dead at 2:26 P.M. His brother Jermaine appeared not long afterward in front of the assembled media cameras in order to announce that his brother, the King of Pop, was dead.

Mystery surrounded Michael Jackson's death, and for days it was not treated by authorities as the result of a possible crime. An investigation that spanned months took place, and, after a complete autopsy and tests and retests of the toxicology results, Michael

Jackson's death was ruled a homicide, due to acute propofol intoxication.

It was not until the late-2011 criminal trial of Dr. Conrad Murray for involuntary manslaughter in the death of Michael Jackson that the truth came out. Testimony by individuals who had some immediate connection to Michael's death on June 25, 2009, was powerful and revealing. Experts testified at length about the toxicology results and the other evidence. The coroner elaborated on his findings regarding the cause and manner of Michael Jackson's death: cause—acute propofol intoxication, and manner of death—homicide.

Bottom line, Michael Jackson died at the hands of Conrad Murray. The doctor administered the drug that killed him; he then let him die by not performing the appropriate medical procedures that could have easily saved him; and he did not call 911, which could have saved him "without injury" if it had been timely done.

On November 7, 2011, the jury in the Conrad Murray trial found him guilty of involuntary manslaughter. This crime carries a maximum sentence of four years in prison. The prosecutors could have charged Murray with a "bigger" crime, but they were seemingly afraid of overcharging him and risking a "not guilty" verdict. In the unrelated Casey Anthony case in Florida only weeks before Murray's trial, the mother of the dead little girl, named Caylee, was found "not guilty" after an intense telecast trial. Many people were appalled and outraged by this verdict, but the mother went free.

Regardless of the length of Murray's sentence, his name will go down in history with the likes of John Wilkes Booth. People will know his name. His worst punishment will likely be that he will be reviled.

The jury that convicted him consisted of 7 men, 5 women; 6 whites, 5 Mexican or Hispanic individuals, 1 African American. Six were "fans" of Michael Jackson; 5 of 12 either worked or had a family member who worked in the medical field. They were everyday people who did an extraordinary job.

The circumstances surrounding the consummately tragic event, the senseless death of Michael Jackson—mourned by his orphaned children, family members, and millions of fans around the planet—can best be understood in the progress of the Conrad Murray trial. An overview of the most relevant testimony and occurrences, in the opinion of this author, is presented in roughly chronological order from those court proceedings. [This author's input, clarifications, and opinions are placed in brackets throughout.]

On September 27, 2011—twenty-seven months after Michael Jackson's death—the trial of Dr. Conrad Robert Murray for involuntary manslaughter began at the Courthouse in Los Angeles. David Walgren, prosecutor, gave an opening statement in which he proclaimed that Michael Jackson "put his life into the hands of Dr. Murray ..., trusted Conrad Murray," who caused Michael's death "through repeatedly acting with gross negligence and repeated incompetent and unskilled acts." Murray, he pointed out, was not Board Certified in anything.

The prosecution played a recording that authorities obtained from Murray's iPhone. It was of Michael Jackson, with slurred speech, saying the following:

We have to be phenomenal. When people leave this show, when people leave my show, I want them to say, "I've never seen nothing like this in my life.... It's amazing. He's the greatest entertainer in the world." I'm taking the money, a million children, children's hospital, the biggest in the world, Michael Jackson's Children's Hospital. Gonna have a movie theater, game room. Children are depressed.... They're sick because they're depressed.... I want to give them that. I care about them, ... angels. God wants me to do it.... I'm gonna do it, Conrad.... Don't have enough hope, no more hope. That's

the next generation that's gonna save our planet ..., United
States, Europe, Prague, my babies. They walk around with
no mother. They drop them off, they leave – a psychological
degradation.... They reach out to me – please take me with
you.... My performances will be up there helping my children
and always be my dream. I love them. I love them because I
didn't have a childhood. I had no childhood. I feel their pain.
I feel their hurt. I can deal with it. "Heal the World," "We
Are the World," "Will You Be There," "The Lost Children."
These are the songs I've written because I hurt, you know I
hurt.
[Some seconds of silence; Murray says, "You OK?"]
I am asleep.

(May 10, 2009)

[There is no reasonable explanation for why Murray taped his
patient in this condition except for the prospect of one day selling
that tape for hundreds of thousands of dollars to a tabloid, or
blackmailing Michael Jackson. It is a felony in California to tape a
person without his knowledge or permission. It is also unethical for
a doctor to tape his patient without his/her permission.]

[In his obvious state of being under the influence of some
intoxicant or sedative—likely propofol—Michael Jackson was
revealing his true self, his deepest feelings. Uninhibited and
unguarded, he was sharing his dream of helping the children of the
world in a hospital that he would establish; he speaks of his deep love
and empathy for the children; and he discloses his own pain, which
he identifies with *their* pain. For a man who was having financial
problems, Michael's core thoughts and primary goal amazingly
remained focused on needy, abandoned, and ill children.]

Two days after this taping, Dr. Murray placed his *third* order
of propofol. [His first orders of the drug were placed on April 6
and 28, 2009.] David Walgren made the point that, as proved by

the recording he had made of his client, Murray knew what he was doing to Michael Jackson, and yet he continued along the unethical, dangerous path that led to destruction. In all, Murray ordered *255* bottles of propofol! That is the equivalent of *more than four gallons* of the potentially lethal drug. He treated Michael Jackson with it for his insomnia for six nights per week for two to two-and-one-half months.

From his phone records, it was shown that Conrad Murray was on 45 minutes of phone calls during the final hour to two hours of Michael Jackson's life—at a time when he should have been next to his patient, his *only* patient, for every second. In the 2-1/2 hour taped interview that the Los Angeles police held with Murray, accompanied by his two attorneys, two days after Michael Jackson's death, Murray said that he left his patient "to go to the bathroom" for a couple of minutes.

"Conrad Murray figuratively and literally abandoned Michael Jackson to fend for himself.... [This] violates the standard of care and decency.... He abandoned Michael Jackson when he needed help ... and all principles of medical care." Michael Jackson's "misplaced trust cost him his life," asserted David Walgren, and he then called the prosecution's first witness....

Kenny Ortega, Michael Jackson's friend, collaborator, and director of *This Is It*, testified that Michael was excited about his upcoming shows. He wanted to share them with his children, who had never seen him perform on a public stage; to do something important for his fans; and to use the concerts as a platform to remind people about the needs of our planet. Because Michael's first priority for his children was their education, they were being home-schooled when he was at meetings and rehearsals. Their father was purposely waiting for—and eagerly anticipating—his children to be able to see him perform live in London. They never did see their dad perform....

On Friday, June 19, Michael appeared to be sick at the rehearsal. Ortega had never before seen him in that kind of condition, and he had known Michael Jackson for nearly twenty years.

Very concerned about his friend, Kenny Ortega wrote an email to Randy Phillips, CEO of AEG (sponsor of the 02 Arena concerts):

Randy,
I will do whatever I can to be of help with this situation.... My concern is, now that we've brought the Doctor in to the fold and have played the tough love, now or never card, is that the Artist may be unable to rise to the occasion due to real emotional stuff. He appeared quite week [sic.] and fatigued this evening. He had a terrible case of the chills, was trembling, rambling and obsessing. Everything in me says he should be psychologically evaluated. If we have any chance at all to get him back in the light. It's going to take a strong Therapist to help him through this as well as immediate physical nurturing.... [H]e's lost more weight. As far as I can tell, there is no one taking responsibility (caring for) for him on a daily basis. Where was his assistant tonight? Tonight I was feeding him, wrapping him in blankets to warm his chills, massaging his feet to calm him and calling his doctor. There were four security guards outside his door, but no one offering him a cup of hot tea. Finally, it's important for everyone to know, I believe that he really wants this ...[;] it would shatter him, break his heart if we pulled the plug. He's terribly frightened it's all going to go away. He asked me repeatedly tonight if I was going to leave him. He was practically begging for my confidence. It broke my heart. He was like a lost boy. There still may be a chance he can rise to the occasion if [sic.] get him the help he needs.
Sincerely,
Kenny

The next day, a meeting was held at Michael's home, during which Conrad Murray chastised Ortega for "playing amateur doctor" and told the director to leave the doctoring to him, that Michael Jackson was fine.

[It was to the great advantage of everyone, including Murray, who liked his $150,000 per-month-plus-expenses, to keep Michael rehearsing at any price to him or to his health. Kenny Ortega had Michael's best interest at heart, but he may have been the only one in that category.]

There were no rehearsals on Sunday, June 21 (Father's Day), the day after the meeting, or June 22, on which day equipment was transferred to the Staples Center and set up for the stage. On June 23rd, Michael Jackson appeared with "energy and enthusiasm," according to Ortega. It was "a different Michael," he said. The next day, too, Michael was "the same," a full participant in all of the preparations—he rehearsed vigorously and consulted in the areas of production. He was "feeling great," according to his friend Kenny; "Michael said he was very happy."

Michael Amir Williams, the personal assistant to Michael Jackson, testified that he was his boss's friend and said that he had worked for him since mid-2007. Saying "He would do anything he could to show his fans he loved them," Williams clarified that Michael Jackson would interact regularly with fans in front of his house and at the auditorium. Michael had gone to the Staples Center about 5 P.M. on June 24th with multiple vehicles, as usual, and he had engaged in work toward the upcoming concerts.

Conrad Murray telephoned Williams on June 25; they spoke at 12:15 P.M. Murray said that Michael Jackson "had a bad reaction," that the assistant should "Get somebody up here immediately." Williams phoned Faheem Muhammed, head of security, who was typically stationed in the trailer outside of the house. Williams then left his home to head toward the Holmby Hills house, while Muhammed sped to Michael Jackson's bedroom after he finished the call from the worried assistant.

Faheem Muhammed, employed as a security guard for Michael Jackson for a period of ten months, testified that at 1:00 A.M., when they returned his boss to the house, the security team carried in the gifts and letters from his waiting fans and then left. He returned to the house at 11:45 A.M. that same day. He had left to go to a local bank, when he got the call from Williams, immediately after which he returned to his employer's home. He entered the bedroom minutes after Alberto Alvarez, his fellow security guard, arrived there. Muhammed testified that he immediately saw Michael Jackson, who appeared to be dead.

Alberto Alvarez, director of logistics for Michael Jackson, worked for his boss as part of the security team for six months. He testified that he had gotten many invitations to interview, and nine or ten offers of money, from media after Michael Jackson's death. One offer was for $500,000 and another for $200,000 (one of those from *National Enquirer*). Alvarez turned down all of the offers and had not spoken to media at all, at the time of his testimony. He stated that he was unable to get full-time employment and was accepting jobs for short periods of time to keep going. He had worked for Michael Jackson for a long time, including in Las Vegas for a few months.

Alvarez confirmed that he was the first one to arrive in Michael Jackson's bedroom after he got the phone call about a problem with his boss. He ran into the room, to see Conrad Murray putting items into a bag. Murray ordered Alvarez to help put vials of medication into a bag to assist him. Michael Jackson was sprawled on the bed; he appeared lifeless. It was Alvarez who [finally] placed the call to 911 at 12:20 P.M.

Michael's two older children, Prince and Paris, came into their father's bedroom and saw him on the bed. They stood just inside the door, but they could see their daddy, lying on his back, arms outstretched, and head turned slightly toward them.

[Both children were weeping, and Paris fell to the floor—"on the ground, balled up crying"—according to Faheem Muhammed's testimony. She was overcome by grief and despair.] Alvarez quickly ushered the children out of the room, and they returned downstairs.

[All of Michael's security guards were not only employees but fans of his. They tried to watch his rehearsals as much as they could.

On the day of Alvarez's testimony, a person who had come from Siberia to show support for Michael Jackson won the court lottery for a seat inside the courtroom. An airplane that pulled a long string of fourteen flags—one from each of fourteen countries—and a fifteenth flag of Michael Jackson's face passed over the courthouse. The plane, commissioned by Michael Jackson fans from those countries, was scheduled to fly overhead three times every week during the trial.]

Kai Chase, the personal chef of Michael Jackson since March 2009, was preparing lunch for the usual time, 12:30 P.M. Mr. Jackson liked to eat with his children at this specific time every day. Ms. Chase prepared meals for the Michael Jackson family six days per week, all three meals. She would arrive between 8:00 – 8:30 A.M. daily.

[It appeared that Michael liked to anchor his day by sharing lunch and conversation with his children; he ate dinner with them also, as he was able, depending upon his rehearsal schedule.]

The chef would make special healthy juices in a blender for Mr. Jackson for his breakfast, which was typically taken to him by Dr. Murray at about 10:00 A.M. A couple of times a week, Mr. Jackson would eat breakfast in the kitchen.

Ms. Chase began speaking on the witness stand with the announcement, "I'm brokenhearted." She said that she loved working for Michael Jackson; his was "a happy home" with children playing and music flowing throughout the house. She was preparing spinach Cobb salad with turkey breast for lunch on June 25th. Conrad Murray did not appear for the usual juices for Mr. Jackson, but he came down the stairs "frantic" between 12:05 – 12:10 P.M. He did not say "Call 911!" but he shouted, "Get help, get security, get Prince!"

Ms. Chase sent Prince upstairs, because she could see the boy not far from the kitchen. Knowing that something was

very wrong, she went into the adjacent room, where she joined
hands with the housekeepers, the teacher, and the children. They
prayed together and cried. Security guards came running into the
house and bounded upstairs. Some minutes later, the paramedics
arrived.

[That evening, September 29, Raymone Bain appeared
on television for an interview about her relationship with her
former boss and "friend" Michael Jackson. "I loved Michael,"
she declared. Her interviewer reminded Bain that she was suing
Michael Jackson, and she mumbled a response; she said that
Michael had been "okay" with her lawsuit. In truth, shortly before
his death, Raymone Bain filed a lawsuit against Michael Jackson,
seeking $44 million-plus.

Thomas Mesereau was interviewed on the *Joy Behar Show*,
HLN, in which he affirmed that Michael Jackson was "always
conversational, articulate, and cooperative" during the months that
he represented him as his defense attorney. Although it was the
most difficult of times for his client, Michael was always lucid and
functional. "He could trust no adult," Mesereau said; "everyone used
him eventually—they showed their true colors." Michael Jackson
attracted one profiteer after another. "I'm appalled by what he took
from all of us," the attorney said, shaking his head.

During that week, Michael Garcia appeared on HLN with a small
panel that discussed Michael Jackson. "He was a very gentle guy," said
Garcia. "He had no entourage" when Garcia worked for Mr. Jackson
in Las Vegas, only security guards. "He had a heart of gold ..., a great
attention to detail ..., and he was a great father." The security guard
affirmed, "I never saw him with any kind of drinking or any kind of
drugs. I did see him intoxicated a few times; what it was I don't know."]

Dr. Richelle Cooper, emergency room doctor at the UCLA
Medical Center, testified that she worked on Michael Jackson for one
hour. Dr. Murray, who was there, having accompanied [the body of]
his patient in the ambulance to the hospital, did not tell the doctor

that he had given Michael propofol. In fact, Murray revealed only that he gave his patient Lorazepam, which was only one of a number of drugs that he had administered. The E.R. doctors were treating Michael Jackson without this critically important information. It was Dr. Cooper who signed the death certificate of Michael Jackson. Murray, having refused to pronounce him dead at the house, thereby passed this responsibility to the E.R. doctor.

Edward Dixon, AT&T employee, testified to Dr. Murray's telephone records from the day of Michael Jackson's death. Among various calls, Murray made one to his office from 11:18 – 11:50 A.M., for 32 minutes. He also made a call to his girlfriend Sade Anding immediately after that phone call of long duration.

Jeff Strohm, a telephone expert from Sprint, testified that Murray also had a working cell phone from that company, which he used during morning hours on the day of Michael Jackson's death.

Dr. Thad Nguyen, cardiologist at the UCLA Medical Center, worked on Michael Jackson along with Dr. Cooper. When she entered the room, she asked Dr. Murray when he had administered drugs to his patient, when he had found the patient not breathing, and when 911 was called. To all of these questions Murray answered, "I don't know." He added, "I have no concept of time; I had no watch."

Dr. Nguyen testified that "Nothing could be done for Mr. Jackson." She stated that she had never heard of propofol being used in a bedroom of a home. Propofol has no antidote … except for the physician. [Without a drug antidote, the attending doctor needs to perform specific acts of resuscitation *immediately* when a patient stops breathing from the effects of propofol. Immediacy and correct procedures are critically important to save the life of the patient.]

Antoinette Gill, a patient of Dr. Murray, called him on June 25 in the morning. Dr. Joanne Prashad also telephoned Murray to ask him a question about one of his patients; her call was placed at 10:20 A.M. and they spoke at that time. [These people were called upon to testify in order to show that Murray was busy on the phone when he should have been attending fully to Michael Jackson.]

Consuela Ng, who served as a volunteer in Dr. Murray's Las Vegas clinic from 2005 to 2009, described her work and responsibilities there. She answered phones, did filing, took the cardiac patients' vital signs, and helped out in other ways. Along with three other women, paid employees, Ms. Ng did everything that was needed in the clinic. Consuela Ng said that she herself and Carol, Sara, and Lia—the other workers—"didn't know where Dr. Murray was"; they didn't know that he was in California. Ms. Ng testified that all four of the women at Murray's clinic were "cross-trained"; she clarified that "everybody does everything." Not one of the women was a registered or licensed nurse.

Murray sent out a letter to his patients, dated June 15, 2009, in which he informed them that he would be "on sabbatical." He failed to set up another doctor to be available for his patients in his absence, according to Ms. Ng. She confirmed that he telephoned his office on the morning of June 25, 2009.

Bridgette Morgan, who met Conrad Murray in Las Vegas in 2003 and continued a relationship with him into 2009, said that she telephoned the doctor at 11:26 A.M. He did not answer. [Murray was on the telephone with his office at this time.]

Michelle Bella, an exotic dancer who dated Murray, had met him in 2008. She testified that she made contact with Murray on June 25 by phone.

Sade Anding, a Houston cocktail waitress who met Murray in 2009, testified that he telephoned her on June 25, 2009. It was 11:51 A.M. when she started speaking with him. During that conversation, the doctor abruptly stopped talking. Ms. Anding said that she heard a commotion—it sounded to her like voices muttering, as if his phone was in his pocket—and she heard coughing. She repeated his name loudly but got no response. She then tried phoning and texting Murray, but still she got no response. [This is likely the time when Michael Jackson was in distress and was struggling to breathe.] It was about 11:56 A.M.

Nicole Alvarez, 29, took the witness stand and explained that she met Dr. Murray in Las Vegas in 2005. [Unknown to the jury, she was reportedly an exotic dancer who gave him a private dance at the club where she worked.] She was living with Conrad Murray, along with their newborn son, who had been born in March 2009. She was the mother of Murray's seventh child. An aspiring actress, Ms. Alvarez said that she spent her time going to auditions. She added, "I am taking care of my instrument." When prosecutor Deborah Brazil asked what she meant by her "instrument," Ms. Alvarez answered, "Myself." Conrad Murray was paying her monthly rent and helping out with her expenses.

Ms. Alvarez testified that she had been excited to be able to meet Michael Jackson at his home. Murray took her there on more than one occasion. Michael told her that he wanted to see her baby after he was born. [This situation reveals the lapses in patient confidentiality by Murray, breaching his professional and ethical responsibility to Michael Jackson, which behavior was verified by other witnesses.]

Conrad Murray telephoned Nicole Alvarez from the ambulance that was carrying Michael Jackson's body to the UCLA Medical Center for resuscitation efforts!

[The jury was never informed about Murray's wife and two children. Judge Michael Pastor had ruled, in pretrial proceedings, that neither Conrad Murray's nor Michael Jackson's personal history could be used in court unless a specific situation or witness was directly related to the manslaughter case and/or the date of Michael's death. Of Murray's four girlfriends at the time of trial, allegedly one was a stripper, another an exotic dancer, and a third an actress.]

Tim Lopez, pharmacist, testified that Conrad Murray ordered a total of *255 bottles* of propofol from him. The doctor told Lopez that he had a clinic in California [which was a lie] and that the pharmacy should ship the propofol and other specified drugs to the clinic. The address Murray provided, however, was that of the girlfriend with whom he was living, Nicole Alvarez. Murray also ordered "lots of supplies," including I.V. bags (for intravenous injections). Conrad Murray's credit card was declined in the spring of 2009, according to the pharmacist. Mr. Lopez admitted to having perceived these problems as "a red flag."

[It should be noted that Murray, as a cardiologist, did not have the credential, experience, or training to administer propofol, and he should not have been able to obtain it at all. *Anesthesiologists* are the specialists who do have these qualifications.]

Stephen Marx, DEA Computer Forensics Examiner, testified to the results of inspecting Dr. Murray's iPhone. On June 25, 2009, Murray emailed the company that was involved in providing the insurance for Michael Jackson relative to his performances for AEG and the London concerts. At 11:17 A.M., Murray sent out an email communication that denied that Michael Jackson was in poor health, "contrary to some reports" in the media. [This is both sad and ironic, as Michael would be dead in less than an hour!] This expert also extricated the May 10th recording of Michael Jackson's slurred speech from Murray's phone.

Elissa Fleak, investigator for the Los Angeles County Coroner's Office, testified to having found a variety of drugs in prescription bottles and twelve propofol bottles in Michael Jackson's bedroom several days after his death. The area was not yet designated as a crime scene; the death was "under investigation."

Paramedic Richard Sennett testified that Michael Jackson was dead by the time that he and his colleagues arrived on the scene in his bedroom. Dr. Murray never told them that he had given Michael propofol; he said that he had given his patient Lorazepam. When the paramedic returned to the bedroom to retrieve his equipment after Michael had been carried to the ambulance, he saw Murray—who looked very surprised to see him—busily putting items into a bag.

The paramedic testified that Michael Jackson "looked like a hospice patient." He was cold to the touch. Sennett saw the I.V. stand, used for administering intravenous drugs, next to the bed. [It is heartbreaking to hear that Michael Jackson looked so bad ... just *twelve hours* after he was working full-steam on the preparations for his *This Is It* concerts. Just hours before, he had been dancing with force and vigor, captured on film that was shown in the posthumous documentary movie. What did Dr. Murray do to this "healthier than average" man?]

On October 7, the interview of two and one-half hours—in which Conrad Murray spoke to two assigned police officers, with two of his attorneys at his side—was played for the jury. It had taken place at the Ritz Carlton in Marina del Rey on June 27, 2009. Murray said that he had given propofol to Michael Jackson at his home in order to treat his chronic insomnia on every night except Sundays across a little more than two months. He claimed that, on the day of Michael's death, he had given him "only 25 mg.," a small dose, at 10:40 A.M. He said that nothing but propofol worked for Michael Jackson, that "he would go anywhere to sleep." [On June 25, Conrad Murray administered to Michael periodic injections of sedatives and anti-anxiety drugs that included Valium, Lorazepam, and Midazolam. Nothing was working, and Michael still couldn't sleep. Murray claimed that he finally gave Michael the propofol at 10:40 A.M.]

Murray stated that he went to the bathroom for two minutes and then returned to Michael's room to find him not breathing but with "a faint pulse." The doctor said that he gave him CPR and tried mouth-to-mouth resuscitation.

Murray said *nothing at all* about the numerous phone calls in which he was engaged during the morning hours. When asked why he did not call 911, he answered that no land line in Michael Jackson's home was working and that, although he knew the address of the home (100 North Carolwood), he did not know the zip code. [This is an incredible story, of course, and from a doctor, a cardiologist. The authorities discovered before too long that Murray had—and was using—*two working cell phones*! And, there was a lot of phone activity during the time when Michael was under the influence of potentially deadly drugs, including propofol. On August 27, 2009, Michael Jackson's death became a homicide investigation.]

Saying that he did everything he could for Michael Jackson, Murray then explained, in detail, how he comforted Prince, Paris, and Blanket in the hospital after their father was declared dead. [Within hours of this audiotape being played in court, a representative of the Jackson family—and also Prince—reportedly denied to the media that this "comforting" by Murray had ever happened!]

Dr. Christopher Rogers, deputy medical examiner for Los Angeles County, testified to the specifics of the autopsy of Michael Jackson. At 5'9" and 136 pounds ["thinner than most"], Michael was within the "normal range" of body mass. Although he had chronic inflammation and scarring of the lungs—[not a life-threatening condition at the time]—Michael Jackson had a healthy heart and liver. "He had no arteriosclerosis," said the coroner; his good heart and clear arteries were highly unusual for a fifty-year-old man.

Michael Jackson was in "better than average health" at the time of his death, concluded the coroner.

The official cause of death was acute propofol intoxication [combined with the effects of other sedatives, chiefly Lorazepam.] The manner of death was determined as "homicide." Michael Jackson did not take his own life, according to the findings; he died at the hands of another person.

[That night, Mo Pleasure, keyboard musician for *This Is It*, gave an interview to Jane Velez-Mitchell on HLN about his experiences with Michael Jackson. Stating that the show was "85 to 90 percent ready" when Michael died, he elaborated, "He was amazing every day …; he was hitting his marks." Mr. Pleasure spoke about Michael Jackson as the "great person" that he knew.]

Dr. Alon Steinberg, a cardiologist with superb credentials, testified that Conrad Murray had "a direct causal role in the death of Michael Jackson." Based upon his intensive examination(s), Dr. Steinberg found Dr. Murray guilty of *seven* serious acts of gross negligence and extreme deviations from medical standards of care. He said that the doctor was "playing [Russian] roulette" with Michael Jackson's life.

Of the seven serious acts of gross negligence, according to Dr. Steinberg, *six* of these independently of each other—#1, 2, 3, 4, 5, and 7—could have killed Michael Jackson. The expert witness listed the gross negligence:

1) administering propofol as a sleep aid in a home was outrageous and unheard of;
2) the patient was unmonitored [even visual monitoring was lacking];
3) the doctor was unprepared for a [likely] emergency;
4) he had no equipment or appropriate medications for resuscitation or rescue of his patient from a bad reaction;
5) a timely call to 911 was not [attempted or] made;
6) the doctor kept no medical records at all (from April through June);
7) CPR was improperly done.

There was no "crash cart," which is required for the administration of propofol, in the event of an emergency. Patients often stop breathing when under the influence of propofol, but when "the breathing is done for the patient" through proper equipment and methods, it becomes routine rather than deadly. Murray had no backboard (for the proper administration of CPR) and he tried to perform CPR on a bed … and with one hand! He had no equipment, such as a simple breathing tube, or anything else for resuscitation of the patient in the event of breathing stoppage. He did not have the appropriate oximeter, with an audible alarm, to gauge the oxygen saturation level of the patient's blood, a critically important instrument.

Dr. Nader Kamanger, a sleep specialist, testified to "multiple extreme deviations from standards of care" by Dr. Murray on June 25, 2009. He called Murray's use of propofol for insomnia "inconceivable."

This highly-credentialed specialist concluded, "Conrad Murray caused the death of Michael Jackson." Dr. Kamanger said that Murray was guilty of "egregious violations of standards of care and abandonment of his patient." He used the words "unconscionable breach" on the part of Murray. The doctor's failure to call 911 was "shocking." Although he was supposed to be treating Michael Jackson's "profound chronic insomnia," Murray had never reviewed Michael Jackson's medical records from any other physicians; did not perform a review of medications that Michael was taking; and never arranged for a sleep study for his patient. A complete, systematic sleep study—that would include his medical history and a thorough review of all medications—should have been performed for Michael Jackson to establish what causes contributed to his extreme and chronic inability to sleep. Once *causes* are established, the appropriate treatments can be prescribed. "Conrad Murray made no attempt to get to the root of his patient's problem."

[One commentator on television that night said that "Giving propofol to a person who needs sleep is like giving chemotherapy to a person who needs a haircut!"]

[A woman from the state of Georgia, who was stationed outside of the courtroom, was interviewed on HLN. She had moved her home to Los Angeles so that she could be at the courthouse every day in support of "Justice for Michael Jackson."]

Dr. Steven Shafer, anesthesiologist and pharmacologist, was described as "one of two people in the world" so highly qualified in the areas of pharmacology and pharmacokinetics in general and propofol specifically. This doctor had done the research on propofol that directs its proper usage everywhere; he wrote the package insert for the drug.

Dr. Shafer testified that propofol does not cause sleep; it causes *unconsciousness*—an entirely different physical state; and it is totally inappropriate as treatment for insomnia. ["Propofol is an intravenous sedative-hypnotic agent for use in the induction and maintenance of anesthesia or sedation"; propofol "produces sedation and amnesia."]

This expert's conclusions regarding Conrad Murray in his treatment of Michael Jackson were that Murray committed *seventeen* egregious acts of violations of medical care standards, "any of which could lead to death." Of these seventeen egregious violations, *four* were "unethical and unconscionable."

He explained how Dr. Murray caused Michael Jackson's death, based upon the scientific evidence, and he stated that Murray violated the Hippocratic Oath that requires all doctors to put their patient first. "Conrad Murray put himself first every night of his treatment of Michael Jackson," Dr. Shafer testified. "He abandoned his patient and caused his death."

Among the egregious violations by Murray were the following:
There was no written informed consent, which is required for the procedures that Murray used.
There was no record-keeping at all by Murray—a fundamental requirement for doctors in their treatment of patients.
The lack of equipment required for the administration of an anesthetic (propofol) was inexcusable:
  no resuscitation equipment,
  no alarm to signal the patient's cessation of breathing,
  no proper control for the flow of propofol from the tube into the patient's body,
  no electrocardiogram monitor.
Murray violated the doctor-patient relationship (by being a "friend" and an "employee").
The doctor was guilty of abandonment by leaving his patient alone in a room where he was being given a potentially deadly anesthetic.

Lack of continuous monitoring and of documentation by the doctor while administering propofol was "unconscionable." Murray's not having called 911 immediately upon finding his patient in mortal distress was "unconscionable."

The doctor incorrectly did chest compressions with one hand on a patient who was on a bed [rather than on the floor or on a backboard].

Murray withheld vitally important information from the paramedics and E.R. doctors, never telling them what he had given the patient.

Dr. Shafer provided a thorough explanation of his findings....

The lack of informed consent, required in written form, "denies the patient of *autonomy*"—his right to make an informed decision about what is being done to him by the doctor.

The lack of any medical records kept by Murray for Michael Jackson, his only patient, across the span of approximately three months, was "ethically egregious and unconscionable." This violation denies the patient and his family of rights under state law— [and morally]—to know what happened to him. There should have been daily/nightly records, kept by hour, that included the specific medications and dosages, responses by the patient, and his vital signs.

The paramedics and emergency room personnel were treating the wrong thing, according to Dr. Shafer, because they lacked the critical information of what substances were administered to Michael Jackson. The rescue teams erroneously believed that the patient had experienced a major heart attack or disorder, while the primary problem was that he stopped breathing.

Murray's abandonment of Michael Jackson would be "expected to result in injury or death; it was completely foreseeable," testified Dr. Shafer. Michael Jackson could have been easily saved, the doctor said emphatically, if only Murray had been by his side when he stopped breathing and done the appropriate things, including calling 911, lifting his patient's chin, and inserting a breathing tube.

Dr. Shafer showed and narrated a film about the proper, required administration of propofol. He testified that Michael Jackson could not have self-ingested the drug, and even if he did somehow, Murray was still responsible for his death for having left his patient alone, under the influence of powerful sedatives and with deadly drugs within reach.

A very compelling portion of Dr. Shafer's testimony was that there are *13,000* articles related to propofol in the available medical literature for the use of the anesthetic. Of these, 2,500 are for sedation and *only one is for insomnia.* That one article is from a highly-controlled study, done in China and published in 2010. In that study, propofol was administered to subjects for only two hours. The researchers stipulated that this work was only *experimental* and needed more studies for any potential validation.

Dr. Shafer stated, based upon all of the evidence, findings, and scientific data, that Dr. Murray administered propofol through an intravenous tube—as he admitted to having done for sixty previous nights. The powerful anesthetic flowed through a bungled I.V. set-up that failed and poured propofol into the body of Michael Jackson, continuing to flood his system after he stopped breathing … and was already dead.

"Michael Jackson could not have killed himself," Shafer asserted, and he presented the reasons for this conclusion. The doctor had run tests and analyzed the data for every possible scenario of self-ingestion of propofol, and he concluded that the level of the drug in the decedent's body was too high for any explanation of self-ingestion. "It was Conrad Murray"—stated the expert witness—"who was responsible" for the fatal dosage ... and it had to have been through intravenous administration.

[Dr. Shafer also testified that, in his opinion based on the medical records, "Michael Jackson was not addicted to Demerol." The defense attorneys tried to make Demerol an issue during the trial even though there was no trace of the drug in Michael's body at autopsy.]

[It is chilling to note that the experts testified that Michael Jackson could have been easily saved, if responded to immediately upon breathing stoppage, and he would be alive today ... if not for Conrad Murray. If 911 had been called immediately—the paramedics arrived in four minutes when they were untimely called—Michael Jackson could have been saved "without injury."

Murray administered the deadly anesthetic to Michael Jackson, abandoned him, and thereby killed him, according to Dr. Shafer.

In addition, by not calling 911 immediately, Murray let him die. Theoretically, if he had given Michael Kool-Aid, to which he had a bad reaction and stopped breathing, *the doctor should have called 911*—the paramedics had necessary resuscitation equipment that was totally absent from Michael Jackson's bedroom. Murray's failure to do so—regardless of the specific substance that caused Michael Jackson to stop breathing—resulted in Michael's death. The doctor let him expire by engaging in other activities, which included spending time telephoning/calling other people and putting items into a bag, to hide them from the awareness of others. He apparently tried to hide the "murder weapon."]

"Dueling anesthesiologists" were the pivotal focus of the trial. Dr. Steven Shafer testified for the prosecution and Dr. Paul White testified for the defense. Interestingly, the two men had been friends and colleagues for thirty-three years! It appeared that, during the trial, their friendship may have been stressed to the point of ending it. After Dr. Shafer testified that Dr. White's findings were both "disappointing" and incorrect, White called Shafer "a name"—in some place outside of the courtroom where he was overheard—and Judge Pastor promptly issued a contempt of court citation to Dr. White.

[Dr. Shafer had unquestionable integrity and credibility because of the fact that, although entitled to thousands of dollars for his research and testimony as an expert witness, the doctor refused to take any money at all. He believed that what he was doing was important. He also wanted to educate the public to the "fact" that propofol is a good drug when used properly "by a doctor who knows what he is doing."]

After sixteen days of court testimony, the Prosecution rested its case on October 24, 2011. The Defense began its case on that same day. [This author is providing only those portions that, in her opinion, are most relevant.]

In his opening statement on September 27, Conrad Murray's defense attorney, Ed Chernoff, stated that Michael Jackson was responsible for his own death, and therefore his client was not guilty of the charge of involuntary manslaughter. The theory that Chernoff advanced was that Michael self-ingested the propofol that killed him, either by swallowing it or self-injection. The decedent supposedly took this action while Dr. Murray was "briefly" out of the room; the other drugs that Michael received on the day of his death, especially Lorazepam, contributed to his death. In combination, claimed Chernoff, they created the "perfect storm" that killed Michael Jackson. And in fact, the attorney alleged, Michael Jackson died so fast that his eyes were still open.

[During his testimony for the prosecution, expert Dr. Steven Shafer debunked the idea that there was any connection between the speed at which an individual dies and his eyes being open. In fact, Dr. Shafer said, he closed his own deceased father's eyes. Sadly and ironically, the doctor's father had died during the weekend previous to his testimony.]

Testifying during the first days for the defense was a number of individuals, most of whom spent only minutes on the witness stand. A 911 specialist testified that the 911 call for Michael Jackson was placed on June 25, 2009, at 12:20 P.M. Alexander Supall, police surveillance specialist, testified about the videotape at Michael Jackson's home on June 25; footage was shown of Michael Jackson's vehicles returning to his home at 1:00 A.M. on the day of his death. Orlando Martinez, detective for the Los Angeles Police Department, addressed questions related to the evidence that was taken from the crime scene.

Dr. Allan Metzger, a physician who had treated Michael Jackson on and off for years since 2003, testified that he had visited Michael Jackson at his home on April 18, 2009. They discussed nutrition, hydration, and stress related to Michael's profound sleep problem. Dr. Metzger said that his patient had suffered from a sleep problem for fifteen to twenty years, particularly when he was on tour and "couldn't come down" from his high-energy output at his performances.

Cherilyn Lee, nurse practitioner, who took the stand as an unwilling witness for the defense, immediately told the judge that she was feeling sick. She was allowed to leave the courtroom for a few minutes in order to recuperate. When she returned, Ms. Lee explained that she had earned a Ph.D., that she specialized in holistic medicine, and that she focused on nutrition and natural products in her nursing practice. She became Michael Jackson's nurse, visiting him in his home—after her initial visit to treat his children for colds—from February 1, 2009, to the latter part of April.

She gave Michael Jackson vitamins and nutrients intravenously on a number of occasions. She also served him nutritious "smoothies" that were especially formulated for him.

"Whatever you tell me, I'll do; I want to be healthy," Michael Jackson told her. She tested his blood on three occasions, and the lab results improved to normal readings on the third, after he had followed the nutrition regime that she prescribed. On Easter, April 10, Michael discussed his sleep problem with her.

Cherilyn Lee testified that, at his request, she watched Michael sleep through the night, during which she observed that he slept for only a few hours—approximately five—and then awoke. [Many nights Michael slept fewer hours and some nights not at all.] Usually, after two or three hours, he was wide awake and unable to fall asleep again.

When Michael told Ms. Lee that the nutritional treatments were not working for his sleep problem, he brought up the possibility of

Diprivan (another name for propofol). After researching the drug on his behalf, she told Michael that he should not take it. She further advised him, "No one who cares about you would ever give you that dangerous drug in your home." While on the witness stand, Ms. Lee became visibly emotional and wiped away tears.

On June 21, 2009, Ms. Lee testified, she received a phone call from one of Michael's bodyguards. Mr. Jackson was experiencing an alarming problem: one-half of his body felt cold and the other half hot. [Ms. Lee believed that this physical reaction was a side effect of propofol. Michael's body was becoming toxic.]

Randy Phillips, CEO of AEG, was called by the defense to testify about the upcoming concert shows and the amount of pressure on Michael Jackson to perform them. Phillips said that he had a meeting with Michael Jackson at the Bel Air Hotel in September 2008. During that meeting, they discussed the possibility of Michael's return to the stage at the O2 Arena, which AEG owned and operated. It was a spectacular venue and only for top-level performers because of its immense size. In January 2009, a deal was struck between AEG and Michael Jackson for the *This Is It* shows.

Michael Jackson had two conditions for doing the concerts. First, he wanted an estate of at least sixteen acres with a pastoral setting, running streams, and horses for his children. Second, he wanted a representative from *Guinness World Records* to be present at his last show [which was later planned to be a *fiftieth* show].

During May, there were no problems related to Michael and the show preparations. He was "laser-focused" on all elements of production, according to Phillips; "he was a perfectionist."

During the week preceding June 19, Michael was missing rehearsals. On June 20, 2009, a meeting was held at Michael's home; it was attended by Phillips, Frank Dileo, Kenny Ortega, Dr. Conrad Murray, and Michael Jackson. Murray assured the group that Michael would be fine. Regarding the concert, Michael told his collaborators, "You build the house; I'll put on the door and paint it." The men felt reassured.

On June 24, Randy Phillips was at the rehearsal at the Staples Center. He said that it was "an amazing rehearsal." In spite of the seasoned professional that he was—and not often excited any more about performing acts—Randy Phillips proclaimed, "I had *goosebumps* watching Michael perform his great songs."

Michael Jackson embraced Kenny Ortega and Travis Payne before he left for home. He hugged Randy Phillips and said that he knew that he could do these shows. Michael was happy, excited, and confident, according to Phillips.

"He was a phenomenal father," Phillips added. "His children were everything to him."

[Murray's attorneys tried to introduce into evidence the contract between Michael Jackson and AEG, but Judge Pastor ruled that it was inadmissible. The defense wanted to demonstrate how pressured Michael Jackson felt over the magnitude of his financial responsibilities and the concomitant need for him to succeed through the fifty scheduled concerts. Michael was ultimately due to repay AEG for millions of dollars that were being advanced to him and also for a number of big-ticket expenses that AEG was "fronting." Michael had recently received $15 million from AEG. He was known for keeping huge amounts of cash with him. Murray's defense likely wanted to raise the potential of robbery as the motive for some mysterious person who killed Michael Jackson by propofol in order to get his money.

The judge had also ruled during pretrial legal activity that Conrad Murray's financial problems would not be admissible. These included unmet obligations for his clinic and his home, and women seeking child support for his children.]

Of the fifteen witnesses for the defense, five were character witnesses. These individuals were former patients and "friends" of Murray. Each of them related their personal story of how Dr. Murray helped them with their heart problems and/or saved their lives. They called him "a good doctor" and "an excellent doctor."

"A bombshell day" for the defense came on October 27, 2011. [Except for the five character witnesses, there had been very few perceived victories for Conrad Murray during the previous four weeks of his trial.] Dr. Robert Waldman, addiction specialist, testified to his interpretation of medical records that were attributed to Michael Jackson, although they had been kept under an alias by the treating doctor Arnold Klein. [It should be noted that reportedly the medical records and prescriptions of *many* celebrities are kept and issued in aliases in order to avoid potential scandals from leaked publicity by greedy, unprincipled people who handle these items.]

These written medical records had been submitted to the court as those of Dr. Arnold Klein, long-time dermatologist for Michael. Referring to twenty-four Demerol treatments that Michael seemingly received, in conjunction with cosmetic and skin-treatment procedures across the months of April, May, and June 2009, Waldman rendered the opinion that Michael Jackson was "dependent on Demerol" and "possibly addicted" to it.

During cross-examination, the prosecutor pursued an answer to the question, "Based on these records alone, can you state absolutely that Michael Jackson was addicted to Demerol?" After a series of attempts by David Walgren to get an answer, the doctor finally responded, "Probably not."

[It should be noted that the only drugs found in Michael Jackson's system after his death were those that were admittedly administered by Conrad Murray. There was *no Demerol* in the toxicology results. The defense was trying to discredit the decedent and intimate that Michael Jackson contributed to—or caused—his own demise.]

In the cross-examination by David Walgren, Dr. Waldman was exceptionally uncooperative and non-responsive. The doctor refused even to disclose the identity of the clinics for which he was working. He also admitted that he had not even read the transcript of the long interview of Dr. Murray by the police, one of the most significant items of evidence in the trial.

[Murray's defense attorneys had managed to divert attention away from their client and onto Michael Jackson in a lurid way. The media predictably picked up on the testimony of Dr. Waldman and blasted lead stories onto television and computer screens about Michael Jackson "the addict."

That evening, on the *Jane Velez-Mitchell Show*, Thomas Mesereau spoke about the day's testimony. He stated, as he had done numerous times in the past, that he never saw Michael Jackson ingest a drug or appear to be under the influence during the fourteen intensely-interactive months when he defended Michael's life in his 2005 criminal trial. If ever there was a time when an individual would want to be taking prescription drugs for relief from anxiety, sleeplessness, and pain, it was during that hellish time in his client's life. Mesereau then appropriately reminded Velez-Mitchell and her viewing audience that the subject of scrutiny should be the accused, Conrad Murray, and not the deceased Michael Jackson, unable to defend or speak for himself in any way.]

Dr. Paul White, retired anesthesiologist, who had impressive credentials and knowledge of propofol and other sedatives, tried to convince the jury that Michael Jackson had self-administered the drugs that killed him. Dr. White had issued to Murray's defense team an early opinion—in March 2011—that Michael Jackson was responsible for his own death by having orally ingested the propofol or having self-injected it. When the medical science ruled out either of these alternatives, Dr. White—during the trial—commissioned a study by a Ph.D. researcher in an attempt to demonstrate that Michael Jackson had self-administered and caused his own demise. For his theory to work at all, however, he testified that Dr. Murray would have been outside of his patient's room for forty minutes instead of the two minutes that Murray claimed to police that he was absent from Michael Jackson's bedroom.

On cross-examination, Dr. White answered that he had already been paid more than $11,000 for his work and testimony in this case—with more expected to come, including his expenses. [Expert witnesses are typically paid well for their work. However, Dr. Shafer had declined any payment for his testimony, which directly and strongly contradicted his colleague Dr. White's position. On October 31, Dr. White was cited by Judge Pastor for contempt of court and fined $1,000—with a hearing to be held on November 16—for making a statement during his testimony on the witness stand that was helpful to Dr. Murray's case but that included an assertion of "fact" that was not in evidence and therefore inadmissible.]

Dr. White did not account for the large amount of propofol found in Michael Jackson's body at autopsy. He also admitted that he had not read the entire recent report from which he had taken the "findings" that he was presenting as valid!

In his closing statement on behalf of Murray's defense, Ed Chernoff did not refer to Dr. White's findings at all, and prosecutor David Walgren dismissed White's work as "garbage science."

Dr. Shafer was recalled to the stand on November 3, 2011, on behalf of the prosecution. He debunked Dr. White's position and asserted that Michael Jackson died from propofol that was administered intravenously from a drip—not a single injection, as Murray had claimed. This was the only valid scientific interpretation for the amount of the drug in the body of the decedent. Michael Jackson was *not* responsible for his own death, Shafer stated firmly. Even in the [unlikely] event that Michael Jackson had somehow increased the flow of the drug into his system, Murray's absence from the scene was abandonment of his patient, and full responsibility for this death was Conrad Murray's and his alone. He had left his patient, with dangerous drugs that the doctor had administered flowing through his veins, and abandoned him to an avoidable death. When he found his patient not breathing, he did not call 911 for help.

On November 3, after a total of forty-nine witnesses and 330 exhibits, the trial of Conrad Murray drew to a close. In his closing argument, David Walgren reminded the jury that Michael Jackson's children were orphans because of Conrad Murray; that the doctor's actions and failure to act—in numerous demonstrated ways—directly caused the death of his patient. Murray violated the sacred trust between doctor and patient "each and every day," Walgren asserted. Murray had demonstrated "consciousness of guilt" by many of his behaviors, including lying to paramedics, E.R. doctors, and the police. Walgren affirmed, "Michael Jackson trusted Conrad Murray with his life … and he paid with his life."

In his closing statement, Ed Chernoff blamed the victim, Michael Jackson, for his own death and asserted that his client, although unarguably guilty of acts of negligence, was not guilty of the death of his patient. Chernoff tried to discredit the testimony of numerous witnesses for the prosecution and implied that there was a conspiracy among these people against Conrad Murray toward a guilty verdict. The attorney asserted that "Conrad Murray was just a little fish in a big dirty pond."

The jury would need to determine whether there was "reasonable doubt" regarding Conrad Murray's culpability in the death of Michael Jackson. The prosecutor pointed out that Murray need only be found as a "substantial cause" of the death for him to be found guilty. Did his gross and egregious acts of negligence and of commission rise to the level of a crime—involuntary manslaughter?

[During his criminal trial, Dr. Murray did not take notes and he always appeared somehow detached. To this author, he looked like a cross between a fox caught in the headlights and a man struggling with acute boredom.]

[All of the members of the Jackson family, including Katherine and Joseph, regularly attended court sessions. They were a united family once again … for Michael.]

"*Guilty!*" After ten hours of deliberation across two days, the jury found Conrad Murray guilty of having caused the death of Michael Jackson. When the verdict was read in court on Monday, November 7, 2011, there was a collective gasp of relief and joy among the assemblage. Outside the courtroom, many hundreds of people wept, shouted, prayed, and hugged each other. Finally, some semblance of justice for Michael Jackson....

[Outside of the court building, people from around the globe were gathered in support of Michael Jackson. Murray had a small number of supporters at the fringe of the multitude of Michael's fans.

A woman from Iran spoke to a reporter about how she was representing her country in support of Michael Jackson. She described how she had bought his records in secret—at the risk of her life—and carried them home under her arm. She came to Los Angeles in gratitude for what Michael Jackson had given her—and her countrymen—during terrible times. "Iran loves Michael Jackson!" she exclaimed into the camera.

A young woman confined to a wheelchair had come from Canada "because Michael Jackson always loved and helped people like me," she said as she bowed her head. Michael comforted and helped the handicapped and disabled wherever he went. She was at the courthouse, paradoxically in her wheelchair, "to *stand up* for him because no one stood up for him in his life."]

In response to the jury verdict of "guilty," Judge Michael Pastor addressed Conrad Murray, declaring that he had been "reckless" and "responsible for the death of a human being." He was potentially a flight risk because he had ties to other states [Texas and Nevada]. Judge Pastor remanded him—without bail—to confinement. Murray was immediately handcuffed and led from the courtroom by the authorities. His sentencing was set for November 29, 2011.

[With a *maximum* sentence of four years in prison, Conrad Murray's punishment seemed outrageously light for his crime. As a convicted felon, however, he will not likely practice medicine again in the United States.]

On November 29th, Judge Michael Pastor sentenced Dr. Conrad Murray to the maximum sentence in the state of California for involuntary manslaughter, four years of confinement. Murray was due to serve his time in the county jail because of overcrowding in the state penitentiary. [His actual time served will be subject to a California law that was recently passed because of overcrowding in detention facilities. Murray's sentence is likely to be no more than two years of time in detention.]

The defense had presented the court with documents related to Murray's life before the "last chapter" with Michael Jackson, in which they portrayed him in a positive light for the court's consideration. The prosecutor, David Walgren, reminded the court of the egregiousness of Dr. Murray's numerous acts of commission and omission that killed his patient Michael Jackson. Brian Panish, attorney for the Jackson family, delivered their message to the judge. He said that Michael's family members grieve for him every day. They miss not being able to hold him, laugh and perform with him. His children miss their father, "best friend, playmate, and dad."

Judge Pastor announced that he had considered the totality of everything submitted to the court by both sides. He concluded that Conrad Murray was guilty of having abandoned his vulnerable, trusting patient Michael Jackson, not on just one day but during the weeks preceding that day. He said that Michael was a "medical experiment" to Murray, who repeatedly risked his patient's life by giving him potentially-deadly propofol in dangerous circumstances. Across many weeks, Murray was also involved in a "pattern of deception" that included his lying to numerous people, including key medical personnel who could have made a difference, police, and Michael Jackson's employees and business associates. This was not a medical malpractice case, the judge made clear—it was a criminal case for manslaughter. Murray caused the death of Michael Jackson. He had been reckless and involved in a "cycle of horrible medicine." He was a "disgrace to the medical profession."

The most compelling aspect of the case for the judge, he explained, was the "surreptitious taped recording" that Murray made of Michael Jackson in his most vulnerable state; he was slurring his words. The judge was "horrified to think of that happening to anyone." This tape was an "insurance policy" for Murray, proclaimed Judge Pastor. If things went wrong in the future between them, Murray could blackmail Michael Jackson with that tape and/or sell it to the media.

Citing "absolutely no sense of remorse" by Murray at any time—including in his "faux documentary, faux reality" program that the doctor made and released via television—the judge called him "dangerous to the community." He was shocked by the behaviors and attitude of Murray, who said that he "had done nothing wrong," "blamed the victim," and "even seemed *offended*" by his death. The judge sharply criticized the "money for medicine madness" to which Murray succumbed. The judge added that he would not accept blaming others—or potential others—or the victim, Michael Jackson, for the doctor's decisions, actions, and culpability.

A hearing on the issue of restitution by Conrad Murray to Michael's family and children would be conducted in the future. Financial restitution would be ordered, said the judge, but he needed more information regarding the appropriate monetary amount than he had received to date. [Michael Jackson's Estate provided data to the court that showed that his prospective earnings for his imminent concert series exceeded one hundred million dollars.]

*   *   *   *   *   *   *   *   *

As in his life, Michael Jackson was treated with disrespect and sensationalism in his death and during the trial of Conrad Murray. The media, as usual, focused on the aspects of his death that were deemed lurid and shocking. Accusations of his having been a "drug addict" and "drug dependent" flooded through the coverage. Ratings and revenues for the media skyrocketed on the days that featured stories about Michael Jackson's alleged problems with prescription drugs, exposed dead body, and slurred speech recorded by Murray. Of course, Michael Jackson was not there to defend himself.

They ripped Michael Jackson open like a bag of birdseed with a knife. Cries of "Foul!" only served to fuel the desires of many in the media to do even more, to go even further.

Power can be intoxicating—and often even more fun than love or sex. The media had full power to do to Michael Jackson, his image and reputation, anything at all that they cared to do … with no accountability or liability. *What a bonanza!* They could eclipse *superstar Michael Jackson* by rushing into the spotlight that followed him everywhere, including in death.

As part of the prosecution's case, a photograph of Michael's body—covered by a sheet, on a gurney—was shown during the opening statement. Some days later, a photo of Michael Jackson's unclothed body—with a strip of cloth covering his private area—on a slab in the morgue, was shown in court. These photos were displayed over and over again—in printed media, across the Internet, and on television programs. [This breach of ethically-based standards was unprecedented. Dead bodies of celebrities, political figures, and everyday people are not displayed for lurid and/or shocking public consumption. The body of Osama bin Laden, for example, was never shown to the public … in spite of widespread cries for validation of his demise.] *Poor Michael Jackson.* The very private Michael would be appalled! His family, friends, and fans *ached* for him and themselves.

Thomas Mesereau wisely said, at a previous time, "The media's goal is never justice. Ratings, revenue, and advertising dollars are the media's only concern. They will constantly look for the entertainment value … and exploit whatever furthers their profit."

The "blame the victim for his own death syndrome" played out before, during, and after the Murray trial. Although defense attorneys are charged with finding ways in which to represent the best interest of their clients, "ethical boundaries can be crossed in their dogged pursuit of that goal," wrote attorney and legal analyst Matt Semino. Using aspects of the victim's life to discredit him to the jury is "a weapon that can be lethal if taken too far, denigrating the victim with each cut and ultimately corroding justice to its bone."

Semino continued, "When it is only the words of the accused against the silence of the deceased, who is there to defend the victim from false accusation and innuendo?"

Judge Michael Pastor had wisely ruled that the details of Michael Jackson's financial and legal affairs and of his mental and physical condition were not admissible at trial except to the extent that any of these had direct bearing on his death on June 25, 2009. It was the responsibility of the twelve jurors to seek the truth "through the smoke and mirrors" so that "justice can be properly served without the victim ever being victimized again," Semino opined. [*Wishful thinking....*]

On September 21, 2011, six days before the start of the Conrad Murray trial, *USA Today* featured a front-page, lead article with the insightful proclamation, "His doctor faces charges, but 'Michael is on trial.'"

The unanimous jury verdict on November 7, 2011 serves to acquit Michael Jackson of culpability in his death. It confirms that he *was* the victim of a homicide. Michael's legacy will include and reflect that fact.

*   *   *   *   *   *   *   *   *

During his last days, Michael Jackson no doubt felt extreme pressure. It must have been for him like being on a treadmill that just keeps going faster and faster. He wanted to perform for his children and his fans ... and it had to be wonderfully good.

He was desperate to sleep; he would do *anything* for a good night's sleep. He "hurt." Michael had never recovered from the deep psychological wounds of having lost his childhood and of having been brutalized in a malicious trial (in 2005). The healer was himself unhealed. Michael internalized his grief; he wanted to be numb, to avoid that pain. He was soul weary, ... and who among us cannot understand that, especially when we learn about some of the truly *unique* struggles that were his alone?

A man with such a nurturing personality—with a burning desire to heal the world and save its children—received no nurturance at all. Although loved by millions, Michael was lacking the love of a significant other, a spouse, a mate, a best friend. He was basically alone.

If someone who loved him had been by his side on June 25, 2009, he would be alive today. If Conrad Murray had not "treated" him, he would be alive today. According to a review of the evidence and testimony at Murray's trial, Michael Jackson could probably have done the fifty concerts at the 02 Arena if he had the appropriate medical treatment and support. He was trying so hard to make his "comeback."

What a loss! He was not able to fulfill his dream, this man who worked so hard for so long to bring to others the fulfillment of their dreams, to bring them hope.

If on that fateful day Michael Jackson had a professional massage, a warm spa-tub bath, some loving conversation with someone who cared about him, would he be alive today? That question may seem Pollyannaish, but it is a common-sense one, and it makes sense to many people who have been salvaged by simple acts of love.

Instead, Michael Jackson got worse than back-alley treatment for his medical needs. His exorbitantly-paid "doctor" was with him overnight rather than a caring, sharing person. Who has ever heard of an otherwise-healthy person dying from insomnia?

Tragically, for Michael Jackson the role of a trusted loved one was filled by a series of sycophants, opportunists, and profiteers who tried to monopolize and control him for their own benefit. Michael Jackson was a *commodity* to those in his inner circle, to many in his life. He was the *currency* for their self-seeking goals. All he really wanted was to be loved.

It is shocking to realize that, while Michael was dying, his beloved children and a coterie of employees were only steps away from his bedroom, and standing at the iron gate in front of his home were people—waiting for a mere glimpse of him—who loved him.

Michael had great plans for the future. He wanted to live in a permanent home once again, one with horses and other animals for himself and his kids. He wanted to tour after the London concerts. He planned to release singles and albums of new original songs. He hoped to make movies, which he had loved and enjoyed all of his life. He wanted to see his children grow up; he wanted so much to go on that journey with them. He wanted to build a hospital for children, where those whose mothers didn't want them could be cared for and provided with a movie theater and game room to escape from their pain.

Michael Jackson was ultimately too trusting of others. He projected his own feelings of warmth and love and trust onto others, believing that they were as well-intentioned and other-directed as he.

The hyenas in Michael Jackson's life have had to make way for the vultures after his death.

The beat goes on....

The lawsuits continue. In civil court, Katherine Jackson has filed a lawsuit against AEG and Joseph Jackson has filed a separate lawsuit against Conrad Murray and AEG. Both of Michael's parents are alleging guilt and blame on the part of AEG for the wrongful death of their son. Hopefully, they will prevail because the homicide of their beloved son should be addressed in an appropriate way; it is a matter of dignity and justice. Lloyds of London is also involved in a legal dispute with AEG related to Michael Jackson's death. There may be more litigation coming.

There is incredible injustice in Michael Jackson's parents, family, and orphaned children not even knowing exactly what happened to their loved one! They not only lost a much-loved son, brother, and father, but they do not understand *how* they lost him … at the age of fifty, in better-than-average health … and with so much to live for.

*   *   *   *   *   *   *   *   *

Michael Jackson was like a modern-day Icarus from Greek mythology. Icarus's father fashioned for his son wings of wax and feathers for Icarus to be able to fly away from imprisonment. Icarus successfully and joyfully flew through the sky, but—alas—he soared too close to the sun. His wings melted, and he fell to his death. He had been *so glorious* as he swept across the heavens.... *Only* Michael Jackson, in our lifetime, has soared so close to the sun.

Now that the difficult and troubling trial of Conrad Murray has become a topic for the history books, we can turn our attention once again to Michael Jackson *in his glory* as an unparalleled artist and humanitarian.

We can grieve for the man again, now that we know that he died at the hands of another … and we realize how senseless and tragic his death was. We can see now more than ever the humanity of the man who was Michael Jackson, and we can recognize our own humanity in his plight. We can love him for what he gave to us, what he left to us, and who he was.

We can remind ourselves that he was happy on the night before he died. He felt a renewed faith in himself and in his future.

We can now turn to *celebrating his life.* And we should.

He would be proud of his legacy—his three beautiful children, the incredible body of work to which he bound his soul, and his tireless and fruitful acts of charity around the globe.

Michael longed to be loved wherever he went. He gave us a mission....

"What More Can I Give?"

— Michael Jackson

Rest in peace,
Michael Jackson,
King of Pop,
King of Hearts.

THE LEGACY
OF MICHAEL JACKSON

**We only live once.
Since we are given the gift of life
it should be our persistent endeavor
to immortalize ourselves.
No matter what field of endeavor we choose.**

Michael,
Michael Jackson

**I know the creator will go.
But his work survives.
That is why to escape death
I attempt to bind my soul to my work.**
— Michael Jackson about himself,
quoting Michelangelo

Rose Giuseppe was escorted by a tall, uniformed young man to the "Reserved" section inside the cavernous Staples Center auditorium on July 7, 2009. She had won a coveted seat, through an Internet lottery system, at this special ceremony of mourning and tribute to Michael Jackson. She was wearing the wristband that was required for entrance into the sprawling building. Rose realized that this would be a gut-wrenching experience for her ... and so many others.

She had traveled from Rome, Italy just for this experience. Rose borrowed the money for the trip from her elderly father. The forty-six-year-old knew that she would have to work for two years, when she returned home to her job as a secondary school teacher, to repay her dad. Rose *had* to be here; she felt both lucky and incredibly sad. She could feel her heart within her chest as if it had greater weight than hours ago; it was beating hard.

Her memories of Michael Jackson were vivid, exciting, and poignant. He was so vulnerable, she knew, and so caring. Her neighbor's dying child Anthony met Michael at a hospital on the day before his concert performance in Rome, Italy. Rose met Michael fleetingly when she was at the fringe of a huge crowd at the Flaminio Stadium, several hours before Michael's *Bad* concert on May 23, 1988. His bodyguards, clearing the way for him, allowed her to extend her hand to him, and, when he saw the bandage covering her left eye, he squeezed that hand and smiled while looking directly into her eyes. Rose felt electrified, and the moment stayed with her forever.

Rose Giuseppe had decided that she would force herself to struggle through the epic-level testimonial service in order to honor, by her presence and participation, her inspiration and her idol, Michael Jackson. Rose taught handicapped children, and she had made it her business to follow, as much as possible, Michael Jackson's involvements with ill and dying children as he toured across Europe and other continents. She most remembered his warm smiles as he interacted with the children of all races and ages.

Rose was struggling with powerful feelings, the depth of which surprised her.

The Staples arena was full to capacity. At least 20,000 attendees were seated and several hundred more were standing. An estimated 50,000 individuals stood outside the Staples Center. Many people claimed their standing spot during the previous evening and then waited overnight so that they would be nearby, even though they were not fortunate enough to obtain a reservation-only seat inside. People had come to Los Angeles via planes, trains, boats, buses, taxis, and automobiles from myriad countries and from cities across the United States—an [estimated] unprecedented two million of them.

During the previous week, 1.6 million Michael Jackson fans and admirers registered online for a chance at 8,750 no-cost pairs of tickets for the Memorial of the Decade. A random drawing determined the attendees, who would be allowed to watch the grand musical tribute to Michael Jackson and to celebrate and mourn him along with 2,500 special-invitation guests.

Within a 25-block radius surrounding the Staples Center, the Los Angeles Police Department assigned 3,000 police officers to secure the perimeter of the area and to ensure the safety of the swelling numbers of public mourners. The freeway to the Center from Forest Lawn Memorial Park was blocked off and was lined with people of all ages for a span of miles.

The large crowd of somber people was not gathering in this filled auditorium for an NBA championship game or the Los Angeles Lakers but for the only memorial services for Michael Jackson that would be accessible to a segment of the population. Untold millions were watching around the world, and the memorial would be repeated on a 24/7 basis via the Internet for many days to come, making it possible for billions of people to view it.

It was apparent that this singer, dancer, superstar, and humanitarian was indeed, in Berry Gordy's words, "simply the greatest entertainer who ever lived," in life and in death. Michael Jackson would be pleased, Rose thought, as she sat amidst the eerily silent crowd, her head bowed. She felt herself fill up with a mixture of pride for having made this journey, grief like she had felt when her mother died, and love. She felt a kinship with everyone in the auditorium, a kind of inexplicable bond....

Michael's closed, solid-bronze casket, plated with 14-karat gold and covered with dozens of blood-red roses—fitting for a king— was not originally expected to be at the Memorial, but his family decided that it should be present.

When Mariah Carey opened the service with Michael Jackson's from-the-heart ballad "I'll Be There," she started out clear and strong. But when the gold casket came out, carried by Michael's brothers, all wearing a single white-sequined glove in tribute to him, Ms. Carey winced and her voice faltered. The ever-professional singer later explained that she was so affected by the sight that she found herself fighting back tears and struggling to continue with the moving song. She later apologized for the lapse in her performance.

Stevie Wonder, Lionel Richie, and Jennifer Hudson sang Michael Jackson songs. With his face contorted by pain, Jermaine Jackson performed his brother's favorite song, "Smile." John Mayer played guitar; Brooke Shields, Berry Gordy, and Smokey Robinson delivered very personal eulogies; and Queen Latifah read "We Had Him," a lovely poem written for this occasion by Maya Angelou. Heartfelt messages were read from Diana Ross, who referred to Michael as "part of the fabric of my life," and Nelson Mandela, who addressed all of those who were grieving for his beloved friend with simple words, "Be strong."

Reverend Al Sharpton delivered a pointed message, during his fiery eulogy, while looking directly at Prince, Paris, and Blanket, who were sitting in the front row with their grandmother Katherine. "There wasn't nothing strange about your daddy," he proclaimed in a forceful voice; "it was strange what your daddy had to deal with." He received a standing ovation. The reverend continued, "Every time he got knocked down, he got back up," and the applauding audience again jumped to their feet.

"Gone Too Soon," Michael Jackson's passionate ballad that was originally dedicated to the memory of his prematurely deceased young friend Ryan White, resounded through the auditorium. Usher sang the poignant words for his friend and mentor Michael, while his hand rested on the golden casket. His voice broke at the end: "Born to ... inspire, to delight. Here one day, gone one night."

The dignified memorial—spiritual and somber—seemed wonderfully personal. It ended with all of Michael Jackson's family members gathered on stage, amid a choir singing his sweet yet stirring ballad "Heal the World."

Making the first public statement of her life, eleven-year-old Paris spontaneously and unexpectedly spoke into the microphone: "Ever since I was born, Daddy has been the best father you could ever imagine, and I just wanted to say I love him—so much." Paris, dissolving into tears, turned into the warm embrace of her aunt Janet.

With that courageous act of twenty-six words heard around the globe, Paris turned her daddy into a real person, turned the King of Pop into Michael Jackson, the man, the father, the son, the brother, the uncle, the friend....

The performers at this church-like memorial service had been chosen to pay tribute not only because they were A-listers, but because each of them knew Michael Jackson and loved him for the gifts he shared with them, his genius, his inspiration, and his friendship.

Tears flowed, not for show but from that core deep inside the heart that stores our humanity, our despair, and our sense of forever.

We will never again see him explode onto a stage, proud, majestic, dazzling and beautiful. We will never again see him dance with such fluid elegance and wonderful precision. We will never again hear him sing with such passion and conviction from his very soul.

We will never again watch him call to us, with both his voice and his bountiful spirit, to join him in loving one another and in working to make the world a better place … for everyone. Michael was boundless in his love for the planet, for animals, and for human beings from every corner of the earth. He worked and sang for the homeless, the discarded, the ill and dying, the unknown and forgotten. He knew suffering and he knew joy, both in full measure.

To those who were hurting around the world, Michael Jackson often said, "I am so sensitive to your pain." And he was.

He also resolved to bring joy through his music to everyone he could reach. The Reverend Lucious Smith closed the memorial ceremony by reminding the attendees, "All around us are people of different cultures, different religions, different nationalities, and yet the music of Michael Jackson brings us together."

*   *   *   *   *   *   *   *   *

People young and old and in between, from countries of all shapes and sizes on six continents, joyfully and sadly played his music and short films (videos) on recorders, radios, computers, iPods, mobile phones, and television sets. Those who had forgotten him remembered; those who didn't know him felt stirrings of curiosity, reverence, and even longing. Millions of his admirers, veteran fans and new coverts, listened to Michael Jackson music over and over again.

If we play his music enough, maybe he will come back to us....

Michael Jackson's spirit has reincarnated, figuratively if not literally, into the hope and joy of more generations. Youngsters everywhere ask, "Who *was* that man?" By the millions, from India to South Africa, from Canada to Brazil, from Oregon to Georgia, they seek the answers and learn to love him ... like their parents and grandparents before them.

With the benefits of hindsight into decades of history, they can review all that Michael Jackson was and experience all that he left us. Via the Internet, they can network with each other, visit and create thousands of websites, and both commiserate over his death and celebrate his amazing life.

Michael Jackson transcended time and space; he wowed one generation with its favorite music and then another and another. He experienced unparalleled popularity and success in North America, Europe, South America, Africa, Asia, and Australia.

Massively talented and precocious, Michael Jackson was thrust into the spotlight as a child, took to it with remarkable grace, and embarked on a spectacular, head-spinning career that spanned forty-five years. He pushed, moved, and then broke the boundaries; slid chameleon-like from one genre to another; and became recognized as one of the most influential entertainers of all time. He defied definition and labels.

Not only has his music invaded cyberspace but it is played throughout the civilized world, in media outlets, restaurants, pubs, nightclubs, shopping malls, elevators, airplanes, gymnasiums, dance studios, and theaters. His dance moves have been imitated, incorporated, simulated, borrowed, and envied. Professional dancers marvel at the creativity, fluidity, and precision of his dance steps and routines. Seemingly "boneless" at times, Michael Jackson performed moves like no one else, full-bodied movements that included crotch-grabbing and across-the-floor slides that made him appear to levitate from the floor.

Michael Jackson was a prolific composer; he created hundreds of songs from sentimental ballads to rousing pop music with driving beats. He not only excelled at a variety of genres but he combined and blended them: classical music, rhythm-and-blues, gospel, country, reggae, disco, rock-n-roll, heavy metal, jazz, pop, hip hop, soul, and even Caribbean and African beats. Some of his most stirring songs are reminiscent of the religious revival mode, enhanced by his exuberant, fall-to-the-floor song-and-dance delivery. "Man in the Mirror" is a prime example; it became Michael's anthem at his concerts.

Today, as in past decades, Michael Jackson continues as an inspiration to musicians of all genres in all countries on the planet. This is a staggering thought ... but it is a truthful assessment.

In October 2010, James Delisco, a young man from a poor neighborhood in Jacksonville, Florida, performed as the headliner in the city's symphony orchestra tribute concert, *Windborne's Music of Michael Jackson*. He imitated Michael's voice and moves as he sang the iconic songs. James did well, to an appreciative audience.

What brought a hush to the crowd was his story about how he came to be in this place on this night, doing this performance. With his head bowed, James spoke softly into the microphone. "When I was just a little boy in 1984," he explained, "Michael Jackson gave a free charity concert at the Gator Bowl for children who were disadvantaged, with no money and no hope. I was one of those kids. We were bused to the stadium on that very exciting day. When I heard Michael sing 'Human Nature,' it was the first time I ever cried at hearing music. It was then that I decided that I wanted to follow in Michael's footsteps."

James did follow ..., and he had just signed a contract with a major show in Las Vegas, "all thanks to Michael Jackson." Emulating his life-long idol, James began the Lil' Angel Project, which works to educate and heal children through artistic presentations, encouraging them to find imaginative outlets for their personal expressions.

Michael's generosity of spirit and behaviors has had ripple effects that no one has mapped or measured, but this young man is only one of myriad people who took Michael Jackson as their example and role model, and then fashioned and followed their dreams.

With a heart as big as his talent, Michael Jackson dedicated himself to serving as the messenger of peace, hope, and joyfulness. He believed that it was his *job* to dedicate himself to healing the world. Through his songs of universal love—such as "We Are the World," "Heal the World," "Man in the Mirror," "Cry," and "What More Can I Give"—Michael touched the souls of so many.

In "Earth Song" he implored us to save our planet—its shores, forests, and animals—from violence, pollution, and war. Long before Al Gore's *An Inconvenient Truth*, before "going green" became a catchphrase, Michael produced "Earth Song," one of the most unusual and audacious protest songs in popular music history. This desperate musical plea, on behalf of a troubled planet, was inspired by moving experiences Michael had during his *Bad* Tour. He composed his "magnum opus," as it has been described, when he was alone in his hotel room in Vienna, Austria. It was a massive hit globally, topping the charts in more than fifteen countries, but, ironically, it wasn't even released as a single in the United States. Perhaps America was not ready for a call to action for a hurting planet. Michael Jackson, from his depths, wanted to transform us, to take us to a better place, *together.*

If you experienced it, you know and you can never return to a time when you were not an admirer of Michael Jackson. If you never experienced it, there is still hope that you will.... His fans get it. They're everywhere, and when they get together, there develops a special bond between them. Sometimes they finish each other's sentences about Michael Jackson.

They feel like they enjoy a personal relationship with the man who so longed for a connection to people. Through his music and messages he reached the hearts of millions with transcendent energy and ineffable charisma.

Many thousands of people have made a difference in their social and geographic environments by becoming involved in charitable causes of all kinds in Michael Jackson's name and in his memory. By his example and his beckoning, Michael has inspired people everywhere to continue his humanitarian work. The Make a Better World Foundation—as one of numerous examples—is a non-profit organization that has promoted non-monetary involvements by people from all backgrounds and cultures in order to recognize the beauty in diversity and to improve our world. Under its auspices, individuals have made a commitment to do volunteer work or demonstrate love for a sick neighbor, stray dog, homeless person, or neglected child. A Million Trees for Michael, through the non-profit American Forests organization, collects donations for trees to be planted in Michael Jackson's name. New forests will eventually be created, beginning with the first "Michael Jackson Memorial Forest" on a dedicated tract of land in California.

*   *   *   *   *   *   *   *   *

His pride and joy, his three children—Prince, Paris, and Blanket—are his greatest living legacy, perpetuating Michael Jackson's memory, humanitarianism, and charity. Already they are following in their father's footsteps by working with the homeless population in Los Angeles. The children have announced their intention to continue his work on behalf of the needy and downtrodden. "It's all about love," they say, echoing Michael Jackson's often-repeated refrain.

Paris dramatically fashioned a piece of Michael Jackson's legacy when she proclaimed to the world at his Memorial that he was the best father that could be imagined and that she loves him so much. It is noteworthy that Paris, at her young age, used the word "love" in the present tense, as opposed to "loved." It is almost as if she realized that her words would catapult her father's image into the perceptual arena of a real, flesh-and-blood human being. Within that one minute, she raised his image from just a demigod or caricature to a daddy and a man who is more and greater than his performing self.

Paris gave her father a great gift. Michael Jackson should be remembered for his *goodness* as much as his *greatness*. Future generations should know him for his humanity and global acts of charity and kindness as well as for his unprecedented artistic accomplishments. As people read, research, and review his life, the nasty and unfounded accusations and tabloid rumors against him will be known for what they were.

In 1997, the official results of a worldwide poll revealed that Michael Jackson was indeed the most recognized person in the world; the Pope was second. Sadly, it was his death and its media coverage around the planet that have served once again to elevate his status, prestige, and recognition—and all deservedly.

His Memorial service forced us to stop and look into our rear-view mirrors, to see Michael Jackson there, … and to say *"Wow!"*

＊　＊　＊　＊　＊　＊　＊　＊　＊

Michael, a collection of Michael Jackson's songs that were completed posthumously by his collaborators and Estate, was released in December 2010. It became the #1 global album after its release, with 3 million units shipped worldwide by the end of February 2011. The album's continuing success proves Michael Jackson's importance as a superstar and global icon; his music continues to transcend languages and cultures.

Within two months, *Michael* achieved platinum status in seventeen countries—the United Kingdom, Germany, France (2 times), Italy (2 times), Spain, Denmark, Poland, Russia (2 times), Austria, Belgium, Czech Republic (5 times), Canada, India (2 times), China, Taiwan, Korea, and the Middle East. The album reached gold status in eighteen countries—Australia, New Zealand, Brazil, Japan, Hong Kong, Indonesia, Malaysia, Philippines, Singapore, Finland, Greece, Hungary, Ireland, Portugal, Netherlands, Norway, Portugal, and Sweden. It continues to sell in profusion. One of the singles from the album, "Hollywood Tonight," reached the Number 1 spot on the *Billboard* charts in May 2011.

Michael Jackson's music is being played in pinnacle-level programs, such as *Glee, American Idol,* and *Secret Millionaire.* His 32-foot-tall statue, the only remaining one of nine such statues from his *HIStory* Tour, is placed permanently in tribute to Michael Jackson in a McDonald's parking lot near Amsterdam in the Netherlands. People visit from far and near to place flowers, say a prayer, or just view and photograph the magnificent sight. A best-selling, interactive Wii dance game by Ubisoft Entertainment, *Michael Jackson The Experience,* has been launched; it teaches Michael Jackson's iconic dance moves. In Japan, the Mobage company has released a new game, in which players must master eighty different dance moves, including the moonwalk; the ultimate goal is to get the King of Pop to perform a concert in outer space.

In 2010, Michael Jackson emerged as the second top-earning celebrity with $275 million going to his Estate; Oprah was first; and all of the others at the top of the annual "What People Earn" list took in less than $115 million. Michael Jackson's place in the chronicles of commercial success is guaranteed once again; he broke many such records in what music historians have described as his "wonder years."

Destined to become as popular in death as he was in life—and perhaps even more so—Michael Jackson joins a limited number of celebrities and entertainers whose body of work continues to be loved and appreciated everywhere. There will be more books, movies, and television specials about Michael Jackson; there will be repackaging of his music catalog. His unpublished music will be massaged and tweaked and then issued for eager fans and admirers. He will likely generate an eight or nine figure annual revenue stream for many years ahead.

Michael Jackson was "the most searched-for male" online in 2009, according to *Guinness World Records 2011*, and he "achieved more world records *after* his death" than before, including unprecedented numbers of downloads and albums sold.

Such statistics are only part of the Michael Jackson picture, however. His influence on the world of music is immeasurable; his impact on modern culture is profound. And why? For his talent, charisma, heart, passion; his philanthropy and humanitarianism; his vulnerability and uniqueness; for his greatness.

The Michael Jackson Tribute Portrait has been undertaken in order to honor Michael's memory. When completed, it is due to tour around the world. This portrait of Michael's face is being painted by internationally-recognized artist David Ilan, using a specific style called *pointillism*, which means that it is done entirely in single same-size dots. On a website designed to promote the portrait, Michael Jackson fans and admirers are invited to contribute one dot to the painting on a no-cost basis. Each dot has a specific placement that becomes known to the contributor, who is also able to write a personal message for Michael. One million dots are needed to finish the portrait.

People from more than 180 countries have contributed to this portrait of Michael Jackson to perpetuate his memory. *What a legacy! He would be proud.*

*   *   *   *   *   *   *   *   *

"Peace, my brother; it is a pleasure to meet you," Michael Jackson said to L. Londell McMillan when the men first met each other. "The pleasure was truly mine," McMillan wrote in his moving tribute to Michael, "The Greatest Ever." As co-executive producer of *The Source* magazine, Londell came to know Michael well.

"Please help me to protect my family and preserve my legacy," Michael said to his publisher friend on more than one occasion.

"I got you!" Londell McMillan responds today, as he adds:

There are millions of people around the world who love you and will never forget. You will live forever ...
Peace to the King!

Michael Jackson cared about his legacy. He often thought about what he would leave behind. Many who knew him relate that he spoke about his actively working to create a body of work—in music and in love—for which he would always be remembered.

J. Randy Taraborrelli captured the essence of Michael Jackson:

... [He] had a unique ability to inspire, to give hope to, to unite. Where others have tried—and often in vain—to use their talents and skills in a way that honors God and the inherent goodness of his nature, Michael Jackson was able to unite millions of people, regardless of race, creed, religion, age, gender, sexuality or nationality, behind messages of service and sacrifice, peace and love, hope and change and the freedom of expression.... He gave a voice to the voiceless, a face to the faceless and hope to the hopeless....
I cannot imagine a world without Michael Jackson in it.

*　　*　　*　　*　　*　　*　　*　　*　　*

It is the intention of the author of this book to add an important, credible, and informative volume to the library—printed and cyber—of works about Michael Jackson. Especially his last years were private and mysterious; he wanted it that way. Now, however, it seems critically important to disclose the information and events that will fill the gap for those who care about him and also challenge the mounds of misinformation and lies in the public domain about this gentle, loving, misinterpreted and misrepresented man.

This book should be evaluated within the context of published material about Michael Jackson, so much of which is based on hearsay, sensationalized tabloid stories, and unverified media accounts of his life and behaviors. Conjecture, rumor, exaggeration, and downright lies run rampant when it comes to Michael Jackson, who kept his life mostly secret for huge spans of time.

Now, some of the very few people who genuinely knew the man—his personality, strengths and weaknesses, comings and goings, triumphs and disappointments, joys and pain—have provided the "guts" of this book.

Michael's defense attorney, Thomas Mesereau, discovered the most private side and intimacies of his famous client, who became his friend through the process. Week after week, before and during the five-month trial, he was privy to Michael Jackson's deepest feelings, the intricacies and complexities of his lifestyle, his sexual behaviors, and all of the sordid accusations made against him.

By virtue of his job in defending Michael Jackson's life, in keeping him from prison and likely death, he became like a clergyman to Michael. With the protection of attorney-client confidentiality, Michael could tell him anything and everything about himself and his life. Theirs was a rare and intensely intimate relationship, forged by Michael's innocence and Mesereau's passionate dedication to the vulnerable, suffering victim who was his client.

His attorneys, Thomas Mesereau and Susan Yu, lived through the most painful, turbulent, and frightening time of Michael Jackson's life, *at* his side and *on* his side. His trial was a game changer, a life-transforming trauma, a torturous lesson like none other. They shared this ride through hell together.

Thomas Mesereau has contributed graciously, generously, and caringly to this book in the hopes of healing Michael Jackson's soiled reputation, of restoring his image to its rightful place, and of vindicating his innocent client to the public at large. He understands better than anyone else not only what the unscrupulous media did to his client but what toll their barbaric attacks took on him. If there is justice in this world, it is time to right this wrong. It is time to restore Michael Jackson to his deserved place in history as a loving, innocent human being.

Michael was a victim who ultimately maintained his dignity and his nobility of spirit.

Boyd Williams, Baron James, and Michael Garcia interacted with Michael Jackson and his children on a daily basis; oversaw his email communications; escorted him everywhere he went; and became privy to conversations, correspondence, and financial records. During the last (approximately) year-and-one-half of Michael Jackson's life—before his move to Los Angeles toward the end of 2008—they stood with him and beside him; they guarded him, his children, homes, vehicles, and belongings; they transported and protected him. They happily did his bidding, ran his errands, and arranged for his everyday needs.

These men came to know the man behind the invisible curtain between him and nearly everyone else in his life. Michael Jackson revealed his real self, through glimpses into his everyday behaviors, to his security men who were entrusted with guarding his very life and the lives of his precious children.

Across time, he came to trust them more and more, and they became confidantes during times of great stress and emotional need. He occasionally sought their opinions, which they gave with gratitude for having been asked. Laughter, tears, smiles, and frowns, from times of seemingly vibrating excitement to moments of quiet respite—Williams, James, and Garcia shared it all with their boss.

The three men accepted a level of responsibility and range of duties for Michael Jackson and his little family that far exceeded their original expectations or the norm for security assignments. To say that they had no idea what they would experience and observe with this amazing man when they embarked on their remarkable journey is an understatement. Three men came together from very different paths to embrace an extraordinary opportunity and to experience a kind of intimacy with Michael Jackson that they rarely witnessed between him and others during their months of service.

Boyd Williams, Baron James, and Michael Garcia were "different men" when they came out at the other end of their *in vivo* education from Michael Jackson. He had taught them more than they could ever articulate. They had learned about him as a man, the exorbitant price of mega-fame, and the inexplicable complexity of his life. They had learned about trust and its ugliest outcomes. They had to learn to deal with their own anger, frustration, and pain throughout the months of their witnessing the outrageous machinations of the people in their boss's world.

Through their revelations, these men can make a significant contribution to Michael Jackson's legacy by providing testimony to his having been a genuinely good man, excellent father, and loving humanitarian. They can provide a context for the behaviors of a man who had to adapt to dreadful circumstances in the best way that he could.

These three people are proud to say that they knew this man. They consider themselves "blessed."

Michael's spiritual adviser during the last months of his life also became his friend and advocate. Reverent June Gatlin came forward in 2010 to share with the public some of the struggles of her beleaguered, yet courageous, client in his quest for spiritual growth and peace of mind. Michael confided in her some of his misgivings and worries about mundane matters, such as his financial representatives and loss of control of his own affairs.

Reverent Gatlin presents insights into the spiritual, seeking Michael, who was also "very human" and committed to working toward unity and peace in the world. He so loved his children and his mother. Reverent Gatlin encouraged Michael through her "readings" for him and strong words of support, summoning their shared African-American heritage of suffering and triumph.

David Nordahl, who first met Michael Jackson to teach him art and painting, became a genuine and loyal friend across more than two decades. When he was approached by this author as a potential contributor to this book, David responded: "I would be honored.... I'm always thrilled to be part of anything that will keep Michael's memory and legacy alive."

David would spend several weeks at a time, visiting Michael at Neverland, and he also traveled with him. He became Michael's full-time artist, doing thousands of sketches for the eventual paintings that he created, working for months on each—beautiful pieces with bold color, incredible details, and vivid themes. Faces of people are especially noteworthy in Nordahl's paintings, which are so true-to-life that they look like stunning photographs. Many of his works represent Michael with children.

During his countless interactions with Michael Jackson and his children, David Nordahl came to know the man intimately. Calling Michael "as normal a person as I've ever met," David recounts many early-morning encounters with his friend. Michael, unable to sleep, would seek out Nordahl for conversation.

"I don't want to wake you," Michael would say at a time around 3 A.M. David would always respond that he could sleep later; the two men would then talk and talk; and Nordahl would "always learn something new and interesting" from his younger friend.

Michael liked to laugh, but he didn't laugh much when Nordahl visited him for a span of three weeks during the time of his trial. "He tried not to dwell on it, but it bothered him deeply," the artist recalls. "He didn't talk much to me about it, but he was disappointed in the U.S. justice system. It was unbelievable. The authorities should have realized how vulnerable he was, that he was the victim of *numerous* extortion attempts. I believe today that the trial sucked the soul out of him." Nordahl's paternal feelings for Michael and his undying love for the man are obvious and deep. The talented artist painted a beautiful *verbal* portrait of Michael for *Defending A King ~ His Life & Legacy.*

The author of this book has attempted to capture the essence of the real man, the Michael Jackson who was a human being in every way. Vulnerable yet persevering, jubilant and despondent, fragile and strong, caring and wounded, Michael Jackson revealed and shared his true, complicated self to his defense attorney, security guards, artist-mentor, and spiritual adviser. Thanks to them, we can put together a composite picture of this king of a man ... and we can cherish it.

*   *   *   *   *   *   *   *   *

Michael Jackson's legacy will be full, rich, and multi-dimensional. It will expand across time. It will bloom like a beautiful flower. Hopefully, it will metamorphose into a softer, gentler thing as the years pass and the truth about Michael Jackson pervades our cultural environment. Other countries are ahead of the United States in this evolutionary process, but we can catch up....

For Gardner Street Elementary School in Los Angeles, Michael donated a large sum of money in the eighties and the Michael Jackson Auditorium was established. During the time of the allegations against him in 2003, the school administration boarded up the "Michael Jackson" letters above the exterior front door of the building. Stubbornly, the Superintendent refused to uncover the name, even in the face of criticism and scorn from people around the world. "Is this the American way?" many asked. "How can Michael Jackson's generosity be so shabbily treated by this ill-advised public disgrace of covering his name?" Michael was found guilty of *nothing*; he was innocent—and the generous benefactor of this school, which he had attended for a short time as a child. His own children were living in Los Angeles. The fans were livid. Finally, in mid-October 2010, only days before a public school board meeting at which the matter was to be decided, the Superintendent directed the wooden boards to be removed, and Michael Jackson's name was again prominently displayed ... and rightfully so.

Today, in sharp contrast to their having dishonored him, the school community has embraced Michael Jackson. Kenneth Urbina, the principal of Gardner School, is proud to show the "Michael Jackson Room," where photos and posters of their "most famous former student" are displayed. A videotape of Michael accepting the honor of the auditorium's naming plays continuously, and the chalkboard that he autographed—"Love the Children, Michael Jackson"—is encased under protective glass. With the substantial donations that the school receives from visitors to this room, a special music program for students has been launched. Children receive musical instruments and instruction, and the second-floor classroom that was Michael's has been transformed into the "Michael Jackson Music Room."

When this author visited Gardner School in June 2011, people from Japan were there. They had traveled to Los Angeles to pay tribute to Michael and to see "his" auditorium and the hallways that he once walked. The same staff member who hosted him during the school's dedication ceremony in 1987 was the welcoming overseer of the Michael Jackson Room. She wept when she spoke about her interactions with the man, whom she described as "so humble, quiet, and nice." Today, she points out the various memorabilia to visitors as if she were a proud mom, and her eyes fill with tears when she watches Michael's videotaped acceptance speech along with the foreign visitors. The students, administration, and staff honor their connection with Michael Jackson; they celebrate him; and their impressive music program continues his legacy by combining children and music. He would be pleased.

There are those who consider Michael Jackson divine. A thread in the fabric of his legacy is representative of people who perceive Christ-like virtues and behaviors in Michael Jackson. Some believe that he was the Archangel Michael incarnate. A sect of the Jehovah's Witnesses espouses this belief.

There is a worldwide movement of ardent fans who have been inspired by Michael, whose lives have changed because of him. In Russia, a recently published book entitled *Michael Jackson P.S.*

advances the theory of Michael's divinity. His persecution by mean-spirited officials and his suffering are acknowledged as redemptive and compelling for devotion by others. Artists' renderings of Michael with a crown of thorns and in crucifixion pose are included with poems and prose about his transcendent qualities and his inspirational example to others.

The consummate tragedy in Michael Jackson's life was that the evil ones against him used the very essence of his goodness, his love for children, against him. They twisted the quality with which he defined himself and fashioned his life-course into something dirty, wrong, and criminal—at least they tried hard to accomplish that sinister goal.

The Russian perception of Michael Jackson as an iconic victim parallels that of American author Dr. Wayne Dyer, who said:

> Not only is that heartbreaking, but immoral in my opinion, that this innocent man was persecuted as he was by this world and particularly the United States—his home country. I am and always will be ashamed of what was done to Michael Jackson by this country.... Michael was essentially lynched in the U.S.... [H]e is not only the man in the mirror, but the mirror itself reflecting back to this country its own ugliness, greed, ignorance, and hate.

An Angel Among Us, written by Louisiana-born Elizabeth Michelle Billeaudeaux and published in 2010, portrays Michael Jackson as a divine being, sent by God to lead us in the healing of the world, and as a messenger and prophet. Using Biblical references, numerology, Egyptian lore, and astrology, Ms. Billeaudeaux explains the rationale for her conclusion that "Michael Joseph Jackson was a divine gift from God ...[,] an angel ... more specifically the archangel Michael or ChristMichael":

> He was sent here to love us, bring us together, and remind us of what was truly important in life: our children, our planet,

ourselves. With the first breath of baby Michael on August 29, 1958, our lives were changed forever....

The author relates her belief that, although Michael "has to take some of the responsibility for His own life path, ... I feel He was less to blame than those chosen to keep Him safe.... Michael had ... childhood trauma and also had very limited experiences with the *real world*...." She continues, "He did not have the proper gauge inside Him to allow Him to choose the best possible 'handlers,' 'gate keepers' or associates." Ms. Billeaudeaux presents Michael's special challenges:

The reason He was less capable of caring for Himself was because Michael was an ancient soul, but a child-like human. I believe that He spent much of His time in the *ethereal* world, as opposed to the *material* one. His thoughts on spiritual matters were amazing, but He needed more support dealing with the physical matters.

Michael's "cosmic energy," "strong life-flow," and spirit continue their influence on our world, even though he has left this physical dimension. Ms. Billeaudeaux wrote her book to memorialize Michael Jackson, to advance his legacy, and to work through her own grief over his passing. Having loved Michael Jackson since she was six years old, Elizabeth has always felt like she had a past life with him. Her relationship with Michael has kept her "warm, hopeful, and perseverant"; her love for him is second only to her love for her young daughter. In her steadfast convictions, she quotes Gandhi, who said, "Even if you are a minority of one, the truth is the truth."

She has become a good friend to this author, consistently supportive and encouraging. Ms. Billeaudeaux affirms that she wants people to find a connection to Michael Jackson, and she will assist in that direction in any way that she can.

"Major Love Prayer," a worldwide network of Michael's followers, has begun a monthly tradition, taking place "in every country on earth" at exactly the same time. Inspired by Michael Jackson's desire to heal the world, the group's mission is "to make a change with love." Every 25th of the month—in memory of Michael's passing on June 25, 2009—all members join together in prayer, meditation, and intention. At 2:00 P.M. Los Angeles time, everyone involved in Michael's "Army of Love"—"Soldiers of Love"—stops in silent prayer and reflection, knowing that they "are one in L.O.V.E."

*   *   *   *   *   *   *   *   *

A unique distinction of a large segment of Michael Jackson's fans, "his soldiers," is the recurring, forceful advocacy role they have embraced on his behalf and for his legacy. From his 2005 criminal trial, at which he faced unjust, unfounded accusations, to the outrages after his 2009 death, his fans have adopted concerted ways to support Michael. They have shown up, carried placards and banners, signed petitions, written and sent various kinds of communications, and boycotted advertising sponsors and media outlets.

His fans, by the millions, demonstrated continuous support in numerous ways, across more than two years, for "Justice for Michael Jackson." They took action while they waited for the September-November 2011 jury trial of Dr. Conrad Murray, with the shared ardent hope that the man who had caused Michael's premature death would be punished and that Michael would be exonerated of the accusations of having caused his own demise. Countless people flocked to the Los Angeles courthouse for various preliminary hearings and for the six-week trial. They rejoiced over the appropriate outcome on November 7, 2011—the guilty verdict.

A probing documentary that covered every aspect of Michael Jackson's autopsy—long before the criminal trial of Conrad Murray—was produced, but it was shelved because of the overwhelmingly negative public response, led by Michael's fans.

Posthumous photos of Michael Jackson were splashed across the media, to a flood of shock and criticism from his supporters and other stunned people everywhere. The documentary that was prepared, with professional assistance, by Conrad Murray—who was convicted of having caused Michael's death—was shown on television even before his court hearing was held to sentence him for having been found guilty of manslaughter. Unscrupulous, ill-directed media telecast the unprecedented material—in which Murray spoke to the general public although he had not taken the witness stand at his criminal trial—but the program was appropriately canceled in some countries before it was aired. Worldwide protests had been registered by Michael Jackson's supporters, and some media outlets responded to the collective outrage by refusing to telecast the Murray documentary.

Michael Jackson's fans and admirers are continually poised to champion decency, decorum, and respect in matters that relate to Michael. He deserves no less.

*   *   *   *   *   *   *   *   *

In the former Soviet Union, Michael Jackson's legacy is especially rich and unique; he has become a legend. Russians remember him for his courage, humanity, and big heart. Today, one of his fan clubs there boasts 10,000 members, who actively perform works of charity that include raising funds for worthy causes in Michael Jackson's name.

The remarkable story spans many years for the Russian people. When Michael Jackson's music was banned by Soviet officials because they feared his capturing "the hearts and minds" of their youth, his records and albums sold briskly on the black market. To the Russians, Michael Jackson became an icon and a symbol of the freedom, creativity, and diversity of America.

When the Iron Curtain came down in 1989, control by the government weakened and softened, if only by degrees across subsequent years. When Michael courageously planned to travel to Moscow to perform a *Dangerous* concert at the Luzjniki Olympic

Stadium (with a seating capacity of 50,000) on September 15, 1993, his organizer was allowed to schedule the performance, but the KGB actively discouraged people from attending. According to Larisa Krasnoschek, the current president of the Michael Jackson Fan Club in Russia, members of the KGB stood at train stations, bus stops, and other transportation centers to sternly tell the people, "There will be no Michael Jackson concert." They also intercepted people at ticket booths, announcing, "There are *no* tickets to Michael Jackson's concert."

The government-controlled media had announced that Michael Jackson would not be coming; anyone who showed up would be an impostor. The Russian people wanted these predictions to be wrong.

At the Moscow stadium, thousands of hopeful people who lived nearby and could not afford tickets to the concert gathered there so that they might perhaps catch a glimpse of Michael Jackson and listen to his performance beyond the perimeter walls of the arena.

When Michael and his crew were due to begin their final preparations for the upcoming performance, they realized that— although they were expecting the typical sold-out status for the show—the paying customers were not showing up. The stadium was virtually empty. Accordingly, the decision was made that Michael Jackson's Moscow concert would be officially canceled.

One determined woman showed up, with her little girl in tow. When she heard the news about the proposed cancellation, she begged to be allowed to speak directly to Michael. She was delighted when he met with her backstage.

"My child has never seen a ray of sunshine," the woman explained to Michael. "Although she is blind, she has drawn this picture of you as a present, and she has looked forward with all her heart to hearing you sing and dance." Michael not only accepted the child's offering as a special present, but he agreed to perform his concert, even if for this one little girl and her mother.

Michael's people opened the doors to the stadium, and the waiting horde of Moscovians streamed in and filled up the open-air arena. Although it was raining and bitterly cold, and the concert started well beyond the scheduled time, Michael Jackson gave an astounding performance, as his crew mopped up the wet stage floor at regular intervals and he danced around them. The lucky and jubilant attendees enjoyed a free concert given by Michael Jackson, who reportedly "didn't miss a beat" in spite of the pouring rain.

Those people remember him today, and, no doubt, that little girl who cannot see can also remember....

On the day following his amazing performance, Michael visited a local orphanage for handicapped children. There he brought excitement and joy to kids who seldom experienced those feelings.

Michael Jackson composed his soulful "Stranger in Moscow" after these events, while he sat—troubled and feeling very alone—in his hotel room, even though hundreds of his fans were gathered outside. At the end of the song, if you listen closely, you will hear a man—a representative of the KGB—speaking in Russian. He is saying, "Go away; we don't want you here; you are taking something from us."

Michael was indeed taking something—the hearts of his Russian fans.

In Germany also, Michael Jackson is remembered and admired for the stunning performance he gave at a benefit concert for the International Red Cross, Nelson Mandela's Children's Fund, and UNESCO, on June 27, 1999. At the Munich Olympic Stadium, on a hot summer evening, Michael's people had set up the usual walls of lights, screens, and tons of elaborate equipment for his performance.

According to Karen Faye, who helped with Michael's hair, make-up, and costumes, the crowd was vibrating with eager anticipation. Michael peeked out at the audience—60,000 excited people—from behind the curtain.

On cue, Michael Jackson emerged onto the stage, to the gasps and screams from his audience. He did their favorite songs, including "Beat It," "Black or White," and "Billie Jean." Then he started "Earth

Song," during which he ran up a bridge, twirled, and stomped his feet to the crescendo of the music. The bridge was being lifted higher and higher, to emphasize the drama of the musical message. Suddenly, smoke and lights exploded around the bridge, which came careening down *fifty feet* to a crash into the orchestra pit in front of the stage! Michael, holding tight to the bridge rail, continued singing that song ... *without missing one beat*, even after it hit the floor with so great a force that his body bounced. The audience believed it was all part of the extravaganza, but Michael's crew and Karen Faye were in a panic.

Michael not only finished that song, but he pulled himself back onto the stage; disappeared behind the curtain briefly; and then insisted to his worried crew and bodyguards that he return to the stage to deliver "You Are Not Alone." After that, he took his bows to his grateful, amazed audience, and then he walked behind the stage curtain, where he collapsed. Michael was rushed to the local hospital and treated for major bruises and minor burns, and released after several hours. "He was in a lot of pain," reported Faye. When she asked him why he continued the concert to completion, in spite of the injuries he had sustained, Michael responded that the voice in his head kept saying, *"Michael, don't disappoint the audience."*

Needless to say, he did not disappoint his audience; he thrilled them. They are still talking about Michael's consummate professionalism and his "the show must go on" endurance.

Even an unlikely group of men—prisoners in a high-security penitentiary in the Philippines—celebrate the legacy and skills of Michael Jackson. In 2007, 1,500 male inmates emulated Michael's classic zombie dance moves from *Thriller*, in unison, and the footage of their tribute went viral, playing on *YouTube* as an immediate Internet hit. It became one of the most viewed pieces on the Internet, receiving 300,000 views per day at its peak and a total of more than 45 million hits as of October 2010.

"Before the dancing," reported the inmate who played Michael Jackson and led the others, "our problems were really heavy to bear. Dancing takes our minds away from our problems.... As for the judges, they may be impressed with us, seeing that we are being rehabilitated and this could help our case. We are being rehabilitated in a good way."

On a grand and professional scale, Cirque du Soleil's musical homage to Michael Jackson opened in Las Vegas during the month of December 2011. In 2013, it will become a permanent attraction in that city. *Michael Jackson: The Immortal World Tour*—the most expensive show in the French company's history—first opened in October 2011, in Montreal, Canada. It was scheduled to travel to dozens of cities in the U.S. and Canada. The tour will also move on to Europe.

Michael Jackson "helped build the company [Cirque du Soleil]," according to its president Daniel Lamarre. Michael greatly admired the shows and the talented acrobats, aerialists, and dancers. He attended Cirque performances in Los Angeles and Las Vegas.

At the Mandalay Bay Hotel-Casino in Las Vegas, a large exhibit opened for the month of December 2011, as a tribute to Michael Jackson and as an attraction for his fans and the general public. "This place … is going to be the home of Michael Jackson in many, many ways," said Daniel Lamarre. A Jackson-themed memorabilia museum and the theater for Cirque du Soleil's performance of Michael Jackson's music are planned to be based at Mandalay Bay in 2013. Objects from Neverland Ranch will likely be on display, including a replica of Michael's "Giving Tree," at the top of which he had a perch built, where he wrote songs and sometimes slept.

Captain EO, Michael Jackson's 17-minute musical space adventure, which originally showed at Disney's Epcot Center from 1986 to 1994, now plays at Disneyland and Epcot. The classic 3-D film, which depicts Michael as a spaceship captain who turns a colorless planet into a world of color and happiness, has also opened at the Disneylands in Tokyo and Paris. New generations of Michael Jackson fans are now able to enjoy what was considered a "remarkable avant-garde film of fantasy and memorable music."

In May 2012, the Estate of Michael Jackson, Pepsi, and Sony Music announced that, in celebration of the 25th anniversary of *Bad*, Pepsi will be issuing a special edition of Pepsi cans with Michael's image on them. There will be a record-breaking *one billion* of these Michael Jackson Bad25 Pepsi cans distributed around the world, "in more than 20 countries."

On a smaller but interesting level, Michael Jackson's jackets have been surfacing from all around. He was very generous with his personal belongings, realizing that each item was a treasure for its recipient. He gave away articles of clothing with frequency, including a single sequined glove, which became his trademark, and many of his iconic jackets. A legendary sequined glove that Michael wore during his *Bad* Tour was the highest-selling item at an auction in Beverly Hills in December 2010; it sold for $330,000.

One of Michael's jackets sold for $1.8 million in June 2011. The red and black jacket was one of two that Michael wore during the filming of *Thriller*. Part of the proceeds went to the Shambala Preserve, where Michael's two Bengal tigers, Thriller and Sabu, have been living. This jacket will go on tour and be used as a fund-raising item for children's charities. Another jacket of Michael's sold for $1.2 million during the summer of 2011. Often Michael Jackson's possessions are auctioned or sold for charity, as he would have wanted. His fashion legacy lives on, as does his commitment to charitable causes.

A heartwarming story was published in May 2011, regarding a Michael Jackson costume that was purchased by Judi Woolworth Donahue for a *dime* in a thrift store nearly ten years before. Although destined to be an heiress to the Woolworth fortune as the great-granddaughter of F.W. Woolworth, Ms. Donahue never got a single penny of inheritance. Instead, she became homeless for most of her adult life, but she found the "miracle from Michael," as she now describes her great luck. When she purchased the multi-colored jacket, she and the seller had no idea that it was

Michael Jackson's, but it has been recently verified as a costume that Katherine made for her young son Michael. It has been valued at $2 million.

During the summer of 2011, this author met with Wendell Thompson, his wife Latisha, and young son Brandon in Jacksonville, Florida, their current home. Wendell became a friend of Michael when he was in junior high school during the eighties. His father owned the hair/beauty salon that Michael Jackson patronized during his frequent visits to Orlando, Florida. Michael even requested the hairstylist-owner to consider moving to the West Coast to become his permanent employee, but the man declined the offer because he was not willing to relocate his family to the other side of the country.

His parents would awaken Wendell late at night, sometimes at midnight, to take him to the salon to visit with the superstar, who would have his hair styled with no one else around to see him except his security guards. Wendell got to know him during these quiet times. He also accompanied Michael, his bodyguards, and his entourage at the time to the Magic Kingdom at Disney World for a good time together. He remembers Michael as "humble, nice, and speaking in a soft voice; he was mild-mannered, very courteous, and polite." Wendell adds, "He really was just like a kid.

"He was into music of all kinds," Wendell says; "he would hum all of the time."

Because Wendell was just a kid himself, he didn't realize the "bigness" of being friends with the King of Pop. At first, he was star-struck and told all of his friends at school, but, perhaps because Michael was so down-to-earth, Wendell came to take the relationship for granted. While they were posing for photographs together one day, Michael requested Wendell to try on his jacket. When he did, Michael simply asked, "Do you like it?" Wendell nodded and said, "Yeah, I do." To that, the superstar murmured, "You can keep it." Wendell gladly did keep it and—feeling just a bit taller than he was before—he proudly wore it home.

On another occasion, which Wendell amazingly does not recall as to its details, Michael gave him another of his jackets to keep. Today, this young man, who is the father in his own family, cherishes these two special gifts from his friend Michael Jackson.

Michael was superlatively generous; giving was his *modus operandi*. His work for humanitarian causes continues with fans and admirers from around the world giving of themselves and their resources in Michael's honor.

With a special penchant for giving to the homeless, Michael Jackson has inspired his fans to emulate their role model's behavior. Many have adopted an ongoing commitment to give money to a homeless person whenever they encounter one. In fact, it might be a good idea for the unfortunate individuals who find themselves without a home, compelled to seek donations from the public, to hold signs that say "Seeking Michael Jackson Fans."

In big ways and small, Michael Jackson's multi-faceted legacy continues and expands. Around the globe, people of all ages— as young as three or four and as old as eighty or ninety—enjoy Michael's music, films, dance, and influences on fashion. Even more important, they are actively advancing his commitments to the betterment of this planet—the environment, animals, and people, especially the children whom Michael so loved.

**Music has been my outlet, my gift
to all of the lovers in this world.
Through it—my music—I know
I will live forever.**
— Michael Jackson

RUMINATIONS

This body of mine
Is a flux of energy
In the river of time....
I am the particle
I am the wave....
I am the Primeval Self
In you and I.
— Michael Jackson

To us, he *was* a king. Not the majestically opulent King of Pop—though we loved him with that crown and deserved title—but the man behind the trappings, pomp, curtain, masks, and veils.

All of us who contributed—remembered stories, cherished memories, heart twinges, and memorable facts—to this book pay tribute to this extraordinary man. We see in Michael Jackson his "old-school" gentleness, a lion's heart for humankind, and an undeniable nobility of spirit. Michael evidenced greatness even during his most difficult of times.

A multitude of people and the American legal system failed and mistreated him. His three children and his fans, however, were always there for him, validating his purpose in life, and he returned their love with vehemence and unswerving passion.

Unlike everyone else in the world, Prince, Paris, and Blanket knew Michael Jackson the man and their "Daddy" completely and intimately. They had not experienced him as the stunning mega-performer King of Pop. He sought to rectify that deficiency by a spectacular return to the stage ... for them and for his legions of loyal fans, who sorely missed him. He was preparing and working hard to recover his rightful kingdom and to gain redemption.

How could Michael Jackson get up every morning to face all of the battles that he had to fight? This peace-loving child-man, who lived to give to others, was besieged from all around—slander, accusations, lawsuits, betrayers, opportunists, profiteers, and greedy assassins at every turn, on every day.

The answer is that Michael awoke to the joyful squeals of his three little children, calling *"Daddy! Daddy!"* with outstretched arms and warming smiles. In spite of his incredible talents and unparalleled creative genius, Michael Jackson was his best self with his children. He wrapped them in his love and devotion. He could suffer anything if he had them near ... and he did.

Michael Jackson achieved more victories than any other person—global, glorious, and transcendent. His defeats, though few in number, were huge, public, and epic. If he had not been so traumatized and stalled by false accusations in 1993 and again in 2003, Michael Jackson would have ruled the world. Heroes of the masses and reigning monarchs often become the targets for iconoclasts, villains, plunderers, and assassins. Michael Jackson was no exception. In fact, he was the prototype.

Yet, he did preside over the beautiful world that he created with his brilliant music and his exemplary good works around the planet for its children, for the needy and downtrodden. His was a moral power; he inspired millions to follow in his footsteps toward brotherhood, caring, and giving. Michael Jackson was not only a global icon; he was a prophet and a messenger of peace, harmony, and unity. Today we are listening to him as never before....

Although he was truly a victim on many levels, with his vast empire continuously under siege, Michael Jackson remained strong, spiritual, determined, and persevering. He ultimately overcame and triumphed over his enemies through love. He never responded in kind against his cruel accusers, savage media, or other attackers. There were no harsh words issued by Michael

Jackson, no proclamations of anger or retaliation. Amazingly, even shockingly, he forgave....

Now that he has become immortal, he has an army of self-declared friends, many more friends than he had in this life. And, deservedly Michael Jackson is a legend.

After you have read *Defending A King ~ His Life & Legacy*, we believe that you will never hear his self-disclosing, intimate song "Will You Be There" in the same way again. Listen to it and let it flood you with strong feelings of your own vulnerability, your own humanity. And, you will understand Michael Jackson's message to this world.

"I just simply want to be loved wherever I go ... all over the world ... [by] people of all races," he revealed in the interview that broke his fourteen-year silence in the domain of media. In early 2009, one million people—an unprecedented multitude from far-flung countries—thronged to make plans for their pilgrimage to London to watch him reclaim his throne. But he never got there.

*   *   *   *   *   *   *   *   *

The time has come to *begin* the healing step of the mourning process over the premature death of Michael Jackson. The doctor who killed him, let him die, tried to hide the murder weapon, and lied to responders who could have saved him has been convicted of manslaughter in a court of law. Tragically, Michael Jackson was also put on trial. The man who was not here to defend himself was exposed to the world in outrageously destructive, disrespectful, and egregious ways; labeled with socially-despised terms; and generally devalued as a human being. Thousands of people had fun and made money—once again—by savaging Michael Jackson and dishonoring his memory.

In the wake of those horrible realities, the terrible photos, the sordid coverage, it is now time to wrestle them aside in our hearts and memory banks. It is time to return to seeing Michael Jackson for who he was before the morning of June 25, 2009.

We should be able to recognize, without judgment, the desperate struggles of a human being over physical pain, the chronic inability to sleep, the ceaseless pressure to please those who loved him. Ultimately Michael was a man in pain and for that he should become human to us, for who among us has not felt pain and considered desperate means to overcome it?

His real fans—old and new—wish that Michael could return to this Earth for one day to see all of the good that he has wrought and how we embrace it....

We feel that, in the end, Michael Jackson knew that he was loved. We cling to that belief.

From Bliss I came....
To Bliss I return.
— Michael Jackson

*   *   *   *   *   *   *   *   *

It's all for
L.O.V.E.

**To live is to be musical,
starting with the blood dancing
in your veins.
Everything living has a rhythm.**
— Michael Jackson

I [am] glad to be tired. Crawling ... into bed, I remember something that I always wonder at. They say that some of the stars that we see overhead aren't really there. Their light takes millions of years to reach us, and all we are doing is looking into the past, to a bygone moment when those stars could still shine.

"So what does a star do after it quits shining?" I ask myself. "Maybe it dies."

"Oh no," a voice in my head says. "A star can never die. It just turns into a smile and melts back into the cosmic music, the dance of life." I like that thought, the last one I have before my eyes close. With a smile, I melt back into the music myself.

"Dance of Life,"
Dancing the Dream,
Michael Jackson

Sources

Most important to *Defending A King ~ His Life & Legacy* have been the people who generously contributed to this book. Among them are Thomas Mesereau, David Nordahl, Larry Nimmer, June Gatlin, Michael Leary, Wendell Thompson, Eddie Jones, Kenneth Urbina, and many dozens of Michael Jackson fans and admirers too numerous to list. Boyd Williams and Baron James are real people (Michael's Las Vegas bodyguards from late 2006 to mid-2008), with whom I spent many hours across four days. I have not used their real names because, to my knowledge, they continue to work in the personal security industry, in which client confidentiality is valued as important. Michael Garcia, the third member of that security team, has also revealed a great deal of information about Michael Jackson *in a variety of forums*. All three security men have made frequent disclosures in the public domain—in television interviews and on the Internet, including Facebook. "Rose Giuseppe" in "The Legacy of Michael Jackson" chapter is a woman who was interviewed on television at the time of Michael's Memorial service in July 2009; her real name is unknown to this author.

The published works that have been most helpful are J. Randy Taraborrelli's biography, *Michael Jackson—The Magic, The Madness, The Whole Story* (1991, 2009); Adrian Grant's *Michael Jackson—A Visual Documentary 1958-2009*; and Aphrodite Jones's *Michael Jackson Conspiracy* (2007). The *MJJ Timeline* Web information has also been very helpful. In the opinion of this author, Taraborrelli's coverage of Michael Jackson's life during his last four years was more hastily written—probably for a fast re-release after his sudden death in 2009—than the earlier material. In only 17 pages (of 765) he adopts a "half empty" view of Michael Jackson, whereas a "half full" view would have likely been more credible and welcome. I have purposely used sources from *every* genre, including social media. Hopefully, the variety and *totality* of the source material convey a real feel of the unique and fascinating world of Michael Jackson.

— Karen Moriarty

Abowitz, Richard. "The continuing fantasy of Michael Jackson's future in Vegas." *The Movable Buffet.* vegasblog.latimes.com, July 11, 2011.

"Adrian Grant Talks About Michael." www.mjfanclub.net, July 10, 2011.

Alexander, Paul. "Inmate 'Thriller' video is Web hit." *USA Today.* www.usatoday.com, August 9, 2007.

"All Michael Jackson Tours and Concerts." www.allmichaeljackson.com, May 14, 2012.

"Angelina Jolie's Carefully Orchestrated Image." www.nytimes.com, March 10, 2011.

"Another Day, Another MJ Creditor's Claim." www.tmz.com, September 11, 2011.

"Attorney Wants $3 Mil, Apology From MJ Estate." www.tmz.com, September 11, 2011.

Banfield, Ashleigh, Angela Ellis and Sabina Ghebremedhin. "Exclusive: Michael Jackson's Secretive Life." *ABC News.* abcnews.go.com, March 9, 2010; April 26, 2011.

"Battle for Michael Jackson's Estate Hits Germany." www.mjjcommunity.com, September 14, 2011.

Beckett Presents: A Tribute to Michael Jackson. USA: Beckett Media LLC, 2009.

"Behind the Mask." As told to Stephanie Wilson by Alvin Malnik. *Haute Living.* July/August 2009.

Billeaudeaux, Elizabeth Michelle. *An Angel Among Us.* Lexington, KY: Ms. Elizabeth Michelle Billeaudeaux, 2010.

Bloemen, Brigitte, Marina Dobler, Miriam Lohr, Sonja Winterholler. *It's All About L.O.V.E.* LaVergne, TN: Books on Demand GmbH, 2010.

Bloom, Howard. "Michael Jackson was the most astonishing person I've ever met on the face of this planet!" www.mj-777.com, January 14, 2011.

"Bodyguards' Q & A: Michael Jackson loved Subway, Had a Facebook, and Other Random Info." ohnotheydidnt.livejournal.com, November 6, 2011.

"Brad And Angelina's Twins: Photos, Details, IVF Denial." www.huffingtonpost.com, February 26, 2011.

"BRANCA is INNOCENT!! MJ hired him back as he TRUSTED HIM." www.michaeljacksonhoaxforum.com, September 28, 2011.

Brenoff, Ann. "Michael Jackson leases Bel-Air mansion for $100,000 a month." www.latimes.com, August 5, 2011.

"Brett Ratner Dot Com." brettratnernewsblog.blogspot.com, May 21, 2011.

"A Call for Love during the Murray trial." www.majorloveprayer.org, September 28, 2011.

Caron, Christina. "Conrad Murray's Girlfriends Testify: Sade Anding, Nicole Alvarez, Michelle Bella and Bridgette Morgan." *ABC NEWS.* abcnews.go.com, October 23, 2011.

"Catherine Bach's husband, Peter Lopez, former Michael Jackson lawyer, found dead in apparent suicide." *The Associated Press.* www.nydailynews.com, April 26, 2011.

Chopra, Deepak. "A Tribute to My Friend, Michael Jackson." www.huffingtonpost.com, September 8, 2011.

Clarke, Norm. "Michael Jackson staying at Palms." www.lvrj.com, July 11, 2011.

Clarke, Norm. "Michael Jackson's home up for sale." www.lvrj.com, July 11, 2011.

Clarke, Norm. "NORM: Michael Jackson landing on Strip?" www.reviewjournal.com, July 11, 2011.

"Conrad Murray and AEG Live, HAD IT NOT BEEN FOR THEM, MICHAEL WOULD BE ALIVE NOW." vindicatemj.wordpress. com, September 11, 2011.

"Conrad Murray (Michael Jackson) Trial: Jury Favor Defense or Prosecution?" trialready.wordpress.com, September 26, 2011.

"Correction to 'In Defense Of The King.'" *What About MJ?* whataboutmj. wordpress.com, September 25, 2011.

"Creditors' Claims Filed and Disposition of Claims." Estate of Michael Joseph Jackson, Deceased. (As of February 22, 2010). 2010.

"Cris Judd Talks About Dancing for MJ." www.mjfanclub.net, July 10, 2011.

"The Death of Michael Jackson." *CNN Justice.* insession.blogs.cnn.com, October 23, 2011.

"Destitute Heiress Finds MJ Costume Worth Fortune." www.mjfanclub. net, July 10, 2011.

"Did Michael Hire Leonard Rowe As His Manager?" muzikfactorytwo. blogspot.com, September 14, 2011.

"Dr. Barry Friedberg: 'Michael's Death: A Predictable, Avoidable Tragedy.'" www.mj-777.com, March 3, 2011.

"Dr. Conrad Murray.biography." *Netflix.* www.biography.com, October 23, 2011.

Dr. Drew Show. HLN. August 8, 2011; August 23, 2011; October 6, 2011; October 16, 2011.

Dr. Oz Show. KABC. October 26, 2011.

"The Estate of Michael Joseph Jackson—Updates." www.mjj2005.com, September 11, 2011.

"The Estate of Michael Joseph Jackson – Updates Taken from http:// lesliemjhu.blogspot.com." www.mjj2005.com, September 8, 2011.

"EXCLUSIVE: Theater Company Sues Michael Jackson's Estate For Breach of Contract." www.radaronline.com, September 13, 2011.

Faye, Karen. "I thought he was surely dead!" www.mjfriendship.de, September 21, 2011.

Friedman, Roger. "Jacko Lived With New Jersey Family for Three Months." www.foxnews.com, May 8, 2011.

Friess, Steve. "Playing It Safe in Las Vegas." www.nytimes.com, July 11, 2011.

Good Morning America. ABC. March 9, 2010; March 10, 2010.

"Goodstone Inn & Estate." www.goodstone.com, July 27, 2011.

Grant, Adrian. *Michael Jackson—A Visual Documentary 1958-2009.* London: Omnibus Press, 2009.

"Grouse Lodge." www.grouselodge.com, August 19, 2011.

Guinness World Records 2011. World Copyright: Guinness World Records Limited, 2010.

Hill, Tim. *Michael Jackson.* UK: Parragon Books Ltd., 2009.

"Hollywood Docket: Billie Jean vs. Michael Jackson Judge ..." www.hollywoodreporter.com, September 10, 2011.

Hughes, Geraldine. *Redemption.* Radford, VA: Branch & Vine Publishers, LLC, 2004.

"In Defense Of The King." *What About MJ?* whataboutmj.wordpress.com, May 20, 2011.

"In Session." *tru TV.* September 16, 2011.

"Jacko bodyguards trying to kill gay rumor." www.nypost.com, April 26, 2011.

"Jackson dies, almost takes Internet with him." CNN. June 26, 2009.

Jackson, Jermaine. *You Are Not Alone*. New York: Simon & Schuster, 2011.

Jackson, Katherine. *Never Can Say Goodbye*. California: Vintage Pop Media LLC & Vintage Pop Inc., 2010.

Jackson, Michael. *Dancing the Dream*. Great Britain: Doubleday, 1992; 2009.

Jackson, Michael. *Moonwalk*. New York: Harmony Books, 1988; 2009.

Jackson, Michael. "Nourish This Child," *Pigtails And Frog Legs: A Family Cookbook from Neiman Marcus*. 1993.

Jackson, Michael. *The Ultimate Collection*. Sony/Epic, 2004.

"Jackson Sued by Disgruntled Choreographer." www.tmz.com, September 11, 2011.

"Jackson sues Granada." www.dailymail.co.uk, September 18, 2011.

Jane Velez-Mitchell Show. HLN. October 11, 2011; October 27, 2011.

Jones, Aphrodite. *Michael Jackson Conspiracy*. USA: Aphrodite Jones Books, 2007.

Jones, Bob. *Michael Jackson—The Man Behind the Mask*. New York: SelectBooks, Inc., 2005.

"Jordan Chandler." mjthekingofpop.wordpress.com, August 17, 2011.

"Jordy Chandler & His Father." www.topix.com, August 17, 2011.

Joy Behar Show. HLN. September 29, 2011.

Kasindorf, Martin. "His doctor faces charges, but 'Michael is on trial.'" *USA Today*. September 21, 2011.

Katherine Jackson, individually & as the Guardian ad Litem of Michael Joseph Jackson, Jr., Paris-Michael Katherine Jackson, and Prince Michael Jackson II v. AEG LIVE LLC; Anschutz Entertainment Group, Inc.; Brandon Phillips; Kenneth Ortega; Paul Gongaware; and Timothy Leiweke; and DOES 1 to 100, inclusive. Superior

Court of California, County of Los Angeles. September 15, 2010. Case No. BC445597. articles.cnn.com.

"Kathy And Paris Hilton Talk MJ." www.mjfanclub.net, July 10, 2011.

Katsilometes, John. "A visit to Michael Jackson's old home, where interloper leads tour and pit bull is shot – for starters." *The Kats Report.* www.lasvegassun.com, July 11, 2011.

Kelly, Antoinette. "Michael Jackson planned leprechaun theme park in Ireland." www.irishcentral.com, August 19, 2011.

King, Jason. *Michael Jackson Treasures.* New York, New York: Fall River Press, 2009.

Koopersmith, Jeff. "Wow 'Em in Heaven, Michael Jackson." *American Politics Journal.* www.apj.us, January 31, 2011.

Kunesh, Deborah L. "Susan Yu … The Unsung Hero of the 2005 Michael Jackson trial." reflectionsonthedance.blogspot.com, July 15, 2011.

"Le blog mjjtimeline." leblogmjjtimeline.com, November 28, 2011.

"Living with Michael Jackson." United Kingdom: Granada Television, 2003.

"Luggala." www.luggala.net, August 19, 2011.

Luzajic, Lorette C. *Michael Jackson for the Soul—A Fanthology of Inspiration and L.O.V.E.* Handymaiden Books, 2010.

"Macaulay Culkin." www.nndb.com, May 17, 2011.

"May – a hard month for MJ." michipato.wordpress.com, April 26, 2011.

Mesereau, Thomas A., Jr. "Defending Michael." www.mesereauyu.com, May 16, 2011.

Mesereau, Thomas A., Jr. "Random Thoughts on Trial Practice," *American Journal of Trial Advocacy.* Cumberland School of Law, Samford University, Summer 2007.

Mesereau, Thomas A., Jr. "The Trial ... Words From Michael's Lawyer." www.reflectionsonthedance.com, May 21, 2011.

"Michael Jackson: A special relationship with Ireland." www. belfasttelegraph.co.uk, August 19, 2011.

"Michael Jackson: A Tribute," *Ebony.* New York: Johnson Publishing Company, Inc., 2009.

"Michael Jackson Adviser Dr. Tohme Tohme Breaks Silence." www.mtv. com, September 13, 2011.

"Michael Jackson: And Justice for Some." mjandjustice4some.blogspot. com, September 13, 2011.

"Michael Jackson Awards." www.michaeljackson.com, May 12, 2012.

"Michael Jackson fans feel at home." Review Journal.com: www.lvrj. com, July 11, 2011.

"Michael Jackson Forever." New York, New York: Word Up! Magazine, September 2009.

"Michael Jackson Has Left the Building." *The Real Estalker.* realestalker. blogspot.com, July 11, 2011.

Michael Jackson Iconic Magazine, #1, 2, 3. Devilcantburn, Mjvibe & DP Productions, November 2010; March 2011; May 2011.

"Michael Jackson Interview: Karen Faye on Her 3 Decades with MJ." www.michaeljackson.com, April 3, 2011.

"Michael Jackson—King of Pop, A Celebration of the Life of Michael Jackson, 1958-2009." Memorial Service Program. USA: July 2009.

"Michael Jackson King of Pop Album." www.allmichaeljackson.com, May 14, 2012.

Michael Jackson, King of Pop—Commemorative Edition. USA Today. PA: Fry Communications, Inc., 2009.

"Michael Jackson Last Years: Timeline." muzikfactorytwo.blogspot.com, September 15, 2011.

Michael Jackson: My Life. New York, New York: IMG Publishing, 2009.

"Michael Jackson Recorded Music in the Cascio Home." www.oprah. com, September 6, 2011.

"Michael Jackson Slurring His Words Recording Played At Trial: 'I Didn't Have A Childhood.'" www.radaronline.com, October 23, 2011.

Michael Jackson, Special Collector's Issue. New York, New York: XXL, Harris Publications Inc., 2009.

"Michael Jackson Sued by Paparazzi." lesliemjhu.blogspot.com, September 10, 2011.

Michael Jackson—The One and Only. Chicago, IL: Triumph Books, 2009.

"Michael Jackson Tops List Of Forbes Top Earning Dead Celebrities." *Radar online.com.* www.radaronline.com, October 27, 2011.

Michael Jackson Tribute—Exclusive Collector's Edition. American Media Inc., 2009.

"Michael Jackson Tribute Portrait." www.michaeljacksontributeportrait. com, November 6, 2011.

"Michael Jackson Wacky Claims Rejected." www.tmz.com, September 9, 2011.

"Michael Jackson $5 Million Claim." www.tmz.com, September 11, 2011.

Michael Jackson's agreement with AEG: EVERYTHING HE HAD for a $6,2 mln. PROMISSORY NOTE." *Vindicating Michael.* vindicatemj. wordpress.com, April 10, 2011.

"Michael Jackson's Art Collection Valued in Millions." crashcollective. com, July 11, 2011.

"Michael Jackson's Bodyguards." abcnews.go.com, March 9, 2010; March 10, 2010.

"Michael Jackson's former Las Vegas home fetches $3.1 million." www.lasvegassun.com, April 27, 2011.

"Michael Jackson's Guinness Book of World Records." www.facebook.com, October 9, 2011.

"Michael Jackson's Last Close-Up." www.vanityfair.com, September 13, 2011.

Michael Jackson's Private Home Movies. USA: Fox Broadcasting Co., Brad Lachman Productions, 2003.

Michael Jackson's This Is It. Columbia Pictures, October 2009.

"Michael Jackson's 'Thriller' Jacket Sells For $1.8M At Auction." www.mjfanclub.net, July 10, 2011.

"Michael Our Icon," *Ebony.* New York: Johnson Publishing Company, July/August 2009.

"Michael's Former Manager: I Was Honest, So Pay Up." www.tmz.com, September 13, 2011.

"A Million Trees for Michael." www.amilliontreesformichael.com, March 19, 2011.

"MJ Estate Made $310 MILLION Since Michael Died." www.tmz.com, July 22, 2011.

"MJ News." www.oocities.org, September 9, 2011.

"MJ Photo Featured in Exhibit." www.mjfanclub.net, July 10, 2011.

"MJ: The 400 Million Dollar Man." www.mjfanclub.net, July 10, 2011.

"MJJ Timeline." mjjtimeline.blogspot.com, September 5, 2011.

"MJJ Timeline: 2005." mjjtimeline.blogspot.com, November 19, 2011.

"MJJ Timeline: 2006." mjjtimeline.blogspot.com, November 19, 2011.

"MJJ Timeline: 2007." mjjtimeline.blogspot.com. November 19, 2011.

"MJJ Timeline: 2008." mjjtimeline.blogspot.com, November 19, 2011.

"MJJ Timeline: 2009." mjjtimeline.blogspot.com, November 19, 2011.

"MJs Bodyguards." www.facebook.com, [various] 2010; 2011.

"MJTP Interview With Michael Bearden." www.mjfanclub.net, July 10, 2011.

"Monte Cristo." www.lasvegassun.com, August 19, 2011.

Netter, Sarah. "Michael Jackson Bodyguards: 'We Were Asked to Leave Hotels.'" *ABC News.* abcnews.go.com, March 8, 2010; November 27, 2011.

"New Michael Jackson Singles Coming From The Global #1 Album 'Michael.'" www.mj-upbeat.com, March 3, 2011.

"New MJ Mobile Social Game." www.mjfanclub.net, July 10, 2011.

Nightline. ABC. March 9, 2010.

Nimmer, Larry. *Michael Jackson: The Untold Story of Neverland.* California: Nimmer Pictures, Inc., 2010.

The Official Michael Jackson Opus. New York: Opus Media Group Ltd., 2009.

"Oprah Interviews Michael Jackson." *Oprah Winfrey Show.* Chicago: ABC, February 10, 1993.

Oprah Winfrey Show. Chicago: ABC, October 21, 2010; November 10, 2010.

Oxford English Dictionary. Oxford University Press, 2011.

"Part II: Tom Sneddon – A Strange Obsession." www.mjjr.net, April 21, 2011.

People Tribute—Remembering Michael. New York, New York: People Books, Time Inc., 2009.

Piers Morgan Tonight. CNN, February 15, 2011; October 3, 2011; November 1, 2011.

"The Prince of Rock." The Daily Journal Corporation: www.callawyer.com, August 12, 2011.

"Propofol." *SGNA.* www.sgna.org, October 24, 2011.

Remembering Michael—Anniversary Tribute. USA: American Media Inc., 2010.

"Reverent June Juliet Gatlin." reverentjune.com, August 17, 2011.

Right On!—Special Commemorative Issue. New York: Magazine Publishers of America, 2009.

Robinson, Lisa. "The Boy Who Would Be King." *Vanity Fair.* New York, New York: Advance Magazine Publishers Inc., September 2009.

Rolling Stone—Special Commemorative Issue. USA: Rolling Stone LLC, 2009.

Rottenberg, Josh. "Last Dance." *Entertainment Weekly.* New York, New York: Time Warner Inc., October 23, 2009.

"Ruska Bergman: The Last Dinner With Michael Jackson." www.mj-upbeat.com, October 30, 2011.

"Ryan White's Mother Remembers Jackson." www.cbsnews.com, July 8, 2009.

Semino, Matt. "Defending the Victim in the Conrad Murray Trial." www.michaeljacksontributeportrait.com, September 23, 2011.

Semino, Matt. "Dr. Conrad Murray Trial, a Bitter Pill to Swallow." www.huffingtonpost.com, January 27, 2011.

"The Silenced Truth ... about Michael Jackson." www.thesilencedtruth.com, November 27, 2011.

Silva, Cristina. "Michael Jackson's Neverland Ranch to be Recreated in Las Vegas." www.billboard.com, May 1, 2011.

The Source—Special Collector's Issue, #233. NYC: BE/GS The Northstar Group, August 2009.

Steinhaus, Rochelle. "Jackson settlement from 1993 allegations topped $20 million." *CNN Justice*. articles.cnn.com, June 16, 2004.

Stiernberg, Bonnie. "Michael Jackson Glove Sells for More than $300K." www.pastemagazine.com, May 1, 2011.

Taraborrelli, J. Randy. *Michael Jackson—The Magic, The Madness, The Whole Story*. New York: Grand Central Publishing, 2009.

Theroux, Paul. "The Original Neverland—Inside Michael Jackson's Private Kingdom." *Architectural Digest*. New York, New York: Advance Magazine Publishers Inc., November 2009.

This Is It. USA: The Michael Jackson Company, LLC, 2009.

Thomson, Charles. "Chandler Suicide Highlights Media Bias Against Jackson." floacist.wordpress.com, May 1, 2010.

Thomson, Charles. "One of the Most Shameful Episodes in Journalistic History." www.huffingtonpost.com, June 14, 2010.

"Those 'Crazy Michael Jackson Fans:' Maybe we should listen?" www.innermichael.com, July 3, 2011.

"Thriller video director John Landis sues Michael Jackson to stop Broadway stage show." www.dailymail.co.uk, September 13, 2011.

"Today in History." newsradio1420.com, July 17, 2011.

"Tohme R. Tohme." www.facebook.com, July 10, 2011.

"Tom Mesereau Gives Thoughts On MJ." www.mjfanclub.net, July 10, 2011.

Verhovek, Sam Howe. "Grammy-Winning Singer Selena Killed in Shooting at Texas Motel." www.nytimes.com, September 5, 2011.

Vogel, Joe. "Remembering Michael Jackson: The Story Behind His Magnum Opus." www.huffingtonpost.com, July 16, 2011.

Vogel, Joseph. *Man in the Music.* New York: Sterling Publishing, 2011.

Wallace, Benjamin. "Monetizing the Celebrity Meltdown." nymag.com, August 12, 2011.

"Woman Wants $50 Million from Michael's Estate." www.tmz.com, September 9, 2011.

Word Up! A Tribute to Michael Jackson, #95. Poughkeepsie, New York: WU Magazine, Inc., 2009.

Word Up! Poughkeepsie, New York: WU Magazine, Inc., November/December 2009.

Wride, Nancy. "Burn Victim Dreads Day His Father Gets Paroled." articles.latimes.com, May 12, 2011.

"2009 Timeline for Michael Jackson [Archive]." www.mjjcommunity.com, September 5, 2011.

"2010 Census Data." www.census.gov, May 12, 2012.

"$300m lawsuit against MJ dismissed." www.thaindian.com, September 8, 2011.

CPSIA information can be obtained
at www.ICGtesting.com
Printed in the USA
BVHW082251240121
598585BV00002B/38